Pud Galvin

ALSO BY BRIAN MARTIN

*The Tecumsehs of the International Association:
Canada's First Major League Baseball Champions*
(McFarland, 2015)

*Baseball's Creation Myth:
Adam Ford, Abner Graves and the Cooperstown Story*
(McFarland, 2013)

Pud Galvin
Baseball's First 300-Game Winner

BRIAN MARTIN

McFarland & Company, Inc., Publishers
Jefferson, North Carolina

LIBRARY OF CONGRESS CATALOGUING-IN-PUBLICATION DATA

Names: Martin, Brian, 1950– author.
Title: Pud Galvin : baseball's first 300-game winner / Brian Martin.
Description: Jefferson, North Carolina : McFarland & Company, Inc., Publishers, [2016] | Includes bibliographical references and index.
Identifiers: LCCN 2016036967 | ISBN 9780786499779 (softcover : acid free paper) ∞
Subjects: LCSH: Galvin, Pud, 1856–1902. | Pitchers (Baseball)—United States—Biography. | Baseball players—United States—Biography. | Baseball—United States—History. | Doping in sports.
Classification: LCC GV865.G258 M37 2016 | DDC 796.357092 [B]—dc23
LC record available at https://lccn.loc.gov/2016036967

BRITISH LIBRARY CATALOGUING DATA ARE AVAILABLE

ISBN (print) 978-0-7864-9977-9
ISBN (ebook) 978-1-4766-2551-5

© 2016 Brian Martin All rights reserved

No part of this book may be reproduced or transmitted in any form or by any means, electronic or mechanical, including photocopying or recording, or by any information storage and retrieval system, without permission in writing from the publisher.

Front cover: Pud Galvin, Pittsburgh Alleghenys, baseball card portrait (National Baseball Hall of Fame & Museum, Inc., Cooperstown, New York)

Printed in the United States of America

McFarland & Company, Inc., Publishers
Box 611, Jefferson, North Carolina 28640
www.mcfarlandpub.com

To the late Joe Overfield,
who reminded baseball
about one of its greatest pitchers
and whose efforts brought Pud Galvin
the recognition he so richly deserved

Table of Contents

Acknowledgments	ix
Preface	1
Introduction	3
1. Of Cheats and Juicers	7
2. The Kid from the Kerry Patch	18
3. Making His Mark in a Changing World	30
4. Introduction to the Big Time	42
5. Playing Through Adversity	53
6. Joining the Show in Buffalo	66
7. A Star Emerges	82
8. 1881–1882: Prelude to Perfection	94
9. Glory Days	107
10. The Little Steam Engine Changes Gears	121
11. Back in the Smoky City	134
12. Making History Amid the Gloom	146
13. Turning Back the Clock	160
14. "The action … was piratical."	179
15. Final Innings	192
Epilogue	209
Appendix One. The Wins of Pud Galvin	217

Appendix Two. The 300 Wins Club 218

Appendix Three. Pud Galvin's Changing Working
 Conditions During His Career, 1875–1892 219

Chapter Notes 221

Bibliography 234

Index 239

Acknowledgments

It has been said so often that a book is the product of the efforts of many people. That is so true. The author is indebted to several individuals who have given of their time and talents to help share the story of Pud Galvin. Research for this book has uncovered some wonderful material and the guardians of it have invariably been helpful, kind and generous. This book could not have been what it is without their assistance. A thank you to all, and apologies to anyone who may have been missed in this acknowledgment.

In Pittsburgh, Craig Britcher, curatorial assistant and project coordinator at the Senator John Heinz History Center, deserves special thanks. He shared a vast amount of information he had meticulously gathered over the years and was always there to answer questions and provide good and timely advice. He helped me find Pud Galvin's grave, no small feat in itself, and provided the names of additional contacts who might have further information. I know both of us have a special interest in the little pitcher who for so long was lost to history. Also in Pittsburgh, Gil Pietrzak at the Carnegie Library kindly shared the image of the 1890 Pittsburgh Burghers and Miriam Meislik, media curator at the archives center of the University of Pittsburgh library system, shared an early map of Allegheny City depicting Union Park.

In Buffalo, Cynthia Van Ness, director of library and archives at the Buffalo Museum was a joy. She is a dedicated and tireless guardian of valuable materials there including the massive Overfield Collection that chronicles Galvin's years in that city. She was always cheerful and helpful as she juggled many tasks and still found ways to accommodate the needs and requests of this writer. She is a fine ambassador for her museum and her city.

In Cooperstown, New York, I received great help from Cassidy Lent, reference librarian at the National Baseball Hall of Fame Library and from John Horne, coordinator of rights and reproductions.

Bill Humber, of Bowmanville, Ontario, Canada's top baseball historian, made me aware of the amazing collection of information compiled by the late Joe Overfield in Buffalo. It has been my pleasure to know such a respected authority in baseball as Bill. Don Murray, of London, Ontario, a true baseball fan, proved to be a great editor, friend and consultant. Diana Copsey Adams, of Denver, another good friend and supporter, proved yet again to be a tireless researcher using her ancestry.com skills to produce amazing results.

Aside from the many people who helped the author, the following organizations deserve a shout-out for making important source material available online, a move that helped this researcher and which will help others seeking to broaden their knowledge of early baseball history: The Society for American Baseball Research for allowing SABR members like myself access to *Sporting News*, by way of the Paper of Record; the University of Illinois for the Illinois Digital Newspaper Collections that include the *New York Clipper*; Google News Archives for access to the *Pittsburgh Press* from 1888 to 1892; the Chronicling America project of the Library of Congress for access to the *Pittsburgh Dispatch*; the LA84 Foundation for making *Sporting Life* available.

Finally, but by no means last in my estimation, I wish to extend my sincere thanks to editor Gary Mitchem and to McFarland. Words can never do justice to express my appreciation.

Preface

Baseball is such an interesting combination of fiction and fact. Historians cringe that some fans of the game still believe it was invented in Cooperstown, New York, by Abner Doubleday in 1839. For decades, Doubleday received credit for something he did not do. The story was a fabrication that served to "prove" baseball mogul Albert Goodwill Spalding's insistence that baseball had a purely American pedigree. It was a convenient untruth, if you will. The creation myth, however, has produced a remarkable Hall of Fame and museum in Cooperstown that celebrates the game and those who have excelled at it over the decades.

Sometimes excellence has been forgotten, facts overlooked. Such is the case with a pioneer pitcher named James Francis Galvin. He was the charter member of the 300-wins pitching club in baseball, earning that milestone victory in 1888, long before baseball itself recognized the accomplishment as a benchmark worthy of celebration. Galvin is generally credited with 365 wins, placing him fifth among the winningest pitchers of all time. He died in poverty at the age of 45 and was soon forgotten as a new century began and a new crop of pitchers and hitters captured the public imagination. The determined efforts of a baseball historian who felt Galvin had been short-changed by history led to his induction into the Hall of Fame six decades after his death. It was long-overdue recognition for the stout little man known as "Pud" Galvin because his outstanding fastball reportedly turned opposition batters into pudding.

After his induction at Cooperstown, Galvin again receded from public consciousness, perhaps viewed as a relic from the past, a man who retired a year before 60 feet, six inches became the standard pitching distance. Four more decades went by before his name surfaced again. This time it was raised in connection with the controversy about performance-enhancing drugs that most observers of the game argue bars Hall of Fame entry for many recent star players. They cheated, baseball purists insisted. Galvin took a testosterone-based potion in 1889 when his level of play began to decline. A precedent had been set with Galvin, some argued, so modern-day performance-enhancers remain worthy candidates for induction. Galvin's name was dragged through the mud during the debate. Needlessly, as it turns out.

This book is an attempt to set the record straight about Pud Galvin, in the first comprehensive effort to chronicle a remarkable career that spanned many changes in rules, leagues and pitching distances in the early years of the professional game. Special attention is paid to his early years in the game, particularly the two seasons he spent with Allegheny and Buffalo in the International Association, a rival to the National League. The IA was an organization that baseball and its historians refuse to acknowledge as a major league, and little effort has been made to understand it. Consequently, Galvin's 36 wins there during league play are also not recognized, otherwise his total would stand at 401 wins and place him comfortably in third place. It is hoped this effort will shed light on his time in the International Association and a lead to a better understanding of his full record.

Thanks to the growing online availability of general circulation and baseball-oriented news publications, this book includes many contemporaneous news accounts of Galvin and his exploits. Through those accounts, sometimes rife with terms and grammar unfamiliar to today's reader, Galvin's own words can be found. It is hoped that the educational and other institutions which are sharing such material will continue collecting and posting invaluable material through the magic of the Internet. This researcher is grateful for what has been done to date and hopeful that such important work will continue. As a print journalist for more than 40 years, the author was always acutely aware that journalism is the first draft of history. Being able to access such first drafts by other reporters without having to travel great distances to dig into library microfilms is an unfettered joy.

Pud Galvin's story is one that is rich in color and accomplishment at a pivotal time in baseball history. It is hoped the reader will share the author's wonder at how he could have been forgotten for so long.

Introduction

His final resting place is atop a windswept hill in Pittsburgh's Calvary cemetery. A small, flat headstone, cracked in two places, marks the hard-to-find spot. Here lies James Francis "Pud" Galvin, baseball's forgotten man, a star of the early game, a player whose easygoing nature earned him the affectionate nickname "Gentle Jeems." He was the first pitcher to win 300 games, long before such an accomplishment was considered the benchmark of pitching excellence. Galvin also threw the first perfect game ever recorded, and repeated the feat twice. In all, he held opposing teams scoreless 57 times, thereby blanking them nearly once in every ten complete games he pitched. Off the field, he was less successful. After baseball, he struggled financially. Despite being one of the best-paid players of his day, he died in poverty in 1902 at a relatively young age, reliant on friends for burial and to help his surviving widow and six children. His headstone is that of a pauper because he had become one.

Largely forgotten for 60 years following his untimely death, Galvin was inducted into the Baseball Hall of Fame in 1965, belated recognition for his stellar career. In more recent times, Galvin's name surfaced during debate about whether players who took anabolic steroids, or were suspected of taking them, should be allowed into the Hall of Fame. Jose Canseco, Mark McGwire and others enhanced their performances with testosterone, a move considered cheating, which many observers insist bars them from the shrine to baseball accomplishments. During the heat of the controversy, it was discovered that Galvin had also taken a performance-enhancing substance. So why ban Canseco, McGwire and the others? More recently, Alex Rodriguez, the slugger for the New York Yankees, admitted using steroids and was suspended for the entire 2014 season. Upon returning to the Yankees' lineup in 2015, Rodriguez joined the 3,000-hit club on June 19 with career home run number 667, thereby resurrecting the debate about Hall of Fame honors for cheats. The issue is far from dead.

The revelation about Galvin's use of testosterone led to renewed scrutiny of his remarkable 18-year professional career in St. Louis, Buffalo and Pittsburgh. "Pud," so named because of his ability to turn batters into "pudding" with his fastball, injected into his body an experimental concoction derived from animal testes during the 1889 season. A Pittsburgh medical school provided Galvin with what was then popularly known as the "elixir of life." This came toward the end of a lengthy career he was trying to extend. After his injection, Galvin enjoyed one of the best games of his career. His outstanding performance prompted a Pittsburgh newspaper to headline its account of the game: "Galvin, The Great." It was pointed out anyone who doubted the powers of the elixir need only consider its remarkable effect on the old ballplayer. Other papers hailed the discovery of the energy-producing potion and endorsed it for all baseball players anxious to restore vigor and vitality. Testimonials about its rejuvenating properties filled the press of the day. But, after a flurry of intense interest, the elixir failed to find widespread use or acceptance and was relegated to history along with other potions of the day claimed to work medical miracles.

Was Pud Galvin a pioneer in playing baseball while "juiced"? Should he be tarred with the same brush and considered no better than modern-day users of performance-enhancing drugs who seek to gain an advantage? Is that fair? The question is out there.

Galvin's achievements on the ball diamond were truly impressive and worthy of recognition by the National Baseball Hall of Fame. A workhorse, he pitched nearly every inning of every game, until the latter part of his career when pitching rotations became more common. He played in several major leagues and saw changes in pitching rules that included the significant switch from an underhand to overhand delivery. Galvin's numbers attest to his success. He threw more than 6,000 innings, made 705 appearances, completed 646 games, and recorded 365 wins against 310 losses. During the seasons of 1883 and 1884, at his peak, he won 46 games both years for the Buffalo Bisons of the National League. In ten of his major league seasons, he won 20 or more games. Galvin is one of 24 pitchers to reach the 300-win milestone in baseball history and ranks fifth. Short and stocky, Galvin had a good fastball along with a wicked pickoff move, a solid bat and a fine fielding glove. He enjoyed a long career at a time when relatively simple injuries often prematurely ended the careers of pitchers who were ridden hard by their managers and were not paid if they could not work. The durable Galvin's 19th-century feat is unlikely to be repeated in baseball's modern era when pitchers and their multi-million-dollar arms are carefully protected from overwork by their managers.

Despite his celebrated career, there has been no comprehensive look at this tireless pioneer of the game. In fact, he remains largely forgotten. It took a determined advocate from Buffalo, where Galvin played his best ball, to persuade baseball that one of its stars had been overlooked and his accomplishments deserved recognition in Cooperstown. That move came more than six decades after Galvin's death. Another 40 years passed before Galvin was again recalled during the controversy that erupted about the use of performance-enhancing drugs (PEDs) in the game and candidacy for the Hall of Fame.

Galvin's easily missed and crumbling headstone is a reflection of baseball's forgotten man.

The time has come to bring to light the remarkable life and career of James Francis Galvin, one of the first stars of the game. His winning record is unlikely to be surpassed in the modern era, and his unorthodox effort to improve his late-career performance deserves close scrutiny and understanding.

A pioneer in the early professional game, it is time to do "Pud" Galvin justice and tell his full story.

Some Notes on Spellings and Style

The game. Until about 1900, baseball was spelled "base ball" and occasionally as "base-ball." This book retains the original spelling in quotations from various publications, but uses the modern spelling otherwise. Similarly, positions such as centerfielder were referred to as center fielder and those spellings are used in quoted material.

Pittsburgh. From 1891 to 1911, the "h" was dropped from the spelling of the city of Pittsburgh, at the behest of the United States Board on Geographic Names, which sought to standardize the spellings of place names. The board argued that *copies* of the 1816 city charter omitted the "h." But a city newspaper, the stock exchange and a university refused to comply with the change. When it was learned the *original* charter for the city included the "h," because of its Scottish, not Germanic origin (like other Pennsylvania communities), the "h" was restored. The city at the confluence of the Allegheny and Monongahela rivers was named after William Pitt, and was intended to be like "Edinburgh." This book uses "Pittsburgh" throughout, including in quotations of the day.

Allegheny City. The smaller city across the Allegheny River from downtown Pittsburgh was home to baseball in its early days. The first professional club played at Union Park, renamed Recreation Park, until replaced by Exposition Park, which was closer to the river. The team name was derived from the city, as was the custom of the day, until the Pirates name was adopted in 1891. Publications beyond the city came to refer to the team as Pittsburgh because it was more familiar to their readers. Allegheny City was annexed against its wishes by Pittsburgh in 1907 and is now known as the city's North Side. To this day, the North Side is home to PNC Park for the Pirates and Heinz Field for the football Steelers.

1

Of Cheats and Juicers

Cheating, it has been argued, is ingrained in baseball. More than one book has been written about the phenomenon. One student of the game argued that cheating has been around the sport forever and that baseball's black arts have made the game more interesting and nuanced.[1] That case can certainly be made. For starters, why are umpires needed to rule on fair/foul balls, strikes/balls, and safe/out? If players were true gentlemen, surely they could agree upon such non–life-altering issues among themselves. Shouldn't a sport that is billed as America's national pastime reflect the country's self-proclaimed values of honesty, integrity, decency and fair play? But America, and the world, are competitive places and those who play baseball—and other games—are always looking for an edge in the unrelenting quest for victory.

"Stealing" bases is not only allowed, but celebrated. The taking of a vital part of the other team's turf is rewarded. It is theft. The fleet-footed Rickey Henderson is in the Baseball Hall of Fame largely because of his all-time record of 1,406 stolen bases. Yet the stealing of the signs between pitcher and catcher is disparaged and considered unsportsmanlike. It is not illegal. Nor is eavesdropping. During their conversations on the mound, pitchers, pitching coaches and catchers cover their mouths to protect themselves from opposition lip-readers anxious to know what's coming next. For their part, hitters have corked their bats to lighten them and speed their swing at the plate. That move, however, is considered going too far. Pitchers have been particularly inventive and devious over the years, and it has taken time for baseball to adapt. They can no longer apply spit to the ball or use abrasives to doctor or deface it to make it more lively—and harder to hit. Nor can they apply pine tar to their fingers to improve their grip and control. Both steps are illegal under the rules of today's game. Pitchers have found other ways to gain an advantage. In the early days of the game, the curveball was considered unfair by some observers. At Harvard University in the 1880s, President Charles W. Eliot wanted to drop baseball as a varsity sport when he learned that one of Harvard's pitchers was throwing the pitch. "I understand that a curveball is thrown with a deliberate attempt to deceive. Surely that is not an ability we would want to foster at Harvard," he huffed.[2] In those days, a pitch that curved in flight was often described as a "deceiver" in press accounts. Clearly, Eliot's was a Victorian mindset and a minority view, because the curve survived. Interesting questions arise about where baseball has traditionally drawn the line between what is considered legal, or acceptable, and what is not. Oftentimes, what has been accepted as part of the game in one era has been outlawed in another.

Players constantly seek a competitive edge to complement the natural abilities they have honed to perfection. Their perspective is from the dirt, grass and sweat of a ballfield, and is far different from that seen from the ivory towers of academia by Victorian moralists. They desperately want to win. And the hunt for new ways to do so has persisted. Cheating is prevalent, according to players themselves. The great hitter Rogers Hornsby, late in his fine career, admitted: "I've cheated, or someone on my team has cheated, in almost every single game I've been in."[3] Hornsby played in 2,259 games from 1915 to 1937. That is a telling and powerful admission from one of the top players who plied his trade with five different teams over more than two decades. Apparently no one held this confession of moral shortcomings against him, because he was elected to the Baseball Hall of Fame in 1942.

Some players have gambled on the outcome of games, and the early professional game was nearly killed off because of gamblers who bought players to "throw" important games for them. Fans, unable to trust that the games they attended would be played fairly, began to turn away from professional baseball. The Louisville Grays scandal of 1877 saw four players barred for life from the National League for selling out to gamblers who had big money riding on Boston in the pennant race that year. Gambling continued to flourish despite the banning of players infected by it. In 1919, eight members of the Chicago White Sox, including "Shoeless Joe" Jackson, were bought off by gamblers whose money was riding on Cincinnati to win the World Series. The "Black Sox" scandal showed how easily players could still succumb to temptation. Many decades later, Cincinnati Red Pete Rose became addicted to betting on games. The prolific hitter nicknamed "Charlie Hustle" spent more than two decades in the game and would otherwise be enshrined in Cooperstown today but for his moral failure. Rose's weakness saw him become deeply indebted to bookmakers while he was still playing the game. He eventually admitted he bet on Reds games while he managed the team, prompting his lifetime ban from the game. Baseball players were still struggling with doing the right thing in the latter part of the 20th century.

As respected law professor and author Roger I. Abrams has candidly observed, we should not be surprised if players prove they have feet of clay.

They are products of their environment. Baseball, he asserted, is merely a reflection of America, with all its warts and imperfections.

> The faults of those who have played the National Game mirrored those who pursued other games in America—in business and in politics. Corruption, bribery, blatant violations of the law, violence in support of business advantage and other repulsive criminal activities have always been a part of American life. While we have deluded ourselves into believing that we alone among nations stand for human dignity and equal rights, we are just part of the matrix of deceit.[4]

Abuse of alcohol among players was also prevalent from the early days of the professional game in the 1870s, when it was considered as much of a scourge as gambling. The National League was founded in 1876 in a bid to rid the game of gambling once and for all and to demand better behavior from players. But, like gambling, alcohol abuse continued for decades. Among the many prominent stars with a fondness for drink was the Yankees slugger of the 1950s and 1960s, Mickey Mantle. An alcoholic for most of his life, Mantle conceded his drinking kept him from being a better player and person. In his later years, he warned about the dangers of alcohol as his liver failed him. It was a factor in his death at age 63.[5] Mantle was inducted into the Baseball Hall of Fame in 1974.

In more recent times, baseball has seen the rise of drug use, particularly steroids, that proponents say enhance athletic performance. As far back as the late 1800s, athletes in a number of sports were looking for a competitive advantage through drugs. They took caffeine, ether, nitroglycerine, ephedrine, tobacco, opiates, cannabis, cocaine, and even strychnine to help them excel or to dull their pain so they could still compete.[6] About a century later, with advances in chemistry, some athletes believed that anabolic steroids—synthetic steroid hormones similar to testosterone that promote the growth of muscle—could enhance their strength and performance.

Major League slugger Jose Canseco admitted publicly he began using them as early as 1984. "Steroids is the future," he insisted, calling himself "the godfather of steroids." Canseco's 2005 book, *Juiced: Wild Times, Rampant 'Roids, Smash Hits and How Baseball Got Big*, described the use of steroids in the game. In his tell-all tome, he named power hitters Mark McGwire, Rafael Palmeiro and Sammy Sosa as fellow users. Canseco had retired in 2001 after belting 462 career home runs and stealing 200 bases for eight major league clubs. His revelations prompted public outcry, accusations of cheating and lying—and denials. A mere three years later, Canseco said he regretted naming names, but more importantly, *using* steroids. Steroids, he admitted, "destroyed my life completely," and he was openly becoming concerned for his health.[7] Palmeiro and Sosa tested positive for steroids, but insisted they had never taken them. Slugger Barry Bonds and pitcher Roger Clemens were also suspected of using them but firmly denied doing so.

What became billed as the "Steroid Era" in baseball saw a significant development during the 1998 season. That year, St. Louis Cardinal Mark McGwire and Chicago Cub Sammy Sosa battled it out in a home-run race that captured the public imagination and filled ballparks. More importantly, it helped rebuild public interest in Major League Baseball that had taken a pummeling because of the 1994 players' strike. The strike, triggered by owners seeking a salary cap and fueled by player distrust, led to the cancellation of the latter part of the season. Upset, fans had been slow to return to the ballpark. The home-run race of 1998 between the powerfully built McGwire and Sosa captured headlines on a daily basis and saw fans streaming back, hoping to witness history.

That same season, reporter Steve Wilstein was covering the McGwire-Sosa battle for the Associated Press. The reporter was not a regular on the baseball beat, having covered, among things, doping scandals in the Olympics. One day, the alert scribe noticed a brown bottle in McGwire's locker with the label "androstenedione." Wilstein, not familiar with the name, carefully jotted it down and began to look into the compound more commonly known as "andro." He discovered it was a perfectly legal drug, sold over the counter in drug and nutrition stores. But it was related to steroids and was believed to stimulate the growth of muscles and increase the production of testosterone. Androstenedione, he learned, was already banned by the National Football League, the National Collegiate Athletic Association, and the International Olympic Committee. Billed as a "dietary supplement," it had recently been pulled from store shelves by the General Nutrition Center chain because of health concerns.

When he reported his findings about "andro," Wilstein found himself ostracized by baseball writers. Cardinals manager Tony La Russa was apoplectic. Trained as a lawyer, La Russa took a legalistic tack. He said the reporter had violated McGwire's privacy and that all Associated Press reporters should be banned from locker rooms of major league teams for the balance of the season. Other players appeared unconcerned, however, as sales of "andro" skyrocketed because of the publicity about its alleged value. Fans were focused more on the home-run race. McGwire ultimately broke Roger Maris' season home-run record of 61, smashing 70 by season's end, compared to the 66 recorded by Sosa. In defending his use of "andro," McGwire said: "Everybody that I know in the game of baseball uses the same stuff I use." In so saying, he was channeling Rogers Hornsby and his defense of cheating. McGwire added that if it were to become illegal, he would stop using it.[8] The burly slugger explained that "andro" had helped his body recover from injuries. He said he had also tried human growth hormone several times and had used other performance-enhancing substances for about a decade in all.

McGwire didn't wait for "andro" to become illegal, however. By August

1999, he said he had discontinued using it four months earlier because he was concerned about the impact his use might have on impressionable children who looked up to him. McGwire continued to insist, however, that there was nothing wrong with the substance. Meanwhile, it was still being sold over the counter in drug stores and on the Internet despite a growing consensus within the medical community that it was "essentially an anabolic steroid."[9]

Major League Baseball Commissioner Bud Selig said he had a lot of faith in McGwire but the player's move would not prompt baseball to abandon its neutral stance on the supplement. Selig said MLB and the Players' Association had retained Harvard University to conduct a study into androstenedione. Reports of health concerns were mounting. A just-completed study at Iowa State University, for instance, found it did little to build muscle in 30 men but did raise the risk of heart disease, pancreatic cancer and breast enlargement. Some doctors criticized the Iowa study because of the small amount of "andro" administered to subjects compared to the amount routinely consumed by body builders (and presumably, ballplayers).

Major League Baseball, embroiled with player and privacy concerns, had decided to lead from behind on the issue of androstenedione. It initiated a modest drug-testing policy in 2002, but it wasn't until mid–2004 that MLB added "andro" to its list of banned substances. Because it had to. Just a few months earlier, the U.S. Food and Drug Administration had moved to stop the sale and distribution of the steroid-based drug still being promoted as a dietary supplement. The federal agency sent warning letters to 23 companies to stop distributing "andro" or face enforcement actions.

"Young people, athletes and other consumers should steer clear of andro because there are serious, substantial concerns about its safety," said Health and Human Services Secretary Tommy G. Thompson, in explaining the federal government decision. His agency noted that one in 40 high school seniors had reported they used "andro" the previous year. Thompson insisted there are "no shortcuts" to building stronger bodies: "The best way to get faster and stronger is through good diet, nutrition and exercise."[10] For its part, MLB offered up Rob Manfred, vice-president of labor relations and human relations, who was succinct: "We've banned andro based on the movement by the federal government this year."[11]

About a month after Canseco's *Juiced* was released in 2005, the House Committee on Government Reform decided it was time to pressure Major League Baseball to toughen its policies against steroids. Some penalties for using them had just been introduced but they were considered insufficient by outside interests. Several members of the committee took note of a recent report from the Center for Disease Control that estimated 500,000 American teens were taking steroids, at least partly because their sports heroes did.

Called as witnesses were Commissioner Bud Selig, executive director of the Players' Association Donald Fehr, and several players including Canseco, McGwire, Palmeiro, Sosa, Clemens, and pitcher Curt Schilling. Also heard from was United States Republican Senator Jim Bunning of Kentucky, a former major leaguer who had been inducted into the Baseball Hall of Fame in 1996. Bunning recorded 224 wins while playing for four teams in his 17 years as a pro and was clearly unimpressed with reports of widespread drug use in baseball and the industry's response to it.

"What is happening in baseball now is not natural and it is not right," Bunning said, noting Congress would have to take action because baseball players and owners were not taking adequate steps to rid the sport of drugs. He suggested players found to have used steroids should have their records erased. "It's not their game," Bunning said of the players. "It's ours. They're just enjoying the privilege of playing it for a short time. What I think many of the players do not understand is that many players came before them, and many will come after them. They all need to protect the integrity of the greatest game ever."[12]

McGwire, citing advice from his lawyer, declined to admit to the committee that he had used steroids. "My message is steroids are bad, don't do them," was about all he was prepared to say. Representative Patrick T. McHenry, a Republican from North Carolina, asked players appearing before the committee if using steroids amounted to cheating, as he sought a simple "yes" or "no" in response. McGwire replied: "That's not for me to determine." Schilling replied with a "yes," while Palmeiro said: "I think it is." Sosa and Canseco both offered: "I think so."[13]

There it was. Steroids were linked to cheating, the bad and unacceptable form of cheating. Hall of Famer Bunning went so far as to suggest that those who had taken performance-enhancing drugs to improve their play ought to have their records erased, as though they had never donned a uniform. The integrity of the game deserved nothing less, he argued.

The debate about whether players who "juiced" should be inducted into the Hall of Fame in Cooperstown was underway. Many observers saw them as cheaters. The bad kind. Many of the top players of the day, who would ordinarily be expected to be inducted into baseball's shrine based on exceptional careers, were tainted by the steroid scandal. Induction is the highest honor that can be bestowed on a player for achievement in his career, but several players were now in jeopardy of being blackballed. They included McGwire, Sosa, Palmeiro, Clemens, Canseco, and Bonds. It would be up to those who vote players into the Hall, about 550 members of the Baseball Writers' Association of America. "Voting," explains the Hall of Fame, "shall be based upon the player's record, playing ability, integrity, sportsmanship, character and contributions to the team(s) on which the player played."[14] This was known as the so-called "character clause," that some said clearly excluded players who had used artificial means to improve their play. There would be plenty of advice, both for and against induction, from many quarters, for years to come.

Sports Illustrated writer Tom Verducci reported that as early as 2001, players who had not resorted to drugs had complained to him that they felt disadvantaged. Some, he said, had lost their jobs and money because they opted to play "clean." A year later, Verducci wrote about the problem of steroids in baseball and claimed that Texas Ranger Ken Caminiti, who admitted steroid use during his 1996 MVP season and for several years afterward, estimated about half of all players were using them. Verducci said he concluded baseball had become an "uneven playing field." And he said voting for Hall of Fame candidates was made difficult because of "the kind of toxicity the players left behind from The Steroid Era." Verducci reminded fans of the extent of juicing and the problems it created for those who elect members of the Hall of Fame as he vowed in 2013 that he would never vote for any player known to have taken steroids.[15] Verducci had plenty of company in his position. Within days, Barry Bonds and Roger Clemens took a beating in their first appearance as candidates for the Hall of Fame ballot. The wildly successful hitter and pitcher fell far short of the 75 percent vote needed from writers for election. Bonds received 36.2 percent, Clemens 37.6 percent. McGwire received a paltry 17 percent vote in his first year of eligibility. For the first time since 1996, no players at all were chosen. The vote was dramatic and was described by the New York Times as "the most resounding referendum yet on the legacy of steroids in baseball."[16] By early 2015, when it was announced pitchers Randy Johnson, Pedro Martinez and John Smoltz were being inducted along with second baseman Craig Biggio, the fate of steroid cheats Clemens and Bonds was clear. Their vote totals remained below 40 percent, while McGwire and Sosa received 10 percent or less and Palmeiro dropped off the ballot at less than five percent. "It now seems certain that the players who have been caught, confessed or have voluminous evidence stacked against them as cheaters will never get into the Hall," Washington Post sports columnist Thomas Boswell wrote.[17]

Players such as slugger Frank Thomas, who spoke out against performance enhancing drugs while the Steroid Era was underway, said users should never darken the hallowed corridors of the Hall of Fame. "They cheated," declared Thomas, the long-time Chicago White Sox player inducted into Cooperstown in 2014, the same year Alex Rodriguez served his suspension for drug use.

Players who took PEDs were not without some support. Darren Rovell, sports business reporter for CNBC, suggested a "Steroid Era" wing could be added at Cooperstown. He said ball fans want to see the stars of the game saluted, and attendance at the Hall had begun to fall when writers turned their backs on players like Bonds, Clemens and others. Failing that, he said, voting should be taken away from writers and placed in the hands of those who understand baseball is business and "it's good business to induct performance-enhancers or suspected performance-enhancers."[18]

Tony La Russa, the manager of the Cardinals when McGwire was blasting home runs, said shortly before his own 2014 induction into the Hall of Fame that the big stars of the Steroid Era should not be excluded from Cooperstown. "It's my two cents, but I think you should let them in, but with an asterisk," he said. He would be happy to have Bonds, Clemens and McGwire join him in the Hall, La Russa said.[19]

Two years earlier, the head of the baseball players' union made a similar argument. Michael Weiner argued that users of PEDs should not be excluded by Cooperstown. "If you want to have some notation on their plaque that indicates that they were either judged to have used performance enhancing substances or accused of having done that, so be it," Weiner told the National Press Club in 2012. The executive director of the Major League Baseball Players' Association said he would also like to see Pete Rose similarly saluted despite his well-documented gambling problems. The Hall, he insisted, "is for the best baseball players that have ever played."

Bob Nightengale, a *USA Today* sportswriter, complained bitterly about the hypocrisy of baseball writers picking and choosing who should be inducted when the use of performance enhancing drugs was so widespread. He noted in 2015 that 113 current or former league players had been suspended for using PEDs. Further, he noted, there were another 103 players who tested positive for steroid use in an anonymous 2003 survey, and 89 players had been identified as PED users in the weighty Mitchell Report issued in 2007. Many players were just rumored to have used chemical help. "I vote for the players who had Hall of Fame careers, regardless of their connections to steroids and performance-enhancing drugs," Nightengale declared. "I will always vote for them, providing they never tested positive after baseball introduced penalties for positive results." He added: "Come on, this isn't the Sistine Chapel. We've let murderers, racists and abusers in the Hall of Fame."[20]

But the hardliners prevailed. Baseball writers continued to shun well-known drug cheats in their voting. It was suggested that catcher Mike Piazza and first baseman Jeff Bagwell, who had only been suspected of drug use, might yet be inducted. By the 2015 vote both were just shy of the 75 percent vote threshold. A year later, Piazza was inducted.

In 2014, the Baseball Hall of Fame moved to change its voting process for the first time since 1991, in what was seen as an attempt to undermine the induction chances of players from the Steroid Era. The number of years a player can appear on the Hall of Fame ballot was reduced from 15 years to ten. It was noted at the time that if a player hadn't succeeded in 10 tries, he wasn't going to be voted in. But it was also pointed out that slugger Jim Rice needed the full 15 years, while pitchers Bert Blyleven and Bruce Sutter needed 14 and 13 respectively. The reduction was seen as one intended to reduce the eligibility of McGwire, Bonds and Clemens, who would simply run out of time, and the knotty problems of the Steroid Era could be flushed away more quickly.[21]

Baseball was determined to keep drug users out of the Hall of Fame, whose members already included cheats and alcoholics, outspoken racists like Cap Anson, and violent sociopaths like Ty Cobb.

But had the gates closed too late?

In 2010, "The Tenth Inning," an updated installment of the acclaimed PBS documentary "Baseball" by Ken Burns, was aired. It had a lengthy segment on the use of steroids in the game. Among those interviewed was Tom Boswell of the *Washington Post.* Boswell said he once witnessed a player in his clubhouse drink a concoction he called "a Jose Canseco milkshake." Boswell didn't say what the drink contained, but it was clear in the context of his remarks that it contained something intended to enhance the player's performance. Boswell didn't identify the player either, other than to say he was already enshrined in the Hall of Fame and had increased his home run output after Canseco joined Major League Baseball. Without evidence, or a name, Boswell could easily have been dismissed. But he had some credibility on the subject, having reported as early as 1988 that Canseco was using steroids, only to find his revelation largely ignored. Boswell's comments in 2010 came at a time when widespread steroid use was acknowledged, and they produced howls demanding Boswell identify the miscreant. At NBC-Sports.com, Craig Calcaterra was vexed. He said if Boswell's milkshake drinker had a plaque in Cooperstown, how could McGwire, Bonds, Clemens and others be barred? Calcaterra said he had no problem seeing PED users honored at Cooperstown. "If what Boswell says is true," he wrote, "a steroid user is in the Hall. If it were widely known that a steroid user were in the Hall—and the world didn't end because of it—it would necessarily change the way that other steroid users such as Bonds and company were treated when they came up for a vote. Or, at the very least, it would lay the hypocrisy of the electorate bare should it continue to bar the door to the Hall for these guys."[22] Calcaterra argued that for the sake of "history" Boswell or someone else should identify the drug cheater. But the secret seemed secure.

Three years before Boswell, Roger I. Abrams had named a player who took a performance-enhancing concoction back in 1889. Abrams, an acclaimed writer on baseball, law professor at Northeastern University and MLB salary arbitrator, published his *The Dark Side of the Diamond: Gambling,*

Violence, Drugs and Alcoholism in the National Pastime in 2007. In it, he wrote about the vices that had permeated baseball over its history, not unlike the vices that had gripped America at the same time, including the current outcry about anabolic steroids and other drugs. "Use of steroid-like substances, however, is not a modern phenomenon. It can be traced back to nineteenth-century baseball. In fact, at least one Hall-of-Fame pitcher of that era used a testosterone treatment to improve his performance."[23] The treatment was said to do wonders to boost strength and rejuvenate those who took it.

Abrams identified the player as James Francis "Pud" Galvin, who was voted into the Baseball Hall of Fame by its Veterans Committee in 1965. Abrams noted that Galvin played a particularly outstanding game with the help of a concoction popularly known as "the elixir of life," and that press reports of the day endorsed it and pointed to Galvin's play as proof of its effectiveness. The *New Haven Register* went so far as to say: "The discovery of a true elixir of youth by which the aged can restored their vitality and renew their bodily vigor would be a great thing for baseball nines. We hope the discovery ... is of such a nature that it can be applied to rejuvenate provincial clubs."[24]

Pud Galvin's plaque in the National Baseball Hall of Fame recounts the record of one of baseball's first pitching stars. He is credited with 365 wins. Four of those wins came in the National Association, which many historians do not recognize as a major league. He earned another 36 wins in the International Association, a league not recognized by historians as major, creating a fine conundrum about his true record. With 365 victories, he is fifth among all pitchers in games won and trails only Cy Young in games lost, with 311 (photograph by author).

Supporters of McGwire, Bonds, Clemens and the others pounced upon the discovery to argue that a drug-user was already in Cooperstown. Abrams had clearly linked Galvin to latter-day juicers. The precedent had been set, it was said. So commentators argued it was untenable to bar the latter-day drug cheats.[25]

Galvin, a five-foot-eight workhorse, pitched more than 6,000 innings and completed 646 starts out of his 705 appearances. He stood fifth in all-time wins, proof of an extraordinary career. When written about in recent times, however, which is rarely, he is linked to performance-enhancing drugs.

Yet is it fair to lump him in with chronic cheaters who relied on chemical help to raise their level of play?

Was he helped along the way by a steroid-like concoction?

To put it bluntly, was "Pud" Galvin a cheat, the pioneering juicer of baseball?

And does he deserve an asterisk on his plaque in Cooperstown?

Galvin is tarred with the same brush as modern-day users of performance-enhancing drugs. Is that fair?

The questions are legitimate about one of baseball's early superstars, forgotten for so long after his impressive 19th-century career, resurrected for praise in the 20th century, then again for vilification in the 21st.

2

The Kid from the Kerry Patch

Among the one million poor Irish who sought a better life in America when the devastating Potato Famine gripped their homeland from 1845 to 1852 were Martin Galvin and Bridgette McTigue. Galvin was born in 1827 and McTigue 12 years later, the places unknown. For anyone born on the Emerald Isle, emigration was one means of escaping misery and the likelihood of death when an airborne potato fungus ruined crop after crop of what had become a staple of the Irish diet. About one million of the total population of eight million starved or died from a variety of diseases related to malnourishment.[1] In about 1850, Galvin and McTigue and their families joined the hordes who arrived on the east coast of the United States seeking a better life. But crowded and difficult conditions in port cities like Boston and New York prompted many of the newcomers to continue westward, anxious to escape the discrimination they encountered that barred them from work and decent housing. Galvin, McTigue and others found themselves in what was then considered the western city of St. Louis. There, the Irish settled in an area north of the core on the west side of the Mississippi River known as the "Kerry Patch." It took its name from County Kerry in Ireland, from which so many of them had fled. They lived in shacks and shanties and later, modest tenement houses erected on land owned by the family of the first successful Irish Catholic businessman in the city. The Mullanphys were willing to accommodate the new arrivals who squatted on their land that straddled today's Cass Avenue.

John Mullanphy, the family patriarch, was born in Enniskillen in 1758 in the southern corner of what today is Protestant Northern Ireland. He fled to America in 1792 to escape new laws that penalized Roman Catholics, stripping them of their rights and their land. He became a cotton merchant in Philadelphia, Baltimore and Frankfort, Kentucky, before he learned about St. Louis and its prospects. Originally chosen as a fur trading post by the French in 1763 and laid out by them, St. Louis was part of the vast Louisiana Territory west of the Mississippi claimed by Spain and transferred to France in a secret 1800 treaty. French leader Napoleon Bonaparte, more interested in his territorial and political ambitions in Europe, sold the Territory to the United States in the 1803 Louisiana Purchase. On March 10 the following year, the French flag was lowered for the last time, replaced by that of the young and expanding American republic.[2] That same year, John Mullanphy arrived in St. Louis, a small community of 180 homes, with vital water access to the South and to points north and west. He relocated to Natchez, Mississippi, and then back to Baltimore, before settling permanently in St. Louis in 1819 and becoming successful selling cotton to Britain. Mullanphy fathered 15 children, many of whom he could afford to send to Europe for their education as profits soared from his cotton trade and real estate holdings. He never forgot the needs of others and became well known for philanthropy as his fortune increased. He favored Catholic charities, upon whom many Irish relied as they adjusted to life in St. Louis. Among the recipients of Mullanphy's generosity were homes for orphaned boys and for poor widows, and a school for young ladies. He helped establish a hospital for the Sisters of Charity and an endowment fund for the Ladies of the Sacred Heart. Mullanphy died in 1833, but his large family continued to manage his land holdings and sympathized with all Irish in need, including those arrivals like Martin Galvin and Bridgette McTigue and their families.[3]

Even before the famine, immigrants from County Kerry had gathered in significant numbers on Mullanphy land and by 1842 they had already named it the "Kerry Patch," sometimes simply "The Patch." Bounded by Biddle Street on the south and Mullanphy Street on the north, it stretched westward from 9th Street to 20th Street and Jefferson Avenue. Several slum and ghetto areas developed within "The Patch," and each had its own gang of toughs. The gangs roamed such colorfully named areas as Clabber Alley, Poverty Pocket, Wild Cat Chute, Castle Thunder and Battle Row. The community was a hardscrabble one, tightly knit, struggling with squalor, deprivation and violence as its inhabitants sought to eke out an existence despite widespread discrimination against them. Native St. Louis residents, who were mainly Protestant, mocked and fought the Catholic newcomers, deprived them of jobs and education, and posted signs saying "No Irish Need Apply." Unless they were looking for fights, St. Louis residents avoided the growing Irish section of the city.

Within "The Patch," pickpockets, pugilists and punks grew to become crime bosses. Street gangs morphed into crime syndicates. Fistfights were common and often escalated into more serious warfare when bricks became projectiles, prompting residents to close their shutters and bar their doors for protection. Cockfights were staged in saloons, while nanny goats roamed vacant lots. The community pulled together for the pageantry of the St. Patrick's Day parade in March, which started, appropriately, at St. Patrick's Church. Landmarks included St. Patrick's and the other parish churches of St. Bridget of Erin, and St. Lawrence O'Toole. Pubs and breweries also had their fair share of supplicants.[4] Some dangerous and unpleasant jobs could be found by the newcomers, but they were generally poor-paying ones that no one else wanted.

The population of St. Louis had reached about 65,000 in 1849 when suffering struck the entire city. A devastating flood, a cholera epidemic and a massive fire swept through, claiming one in every ten residents. Despite the tragedy, there was good news for the Irish, whose labor, along with that of the more skilled tradesmen arriving from Germany, helped rebuild the city. There was plenty of work to be done because the building of frame homes was banned. Brick was the building material of choice because it was better able to withstand fire. All the while, the millionaire Mullanphys continued to help Irish immigrants adjust to life in the city. Mullanphy House, located in the midst of the Irish community, acted as a sort of social agency for those needing help. And help was needed. Life expectancy was short for those who lived in the ghettos within "The Patch."[5]

In this difficult environment, laborer Martin Galvin met and married Bridgette McTigue, and they began raising a family. On Christmas Day, 1856, James Francis Galvin was born.[6] He would be the first of nine children for the couple, of which only five survived infancy. Michael followed in 1860. Three more boys, William born in 1861, Martin in 1865, and Patrick in 1866, all failed to survive. Then came Joseph in 1868, Julia in 1870, and Stephen in 1873. Anna, born in 1875, also died. First-born James was an easygoing boy by all accounts, and managed to steer clear of the danger and temptation around him. Unlike many of his peers, he was more likely to talk his way out of trouble than rely on his fists. Given his small stature, this was not surprising and likely a key to his ability to steer clear of violence. Little is known about his formative years other than that he had some rudimentary training as a steamfitter or blacksmith, depending on the source.[7] He had little education and was likely expected to help support his family as the oldest boy in a large household. Like many young men, he gravitated to baseball as an escape from his grim surroundings. In manner, little Jimmy Galvin was a rough-hewn character. His personal habits left much to be desired by the time he became a teenager. He wore only flannel shirts and preferred to eat with his fingers. In years to come, when he began playing baseball and traveled with the team, his teammates often demanded that he eat by himself in the kitchen rather than alongside them.[8] In the fullness of time, however, as he became a success at the game and money came easily, Galvin became almost dapper, often seen wearing white duck pants, shiny patent leather shoes and a stylish straw hat.[9]

2. The Kid from the Kerry Patch   21

By 1860, the year Jimmy Galvin turned four, booming St. Louis had reached a population of 160,000 and was considered the most important city in the American West. While technically and nominally a slave state, Missouri voted to stay on the Union side during the Civil War. The war reduced northbound traffic on the Mississippi and retarded the city's growth, allowing Chicago to make up for lost time and vie to become the leading city in the Middle West and gateway to points farther west.[10]

Shortly before the war, the first baseball clubs were formed in St. Louis: the Cyclones, Unions, Morning Stars, Empires and Commercials, some as early as 1859. They played on Gamble Lawn, just south of Gamble Avenue and West 20th Street, a field long used for cricket. Things changed that year when Merritt Griswold arrived from Brooklyn and established the Cyclone Club to play the form of baseball he knew from New York. A new employee of the Missouri Glass Company, Griswold had played the game in Brooklyn and became a sort of evangelist for the game as played there. He persuaded other St. Louis clubs, then playing another form of baseball known as town ball, to switch to the rules for the New York game, which he published for reference purposes. By 1860, an active baseball season was underway in St. Louis, but with the outbreak of the Civil War, all but the Empire Club suspended play.[11] After hostilities ended, teams quickly re-formed and sought playing fields in a city that was experiencing an economic boom. In 1866, businessman and ballplayer August Solari purchased farmland in North St. Louis along North Grand Avenue at Dodier Street for the first park dedicated to baseball in the city. It became known as the Grand Avenue Ball Grounds, sometimes the St. Louis Base Ball Park. By 1874, it became home to the city's first professional club, the St. Louis Brown Stockings. A wooden grandstand was erected in 1881, when it was renamed Sportsman's Park. It served until 1892, the last year for the American Association in which the Browns played. The following year, the club joined the National League and opened a new park several blocks away.[12]

After seeing the success of baseball's first professional club, the Cincinnati Red Stockings, established in 1869, and others that formed in Rockford, Illinois, and Chicago, St. Louis fans of the game banded together and raised funds to establish a professional nine. St. Louis had surpassed a population of 310,000 in 1870, becoming the fourth largest city in the United States, and was looking to assert itself in trade, commerce—and baseball. Chicago was close behind at 300,000 and about to surge past St. Louis, despite the devastating Great Fire of 1871 that struck the Windy City. During 1872, St. Louis businesses began closing early on Saturdays, freeing their employees to play baseball for company teams in the afternoon. By 1873, teams had proliferated across the city and it was a busy season.[13] Interest was high in fielding a good professional club to battle other cities. Following the example of its great rival

Chicago, St. Louis organizers pursued proven baseball talent in cities along the Eastern seaboard, many of whom were members of the National Association of Professional Base Ball Players, which in 1871 became the first professional league. The St Louis Brown Stockings club was established late in 1874, capitalized at $10,000, and promptly signed four members of the Brooklyn Atlantics to play in St. Louis for the 1875 season.[14] The four were shortstop Dickey Pearce, first baseman Dutch Dehlman, pitcher Frank Fleet and right fielder Jack Chapman. With this nucleus of experienced players, the Browns applied for entry into the National Association for what would be its final year in 1875. Upon the foursome's arrival in St. Louis, Chapman sent a letter to Henry Chadwick, the baseball writer at the *New York Clipper*, saying they were being well treated by "as fine a set of men as I have ever met. They are very anxious for us to beat Chicago. If we only do that—which I know we will—they will be satisfied. This will be the greatest city in the country for baseball the coming season. Everyone appears to be red-hot on it here."[15]

Not to be outdone, another group of baseball enthusiasts also decided to form a professional nine, and in early March 1875 capitalized the St. Louis Red Stockings at $12,000 as they assembled a team of mostly local talent. The Red Stockings, also known as the Reds, likely derived their name from the Cincinnati Red Stockings. That club inspired many other clubs to adopt their name, or variations on it, at a time when originality was in short supply. That same month, at its convention in Philadelphia, the National Association accepted both St. Louis clubs as among its 13 members for the upcoming season. The Brown Stockings, feeling optimistic about their prospects, paid an extra fee to compete for the Association pennant against rival Chicago and others.[16] The Browns, with their imported players, would become one of the loop's stronger teams, winning 39 games to finish in fourth place. The Red Stockings proved far less successful. Their name was shortened to the Reds to avoid confusion with the Boston Red Stockings, who had dominated the NA since its inception. The Reds found a ballpark for their home in central St. Louis along Compton Avenue beside the Missouri Pacific Railroad yard. The weaker St. Louis nine included a future star, teenager Frank "Silver" Flint, at catcher. He was embarking on what would become an outstanding professional career that saw him help the Chicago White Stockings win five National League championships. For the Reds, the sure-handed Flint caught for pitcher Joe Blong, who was kicked off the team in June, suspected of crooked play, by which time he had won three games and lost 12. The team was not very strong and finished tenth in the Association standings in 1875, winning only four games.[17]

On May 4, at the outset of the season, the two St. Louis clubs faced each other before a sizable crowd whose only wagering was on how badly the Reds would lose. Flint, until recently the catcher for the amateur Elephant club in

2. The Kid from the Kerry Patch

town, was installed at third base at the last minute and struggled at the unfamiliar position, although he managed to hit two singles. For the Browns, the game marked the professional debut of pitcher George Washington Bradley, who was on the cusp of a successful career. The newspaper correspondent at the game noted the striking difference between the two clubs who took to the field. He wrote that "the physical contrast between the Eastern professionals and the eight St. Louis players in the scarlet-hosed team was very evident, the former being men of massive mold, while the latter, with one or two exceptions, are mere striplings."[18] The Reds were held scoreless for the first five innings, making several errors, while the Browns drove four runs across the plate. Further defensive lapses in the sixth inning let the Browns score eight more times. The Reds' bats roared to life in the ninth inning to score eight runs but it was too late, and the more powerful Browns won the game, 15–9.

Two days later, on May 6, the Chicago White Stockings came to town to face the Brown Stockings for the first time. What was described as "an immense concourse of spectators," estimated at 5,000, was on hand and betting was heavy on the visitors, fifth-place finishers in the National Association's 1874 season. Browns pitcher Bradley overpowered the visitors' bats, surrendering four hits but not allowing a run, for a 10–0 "whitewash" of Chicago. It was the first time Chicago had been held scoreless since 1873. Bradley's counterpart for the Whites, the veteran George "The Charmer" Zettlein, 32, had a bad day, giving up 18 hits.[19] On May 8, a Saturday, the two teams were at it again and St. Louis turned out in force to see the city's new heroes in action. The Brown Stockings were now favored to win, and an estimated 15,000 to 20,000 fans flocked to the park to witness it. Among the crowd were distinguished visitors such as William Tecumseh Sherman, the Union general in the Civil War whose activities included burning Atlanta to the ground. Commander of the U.S. Army until 1874, he left Washington for his home in St. Louis.

For the rematch, Chicago, anxious to avoid another embarrassment, put Jim Devlin in the pitcher's box and moved Zettlein to first. Devlin fared only slightly better than Zettlein had in the earlier outing. He surrendered eight hits while Bradley held the White Stockings off the scoreboard until the ninth inning. Shutting out a team for 17 consecutive innings was quite an accomplishment and had never before been achieved in baseball.[20] St. Louis had plated single runs in the third and fourth innings and two in the fifth, and it seemed another shutout of the powerful visitors was imminent. But in the ninth, Chicago brought in three runs as the Browns held on for a 4–3 victory. A correspondent noted that "multitudes" flocked to newspaper offices and "prominent saloons" for updates telegraphed from the Grand Avenue grounds "and received with the wildest cheers the results as announced. St. Louis is enthusiastic over its second triumph, and nothing else is talked about on the street or in the hotels or in the barrooms."²¹ Another account suggested the lack of success for Chicago was due to internal strife, with two feuding "cliques," one led by catcher Dick Higham, the other by utility player Scott Hastings. "Captain (Warren) White's efforts to work these elements into a harmonious whole have not, apparently, been successful," it was reported.²²

Despite the lack of hospitality shown them on the ball field, the White Stockings remained in St. Louis for a game against the Reds on May 11. This game proved to be an unexpectedly noteworthy contest between the experienced Chicago club and the mainly local lads upon whom little hope or money was placed. Conditions were poor for play that day, as about 200 fans endured a windstorm that swept the Compton Avenue grounds. Zettlein took his usual position in the pitching circle for the Whites, opposed by Blong for the home nine. The only scoring of the game came in the second inning when Zettlein drove a base hit to score rightfielder Oscar Bielaski, who had hit his way to first, stolen second and advanced to third on a single by leftfielder John Glenn. Silver Flint was thrown out at home plate in the fourth inning, a run which would have tied the game for the Reds. Each team recorded six hits, but sharp fielding prevented any further runs and the game ended with a hard-fought, 1-0 victory for Chicago. At that time, low-scoring games in which fielding trumped batting in the eyes of observers were considered among the best. One newspaper described the game as "the finest ever played anywhere."²³

Clearly, St. Louis had contracted a serious case of baseball fever. Catching it as badly as anyone in the city was the oldest son of Martin and Bridgette Galvin. Jimmy Galvin was likely among the crowds at the ballparks in those early days of May. When he wasn't watching games, he was playing in them. Rather than the minor larceny and violence of gangs, it was the hitting, catching and throwing of a baseball that appealed to the teenager. Especially the throwing. In 1874, at age 17, Galvin was playing for amateur teams in St. Louis—the Turner and Niagara clubs—and the next year for the Niagaras and the more prestigious Empire Club. The earliest record of him playing in a game comes from a box score from April 28, 1874, when he appeared at second base for the Turner club in a game against the visiting Chicago White Stockings, who played several local clubs during a visit. Not surprisingly, Chicago won, 22-5.²⁴ The box score was reproduced by Edmund Tobias, who played for the Empire Club in the 1860s and kept close track of the game as it developed in the city, keeping his notes and box scores. In late 1895 and early 1896, Tobias shared details of those early games and clubs with *The Sporting News*, which was published in St. Louis. His accounts were published every week for four months and were a boon to future historians. Another of his box scores was for a June 11 game in which Galvin pitched for the

Turner club in a 12–2 loss to the Empires. Tobias, who apparently witnessed the game, noted that good fielding was the feature of it and "Galvin played finely" even though he gave up nine base hits. He noted that the Turners were crippled by the absence of their regular catcher and another player to injuries.[25]

Galvin, meanwhile, was still growing into a stocky body with a short neck, broad shoulders, small hands and size-nine feet. Galvin had reached his ultimate height of five-foot-eight and was beginning to put on weight on his way to the 250 pounds, or more, that he would record later in life. The young man proved to be strong, durable and tireless. He also played the outfield, but it was at pitcher where he shone. He threw the underhand pitch of the day hard enough to strike out much older and more experienced batters. Galvin likely watched and played in games at the Grand Avenue Ball Grounds, a dozen blocks or so northwest of his rough-and-tumble neighborhood. He may have also traveled a bit farther south to Compton Avenue to watch the Red Stockings. The young pitcher with a surprisingly fast delivery caught the attention of the Brown Stockings before the more local Reds.

After the May 8, 1875, defeat of Chicago, the Browns' ace, Bradley, took ill and did not return until May 29. The 22-year-old Pennsylvanian had pitched the previous season for the semi-professional team in Easton, and he was beginning a season in which he would win 33 games. His loss left his team in a bad way. The Browns headed out of town on a western trip in mid–May to play the Keokuk Westerns in Iowa and then on to Chicago. Backup pitcher Frank Fleet was unimpressive even though St. Louis defeated the weak Keokuk nine by scores of 15–6, 16–6, and 4–2. The Brown Stockings played the White Stockings in Chicago on May 19, and this time Zettlein was back in form. The White Stockings had their way with Fleet, making 18 hits off him, while Zettlein surrendered only five. Chicago scored three runs in the first inning and never relinquished the lead. The final score was 9–4 for Chicago. Pitching was the difference in the game, about which it was said: "The team from the Mound City were badly crippled by the absence of their pitcher, Bradley, whose substitute, Fleet, was batted all over the field."[26] Late in the month, it was reported: "The management of the St. Louis Club have become dissatisfied with Fleet, and have cancelled his contract. His successor has not been named, but Galvin will probably be the man."[27] It seems strange that the club would let a pitcher go who appeared in three games and won two of them. Management must have had other issues with Fleet. Or they were anxious to see what Galvin could do.

Immediately after their 9–4 loss, the Brown Stockings telegraphed Galvin to come to Chicago. It was no surprise Galvin was summoned. He was one of the outstanding amateur pitchers in St. Louis at the time and was making a name for himself. As late as May 16, while St. Louis was on its road trip, he pitched for the Niagaras against the solid Empire club in a game his club lost, 11–9. On May 22, he appeared in the pitching box for the Browns at the 23rd Street Grounds in Chicago for his professional debut. He was 18.

Under threatening clouds with a distinct chill in the air, the game got underway before a crowd estimated at 5,000. Chicago, seeing Bradley was still absent, had hopes of tying the series with St. Louis at two games apiece. Fleet had been moved to third base and Galvin had replaced him. The *Chicago Tribune* noted that the absence of Bradley "is certainly injurious to the efficiency of their nine" and recalled the difficulty he had provided White Stockings batters in St. Louis. The game proved to be an eye-opener for the Whites and for the *Tribune*:

> The Browns yesterday played an unknown pitcher named Galvin. He has been a member of the St. Louis amateur Niagaras. He was picked by the St. Louis people a short time ago on account of his promising work in the pitcher's position. What they think of him is clearly shown by the fact that they brought him here in great haste to play in this game. For several weeks past he has been steadily practising in a handball alley. He proved to be a player of no ordinary ability. He uses the underhand throw, delivers a ball with great speed, and is not unlike Bradley in his general style. The White Stockings did not find him as easy a customer as might have been expected from an unknown amateur.[28]

Galvin did far better than Fleet at holding the Chicago bats in check. The home team was particularly sharp at fielding but fell behind 1–0 in the second inning when Chicago committed two errors and allowed hits by St. Louis right fielder Jack Chapman and second baseman George Seward. Centerfielder Lip Pike hit a Zettlein pitch to the right field fence and scored St. Louis' only other run when Chapman singled in the seventh. However, the Brown Stockings managed only five hits and booted the ball around, making 12 errors, providing little support for their rookie pitcher. Chicago recorded a dozen hits and seven of their players reached first base on St. Louis errors. They scored single runs in the third, fourth and seventh innings before erupting for three more in the eighth as Galvin tired. The ninth inning was scoreless to give Chicago a 6–2 victory and tie their season series with St. Louis at two games apiece. In a dispatch from St. Louis, the *Tribune* reported it wasn't expected the Browns could win without Bradley. "'Wait till Bradley gets well,' is heard on all sides."[29]

With Bradley still unable to pitch, the St. Louis club returned home for two games against the lowly Westerns of Keokuk. Despite Galvin's loss in Chicago, the Browns again turned to him. His teammates helped him snatch victory from what looked like another defeat on May 25. Trailing 2–0 after seven innings, the Browns' bats came alive in the eighth with three unanswered runs for a 3–2 win, giving the youngster from "The Patch" his first professional victory.[30] In the fullness of time, there would be many, many more.

2. The Kid from the Kerry Patch 27

Two days later, St. Louis romped to a 12–4 win over the same club and Galvin helped his own cause with a single. The Westerns, of tiny Keokuk, population 12,000, disbanded about three weeks later, having won only one game while losing 12. By the time Bradley returned to the lineup on May 29, Galvin had made a strong impression by winning two of his three appearances. The likeable kid returned to the amateur ranks with the Niagaras and the Empires, but he would be called back ten more times before season's end. He was one of the few locals to appear with the Browns that season.

While Galvin awaited his next chance with the professionals, the Browns played host to the Boston Red Stockings on June 5. Boston was a perennial powerhouse and repeat champion in the National Association. Coming into St. Louis, they had not lost a game yet in the 1875 season, with 26 wins and one tie. Albert Goodwill Spalding, the stalwart pitcher for Boston, was in his usual position but his catcher, Deacon White, was unable to play because of a thumb injury. He was replaced by Cal McVey, who moved from first base. The home team fielded and batted well and capitalized on a few Boston errors. The Browns led off the first inning with a single run, but Boston replied with four of their own in the bottom of the inning (they batted last as determined by a coin toss), leading spectators to fear the worst. But the visitors were held scoreless the rest of the way while St. Louis added a single run in the fourth inning and two more in the fifth to tie the game. The excitement at the ballpark was intense through the scoreless sixth and seventh innings. In the eighth inning, Browns shortstop Dickey Pearce led off with a "fair-foul" single, a hit that starts in fair territory but rolls foul, a hit that would be outlawed after the 1876 season. Pearce made it to second on a passed ball by McVey. Centerfielder Lip Pike popped up to Spalding. Jack Chapman then hit a grounder past Jim O'Rourke, the centerfielder playing at third base for this game. Browns third baseman Bill Hague drove a ball to shortstop Warren White, who threw to Ross Barnes at second, forcing Chapman. Barnes relayed the ball to Frank Heifer at first but his throw was wild, allowing Pearce to score what proved to be the winning.

After Bradley made the last putout for the Browns, fans rushed the field and hoisted the conquering hero onto their shoulders. The St. Louis fans cheered themselves hoarse at the unexpected turn of events. The *New York Clipper* correspondent wrote, "the Western team again covered themselves with glory, and gained the greatest victory they have achieved since their organization by vanquishing the champions." The report said the impact on St. Louis supporters was dramatic. "Hats were thrown high in the air, and the victorious players were carried around on the backs of their admirers."[31] The St. Louis accomplishment cannot be underestimated. In its first season as a professional club it downed arguably the best team in the game. It was a minor setback for the Boston nine, however, which went 34–8 on the road and won all 47 of its home games in 1875, rolling to a fourth straight NA pennant.[32] Boston quickly recovered from the June 5 loss, pasting the Browns 15–2 a mere two days later.

In early July, St. Louis played two more games in a home-and-home series with the White Stockings. The first, on July 3, was in Chicago where hometown fans saw the home team win, 8–5, by scoring three runs in the 11th inning. Two days later in St. Louis, a huge crowd estimated at 15,000 was on hand for a rematch. This time, the inconsistent Zettlein give up 23 hits to the Browns, who won, 13–2.[33] The Browns scored a triple play when Zettlein struck out swinging but catcher Tom Miller deliberately dropped the ball. He touched home plate to force out a runner charging in from third, then tagged Zettlein and threw to third base, where Whites shortstop John Peters was called out as he ran from second. Witnessing the July 5 rout of Chicago were members of the Washington club, sometimes known as the Nationals, who were in town for a series of games against the Red Stockings and the Browns. Washington had been struggling both on the field and financially. After defeating the Reds, 12–5, on July 4, members of the team learned their business manager had absconded with team funds and they were stranded with no means to get home. Directors of the St. Louis Browns came to their aid, providing them with train fare and paying expenses.[34]

Galvin again joined the Browns, who were missing Bradley and catcher Miller, for a July 12 start in Brooklyn against the woefully weak Atlantics. George Seward, the backup catcher, was tapped to catch for Galvin. The Browns noticed that Frank Fleet, the pitcher they had released in June, appeared for the Atlantics at the catching position, prompting them to file a protest that paperwork relating to his release was improper and he shouldn't be allowed to play. But the protest proved unnecessary as the Browns rolled to a 6–2 victory. Galvin held the Atlantics to four hits to take his third win.[35]

On July 20, Galvin was called upon again to pitch as Bradley moved to right field for an exhibition game in Lynn, Massachusetts, against the Live Oaks. Galvin gave up five hits as St. Louis doubled the score on the home team, 10–5. At the beginning of August, Bradley injured a finger on his pitching hand and Galvin again entered the pitching box for a game on August 9. This time the opposition was the Philadelphia Pearls, for whom Joe Borden (also known as Josephs) replaced veteran pitcher Cherokee Fisher. Borden was an upcoming star and made seven starts this year, including a no-hitter he threw against Chicago on July 28. It was reported that Galvin pitched well but his teammates struggled with Borden. The Browns managed only five hits and were shut out as Philadelphia, showing their best batting of the season, cruised to a 16–0 victory.[36]

As he pondered his plans for the next season while summer slipped away, Galvin may have seen a short notice in the *New York Clipper* on October

2. The Kid from the Kerry Patch 29

9 that the Brown Stockings had already engaged most of their players for 1876, including the battery of Bradley and Miller, and most of the other members of the 1875 club.[37] Given the fact that Bradley was only three years older than Galvin, then approaching his 19th birthday, the kid from the Kerry Patch may have felt it was time to pin his hopes for a permanent pitching job elsewhere.

Whatever his thoughts about the management of the Browns, or their plans for him, Galvin was not done playing with them as the season wound down. He played right field in an October 22 game against the New York Mutuals in Brooklyn and had one of his club's four hits as the Browns won, 4–3, in a poorly attended game that went ten innings. First baseman Dutch Dehlman, who had all the other St. Louis hits, scored the winning run on a hit to short right field by Lip Pike.[38] In Philadelphia on October 25, Galvin was called in to replace catcher Tom Miller after four innings. The Pearls had their bats working again and downed the visitors, 17–2.[39] Two days later, Galvin played right field as the Browns took on the other Philadelphia club, the Athletics. The Athletics' bats pounded Bradley for nine hits, led by center fielder Dave Eggler with three. The Browns posted eight hits but could bring in only three runs as the Athletics prevailed, 9–3.[40] Galvin made his final pitching appearance for 1875 on October 29, for the Browns. The game was at the Union Grounds in Brooklyn against the Mutuals, a team to which the Browns had not yet lost. Brooklyn scored two runs in the first inning, another in the third and two more in the sixth as Galvin allowed nine hits. St. Louis, trailing 5–3, scored two runs in the seventh inning to tie the score. It soon became too dark to play and the game was called. The score was recorded as 5–5.[41]

Overall, Galvin made eight appearances in the pitcher's box for the Brown Stockings, winning four games, losing two and tying one. He also played two games in the outfield alongside the veteran Pike and worked several innings as a catcher.[42] Jimmy Galvin pitched 62 innings, struck out eight batters and walked one, with an earned run average of 1.16. He was off to a great start.

3

Making His Mark in a Changing World

The National Association collapsed after completing its fifth season in 1875 when Chicago's William Hulbert collared four of its top stars from perennial champions Boston for his White Stockings: Al Spalding, Deacon White, Cal McVey and Ross Barnes. Rather than face repercussions from the Association for his larceny, the Chicago president persuaded like-minded baseball moguls to establish the National League on business principles for 1876. They vowed to put an end to the twin evils of gambling and contract-jumping by players. The Brown Stockings signed up as one of its eight founding teams, but the Red Stockings were not wanted and opted to continue as an unaffiliated team.

Galvin decided to join the homegrown Red Stockings for 1876. Perhaps he realized he would never supplant the impressive Bradley, who was again pitching for the Browns and on his way to amassing 45 wins in 63 complete games and a league-leading earned run average of 1.23. As it turned out that year, Al Spalding, now wearing a White Stockings uniform, recorded two more wins than Bradley. Galvin knew he would do more pitching with the Reds, who retained several players from their disappointing 1875 season but were looking to improve. One of their best, however, six-foot-tall catcher Frank Sylvester "Silver" Flint, a reliable receiver, had signed with the Covington, Kentucky, team. When that club folded, he was hired by Indianapolis and first caught for them on July 11, the day they opened their new stadium.[1] Replacing him on the Reds was Tom Dolan, who performed solidly and had a better bat. In their first foray into professional sport, the Red Stockings hadn't attracted a strong following so they were being cautious as they looked ahead. There was reason to be, given the experience of 1875 when things went downhill after July 4. From Independence Day onward, NA teams stopped making the long road trip west to St Louis to play a weak nine that was rumored to be close to disbanding. No club was willing to make a time-

3. Making His Mark in a Changing World 31

consuming and costly trip to play the Reds because, even with a win, any points awarded for a victory would be removed from its championship record if the Reds later dissolved. The St. Louis nine struggled on and did not disband, winning only four games with 15 losses. Essentially its season had ended early in the 1875 campaign.[2] So the Red Stockings chose to become an independent team for 1876 and play teams that passed through St. Louis, arrange barnstorming road trips and compete in tournaments for cash prizes. As an independent nine, its record would be harder to track than if it had been in a league, and the accomplishments of its players would not appear in record books like those who played for league teams.

During the patched-together 1876 Reds' campaign, Galvin won 31 of the 47 games he pitched.[3] Because it was an independent club, his wins would not be included by historians in his impressive lifetime tally. In the pitching box, he was spelled occasionally by Daniel "Pidge" Morgan, who had appeared in four games the previous year for his hometown Reds, losing three of them. Comprehensive records and game accounts are rather scarce for Galvin's new club, but it proved to be a breakthrough year for the young man, with three of his performances being particularly noteworthy.

The first came during an eastern road trip of nearly three weeks in late June and early July when the Reds barnstormed across Indiana, Ohio and Pennsylvania. They played 15 games and won all but four of them.[4] Midway through the trip, on July 4, the St. Louis club appeared in Philadelphia for a game against the hometown independent team formerly known as the Pearls. The local nine was struggling financially, like its cross-town rival the Athletics, both having to compete for spectators with the Centennial Exposition in Philadelphia which attracted nearly nine million people as the United States celebrated a century as a nation. The Athletics were so cash-strapped that they were expelled by the National League later that season (along with the New York Mutuals) for refusing to make a western tour to complete their schedule. Both Philadelphia clubs went bankrupt.[5] July 4 was full of optimism and celebration, however, as the city of Philadelphia was abuzz with Centennial celebrations, providing competition for the ballgame in which Galvin made some history of his own. He pitched a no-hitter that day as he dominated Philadelphia batters, who reached base only twice. Galvin enjoyed significant support from his Reds batters, who swatted 14 hits, including three apiece by center fielder Dan Collins and shortstop Billy Redmond. Galvin joined the hit parade with two of his own. He had five assists and one putout as his club capitalized on 11 Philadelphia errors for an 11–0 victory.[6]

Galvin's feat came 11 days before George Bradley recorded the first no-hitter in National League history. That benchmark came as the St. Louis Brown Stockings shut out the visiting Hartford Dark Blues and their pitcher Tommy Bond for the third time in a three-game series.[7] On July 11, the Browns won, 2–0, and on July 13 the score was 3–0. The no-hitter game came on the 15th with another 2–0 result. Bradley's work was outstanding, and it was becoming clear Galvin had made a wise decision to switch to the Reds. He would have been stuck in the outfield had he stayed with the Brown Stockings, now playing well under their new manager, Mase Graffen. Dickey Pearce, the 1875 manager, was spelling Denny Mack at shortstop.

Galvin achieved two more outstanding pitching performances six weeks later at a baseball tournament in the small west-central Michigan city of Ionia, midway between Lansing and Grand Rapids. The tournament, with a top prize of $400, attracted the Cass club of Detroit and the Mutuals of Jackson, two of the state's best teams, who often played National Association and League teams. Also expected to attend was the successful Tecumseh club of London, Ontario, across the border to the east. The Tecumsehs were about to become Canadian champions and within a year a charter member and winner of the International Association pennant. The Canadian club did not appear, however, opting instead at the last minute for a more lucrative road trip through eastern Ontario. The Red Stockings took to the field for the first time on August 17, the third day of the tournament, facing the Mutuals in the morning and the Cass club in the afternoon. Galvin's St. Louis nine put on a fine display of hitting and fielding as he pitched like a man possessed. Galvin's blistering underhand fastball proved too much for the Mutuals to handle in the first game. Behind him, his steady defense committed only three errors. Galvin threw a no-hitter at the Jackson club for a final score of 3–0.[8] Hours later, the Red Stockings faced the Cass club, named in honor of Lewis Cass, a Michigan political hero who had been a general in the War of 1812, former governor of the Michigan Territory, U.S. Senator, statesman, and presidential candidate. A close contest was expected because on August 9 in Jackson, the Reds needed ten innings to find their bats and dispose of the pesky Detroit nine, 6–2.

The weekly *Ionia Sentinel* gave the local tournament prominent coverage but failed to fully grasp the importance of the key feature, or report who pulled it off:

> The last game of the day was played by the Red Sox, of St. Louis, and the Cass of Detroit. This was for first money in the first class. The Detroit Club seemed a little disheartened on account of the defeat of the Mutuals in the morning; but they played exceedingly well. The game was in some respects one of the most remarkable on record. The Cass boys did not make a base hit or reach first base during the game. Each man of the club batted three times and each was put out three times. Of the Red Sox Redman [shortstop Billy Redmond] had the best score. He made three runs and struck out twice. J. Gleason [outfielder Jack Gleason] was put out four times and did not get a run.[9]

The box score showed nine goose eggs for Cass, while the Reds scored twice in the second inning, five times in the sixth, once in the seventh and three more times in the ninth, for a final tally of 11–0. This was Galvin's first perfect game, a feat accomplished long before the term was used to describe a remarkable and rare pitching feat. He had faced the minimum 27 batters, giving him the first recorded perfect game in baseball history.[10] And it came mere hours after the tireless hurler shut out the Mutuals. It had been quite a day for the 19-year-old. The *New York Clipper*, the first publication to provide extensive coverage to baseball, shared his dual accomplishments more widely with readers of its August 26 edition, noting the shutout of the Mutuals followed by the defeat of Cass, "the latter club not reaching first base once."[11] The effort was seen as noteworthy, but not enough to give credit to the pitcher or provide a name for that level of pitching perfection. The professional game was still fairly young and coverage of it was evolving. The Red Stockings picked up $400 for their first-place showing and second-place Cass went home with $200.[12]

While Galvin was establishing himself as a rising star, the Brown Stockings and George Bradley were also turning heads in the baseball community. On May 5, the Chicago White Stockings appeared in St. Louis for their first clash of the season. The Chicago club, with its "Big Four" from Boston, was off to a great start, and St. Louis supporters were apprehensive. Earlier, on April 25 in Louisville, White Stockings pitcher Al Spalding threw the National League's first shutout at the Grays in a 4–0 win. Two days later, he repeated the feat in a 10–0 rout of Louisville. Meanwhile, on May 2 in Cincinnati, the White Stockings' new hitting star, Ross Barnes, hit the league's first home run, an inside-the-park blast off Red Stockings pitcher Cherokee Fisher, as Chicago romped to a 15–9 win. Barnes was on fire that day and also hit a triple and single, stole two bases and scored four runs.[13] Spalding and Barnes were justifying the faith placed in them by team president William Hulbert when he lured them from Boston along with McVey and White.

In that first May 5 meeting between Chicago and St. Louis, the pitching of Spalding and Bradley was brilliant, but the Brown Stockings had the edge in fielding and hitting. The only run of the game scored in the first inning when St. Louis catcher John Clapp reached first base on a bad throw by Spalding and advanced to second on second baseman Mike McGeary's "fair-foul" hit. Center fielder Lip Pike then drove Clapp home. The 1–0 result marked Chicago's first loss of the season and produced unbridled joy in St. Louis. Bradley was able to claim his own shutout over the celebrated veteran Spalding. He would have many more that season. Until 1876, shutouts were not common. At the time, they were known as "Chicagos," named after a humiliating no-run loss suffered by Chicago back in 1870. The inaugural 1876 season of the National League, however, saw plenty of "Chicagos." Spalding threw eight shutouts that year as his playing career neared its end. The eight would have been a record. But Bradley logged 16, still a major league record, tied only once, in 1916, by Pete Alexander, the Phillies' Hall of Famer.[14] Bradley was dubbed the "Chicago King" for good reason.

St. Louis, led by Bradley, was on a roll, shutting out Cincinnati, 11–0, on May 13 and the Philadelphia Athletics, 17–0, on June 1. The Browns were among the elite teams in the new league. The National League's pennant race was eventually won by Chicago, however, with 52 victories against 14 losses for a winning percentage of .788. The 47 wins earned by Spalding led the league as he and another newcomer to the team were largely responsible for its success. Ross Barnes led hitters with a batting average of .429 and was first in most hitting categories. It seemed St. Louis would place second after defeating the Hartford Dark Blues, 6–4, on September 16 in Hartford's last home game. But Hartford embarked on its final road trip and won nine straight games, including one in St. Louis, to edge past the Brown Stockings. In the final standings, Hartford had 47 wins and 21 losses for a winning percentage of .691. St. Louis had 45 wins and 19 losses for a winning percentage slightly better at .703. Today, the team with a higher winning percentage would prevail and St. Louis would awarded second place. But until 1882, standings were determined by total wins alone, so Hartford was considered the runner-up to Chicago and the Browns took third.[15]

Like other non-members of the National League, the Red Stockings saw players lured away by higher salaries, even while they were still under contract. The National League had little regard for outside teams, even though it had condemned the practice of players jumping from one team to another, a practice known as "revolving" and common in the old National Association. Collins, the centerfielder for the Red Stockings, accepted his latest pay packet at the end of July and promptly jumped to the Louisville Grays in the National League. This prompted Henry Chadwick, baseball writer at the *New York Clipper*, to huff: "An idea seems to prevail with some players of the professional class that, though it is not safe to 'revolve,' or forfeit and break contracts with the League clubs, it is quite legitimate to do it with 'outside' organizations." He noted that some players obviously felt non–League organizations had no power to prevent contract jumping. A letter protesting the Louisville action by Thomas McNeary of the Reds to Louisville president W. N. Haldeman accompanied Chadwick's article.[16] For his part, Collins played seven games with the Grays.

On August 7, the St. Louis Reds embarked on their fourth road trip of the season and continued their run as one of the strongest non–League teams. By September 5, they completed 20 games on the trip and had lost only four, three of those by a single run. Of the 70 games played to that point, they had won 55, lost 14 and recorded a tie. They shut out 11 teams and suffered that same fate four times.[17] At the end of the season, the final tally was 67 wins, 23 losses and one tie. They shut out 12 teams and were shut out six times.

They had not done well in St. Louis, however, where they lost all six games played against the crosstown Brown Stockings. Among their notable wins scored that year were those against the Cass, Philadelphia, Allegheny, and Indianapolis clubs.[18]

The National League, whose eight teams had been reduced to six after the expulsion of the New York Mutuals and Philadelphia Athletics, was not the only game in town when it came to professional baseball. The league hadn't been successful financially in its first year and some were wondering if it could survive. Only Chicago had made money. Boston, which had been happily solvent in the National Association, lost $777.22 in 1876 and would lose another $2,230.85 the next year.[19] Philadelphia had gone bankrupt. The league entered 1877 with only six teams: Chicago, Boston, Louisville, St. Louis, Hartford and Cincinnati. Many large population centers were missing, like New York, Philadelphia, and Washington, and the viability of Hulbert's exclusive league was anything but assured. Baseball, generally, was thriving, however. It was estimated there were as many as 50 professional organizations at the time, and *Beadle's Dime Base-Ball Player* listed 30 of them in 1876. They included Philadelphia, New York, the Red Stockings of St. Louis, Allegheny of Pittsburgh, several clubs in New York state and Massachusetts, along with those from Rhode Island, Connecticut, New Jersey, West Virginia, Ohio, Indiana, Tennessee, California and two in Southern Ontario—London and Guelph.[20] With only six playing in the tightly controlled National League, other options were sought by the many clubs who were excluded. L. C. Waite, secretary of the St. Louis Red Stockings, was unhappy that the National League was trying to monopolize the professional game and cherry-pick only those teams it felt were suitable for its purposes. A transportation agent at the United States Quartermaster's depot in St. Louis, he understood clearly what fair dealing was all about. Waite was still stinging from the loss of the "revolver," Collins, to Louisville. The league moguls had decreed that only one club was allowed from each city, for instance, so his nine was excluded while the crosstown rival Brown Stockings were granted membership. Waite was not alone in his grudges or in his thinking.

During their road trip of June and July, the Reds played the unexpectedly strong Allegheny Club twice, winning 12–8 and losing 5–4. On a third occasion, the Reds won, 10–3. Galvin of the Reds was a more formidable hurler than Allegheny's Russ McKelvy, and the St. Louis club's only loss was due largely to errors. Waite developed a friendship with Harmar Denny McKnight, a director of the Allegheny club and a great promoter of baseball in Pittsburgh. The Steel City was also dubbed "The Smoky City," because its iron and steel industries dirtied its air, but also brought prosperity and civic boosterism. Residents felt Pittsburgh could compete with major U.S. cities, and by the mid–1870s its population had surged past 100,000. Its neighbor to the north across the Allegheny River, Allegheny City, had 50,000 inhabitants, bringing the total population of the metropolitan area to a bit less than half that of St. Louis. Allegheny City was where many Pittsburghers worked and played. Heavy industry in both cities attracted workers from a wide area, and by 1874, Pittsburgh was the home of 29 wrought-iron works and eight crucible steel mills. Allegheny City had 15 foundries and machine-and-engine-building shops. The two cities were a hub for railroads, while large mills produced paper and lumber along the Monongahela, Allegheny and Ohio Rivers. Industry was powered by the region's abundant supply of coal.[21]

Baseball came as a welcome relief from the long hours and tedium of industrial work, its pastoral connotations a nice change for those who toiled in the hot mills, furnaces and factories. Baseball had flourished in Allegheny City since the end of the Civil War with strong amateur clubs like Enterprise, Olympics and Xanthas. Most games were played at Union Park, later known as Recreation Park, lying south of Pennsylvania Avenue and alongside the Pittsburgh, Fort Wayne and Chicago Railroad. In 1869, the Olympics ventured down the Ohio River to play the Cincinnati Red Stockings, baseball's first openly professional club. The Olympics were pounded 54–2 in the 43rd consecutive victory for the storied Red Stockings, whose streak of 69 in a row ended with a loss to the Atlantics in Brooklyn in 1870.[22] Undaunted, Pittsburgh and Allegheny City baseball fans still dreamed of fielding a club competitive with other cities. By 1876, local ball enthusiasts, including Denny McKnight, decided the time had come for Pittsburgh to have a professional club and approached the National League. But the National League wasn't interested in granting a franchise.

That didn't dissuade McKnight and his friends. In late February, three weeks after the league was formally established, the Allegheny club became the first professional baseball organization in the city, with McKnight as a director. The Alleghenys would be an independent nine. On April 15, their first game was played at Union Park, which had a serviceable, 2,500-seat grandstand. Allegheny defeated the local Xanthas, 7–3.[23] McKnight, a keen civic booster who enjoyed baseball as a teenager, was a member of two prominent families. His father, Robert McKnight, a lawyer, was a city councilman and member of Congress, while his mother, Elizabeth O'Hara Denny, was from a wealthy land-owning family. Her family owned Union Park, so her son was assured of an understanding landlord. Denny McKnight, the oldest of their ten children, obtained a degree in mining and metallurgy from Lafayette College, in Easton, and after a stint as an industrial bookkeeper at Third National Bank, established an iron smelting company, the Eclipse Steam Works, in the late 1870s.[24]

The Allegheny Club, as a semi-professional nine, had a successful season in 1876, winning 39 games, losing 25, and tying three. Among its victories

3. Making His Mark in a Changing World 37

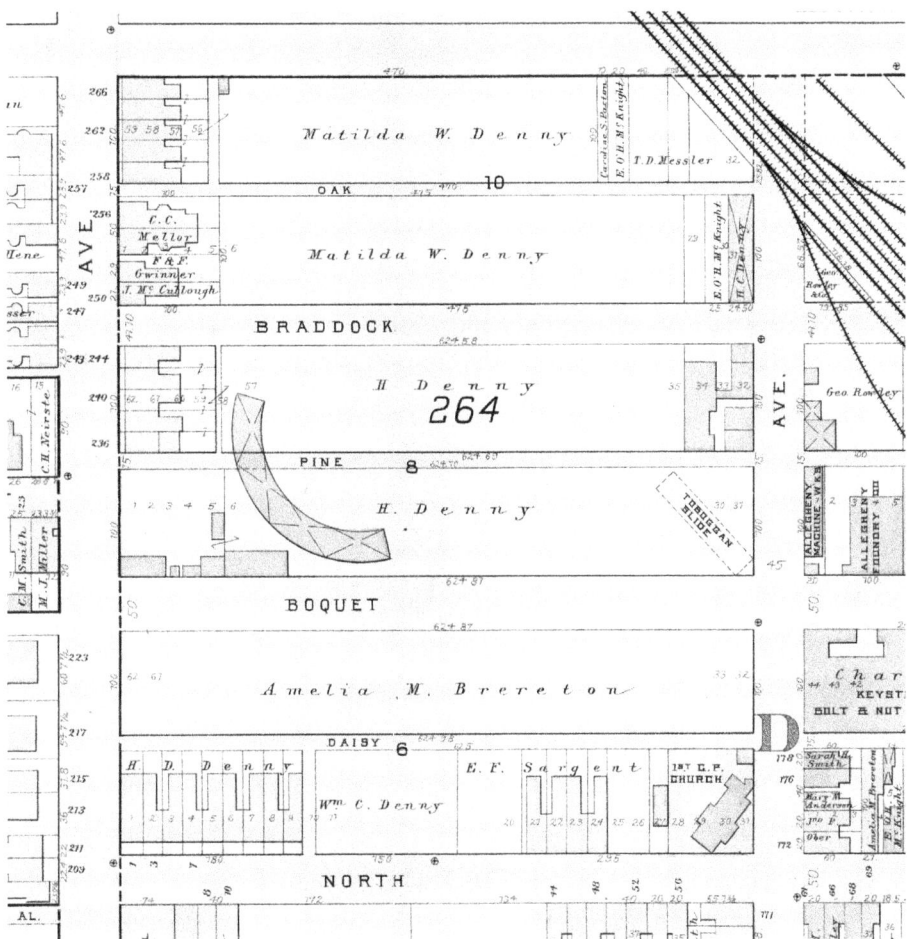

When Harmar Denny McKnight went looking for a home for his Allegheny baseball club for 1876, he didn't have far to go. His mother's family, the Dennys, owned many parcels of land in Allegheny City, just across the Allegheny River from Pittsburgh. This land, bounded by Pennsylvania Avenue to the north, Bouquet Street (today, Behan Street), Allegheny Avenue to the west and Grant Avenue (today, Galveston Avenue) to the east, was chosen. First named Union Park, it became Recreation Park in the early 1880s (G. M. Hopkins & Co. real estate maps, 1872–1940. Archives Service Center, University of Pittsburgh).

were those over the Buckeyes of Columbus, the Philadelphias, New Haven, Indianapolis (three times), the St. Louis Browns, and the Cincinnati and St. Louis Red Stockings.[25] Aside from McKelvy, it tried two or three other pitchers as the club struggled for consistency in the pitching box.

Pittsburgh's team, like the second one in St. Louis, was looking for challenges and unwilling to wait until the National League decided to invite them into its ranks. Allegheny president McKnight saw eye-to-eye with Waite of the Red Stockings as they discussed the discrimination they felt they faced. The pair became allies as they considered some sort of alternative to the National League. After much discussion and consulting other teams, they came up with a plan and agreed to test the waters of professional baseball. In a letter dated September 23, sent to the leading non–League baseball teams of the day and published in the *New York Clipper*, Waite said he was soliciting opinions from the baseball community to determine if there was support for creation of a new baseball organization out of concern for "the welfare of the national game." He was still upset at how the National League was trying to monopolize the game and contributing to high player salaries. Waite looked ahead to the next season:

> We should go systematically to work to remedy the evils that beset us during the past, and also to take some action in regard to the League, the few clubs composing which seem to be so anxious to have a monopoly of the business, and to dictate terms to the hundreds of good clubs outside its code of laws. It will not take long to convince any man of common sense that, if the first class non–League clubs will band together, with rules as stringent as those of the older organization—binding not only on the players, but on their employers also—an association can be formed larger and stronger than any that has ever existed in this country. Such an association should be formed at as early a day as practicable ... under no circumstances whatever should we play League clubs, and only twenty-five cents admission should be charged to our games. It has been practically demonstrated this season that non–League clubs can play every bit as pretty a game of ball as their older rivals; and when but half-price is charged, we are sure to receive our share of public patronage.[26]

Waite stressed that his views represented those of his Red Stockings club and he wanted feedback as soon as possible from other teams about whether the notion of a new organization was worth pursuing. *Clipper* baseball editor Chadwick, in his review of the National League's first season, echoed many of the concerns expressed by Waite and McKnight. Chadwick insisted clubs had lost money because of the 50-cent admission fee, which failed to acknowledge the tough economic times. He said hiring players while still under contract elsewhere was "demoralizing," and such moves contributed to high salaries that some clubs proved unable to pay. Chadwick said that revolving continued to be a problem in the semi-professional arena, and he was aware of men who had played for eight different clubs within three months and others who played for three different teams in as many weeks. He argued that things must improve.[27]

Also looking for change were the principals of the Cass club of Detroit, the West End club of Milwaukee, the Tecumseh club of London, Ontario, and McKnight's Allegheny club. All sent letters of support to Waite, which were published in Chadwick's *Clipper* on November 4. "Go ahead and push

3. Making His Mark in a Changing World 39

it through," wrote R. B. Sheeran of Cass; "We are in favor of the organization your circular speaks of," said Theo Myler of Allegheny; "It is a good idea," said W. P. Rogers of West End; and "We are prepared to become one of its members," offered Harry Gorman, secretary of the Tecumsehs. In his commentary about the positive feedback, Chadwick suggested the new organization should have a "liberal policy," by inviting Canadian clubs to join and not ban games against National League clubs. He urged a cap on player salaries along with a maximum 25-cent admission fee, and he encouraged other clubs to contact Waite.[28]

Waite's letter struck a responsive chord. There was an appetite for change in baseball and his timing was perfect. In early 1877, Waite, based on the feedback he received and following consultation with McKnight, sent the following letter to about 50 baseball organizations and the *New York Clipper*, calling for the creation of a new, broad-based organization:

> Dear Sir: Let me give you a little idea of what kind of an association we ought to form. It would take in all clubs in the United States and Canada who hire part or all of their players on the broad ground of protection to clubs and players alike, and allow them a full representation in the convention, say, about two votes each, all of whom should be governed by the constitution and by-laws of the Association. Then have a ring within the ring, composed of clubs who desire to compete for the championship, who should be governed by a code of rules something like the League's. This would allow and bring under some kind of restraint and responsibility the vast number of clubs who play as they please, under such rules as they please, with what men they can get, and a new nine every game. This peculiar kind of play and club tactics has a demoralizing influence on the rising players, upon whom we here hope to depend in the future. It would also be beneficial to fostering good nines at various points who would be able to keep up, knowing they could not be broken up every day by secession of players, inveigled away by weaker clubs.[29]

The new organization, as envisaged by Waite and McKnight, would adopt a "big tent" approach, rather than the exclusive one of Hulbert's league, while using similar playing rules but would provide greater democracy for member clubs. It was an ambitious venture, proposed during the prolonged economic downturn that was challenging the capitalists behind the fledgling National League.

McKnight and Waite had an influential friend in Chadwick, who was also anxious to ensure that the game of professional baseball was broadly based and not restricted to a few business tycoons in a handful of cities. Chadwick, who became known as "The Father of Baseball" for his contribution to the game and promotion of it, was fully onside:

> The probability is that over forty professional clubs—stock company, co-operative, gate-money, amateur and semi-professional—will enter the arena in 1877, and to accommodate these clubs with the necessary controlling legislation there is at present time of writing but one Association governing professional clubs practically in existence, and that is the League association.[30]

The National League had been created in relative secrecy without any input or advice from Chadwick, suggesting he was holding a grudge against it.[31] He encouraged competition for it based of his belief that the game was owned by the public generally and not reserved for a handful of business moguls focused on profit. Chadwick liked the idea floated by Waite and McKnight for an international association and thought it would be a noble experiment.

Interest proved sufficient in the baseball community for McKnight to call a meeting of all interested professional baseball clubs in Pittsburgh to pursue the idea of a new organization. Representatives of 17 clubs gathered at the St. Clair Hotel on February 20 for two days of talks. Many were from smaller cities and co-operatives whose players were paid a share of gate proceeds rather than a salary. Delegates and proxies favored a league organization similar to the old National Association in which players, merchants, local politicians and others played key roles in their teams and in association business. Aside from the clubs of Waite and McKnight, the following were represented personally or by proxy at the Pittsburgh convention: Buckeyes of Columbus, Ohio; Chelseas of Brooklyn; Fairbanks of Chicago; Rochesters of Rochester, New York; Essex of Buffalo; Live Oaks of Lynn, Massachusetts; Manchesters of New Hampshire; Alaskas of New York; Resolutes of New Jersey; Brown Stockings of Erie, Pennsylvania; San Franciscos of San Francisco; Reading of Reading, Pennsylvania; Mountain City of Altoona, Pennsylvania; Tecumsehs of London, Ontario; and Maple Leafs of Guelph, Ontario.[32] At the end of the discussion, it was agreed to form the International Association of Professional Base Ball Players. The name reflected the willingness of the two Canadian clubs, represented by Tecumseh manager Harry Gorman, to affiliate, and an acknowledgment that the league was for the benefit of players, not the clubs owned by businessmen. It harkened back to the National Association of Professional Base Ball Players on which the new organization was loosely based. Unlike the tightly controlled National League of Professional Base Ball Clubs, the IA would be player-centered and a federation of likeminded organizations. Rather than reinventing the wheel, and because of time constraints before the start of the season, delegates adopted nearly all of the playing rules of the National League. This move would also reduce problems when League and Association teams played each other.

Among the important decisions taken were to ban the "revolving" of players in pursuit of more money while they were still under contract. The entry fee for teams was set at $10 for the season, and those wishing to compete for the Association championship pennant were to pay a further $10 by April 1. The title of IA champion would be bestowed on the team winning the most designated "championship" games by season end, and those competing had to play four games against each other, two at home, two away. Admission price for spectators was set at 25 cents, the same as the old National Association and half that stipulated by the National League. The amount could be increased for games against National League teams, however, and was to be negotiated. Visiting IA clubs would split the gross game proceeds with the home club if the $75 minimum share was exceeded.[33] Seven teams decided to enter the championship race for the inaugural IA pennant: Allegheny, Buckeyes, Live Oaks, Manchesters, Rochesters, and both Canadian clubs, London and Guelph. Interestingly, although signed on as a member, the St. Louis Red Stockings club opted against competing for the championship, likely because of concern about travel costs because it was by far the most westerly club in the new loop. In all, about two dozen clubs signed up as IA members.

Elected president of the new organization was William A. "Candy" Cummings, the delegate and newly signed pitcher for the Live Oaks. His election was symbolic and intended to show that a player was in charge. A future Hall of Famer credited with developing the curve ball, Cummings played the 1876 season with the Hartford Dark Blues in the National League, where the veteran hurler was outshone by their rising star, Tommy Bond. Cummings pitched 24 games and won 16 of them. He signed with the independent Live Oaks in Lynn, Massachusetts, for the 1877 season and was asked by them to represent the club at the International Association founding convention in Pittsburgh. He wouldn't remain long in Lynn, however. The nomadic Cummings signed with Cincinnati of the National League in late June, but, strangely, retained his post as IA president.[34] He returned to the IA briefly in 1878, but his arm was worn out by then and his career over. Cummings, 28, had been pitching since 1865, professionally since 1871. Chosen vice-president by delegates was Tecumseh secretary and manager Harry Gorman, a move that reinforced the international nature of the new league. James A. Williams, a key figure in the Buckeyes of Columbus for many years, was elected secretary and chief administrative officer, posts he held for the life of the IA.[35] Appointed to the judiciary committee were Denny McKnight of Allegheny, L. C. Waite of the St. Louis Reds, George Sleeman of Guelph, A. B. Rankin of Chelsea and N. P. Pond of Rochester.

The St. Louis and Allegheny clubs and their players came together with others in a bid to promote their cities and their brand of baseball. All were anxious to provide an alternative professional model to the National League, to share the game more widely, to make it more affordable for spectators, and to move baseball forward. They had a challenge ahead of them and a chance to make history.

The table was set. All that was left now was to play the games.

4

Introduction to the Big Time

Optimistic that the notion of the International Association would gain ready acceptance, Denny McKnight began signing players for his Allegheny club well before the February convention that he and L. C. Waite convened in Pittsburgh. McKnight soon discovered he had to make competitive offers to attract talent, offering from $800 to $1,200 to get names on player contracts.[1] On January 13, the *New York Clipper* reported Allegheny would field "a very strong team," as the paper listed its roster for 1877.[2] Featured was a young pitcher from St. Louis who was making a name for himself with a great fastball and an excellent changeup that made it even more effective. James Francis Galvin, just turned 20, had also developed a wicked pickoff move that often caught base runners napping. His fellow players, many with nicknames related to their physical appearance, habits, or play, would soon be calling him "Pud," short for the pudding to which he reduced batters. McKnight and the Allegheny directors were taking a bit of a gamble on the young man with great potential but limited experience. From what they had seen in games the previous season, however, they felt comfortable with their choice. Galvin would soon have his chance to succeed with a newly competitive club.

Signed as catcher was Bill Holbert, 22, who had caught and patrolled the outfield for the Louisville Grays of the National League the previous season, seeing action in a dozen games. Another Gray, Philadelphian Chick Fulmer, 24, a veteran infielder with a good bat, also joined the roster. He traced his career back to the 1871 Rockford team of the National Association, bringing valuable experience to the new club. Another veteran, John "Candy" Nelson, 28, a native of Maine, was a first baseman and outfielder with four years of professional experience, mainly with the New York Mutuals. Al Nichols, 25, from Brooklyn, was hired to play third base. Nichols played 57 games for New York's National League team in 1876, but dressed for only nine games with Allegheny before signing with Louisville. In the latter city, he found trouble. Nichols became one of four players accused of fixing games in a scandal that rocked the National League and saw them expelled from baseball for life. Also signed by McKnight was George Creamer, a 22-year-old infielder from Philadelphia who was just starting his professional career, along with three other rookies: Tom Dolan, 18, of New York, a catcher and outfielder; Jake Goodman, 23, of Lancaster, Pennsylvania, a first baseman; and Ned Williamson, 19, yet another Philadelphian, a utility infielder. Back for a second season with Allegheny was Russ McKelvy, 22, a northern Pennsylvanian who had been one of four pitchers used by the club in 1876. Intended to be the backup to Galvin, he saw only one appearance in the pitching box because of Galvin's dominance. Overall, it was a balanced lineup for Pittsburgh's first fully professional club, a mix of promising youngsters and proven veterans. McKnight had assembled a competitive group.

Up north, a team that would prove to be the great rival for the Allegheny club in the International Association was also loading up on talent. The Tecumsehs of London, Ontario, had fielded a strong nine the previous year, winning the Canadian championship from their archrivals, the Guelph Maple Leafs, after years of trying. They copied the Maple Leafs by hiring a "foreign legion" of American professionals to get the job done. London found three players from south of the border for that 1876 campaign after introducing its first American the previous year, Warren "Juice" Latham. He joined the Tecumsehs for the dying weeks of their 1875 season. A native of Utica, New York, about 350 miles east of London, Latham played first base for the New Haven, Connecticut, team that had barnstormed across Southern Ontario. He had also played 16 games for Boston. Latham had extensive contacts in the wider baseball community that he agreed to tap to help the Tecumsehs become stronger. Latham helped attract a promising young player from Utica, 18-year-old Joe "Dutch" Hornung, an outfielder who played his position without a glove until late in a professional career that continued until 1890.

It is also likely that Latham helped the Tecumsehs find outstanding young pitcher Fred Goldsmith just a few months later, in May 1876. Latham and Goldsmith had both played for New Haven. Goldsmith was one of the first curve ball pitchers and was enjoying great success throwing what became known as his "deceivers." A native of New Haven, where he had pitched for the Elm Citys, Goldsmith turned 20 the month he showed up in London. He had been lured north by the promise of $100 in gold every month from Tecumseh manager Harry Gorman. That same season, Phil Powers, 21, a durable catcher from New York City, was brought on board, initially expected to receive for local pitcher Hugh McLean, who stood aside when Goldsmith arrived. Powers picked up the nickname "Grandmother," sometimes "Grandma," during a lengthy career that saw him play with Chicago, Boston and Cincinnati after leaving London. Also joining the club for the 1876 campaign was yet another Utica player, Mike Dinnen, age unknown, a light-hitting infielder who became a crowd favorite with his dazzling defense.[3]

To that core which had helped the Tecumsehs secure the Canadian championship and defeat the touring St. Louis Browns during 1876, the team added several more imports to its roster for the International Association campaign. Latham had quietly left London but was replaced by several outstanding Americans. George H. "Foghorn" Bradley, 22, was hired to become backup for Goldsmith. He had pitched 22 games for Boston in 1876, winning nine of them. Also joining London was Philadelphia-born shortstop Ed Somerville, 24, who lived in New Haven and had played on its National Association team alongside Latham and Goldsmith. In 1876, Somerville played second base for the Louisville Grays of the National League and while his bat was weak, his work in the field was first-rate. Another newcomer was Jake Knowdell, 22, who had played with his hometown Brooklyn Atlantics in 1874 and 1875 and was expected to back up Powers at catcher. John Henry "Herm" Doscher, 24, a New Yorker and former member of the Atlantics and Washington who could easily switch between infield and outfield, joined the Tecumsehs along with veteran Fred Waterman, 32, another New Yorker who had been a member of the famous Cincinnati Red Stockings of 1869–1870. A third baseman who also played outfield, Waterman had been a member of several professional clubs including Washington and Chicago.[4] With the addition of the five new faces, the London club was stronger than before and ready to play against the top teams of the day.

Some very talented players with experience in the National Association and National League were signed up by the new teams of the International Association. Many of them later moved seamlessly into the National League. The top players of the day were found in both organizations, and when NL clubs played other professional clubs in that 1877 season, including those in the IA, they won barely more than half of them. The International Association, in particular, was a thorn in the side of the six teams of the National League. As historian Ted Vincent observed: "Despite its high-priced tickets and other classy features, the League was no more than the equal of the 1877 International Association in playing talent, with the players in the top six IA clubs having more past and future years of 'big league' baseball among them than had the six clubs of the NL."[5]

Scanning the rosters of some of the other IA teams makes Vincent's case. The Columbus Buckeyes went into the season with two pitchers who would each amass nearly 300 career wins while playing in the NA, NL, Union Association and American Association. Bobby Mathews, who had been in the National Association since 1871, would spend 15 years in the "majors" and notch 297 victories. Jim McCormick was beginning a career that would produce 265 wins in 10 years. Another Buckeye, Mike "King" Kelly, a rightfielder,

4. Introduction to the Big Time 45

catcher and third baseman, was embarking on a 16-year career in the "majors" where he recorded an overall batting average of .308. Kelly played on eight pennant-winning teams and was inducted into the Baseball Hall of Fame. Rochester had Doc Kennedy, a catcher and outfielder whose career would span five years in the National League with a .260 batting average. Manchester featured Lou Say, a shortstop whose professional play outside the IA lasted seven years and Oscar Walker, the center fielder and first baseman whose career in the NA, NL and AA lasted six years with a batting average of .254. Guelph hired versatile player Scott Hastings, who had played professionally with Rockford of the NA in 1871 and then with Cleveland, Baltimore, Hartford, and Chicago. Hastings went to the National League team in Cincinnati before 1877 was over, ending his career after seven years.

Goldsmith in London would later to move to Troy and Chicago of the National League, and Galvin in Allegheny would enjoy a successful and lengthy career with National League clubs in Buffalo, Pittsburgh and St. Louis before retiring. Many other players were at the beginning or end of their professional careers, while still others were at the midpoint and easily moved from one league to another. Those who chose to spend time in the International Association, however, would not find their accomplishments documented in the major league record books because historians afterward decreed it was not a major league. This view persists despite the fact that every other league that arose to challenge the National League in its first decades has been accorded major league status. Those organizations include the American Association, the Players' League and the Union Association (both with single seasons), the American League and the Federal League. Players wouldn't have known about such discrimination at the time because they, and the IA itself, did not see themselves as inferior to the National League and its players in any way. As another historian, David Pietrusza, put it:

> From a modern perspective, it would be tempting to term the Association a "minor league." Yet at the time, it could not be so easily pigeonholed. Despite a rather miserable form of organization, a good caliber of ball was played by these nines. International Association and National League players were equally named to nationally recognized all-star teams. Additionally, of course, the very idea of a minor league simply did not exist.[6]

Pietrusza quoted the *Philadelphia Times*, which in 1878 reflected on two years of IA play and opined, "There are clubs in the International Association fully as strong as League clubs."

All was new and the air full of optimism as the 1877 season approached for the cities of the International Association. This was despite a lingering recession that hit in 1873 and continued to make all business challenging. Changes were being made at the National League to improve the financial picture of its teams. Founding president Morgan Bulkeley of the Hartfords resigned to pursue a political career, and Chicago president William Hulbert took over. Bulkeley had been chosen to bring some eastern flavor to the league, but was its leader in name only. Hulbert made all the important decisions and began taking steps to cut costs and produce positive bottom lines. Salaries were trimmed and players were required to place a $30 deposit for their uniforms and launder and repair them at their own expense. While on the road, players were required to pay 50 cents each day toward the cost of their room and board.[7] Hulbert's Chicago club had been the only one in the league to make money, and if others couldn't, the shrunken loop's very survival was at stake. Hartford, for instance, had lost $2,230 on its operations in 1876. In a bid to turn things around, the club arranged to play its 1877 home games in the baseball hotbed of Brooklyn. It continued to call itself Hartford, however, creating some confusion for its opposition and for newspapers.[8] Historian David Q. Voigt put the overall situation facing the League this way: "Although managerial austerity, salary cuts, and new stock issues lightened the burden somewhat, it was a discouraging picture.... Ranged alongside the profitable [National] Association era, it goes far to debunk the myth of League superiority."[9] The National League, preoccupied with its serious problems, tolerated the new International Association and allowed teams in the two organizations to interact, provided they charged the league-mandated 50 cents admission to games. The league would tighten the screws for 1878 when it saw how well its upstart rival was doing.

The opening pitch for the International Association was thrown by its president on April 26 in Lynn, Massachusetts. And he kept throwing for the entire game. But Candy Cummings, credited with developing the curve ball by the Baseball Hall of Fame, found himself on the losing end of a 14–3 rout at the hands of Manchester. Louis Say, shortstop for the visitors, scored four of their runs in a game that foreshadowed disappointment for Lynn hopes that year. The club had managed only one win and lost seven games when it dropped out of the IA. On June 30, Cummings jumped to Cincinnati of the National League, where he won five games and lost 14 while still retaining his post as president of the Association.[10] The situation was bizarre, but league president Hulbert likely smiled that among the many players his organization controlled was the president of the rival loop.

The Allegheny club had high expectations for 1877 and, in an April 19 pre-season game, were ahead of the visiting Cincinnati Ludlows, 10–0, when the game was washed out in the sixth inning. About 1,200 spectators saw a much-improved home club play error-free ball and hit strongly. Galvin pitched the shutout and scored a run. The report of the game said it was the opinion of all on hand that "the club is a vast improvement over last season's nine," a reflection on the handiwork of club president McKnight.[11] Allegheny opened its season on April 23, surprising itself with a 3–2 victory over the Syracuse Stars in Union Park. After five scoreless innings, Galvin made it to first on a throwing error in the top of the sixth, stole second, advanced to third on a hit by Candy Nelson to right field and scampered home on an errant throw to Stars pitcher Harry McCormick. McCormick himself replied with a Syracuse run in the bottom of the same inning on a hit, a stolen base and another hit. Galvin allowed only two base hits in the game while McCormick allowed nine. Allegheny added another run in the seventh, and the Stars tied the game in the eighth. The ninth inning was scoreless and it was in the tenth that Allegheny scored to take its first-ever professional victory.[12]

Syracuse was a member of the League Alliance, a collection of teams loosely affiliated with the National League. Two days later, the National League's Louisville Grays came to town and were defeated, 3–1, Galvin being "too bothersome a pitcher for the professionals to get onto with effect," reported the *Clipper*. The hometown *Pittsburgh Gazette* also took note of the new pitcher's performance before a crowd of 2,000. "The visitors found Galvin's balls just about as hard to hit as [veteran Louisville pitcher Jim] Devlin's are known to be, and two of them managed to strike out."[13] Allegheny and Galvin were off to a fine start. They had beaten one of the leading teams in the National League, which led its loop for most of the season. The Grays, however, had an unexpected late-season swoon to finish second because gamblers with money riding on Boston had persuaded Devlin and three other Grays to see things their way. Boston won the pennant. On April 28, Galvin won his third game of the season when Allegheny defeated a surprisingly strong club from Erie, 1–0, in a seven-inning, rain-shortened contest.

April 30 proved to be a memorable day for baseball on two counts.

It marked the first day of the 1877 season for the National League. The Hartford Dark Blues were in their new home park in Brooklyn to face the Boston Red Caps. Pitching for Boston was Tommy Bond, who had hurled for Hartford the previous year. The game was called after 11 innings, the score tied at 1–1.

That same day, Pud Galvin threw the first shutout in the International Association when his Allegheny nine defeated the visiting Columbus Buckeyes, 2–0. Third baseman Al Nichols drove in both runs during the first inning, after which goose eggs filled the score sheet. Galvin gave up four hits in Allegheny's fifth straight victory. On May 1, Allegheny again played the Buckeyes in the first game of their race for the International Association pennant, designated, in the lingo of the day, as a "championship" game. Play was called after four innings because of heavy rain mixed with snow, with Columbus leading, 1–0. In St. Louis the same day, the Browns and Syracuse Stars went 15 innings with neither team scoring a run in a game marked by heavy batting and terrific fielding. The game, the longest professional contest to that point in baseball history, was called on account of darkness.

On May 2, the Boston Red Caps of the National League faced Allegheny before about 2,000 spectators. Inning after inning passed without a run crossing the plate. The eighth inning looked to be more of the same after George Creamer, playing left field, fouled out to Boston pitcher Bond. McKelvy, playing center field, was thrown out at first. Galvin came to the plate and was quickly down two strikes with one ball. He connected solidly with the next pitch, but the ball sailed foul in far left field. With two men out and two strikes, Galvin suddenly became a hero. He connected with another wicked swing, and this time the ball sailed high above leftfielder Andy Leonard and carried over the fence. It was the first home run knocked out of Union Park, and the crowd was ecstatic. "Galvin took his cap in hand and crossed the home-plate, amid the cheers of the entire crowd," reported the *Pittsburgh Dispatch*. "Galvin now addressed himself more effectively to his work, as he considered the game won, and the excitement continued to increase."[14] Boston, which batted last because of the coin-toss then used to determine such matters, failed to reply with any runs in the bottom of the eighth or the ninth. Leonard made it to third in the final inning, capitalizing on a couple of fielding errors, but the home team wouldn't let him advance. The 1–0 game was a pitching duel between Bond and Galvin that the newcomer had won, surrendering one hit to the two allowed by Bond. "The victory of the Alleghenys yesterday over the Boston Red Stockings [sic] one of the best clubs in the League organization, was a very gratifying surprise," the *Pittsburgh Commercial Gazette* crowed on its front page.[15] The highlight of the game had been Galvin's home run, it reported. "The friends of the home club, as well as the players themselves, were immensely tickled over the feat. Policeman Thomas nearly shook Galvin's arm off, and Williamson hugged him as lovingly and fondly as though he was his own dear sweetheart. It was doubtless the first home run that has been made in the country since the commencement of the season." Aside from the hitting heroics, the win against the powerful Red Caps marked Galvin's third shutout in three games.

Allegheny came down to earth the next day, May 3, when Boston recovered to blank the home nine, 2–0, before 3,000 spectators, capitalizing on ten errors. For his part, Galvin's bat was cold this time. He struck out three times and surrendered four base hits. Having mostly dazzled the hometown fans to start the season, it was time for the team to hit the road for more than two weeks to play in Erie, Pennsylvania, London and Guelph (both in Ontario), Auburn, Syracuse, Ithaca and Rochester.

The tour began promisingly with a 4–2 win in Erie on May 7 before Allegheny crossed the border for a game May 9 against the Tecumsehs of London and their curveballer, Fred Goldsmith. London, playing one of the first games in their new baseball park, were without the services of catcher Phil Powers, who had injured his hand. Galvin threw a one-hitter against the

4. Introduction to the Big Time 49

Tecumsehs, a single by Goldsmith. Meanwhile, Goldsmith surrendered three hits in a game that featured sharp fielding by both clubs. The final score was 2–0 in the first of four games the two teams arranged to play that season for the International Association championship. The following day in Guelph, Allegheny ran into another curveballer named Sullivan who made life difficult for the visitors' bats. Sharp fielding was noted by both sides but the Maple Leafs prevailed, 3–2, despite committing 11 errors. On May 11, Allegheny turned the tables on their hosts, as Galvin issued only two hits as the visitors blanked Guelph, 5–0. A 2–0 loss in Rochester followed on May 12, but Allegheny bounced back on May 14 for a 6–2 win in Auburn. On May 15, Galvin and company rolled into Syracuse, which was seeking to avenge its ten-inning loss three weeks earlier. Pitcher Harry McCormick was on his game while Galvin gave up nine hits to the Stars, who won, 5–2. Four days later, the same two teams met in Ithaca and Syracuse again won, 8–4. Allegheny finished its tour on a winning note May 21 when it defeated Rochester, 10–2, salvaging a split in its championship games with the New York club. Galvin doubled in the game and took a ball to the face, which he shook off with no apparent lasting damage. Allegheny's first road trip produced five wins and four losses.

Candy Cummings, president of the Association, arrived in Allegheny City on May 23 with his Live Oaks of Lynn. The curveballer was not on his game that day, giving up 11 hits in a 7–0 loss to the home nine. Allegheny entertained the unaligned Philadelphia Athletics on May 24 and 25, winning by scores of 7–3 and 9–8. In the first game, Galvin hit a home run over the left field fence in the fifth inning and three innings later brought in two more runs with a hard hit. The back-to-back victories put some wind in the sails of the Alleghenians as they welcomed the National League's Hartford Dark Blues on May 26. Galvin and his mates were winning, 3–2, after eight innings, but the visitors' bats suddenly came alive in the ninth for four runs to take the game, 6–3. Three days later, Hartford, one of the strongest teams in the National League, pummeled Allegheny, 9–1. Galvin surrendered 15 hits in a forgettable outing before a large crowd. After the game, William Coates resigned as team manager and backup pitcher Russ McKelvy took over his duties.

More than 4,000 spectators packed Union Park on May 30 for a game against the Indianapolis Blue Legs, also known as the Blues, from whom the Allegheny fans expected a strong showing and upon whom they bet heavily to win. Allegheny made the first run of the game on a hard shot by Galvin over shortstop that scored McKelvy in the fourth inning. A line drive down the third base line by Dolan in the fifth inning scored Nelson. Indianapolis managed a single run in the ninth as Allegheny held on for a 2–1 win. Nearly 3,000 fans returned to the park the following day when the same two teams were tied, 1–1, after nine innings and 2–2 after 12 innings. A draw was proclaimed after 13 innings were completed when the Blue Legs had to leave to catch a train to Philadelphia. Allegheny welcomed June with a 14–5 thrashing of the touring Memphis Blues in a game pitched by McKelvy as Galvin occupied center field. Payback came the next day, June 2, when Memphis won, 3–2, in a grueling 19-inning marathon that went so long the game ball became "soft and flabby," according to one account.[16] Galvin again occupied center field and McKelvy took the loss.

The *New York Clipper* published the International Association standings as of June 3, which showed Allegheny with five championship wins, one each against the Buckeyes, Live Oaks, Maple Leafs, Rochesters and Tecumsehs. The club was tied for the lead with Rochester. Two wins back were the Buckeyes and Tecumsehs. Live Oaks and Manchesters followed with two wins apiece, and the Maple Leafs trailed the pack with a single victory.

An era ended on June 5 in Chicago when veteran pitcher Albert Goodwill Spalding made his last appearance as a starter. At age 26, he had been hampered by injuries and distracted by his efforts to establish a sporting goods business. The top National League pitcher in 1876, he had appeared in three games this season and had only one victory to his credit. After Spalding gave up four runs in the first inning against the Cincinnati Reds, the White Stockings replaced him with backup George Washington Bradley. Things did not improve and the Chicago club suffered a 12–5 defeat. Spalding, whose days as a player were numbered, moved to first base, where his abilities proved to be average at best.

Allegheny took to the road again in early June for an eastern swing through Massachusetts and New Hampshire. On June 9, Candy Cummings scored a one-hit shutout for the Live Oaks in Lynn as they prevailed 1–0 over the Smoky City crew. Allegheny lost to Manchester, 5–2, two days later. On June 12 Galvin and his mates downed Lowell, 3–2, before rolling into Boston for games June 13 and 14 against the Red Caps. Allegheny found Boston a much different opponent from the club they had edged 1–0 back home on May 2. Boston bats scored ten hits off Galvin in the first game as they won, 7–2. The following day, Galvin was batted "from pillar to post" and was relieved by McKelvy in the seventh inning.[17] Boston recorded 17 hits in the 10–2 shellacking, three apiece by second baseman George Wright and catcher Tim Murnan. It was a shell-shocked Allegheny club that left Boston for a return to Manchester. There, on June 15, Allegheny found its winning ways again with a 7–3 victory. Galvin and McKelvy shared pitching duties in a 9–2 loss to Lowell on June 16. Two days later in Lynn, Galvin pitched another shutout as Allegheny defeated Cummings and the Live Oaks, 2–0. On June 19, as they headed for home, a tired Allegheny nine ran into a heavy-hitting Philadelphia Athletics club which easily downed the weary travelers, 6–2.

Allegheny was relieved to return home after a long and grueling trip in which they lost twice as many games as they won. Once back home, third baseman Al Nichols was let go by directors who learned he had tried to bribe Galvin on behalf of gamblers.[18] Presumably, Galvin reported Nichols, who turned up in a Louisville Grays uniform beginning July 13. He took his moral shortcomings with him and was implicated in a bribery scandal in Louisville that season which saw Nichols, identified as the "go-between," and three other players banned for life from the National League.

Home cooking and familiar beds agreed with Allegheny City. The Chicago White Stockings appeared at Union Park for two games against the Smoky City boys and lost both of them. On June 22, Chicago made eight hits off Galvin while the home team managed only three. Allegheny showed superior fielding and clustered their hits to maximum advantage in the third and fourth innings for a 3–1 victory. George Washington Bradley was in the pitching box now for Chicago since Al Spalding's move to first base less than three weeks earlier. The following day, it was a more confident local nine that took on the reigning champions of the National League. Allegheny made six hits off Bradley while the Whites managed half that many off Galvin. The home team took an early lead and did not relinquish it, while Chicago left runners stranded at third base, once with no one out, and failed to bring any of them across the plate. Among them was shortstop John Peters, who belted a triple. For his part, Galvin had three base hits, including a double, as he shut out the visitors, 6–0. Allegheny fans were able to rejoice at defeating the powerful Chicagos after what had been a tough start to the month. As for Galvin, his performance against some of the top National League teams was beginning to draw attention.

About 4,000 spectators poured into Union Park for a July 4 game against the Columbus Buckeyes and their top pitcher, Bobby Mathews. For this holiday game on a beautiful day for baseball, 50 cents admission was charged, double the usual amount, but the fans received full value for their money as Galvin scored yet another shutout, allowing four hits, for a final score of 2–0. The *Pittsburgh Gazette* reported that Allegheny outplayed the visitors in every aspect of the game and that the Buckeyes struck so "savagely" at Galvin's pitches that they broke three of their bats in their efforts to get on base.[19] Syracuse returned to Allegheny on July 7 for the first time since its pre-season 3–2 loss, and Stars batters found Galvin to be an easy touch, collecting 16 hits off him. Allegheny was held to two runs by Harry McCormick, who had two hits of his own. Rightfielder Pete Hotaling cranked out four hits to lead the Syracuse hit parade in the 5–2 win for the visitors. Two days later, sloppy fielding by Allegheny contributed to a 2–0 loss. On July 10, it was the Stars' turn to catch the error bug, making ten in an 8–2 loss to Allegheny. Six of them were passed balls as Hotaling struggled behind home plate. Galvin's three hits, one of them a double, helped his cause. Only two of the Allegheny runs were earned.

Next up was Manchester, who arrived in town for two games. Allegheny helped distance itself from the New Hampshire nine which was hot on its heels in the IA championship race, beating them 5–1 on July 11 and 6–4 on July 12. The Tecumseh club of London, which was steadily moving up in the IA standings, appeared at Union Park for games on July 14 and 16. In the first game, Galvin allowed five hits, four of which were recorded by London pitcher Fred Goldsmith, but Allegheny bats were superior and cashed in six of their seven hits for runs as the home club won, 6–2. In the second contest, London played poorly and Allegheny won, 5–1, for its third straight championship win against the Canadian club. In standings published late in July, Allegheny had a commanding lead in the International Association with 12 wins. Columbus and Rochester each had eight, while Manchester and London had seven, Lynn had three and Guelph continued to trail the loop with two.

At the mid-point of the IA's inaugural season, it seemed Allegheny was well on its way to capturing the pennant.

5

Playing Through Adversity

The Champion City club of Springfield, Ohio, arrived in Allegheny City for games July 20 and 21, at a turbulent time in history for the American railroads upon which the country depended for commerce and baseball teams for travel. As a railroad hub, Pittsburgh had become a focal point of unprecedented labor turmoil. The games were played against a backdrop of violence across the river in Pittsburgh. The first game was a 5–3 win by Allegheny, but few fans appeared at Union Park. "The excitement in regard to the railroad war kept many away so that there were not more than 500 spectators present," the *Pittsburgh Commercial Gazette* explained.[1] The poor turnout was repeated the following day when Allegheny whitewashed the visitors, 1–0. The box score from that game, as published in the *New York Clipper*, showed that Galvin hadn't allowed a hit and had pitched another no-hitter. Nothing but goose eggs appeared in the hits column for the visitors, although a single error was attributed to Allegheny. Later it was suggested that a single hit had been made by Springfield that day, with the failure to record it attributed to the major distraction facing the city and its newspapers.[2]

On July 16 in Baltimore, angry rail workers and their supporters blocked trains of the Baltimore and Ohio Railroad, which had cut wages by 10 percent for workers earning more than $1 a day. The company also reduced the work week to two or three days. At the time, a wage of $1 a day was considered "absolute poverty" in Ohio.[3] Workers were infuriated because railroads said they had to cut costs to deal with the lingering effects of the economic collapse of 1873, but B&O had boosted dividends for its shareholders by 10 percent. The optics of that move proved to be incendiary, and workers felt railroads were trying to profit at their expense at a time when jobs were scarce. In May, the Pennsylvania Railroad had imposed its second 10-percent wage cut in two years. It also doubled the length of its trains without increasing the size of the crews. The flashpoint came in Baltimore, where rail workers decided the time had come to act. Inspired by their blockade, rail employees struck

53

in West Virginia and the labor disruption soon spread to Reading, Scranton, Harrisburg, Erie, Washington and Pittsburgh. Violence accompanied the strikes in Baltimore, Chicago, St. Louis, Kansas City, and Pittsburgh, bringing commercial train traffic to a halt. Public sympathy tended to lie with the workers rather than with the rich rail barons of the day. Rumors spread that those fomenting the uprisings were foreign agitators as the authorities fought back and tried to preserve order.

On July 19, mobs in Pittsburgh disrupted rail operations and occupied Pennsylvania Railroad property. Much resentment about the Philadelphia-headquartered rail company already existed in Pittsburgh, where many residents felt it had been squeezing their city and its people for profits for many years. Authorities were unable to deal with the hundreds of rail workers and their supporters drawn from the steel plants and iron foundries in a largely blue-collar city. Budget cuts at city hall had reduced the police force to 11 men in the city of about 150,000. Another ten laid-off officers were called in. The Pittsburgh militia was mobilized to disperse the demonstrators, but members opted instead to lay down their arms, refusing to act against their neighbors and friends. Among those in the militia was Denny McKnight, president of the Allegheny City ball club. He wasn't interested in antagonizing or threatening people who attended his ball games.

Pennsylvania Railroad officials demanded action and when local efforts failed, they pressed Pennsylvania Governor John Hartranft to intervene. The governor mobilized the National Guard troops in Philadelphia, sending nearly 1,000 of them to Pittsburgh by rail to restore order. Upon arriving, the troops were confronted by an angry mob more intent on taunting the unwanted Philadelphians than returning peacefully to their homes. Strikers set fire to dozens of railroad cars and buildings as crowds hurled abuse at the guardsmen who approached them with bayonets fixed. At one point, without warning, the troops fired into an unarmed crowd that had gathered on an embankment to watch the action, killing 20 persons, including a woman and three children, and wounding 29 others. Incensed and bloodied, the crowd pursued the troops, who sought refuge in a railway roundhouse. Gunfire was exchanged on the nights of July 21 and 22 as another 20 residents and five guardsmen were killed in the tense standoff. The mob then set fire to the roundhouse in a bid to force the guardsmen out—or roast them alive. When the situation grew dire, the guardsmen charged out of the blazing structure, scattering Gatling gun fire into the crowd, creating panic and forcing the mob back. The troops sought shelter at the Allegheny Arsenal, but the officer in charge turned them away. Meanwhile, shots were fired at the Philadelphians from the nearly police station.[4] The troops managed to flee the city, leaving it a smoking shambles. A total of 39 buildings, including Union Station, had been set on fire. In all, 104 locomotives had been burned or damaged, along

5. Playing Through Adversity 55

with 46 rail passenger cars and 506 rail cars. The Pennsylvania Railroad later put the damage at $4 million and estimated the mob at from 10,000 to 30,000 strong. By July 28, when Governor Hartranft arrived in Pittsburgh with thousands more National Guard troops, order had been restored and cleanup operations were underway. In the aftermath of the violence, few charges were laid and meetings between strikers and railroad officials resolved many of the worker grievances. The Great Rail Strike was the largest outbreak of labor unrest ever seen in Pittsburgh, or America. Violence had also characterized strikes in Buffalo, Harrisburg and Chicago, but Pittsburgh had seen by far the bloodiest confrontations.

Across the bridges in Allegheny City, citizens watched in horror as their civic sister was swept by violence and erupted in flames. Things were relatively peaceful, however, in large part because of the respect workers there had for the Pennsylvania Railroad's general manager.[5] During the height of the violence raging just across the Allegheny River, Pud Galvin and his teammates twice took to pastoral Union Park and downed the Champion Citys. With the pages of Pittsburgh newspapers full of detailed accounts of the anarchy and mob rule that gripped the city, it is understandable some confusion might relate to how perfect Galvin had been in the second of those games.

With rail travel impossible throughout the turmoil, the Allegheny City club didn't resume play until July 28, when the Syracuse Stars arrived and defeated the well-rested nine, 6–3. It didn't take the locals long to regroup. Galvin was back on his game in the first of three contests with the Hartford Dark Blues. On July 30, he shut out the visitors in a hard-fought 2–0 victory in which he allowed only two hits. "The excitement over the railroad war having begun to wane, the attendance at ball games is increasing," observed the *Pittsburgh Commercial Gazette,* which put the crowd at between 800 and 1,000.[6] On July 31, Hartford bounced back with a late rally to blank Allegheny, 6–0, and the next day prevailed again, 4–3, the local club weakened by injuries to catcher Tom Dolan and outfielder Bill Holbert. The Boston Red Caps were next into Union Park for a game that drew yet another light crowd. On August 2, the visitors hammered Galvin mercilessly for 12 base hits and capitalized on 11 errors by his supporting cast to romp to a 5–1 win. The loss prompted the *Commercial Gazette* to observe: "Galvin seems to be pie for the Bostons. In the two games played at Union Park early in the season, they didn't bat him to any extent, but in every game since then they have fallen upon his delivery and punished it without remorse.... The Bostons and Hartfords are the only clubs that have ever rattled Galvin, and they have done it completely."[7] The bad press didn't seem to inspire the Allegheny pitcher. The following day, August 3, Boston won, 5–2, scattering nine more hits off Galvin. First baseman Jake Goodman took Boston pitcher Tommy Bond out of the park for a home run but it was too little to make a difference in the outcome.

Allegheny City was organizing a three-team tournament with the Syracuse Stars and Indianapolis Blues. The two clubs were members of the League Alliance, a group of more than 30 professional clubs loosely affiliated with the National League. The tournament, expected to be a winner financially, was originally scheduled to begin on August 6, but the rail strike pushed it back a month. Meanwhile, that same day in August, an interesting snippet appeared in the *Commercial Gazette* suggesting all was not well with the Allegheny nine: "Internal dissensions are said to rend the Allegheny club. Hadn't they better be stopped." The same edition reported the club had already selected most of its team for the 1878 season. Galvin, Holbert, Williamson, McKelvy and Nelson were listed as returning, along with four newcomers and a backup catcher not yet decided upon.[8]

On August 8, Allegheny met the Columbus Buckeyes for a game counting toward the championship race it continued to lead. The game was close but the visitors were edged, 2–1, thanks to a two-run outburst in the ninth inning. Galvin and Buckeyes pitcher Jim McCormick proved hard to hit that day, demonstrating again that they were among the top hurlers in the International Association. The next day, Allegheny won its second game against Columbus, 3–1, completing the four-game series needed with that club in the championship. Allegheny, without a loss to Columbus, now had 14 wins and four losses to improve its lead. Auburn, a non–IA club, came to town and two games with it were split before Allegheny left on a western road trip. As the team left town, the *Commercial Gazette*, citing the *Indianapolis Journal* as its source, reported: "The Allegheny managers have accepted the terms of Galvin, Williamson, Nelson and Holbert for next season, but they have not signed yet. If they want to keep them they had better close the contract right away. Several clubs have their eye on Galvin, who is one of the finest pitchers in the country."[9] The paper said it appeared McKelvy would be signing with Indianapolis.

In Columbus August 14 for a non-championship contest, Galvin was pulled after four innings as the Buckeyes had their way with him, securing eight hits. He was replaced by McKelvy, who surrendered three more in the 8–7 loss. Next up was Indianapolis, where the Alleghenys lost, 3–2, then bounced back to win, 7–2. Meanwhile, it was reported club directors had engaged only Galvin, Dolan and Nelson for next season. Williamson said he wouldn't be back because he didn't like being accused of "crookedness" by directors. The comment showed that concern still existed that players of the day were selling out to gamblers. It wouldn't be long before the issue of crooked play would take center stage for the club. In a reference that would have caught the attention of Galvin, it was reported in the *New York Clipper* that team directors "have been making every effort to secure the services of Goldsmith, pitcher of the Tecumsehs."[10] If true, Galvin would have grounds

5. Playing Through Adversity 57

for concern at a time when teams generally rode the arm of one pitcher, game in and game out. Backup, or "change" pitchers generally made few appearances in the pitching box, and he may have wondered about his future and what directors were thinking.

An upcoming game soon preoccupied him. On August 20, Galvin returned to St. Louis to meet his former team, the Browns. He was highly motivated. Allegheny scored nine runs off Joe Blong, while Galvin surrendered only five. Galvin also homered, while Williamson and McKelvy tripled and Williamson and Nelson doubled. The final score was 9–5 for the hard-hitting Smoky City crew. Allegheny rolled into Chicago for games August 21 and 22, feeling pleased with their performance in St. Louis. In the first clash, the fielding by both teams was very sharp as Allegheny won, 6–5. Galvin collected two hits and gave up eight hits to the nine issued by George Washington Bradley. It marked the third time Allegheny and Chicago had met that season, and Allegheny had won on all three occasions. The following day, the bats were lively for both teams, beginning in the first inning when Chicago scored six times to the visitors' five. Allegheny scored five more runs in the ninth inning to one for the White Stockings, giving the home team a 19–18 win. Galvin was relieved by McKelvy in the sixth inning and between them the pair allowed 24 hits to the 23 made off Bradley. A short hop up to Milwaukee and Janesville, Wisconsin, to play two League Alliance clubs produced four more victories and a single loss between August 23–28.

On August 25, shortly after Allegheny left St. Louis, Browns pitcher Joe Blong and third baseman Joe Battin were named by Chicago gamblers as "willing partners." St. Louis had played Chicago three times in the previous week and lost every game, including August 17 in the Windy City when Blong pitched poorly and made four of his team's 12 errors. In an August 24 loss at home, St. Louis second baseman Battin and shortstop Davy Force made errors that saw Chicago win, 4–3. After an investigation, Blong, Force, Battin and third baseman Mike McGeary were blacklisted by the National League. All but Blong, who never again played at the top level of the professional game, eventually found their way back onto League teams.[11]

At the end of August, the *Chicago Tribune* took note of the success of the Allegheny club, finding it was superior to the White Stockings when playing both National League and major non-league opponents. The paper pointed to Allegheny's one win without a loss against each of the Louisville and St. Louis nines, three wins and one loss against Chicago, one win and two losses to Hartford, one win and three losses to Boston. This gave Allegheny a 7–6 record against National League teams. Against other teams, Allegheny won two and lost one against Indianapolis, won two and lost four against Syracuse, and won three against the Tecumsehs of London. This was a record of 7–5. In light of this, the *Pittsburgh Commercial Gazette* repeated the item in which the *Tribune* argued that the Chicago club was overpaid and that player pay should be reduced. Salaries for the White Stockings totaled $22,750, it noted, while Allegheny players received a relatively paltry $8,300.[12]

On September 1, Allegheny welcomed the St. Louis Browns to Union Park for what proved to be a titanic struggle for 14 innings with neither team able to cross the plate. In the 15th, Allegheny's McKelvy doubled and scampered toward home on a fielding error. A throw to Blong, covering the plate, was late and the home team took a 1–0 lead. The visitors were held hitless in the bottom of the inning. Galvin had thrown another no-hitter and the fielding behind him was without error, while St. Louis recorded seven miscues. For Galvin, this was a particularly sweet defeat of his old team. The International Association standings as of September 2 showed Allegheny retaining its lead in the loop, with 14 games won. Hot in pursuit with 13 victories were the Tecumsehs, followed by the Rochesters with 12 and Manchesters with 10. The Buckeyes had eight wins and the Live Oaks were tied with the Maple Leafs at the bottom with three wins apiece. Every victory was important for Allegheny if it wanted to hold onto its pennant hopes. Louisville came to town for games September 3 and 4, losing the first to Allegheny, 3–2, but blanking their hosts, 3–0, in the second match. Jim Devlin, the Louisville Grays' pitcher, was particularly effective, silencing the host bats in a shutout. Al Nichols, formerly of Allegheny, appeared at shortstop and second base in the two games. The Louisville win marked its first of the season against Allegheny, coming at a time when the Grays were leading the National League standings.

The final two games against Rochester that were required for the IA championship were both played September 8 in Allegheny City. The home team took the first game, 3–2, making only two errors. Chick Fulmer, now playing at second base, which Nichols once manned, smacked a ball over the left field fence in the first inning with two runners on base to score all the Allegheny runs. In the second game, Rochester took advantage of 12 errors and a weak performance by Galvin for an easy 6–1 victory.

On September 10, the rescheduled and much anticipated tournament hosted by Allegheny got underway with a game against the Syracuse Stars. The tournament was billed as one to determine "the non–League championship of the United States."[13] The other team taking part was the Indianapolis Blues, like Syracuse a member of the League Alliance. Given the number of top-notch professional clubs not included, among them Rochester, Manchester, Lowell, and Philadelphia (but not Columbus, which disbanded September 16), the tournament billing was inflated and wishful. One game was played each day until September 15. When it was over, each of the three participants had won two games and lost two, prompting the *New York Clipper*, which

5. Playing Through Adversity 59

understood the winner would be crowned champions of the League Alliance (even though Allegheny was not in the Alliance), to call the outcome "rather curious." Financially, the tournament was deemed a success, producing about $600 for each of the participating clubs.[14] Even before the last game was played between Indianapolis and Syracuse, which Indianapolis won 4–2 to ensure all three teams had two wins, the *Pittsburgh Commercial Gazette* claimed the tournament was "a put up job." Managers of all three clubs felt compelled to issue an affidavit denying the charge, saying each had done its best to win. The newspaper quickly backed down in its next edition:

> In the absence of any evidence to the contrary this affidavit must be accepted as conclusive. And it is well that it was made, for if the general impression that the tournament was set up had been allowed to go uncorrected it would have been the death of base ball in this vicinity. There is nothing like fair-play, and if this paper should ever discover anything like fraud it will be promptly shown up. The tournament is to be repeated this week in Chicago, for which place all three clubs left yesterday afternoon.[15]

Chicago had offered to host a repeat of the event, from September 17–21. This time, Syracuse came out as the winner with three victories, Indianapolis placed second with two and Allegheny managed only a single win, downing Indianapolis, 15–5. Galvin and his team played poorly throughout the event, beaten 6–1 and 6–4 by Syracuse and 5–2 by Indianapolis. After the 6–4 loss to Syracuse, the *Commercial Gazette* printed allegations from Chicago that Allegheny had thrown the game to Syracuse. But there was more, the Pittsburgh paper said, noting that the Stars were also guilty of misconduct. "This allegation would seem to be sustained by the fact that the Alleghenys made thirteen base hits, against eight for the Stars. The *Chicago Inter-Ocean* boldly asserts that Friday's game was sold [thrown] by the Stars to the Indianapolis team and that [catcher Dick] Higham was the chief seller."[16] The Pittsburgh newspaper had obviously caught a whiff of crooked play and wasn't going to let go. It went on to note that on September 24, Syracuse was scheduled to appear for several games at Union Park. "It will be interesting in view of the double dealing that has been alleged, to note the dimensions of the audience that will be present." As it turned out, attendance was poor at the first of four games against the Stars, which Syracuse won, 1–0, with a ninth-inning run. "The gate receipts did not amount to a hundred dollars which shows that selling tournament games don't [sic] pay," the newspaper opined. It went on:

> Base ball is dead in this city unless something is done to wipe out the disgrace that now justly clings to the Allegheny club. In a conversation which our reporter had last night with two Allegheny players, they frankly stated that the game in Chicago on Saturday was sold, and named the men who sold it. It is unnecessary to mention them here, but they have always been looked upon, and undoubtedly are, among the best players in the club. The other players keenly feel the position in which they are placed by the action of their

colleagues, and one of them, who has already signed with another club for next season, says that even if he could get his release from it nothing could now induce him to remain here. He depends largely upon base ball for his living, and says he cannot afford to have the name of belonging to a club that plays crooked games. He claims to be an honest player, and no doubt is. He says that he was offered money to assist in selling of the Chicago game on Saturday, but refused. There is a great deal of indignation among the lovers of the game in this city over the conduct of the Alleghenys, and the stockholders and directors of the nine express themselves as determined to institute a rigid investigation, and make public every dishonorable act which they can ascertain was committed, no matter by whom, and no matter who may be hurt. The only way left for the redemption of the Allegheny club, and its restoration to public confidence, is by the summary expulsion of the players who sold out and the resignation of those alleged to have been implicated and financially interested to a large extent in the sale.[17]

The newspaper said Syracuse was just as bad for selling out to Indianapolis in Chicago, and its reporter found a Stars player who confirmed it. As if stung by the allegations of crooked play, Allegheny went to work with a vengeance. The team downed Syracuse in each of the next three days by scores of 6–4, 13–7, and 16–6. In the 13–7 victory, Allegheny pounded out three home runs, and in the final contest no less than five triples.

Allegheny visited Buffalo on September 28 and learned that baseball fever was rampant there and fans had embraced its newly formed first professional club. Allegheny scored four runs in the first inning as it cruised to a 7–2 victory. Pitching for the Bisons was a youngster named Larry Corcoran who showed much promise despite the rough reception by Creamer, Fulmer and McKelvy, who touched him up for seven of the Alleghenys' nine hits. The next day, the *New York Clipper* reported that the International Association had formally announced that Allegheny had signed Galvin, Dolan, Goodman, Nelson and Ryan for their 1878 campaign. It also noted the collapse of Columbus for financial reasons and reported that their star pitcher, Jim McCormick, would finish the season with Indianapolis, while the hard-hitting King Kelly signed with Hornellsville, New York.[18] The disbanding of the IA Buckeyes and the Live Oaks of Lynn, Massachusetts, meant the Association standings had to be adjusted by removing the results of their games won and lost by teams still in the championship hunt. The recalculation put the Tecumsehs of London in the lead with 13 games won, to 11 for Allegheny. Rochester was in third spot with eight wins, Manchester stood fourth with seven, and the Maple Leafs of Guelph, with four, were at the bottom of the heap. Galvin, Goldsmith and other IA pitchers lost credit for games they had won from teams that later dropped out.

To complete its requirements for the championship race based on total wins, Allegheny had to play one more game against London. Having won all three previous contests, it was a confident Pennsylvania team that crossed the border into Canada on October 1 for a game the next day that had been

5. Playing Through Adversity 61

arranged on short notice. Arriving in London, the Alleghenys learned that Ed Somerville, the sure-handed Tecumseh shortstop, had just died of pneumonia, at age 24. Somerville's funeral attracted Tecumseh stockholders and directors and members of baseball teams from across the city. His teammates acted as pallbearers as the player's casket was placed on an eastbound train for burial at his home in New Haven. Tecumseh manager Harry Gorman quickly found Cincinnati native Mike Burke to fill Somerville's spot at short. But a pall lingered over the home team as it regrouped to meet Allegheny on October 2. Aside from the loss of Somerville, second baseman Mike Dinnen was hurt and was replaced by utility player Marshall Quinton. There was faint hope in London that the Tecumsehs could finally defeat the powerful visitors. Allegheny, however, was dealing with its own black cloud, removed by only a few days and several hundred miles from the allegations of crooked play in the Chicago tournament. Both teams felt a win that would bring them the IA pennant was just the tonic they needed.

Game day was a Tuesday, a difficult time to generate a crowd in the city of 18,000 where work beckoned. The local newspapers estimated the turnout at from 1,500 to 2,000 at Tecumseh Park, directly across the Thames River from downtown. Appointed umpire was the injured Tecumseh Dinnen, whose work had been commended to the Alleghenys by the Milwaukee club, which was leaving town after a string of three games in London. The championship game featured a pitching duel between the fastballer Galvin and curveballer Fred Goldsmith, along with some sharp fielding. It was described by the *London Advertiser* as "the most exciting contest ever seen on the London grounds."[19] Neither team was able to score a run for six innings as few hits were made off the determined pitchers. In the top of the first inning, Tecumseh's Burke hit a hard drive to center field which was pulled in by a sparkling one-handed catch by Russ McKelvy. The crowd appreciated the effort and erupted with cheers and applause. In the third inning, Goldsmith struck out Bill Holbert, Jake Goodman and McKelvy in order. Newcomer Burke was aggressive on the base paths throughout the game for the Tecumsehs, while behind the plate the home team's Phil Powers was sharp and fielded a particularly difficult pop-up foul in the fourth inning.

The fifth inning was marked by controversy. At the plate, Allegheny second baseman Chick Fulmer stepped outside the lines marking the batter's position during his swing. Powers had noted Fulmer's habit and drew it to umpire Dinnen's attention. Fulmer was called out by Dinnen for the transgression, prompting howls of protest from the Allegheny bench. An uproar ensued that lasted for some time, but Dinnen refused to back down. At another point in the game, the usually even-tempered Galvin lost his cool. The *London Free Press* described it this way: "A regrettable circumstance in connection with the game was some filthy language used by Galvin, the pitcher of the Alleghenys, to the audience, and he may thank the forbearance of Londoners for not receiving some physical reminder that such insolence is not appreciated."[20] It wasn't clear what prompted his outburst using language he no doubt learned back in the Kerry Patch.

Because it won the coin toss and chose to bat last, Allegheny put a scare into the home club in the bottom of the sixth inning when Goodman made a base hit off Goldsmith. McKelvy followed with a double, but Goodman was held at third. Galvin came to the plate with two out and a chance to put his team in the lead. But it was not to be. For the third time in the game, Goldsmith struck out his opposite number. In the top of the seventh inning, Burke reached first on an error committed by Fulmer at second. He advanced to second when Hornung drove a single past shortstop Candy Nelson. Burke stole third, and both he and Dutch Hornung crossed home plate when Tecumseh first baseman Foghorn Bradley tripled. Quinton sacrificed to bring Bradley home and put the score at 3–0 as the home crowd erupted in delight. Allegheny failed to reply in the bottom of the inning. The eighth inning saw goose eggs registered by both teams. In the top of the ninth, London centerfielder Tommy Smith was struck out by Galvin. Powers connected for a double, followed by Goldsmith with a single. Powers raced home when Allegheny catcher Dolan bobbled the ball and missed tagging him. Burke made a hit to right field that allowed Goldsmith to score another run, prompting "deafening applause."[21] The at-bat for London ended without further scoring. Up to that point, the Tecumsehs had played error-free ball. In the bottom of the inning, however, Nelson managed a single with one out and advanced to second on Goldsmith's first wild pitch of the game. Galvin struck out, but Williamson singled. Powers tried to catch Williamson at second but overthrew into center field, where Smith mishandled the ball, allowing both runners to score. The only Tecumseh errors in the game came late and proved costly. The inning ended on a foul by Fulmer that was grabbed by Powers. The final score was 5–2 for London, and the first International Association pennant was theirs. Both Galvin and Goldsmith had given up six hits, but the Tecumsehs were better able to convert theirs into runs. The London team had finally been able to defeat Allegheny after three losses, and they couldn't have picked a better time to do so.

That night, the Tecumsehs were entertained at the Tecumseh House Hotel, guests of team vice-president W. H. Birrell and his wife. They received flowers and bouquets of praise for bringing glory to London. The players, more subdued than they would otherwise have been, wore black crepe in memory of Ed Somerville, their co-captain who had been such a key part of their successful season.

Back in Pittsburgh, the *Commercial Gazette* carried only a brief item about the loss, perhaps reflecting the waning interest in the local nine because of the revelations of crooked play. There had been few stories about the home team in the paper since its September 25 article about "sold" games.

The Championship Lost
Defeat of the Alleghenys Yesterday by the Tecumsehs—How it Was Done.
  A private dispatch received in this city last night states that the Allegheny ball club played yesterday at London, Ontario, with the Tecumsehs, and were defeated by a score of 3–2 [sic]. This is bad. By this defeat the Alleghenys will doubtless lose the International Association championship. The telegram states that the game was not won by the superior playing of the Tecumsehs, but by the partiality of the umpire, who gave all decisions in their favor. The umpire is reported as a member of the Tecumseh club. The Alleghenys were all the more fools for playing such an important game with an umpire that belonged to the opposing team. Base ball admirers in this city will be inconsolable over the loss of the championship. "Thou wert so near and now thou art so far."[22]

  The following day in London, in a game that was meaningless, Allegheny roared back, taking advantage of Goldsmith, who complained of a sore arm and was replaced by Bradley in an error-filled game that drew a small crowd. Galvin homered for his team and Quinton did the same for London. The final score was 22–6 for Allegheny.
  Some controversy would develop about who was entitled to the International Association pennant, but there was no question in the mind of Henry Chadwick in the *New York Clipper*. In its October 13 edition, Chadwick wrote, "nothing better could have happened" to promote baseball in Canada or the International Association "than the success of the Canada Tecumsehs in winning the International Association championship, as they have done."[23]
  On their way home, the Allegheny nine stopped in Buffalo for some well-attended games on October 4 and 5, winning by scores of 1–0 and 2–0. Upon their return, Denny McKnight, now vice-president of the club, disputed the validity of bestowing the championship on London. He argued that the Guelph Maple Leafs had disbanded before playing two games that they were required to play against Allegheny, so, in fairness, two victories London had over Guelph should be disregarded in the standings. McKnight said Allegheny also deserved credit for winning two games over disbanded Lynn. That would leave Allegheny with the best overall record in the Association, he argued, and entitled to the pennant. The *Commercial Gazette*, which earlier declared the IA pennant to be London's, gamely carried McKnight's assertion and added: "the championship will remain in a state of delightful perplexity until finally decided by the International Association."[24] Within five days, Chadwick stated his view that London had won, but later in the month generously provided space in the *Clipper* for the Allegheny argument from its secretary. In a preamble, however, Chadwick noted that the Guelph team had not disbanded at all, but had released most of its professional players late in the season and continued with replacements. The "Father of Baseball" was dismissive

of the Allegheny claim.[25] Chadwick gave space for a reply by the Tecumseh club secretary on October 27, in which the official suggested Allegheny didn't understand the championship rules. A week after that, a correspondent giving the pen-name "Canadian," wrote the *Clipper* to say he had inside knowledge of the situation and insisted Guelph had completed its schedule, except for two games it wanted to play in Allegheny. When the Maple Leafs went south to meet their championship requirements, he wrote, they couldn't because McKnight opted to play games against Indianapolis on dates originally allocated to Guelph. Given the extent of detail shared by the writer, "Canadian" was likely Maple Leafs president George Sleeman.[26] The issue was left for the judiciary committee of the International Association to resolve. After considering the arguments on all sides, the judiciary committee awarded the championship to London at the IA's annual meeting held in February.[27]

The Boston Red Caps won the National League championship by seven games over the Louisville Grays, taking advantage of Louisville's late-season collapse tied to the influence of gamblers. In late October, Louisville expelled pitcher Jim Devlin, leftfielder George Hall, and infielders Bill Craver and Al Nichols, the latter of whom began the season with Allegheny. The league, determined to send a message that crooked play was unacceptable, upheld the action and banned the foursome from baseball for life.[28] Meanwhile, the Syracuse Stars were declared champions of the League Alliance.

As the bickering continued among Allegheny, Guelph and London, the *Clipper* reported that Pud Galvin had signed with Buffalo for the 1878 season. It was a shock for Allegheny fans who admired his work and had been repeatedly assured he was going to sign—or had signed—with Allegheny for a second season. Also hired by Buffalo, it was said, were Allegheny catcher Tom Dolan and second baseman Chick Fulmer. Buffalo had been busy signing players for the coming campaign in "new and much larger grounds [that] have been leased for three years and will be fitted up in first-class style." The *Clipper* also reported that the promising young pitcher Larry Corcoran had been signed to play again with Buffalo but was later released at his own request.[29]

Toward the end of the year, Chadwick's paper took note of the estimated losses by some of the major professional nines during 1877, a clear indication that difficult economic times continued. For National League teams they were: $6,000 for St. Louis; $4,000 for Cincinnati, $2,500 for Hartford; $2,000 for Louisville. Outside the league they were: $4,000 for Indianapolis; $3,000 for Allegheny and London; $2,000 for Syracuse and Milwaukee; $1,500 for Columbus.[30] A Syracuse newspaper reported that a much more dire situation existed in Allegheny, which owed $8,000 to its creditors and had "gone by board" in October.[31] Another source suggested the St. Louis loss totaled $8,000, while Chicago lost $6,000 and Boston $1,500.[32] Professional baseball was still struggling to succeed as a business.

5. Playing Through Adversity 65

The *Clipper* also published a recap of the overall records of major clubs in the season past. It showed Allegheny with 59 wins and 37 losses with two draws. The Tecumsehs had 41 wins with 26 losses and seven draws.[33] Based on their pitching records, the paper ranked Galvin the top pitcher, with Charles Purroy of Rochester second and Fred Goldsmith third. But that ranking was based on average base hits allowed per game. Earned run averages weren't provided, or their win-loss records. Records available today show that in games played for the IA championship, Goldsmith came in first with 14 wins and four losses, Galvin was second with 12 wins and six losses,[34] and Purroy had eight wins and five defeats.

It was a breakout season for Galvin, who had risen to the very top rank of pitchers in professional baseball, without being a member of a National League team. Allegheny gave him a chance to show what he could do and wanted him back for another season as it planned to reorganize. But Buffalo presented a new challenge and a fresh start for him. The club turned a profit of $490.60 in its short 1877 season and was buoyed by optimism and throngs of enthusiastic fans.[35] It has been said that the Bisons club was the only professional organization in all of baseball to turn a profit that year.[36] This was quite a feat when the traditional money-makers of Boston and Chicago lost thousands. There was talk about Buffalo plans to enter the International Association for 1878, and the city played host for its annual meeting in February.

In Allegheny City, the scent of crooked play lingered like the smoke from Pittsburgh's steel mills and iron foundries. It was far from certain the ball club there could rise from its financial ashes and again field a professional nine that could be competitive. It had given the young man from St. Louis his opportunity to shine and he had seized it. But a future there did not appear very promising to him.

For Pud Galvin, the decision to play his next season in Buffalo, with a clean slate, was not difficult.

6

Joining the Show in Buffalo

Pud Galvin may have received some overtures from Buffalo during the late September stop his Allegheny club made in the border city on its way west to play the final championship game at London. At the time, the signing of players under contract was common. The practice was criticized, however, for fear a player might go easy on his future club if both his current and future teams were to meet. Rules were soon changed to forbid such signings until a season was over. In October, an offer of some sort was apparently made to Galvin by Bisons manager Bill Barnie. On October 20, Galvin wired Barnie from Pittsburgh with the following message: "I will play for twelve hundred & Tom [catcher Tom Dolan] will play for nine hundred but I want to get some in winter. Answer soon and [infielder Chick] Fulmer will let you know soon. J. F. Galvin."[1] Barnie moved quickly because within days the *New York Clipper* revealed that all three would become Bisons.[2]

Organized baseball had been played in Buffalo since 1857, when the Niagaras club "chose up" sides from among its members for their amateur contests. A year later, the first game was played with an out-of-town nine when the Buffalo team downed Rochester, 30–20. Two years later, in what is believed to be the first international game, the Queen Cities, another Buffalo club, defeated the Burlingtons of Hamilton, Ontario, 30–25. Soon afterward, the Niagaras traveled to Hamilton, where they defeated the Young Canadians club, 87–13. The Civil War brought a halt to baseball, but by 1867 about 100 amateur teams were again playing the game in the city of Buffalo. The Niagaras became the pre-eminent ball club and played many of the better teams in the East and Midwest at home and on the road.[3]

The professional game was rather late coming to Buffalo, the booming Lake Erie city where western raw materials, lumber and grain were shipped to eastern markets and manufactured goods and adventurers from the east paused on their way to the Midwest and beyond. The city was strategically located at the western terminus of the Erie Canal, an important shipping route completed in 1825. It would be surpassed by rail, for which Buffalo also became an important hub. During the 1870s, Buffalo experienced its Golden Age as the population grew from 117,000 to 155,000. More than 1,000 industries had been established and retailers flourished in what had become known as the Queen City.[4] Civic pride was growing as Buffalo sought to establish its place among the leading cities of the U.S. northeast, many of which played out their rivalries on the ball field. Residents of Buffalo began clamoring for their own baseball team, tired of merely playing host to games between teams from Erie, Rochester, London, Guelph, Hornellsville, Syracuse and other places, that drew good crowds.

The baseball season of 1877 was well underway when the Buffalo Base Ball Club was organized as an independent, professional nine. A group of professional men had failed to buy the disbanding Erie club and move it to Buffalo, apparently scared off because of the sad state of its books. A rumor had spread in the spring that the Cass club of Detroit was disbanding and its manager and best players were eyeing Buffalo for a new start, but nothing had come of that, either. The *Buffalo Courier* reported on August 2 that "the managers of the club have spared no pains in organizing a nine which if what we hear of them is true, will prove a credit to the city.... The organizers of the nine intend that their club shall be above reproach and that it will avoid those things that proved so disastrous to many other similar organizations."[5] President of the club was Edward R. Spaulding, a cashier at the Farmers' and Mechanics' National Bank. Secretary was Elihu Spencer, a local agent for Equitable Life. Other directors were young professional and business men in Buffalo.[6] The organizers soon announced the players who would represent the city in the loose organization known as the League Alliance. The pitcher would be Larry Corcoran, a rookie from Geneseo, 60 miles to the east, who turned 18 that month. Named as catcher was Sam Field, 28, who had played with Philadelphia Centennials and Washington in the National Association and Cincinnati's National League team in 1876. Field was one of the few experienced players on the team, along with manager Bill Barnie, who had appeared with four different teams in the National Association.

The rest of the roster consisted mainly of young players, several of them locals, only a few with professional experience. Three came from the disbanded Erie club. As weeks went by, Buffalo management tried more players with greater experience to support the hard-throwing Corcoran. The first game was played August 3 on the grounds of the former Prospect Skating Club, on the east side of Niagara Street between Rhode Island and Vermont Streets, not far from the Niagara River. Catcher Field had not yet arrived, so his position behind the plate was filled by a local, 20-year-old John Purrington, formerly of the Auburns. The experienced Rochester Flour City team was the opposition "and the game proved one of the most brilliant that has ever been played in this city," reported the *Buffalo Courier*, attracting 1,000 fans who were accommodated in newly constructed stands.[7] Hitting was anemic by both sides as one scoreless inning followed another. Corcoran, the *Buffalo Express* reported, "fully established his claim as a pitcher. He did the work admirably yesterday and is the right man in the right place."[8] The visitors objected to the umpiring throughout and in the sixth inning refused to take the field. After a brief standoff, the issue was resolved and play resumed. Rochester nearly scored in the ninth inning but stranded a runner on third, and the teams continued into a tenth inning. After ten complete innings, the visitors begged off, having to catch a train for home, and the score was recorded as a 0-0 tie. It was considered a strong start for the Buffalo club, to be known as the Bisons, for which a loss had been generally expected.

Buffalo won its first game nine days later, defeating Hornellsville, 7-5. A highlight in the early days of the team came August 14 when the Louisville Reds were in town. More than 2,000 fans crammed into the new ballpark and hundreds more peered over its low fences. The Bisons gave Louisville a good battle but lost, 3-0, for another strong showing. During the game, a section of the new grandstand collapsed, but no one was seriously hurt. On August 28, the Bisons welcomed the Chicago White Stockings for a game that attracted 3,000 fans. Horace Phillips, who would become manager of the Troy, Columbus and Allegheny clubs, pitched for Buffalo as Corcoran rested. Cal McVey appeared for the White Stockings, giving George Washington Bradley the day off. The reigning National League champions won, 4-2, against the Bisons, but it was another credible showing for the new team. After a September 8 loss to Indianapolis, a 7-0 whitewash with Phillips again pitching, the correspondent for the *New York Clipper* said this marked the 13th defeat in 16 games.

> In the two months of its organization the Buffalo managers have taken on trial nearly twenty players, and the team have never yet been able to get acquainted with one another before changes would be made and the new men substituted.... The team as now constituted, if allowed to work together, bid fair to do well the remainder of the season, and it is understood that the managers entertain an idea of making no further changes during September.[9]

With Corcoran in the pitching box, Buffalo shut out Rochester, 3-0, on September 24. His pitching was at times wild and on August 15, less than two weeks into the Bisons season, catcher Field suffered a double fracture of his thumb while trying to corral one of Corcoran's errant missiles. The catcher was out for the season and several players were tried as replacements.

Despite its late start, the Buffalo club played a schedule of 40 games as it added and dropped players in a bid to strengthen its roster. Among those picked up in September was a 17-year-old Pennsylvanian, John Montgomery Ward, an infielder and pitcher with an effective curve ball. Ward was on the

6. Joining the Show in Buffalo   69

Riverside Park, along Rhode Island Street, a few blocks from the Niagara River in Buffalo, was home to the Bisons from 1877 to 1884. Here Galvin recorded his best seasons, winning 46 games in 1883 and 1884 when Buffalo was a member of the National League. The team's move a few blocks east to Olympic Park for 1885 led to financial problems that contributed to its collapse that same year (Buffalo History Museum).

cusp of a long and successful professional career that saw him credited with 2,107 hits, 164 major league pitching victories and a place in the Baseball Hall of Fame. Directors of the Bisons were not done yet, and in months to come their keen eye on talent would soon find other future stars.

In October, Buffalo continued to lose more games than it won, defeated by Boston, 5–0 and 8–0, Hartford, 12–1, and Rochester, 8–4 and 3–0. In the latter game, an October 18 shutout that marked the end of the season, Ward pitched and gave up seven hits. When play ended for the season, the Bisons' overall record was ten wins and 27 losses, with three ties. As they looked to further improve their club, directors took satisfaction from the $490 profit from operations. Encouraged, they began to make inquiries about joining the International Association as they looked ahead. One of the first players signed for the 1878 campaign was pitcher Corcoran, at $600 for six months. Before the year was out, however, directors had a change of heart and decided to buy back his contract. Perhaps the signing of Pud Galvin by the beginning of November was a factor and management felt it couldn't afford two pitching stars. The reason, as given in the *Buffalo Courier*, was that Corcoran was a good pitcher, but a poor team player "who showed no sympathy for his catcher after getting two strikes on a batter."[10] That may have been code for saying his delivery was too wild to be relied upon. He proved to be a budding star that Buffalo let slip away. Corcoran went on to enjoy an eight-year career in the National League, mainly with Chicago, where he found himself paired with Fred Goldsmith in one of baseball's early pitching rotations. Corcoran won 177 games with 91 losses. Yet another standout pitcher contacted the Buffalo directors before the year was out. Candy Cummings, still president of the International Association, wrote from Brooklyn on December 20, offering his services as manager, pitcher or fielder, giving Henry Chadwick of the *Clipper* as one of his references.[11] Buffalo took a pass and Cummings landed with Association teams in New Bedford, New Haven, and Hartford in 1878. John Montgomery Ward went to Binghamton's IA team for 1878, but before the year was out he jumped to the National League team in Providence.

For 1878, the National League took aim at the upstart International Association. It decreed that no games against non–League teams could take place on League team grounds, that the Spalding League ball had to be used and a League umpire in place in all meetings. Pre-season exhibition contests could be played against teams outside the League in League parks, but that was the only exception. The League insisted on being able to cancel games with outside teams to make up for rained-out league contests. But $50 would be demanded from outside teams who cancelled for any reason. William Hulbert and the league he presided over were determined to put the squeeze on the Association they saw as a threat. Hulbert and his teams did acknowledge the loosely affiliated League Alliance and were willing to recognize contracts of its teams with players and agree on issues of player eligibility. The same courtesy was not extended to the IA, from whom National League teams would continue to lure players. Some territorial rights and a guarantee of some games against League teams were also extended to Alliance members, another slap at the International Association.

Several members of the Association were livid at the power play launched by Hulbert's western-based NL that was about to enter its third

6. Joining the Show in Buffalo   71

Pud Galvin became a Buffalo Bison for the 1878 season, its first year in the International Association. Galvin recorded 72 wins overall, with 25 losses and three ties. In league play, he won 24 games as the Bisons took the Association pennant. From left to right, back row: Tom Dolan, Dick Allen, Bill McGunnigle, Galvin. Middle row: Bill Crowley, Dave Eggler, Steve Libby, Chick Fulmer, Denny Mack. Front row: Davy Force, Trick McSorley (Buffalo History Museum).

season of existence with only six teams. Directors of the Auburn, New York, club urged fellow IA clubs to "stick together and kick together" while A. B. Rankin of Brooklyn urged non–League clubs to stand together and stay away from getting roped into the League Alliance. He said the National League was being "unreasonably absurd in its attempts to control all of baseball. Are we to submit to the caprice of a clique or ring? Or are we to assert our own independence?" he asked.[12] Even players were upset. When he learned Buffalo (and London) were considering National League membership, newly signed Buffalo shortstop, Davy Force, wrote to the club: "I heard that we were going to join the League. I hope & pray not, for if we do we are gone financially ... for there is nothing in it."[13] In the end, the IA and its clubs opted against waging war. They would extend to other teams and leagues exactly the same treatment as they received.

Buffalo joined the International Association for 1878 and agreed to enter the championship race, which attracted Syracuse, Allegheny, London, Utica, Rochester, Hornellsville, Manchester, Lynn, Lowell, New Bedford/New Haven/Hartford (the franchise kept folding and moving), Binghamton, and Springfield (Massachusetts). Allegheny appeared unable to field a professional nine to replace the disbanded one from the previous season, but scrambled to submit its $50 entry fee a mere two days before the deadline.[14] The Guelph Maple Leafs had decided to stay home, having found the 1877 season too financially draining. That left the defending champions Tecumsehs of London as the only "international" team in the International Association.

Directors of the Bisons were determined to put on a good show as they pursued players. To the battery of Galvin and Dolan, and infielder Fulmer, they added first baseman Steve Libby, second baseman Denny Mack, third baseman Dick Allen, shortstop Davy Force, leftfielder Bill Crowley, centerfielder Dave Eggler, outfielder/backup pitcher Bill McGunnigle and utility player John "Trick" McSorley. It was a talent-laden crew. Mack, 28, had been playing professional ball since joining the 1871 Rockford club in the National Association. He was a member of the Philadelphia nine in the Association and the 1876 St. Louis Browns of the National League. Force, 28, had played for five National Association teams and the National League teams in Philadelphia, New York and St. Louis. In 1874–1875, Force signed a contract with Philadelphia after signing one with Chicago, triggering a nasty fight and controversy that saw Chicago president William Hulbert lose Force to Philadelphia. This so incensed Hulbert at the Eastern-dominated National Association that he began to formulate plans for what soon became the National League.[15] In 1877, Force was tainted by the allegations of selling games that had rocked the St. Louis club. Force and three teammates were blacklisted and he was looking for a team outside the league. So perhaps some residual bitterness was behind Force urging Buffalo against joining the National League. His hitting had begun to decline but he still had the good hands essential at shortstop. At five-foot-four, Force was one of the smallest men ever to play the professional game. The Bisons paid him $1,200, the same as Galvin, the top earner on the team. Crowley, 21, had played with Philadelphia in the National Association and Louisville in the League. A good hitter, he would record a batting average of .304 for Buffalo in the upcoming season. Eggler, 27, had been playing professionally since 1871 and was a member of three National Association clubs and the Philadelphia and Chicago nines in the National League. He was an outstanding fielder, but his batting average had begun to skid (to .187 for the upcoming season). Buffalo signed him for $1,000. McSorley, 25, a utility infielder, often played first base as well as shortstop. He had played for the St. Louis Reds from 1873 to 1875 (the year they joined the National Association), and was familiar with the young St. Louis

6. Joining the Show in Buffalo 73

pitching prodigy Galvin. McSorley proved to be a notorious "kicker," complaining about the calls of umpires who replied to his outbursts by fining or ejecting him, or both. He would be paid $700.

The Buffalo Bisons for 1878 would become one of the best clubs in professional baseball, largely because of the pitching of Galvin, who soon picked up another nickname, "Gentle Jeems," because of his generally easygoing nature.

The Bisons were scheduled to play their season opener April 22 on their newly sodded grounds along Rhode Island Street now, renamed Riverside Park. But the field, a former swamp, was too wet for play and the game was cancelled. Their first game, an exhibition match, came four days later in London, where they lost to the Tecumsehs, 7–3. "Galvin pitched very fine, umpire very bad," team captain Chick Fulmer wired home afterward.[16] The game marked Galvin's first time back in London since his Allegheny team failed to win the IA pennant six months earlier. The Tecumseh roster had been bolstered by hard-hitting Ross Barnes, formerly of Chicago, the new team captain who played mainly at second base. Barnes managed only a single hit off Galvin, but his team collected 11 in all, mostly during an eighth-inning rally that produced five of London's seven runs.[17] Catcher Phil Powers did most of the damage that inning with a bases-loaded triple. The following day, in another exhibition, Buffalo capitalized on Tecumseh fielding errors to win, 2–1. On May 1 in Buffalo, both teams went at it again for a third exhibition tilt in a week. This time, the Londoners won, 5–2. The defending champions and newcomer Syracuse proved to be the strongest competition for Buffalo as the IA season unfolded. Buffalo would see them early and often. The following day, May 2, the Bisons lost, 5–1, in Syracuse. Galvin gave up five hits, four in succession during the seventh inning. On May 3, Syracuse again won, 1–0, scoring its only run in the ninth inning. Stars pitcher Harry McCormick had the highlight play of the game, snagging a hard line drive by Buffalo first baseman Steve Libby.

Buffalo got off to a slow start as it began to play games to count for the championship. Published IA standings as of May 6 showed the Bisons were 12th of 13 teams with no wins, three losses and a tie. Syracuse was first with six wins and one loss. London was ninth, having won the only game it had played. But the *Clipper* confessed it was having trouble separating games played for the IA championship from those counting toward the New York State championship. It urged team officials filing results of games to indicate clearly which games counted toward which championship—and which were merely exhibitions. With no centralized scheduling, teams were expected to arrange their four championship matches with each other contending team.

Regardless, the early days of play showed Buffalo that it had to pull up its socks to be competitive. It supporters were many, but they would need to see some on-field success to continue patronizing the club. In early May, Henry Chadwick, never a fan of the National League, penned a piece in the *Clipper* in which he pointed out how busy April had been for Association teams as they filled their coffers with game proceeds, while National League teams resorted to playing "picked nines" or other lesser clubs because of the new ban on non–League teams in league parks. "The successful establishment of the International Association as the ruling professional association of the country—which it now unquestionably is—has been followed up by the opening of the campaign in a style never before equaled in the professional arena," he wrote. Buffalo, by joining the Association, found itself in good company, at least in the eyes of the Father of Baseball.

On May 21, more than 400 Buffalo fans traveled to a game in Rochester, taking advantage of a special rail excursion fare of two dollars. They would be disappointed. The Bisons were weary from an eastern trip and it showed. Rochester pounded Galvin for eight hits, scoring four runs in the ninth inning for a 7–1 win. Losing to their arch-rivals to the east was a bitter pill to swallow for some Buffalo fans, who said it appeared the game had been "sold."[18] While there was no evidence to support the contention, it showed how easily confidence could be lost in home teams in an era where gambling and corruption still flourished, despite efforts to stamp them out. The following day in Buffalo, fans hoped for better things in another clash between the same teams. Galvin was badly abused by Rochester hitters in the first inning as they scored two runs, and he was moved to right field and replaced by McGunnigle. Rochester made eight hits off the two pitchers as it won, 5–3.

Buffalo traveled to London for its first championship game with the Tecumsehs on May 24, the Queen's Birthday, Victoria Day in Canada. A large holiday crowd of 3,500 witnessed a 7–1 loss to the Bisons. The visitors scored two runs off Goldsmith in the first inning and from then on capitalized on London errors. Galvin was sharp in the pitcher's box, giving up only two hits to the powerful Tecumsehs. His own line drive past third base in the fourth inning scored another of Buffalo's runs. Goldsmith tallied the only run for London on a series of throwing errors. His catcher, Powers, had one eye swollen shut from taking a hit in the face in Utica and he wore a mask, which seemed to cause him trouble. One of the local papers attributed the uncharacteristically weak showing and poor hitting of the Tecumsehs to fatigue. The team had returned to London from an eastern road trip at 6 a.m. that same day.[19] Buffalo immediately returned home for a May 25 game against Allegheny, Galvin's old team. The Bisons made only one error and Galvin and McGunnigle allowed four hits as they shared pitching duties. Buffalo won the game that featured some excellent fielding, 2–1. The Bisons were down, 1–0, before Crowley and Libby crossed the plate in the seventh inning to seal the win. Decoration Day (later renamed Memorial Day), May 30,

6. Joining the Show in Buffalo 75

attracted a holiday crowd in Buffalo, estimated at 5,000 to 6,000, to witness a championship game with London. The visitors returned the holiday-game favor by beating the Bisons, 2–1. McGunnigle began pitching for the home team and gave up five hits in three innings before being relieved by Galvin, who allowed only two more. Galvin reached Goldsmith for a double in the second inning to bring home Libby for the first run of the game, Buffalo's only tally. In the following inning, London's Dutch Hornung doubled to bring Herm Doscher home and then scored himself when a hit to left field was dropped. The *London Advertiser* sent a reporter to the game that attracted a good number of London fans and filed a report full of local color.

> London is looked upon as a "base ball town," and with some reason, too, but it can't touch Buffalo. The epidemic rages there—everybody has the base ball fever! Even the ladies examine the score cards critically, know what a base hit is, and dispute the umpire's decision, when necessary, with all the readiness of professional ball tossers.[20]

The reporter also noted something he found most interesting in the large crowd that packed the ball ground that day.

> This Buffalo audience have one particularly good joke all to themselves and enjoy it immensely. Sitting so long in the cramped seats, and a good many on the ragged edge of anxiety, the audience feel naturally a little stiff. In the space between the third and fourth innings a good looking, middle-aged man in the grand stand rose gravely to his feet, extended his hands to heaven and in the most yawny voice ejaculated "Stretch!" The effect was instantaneous. In a moment three thousand good-natured people—ladies and all—were on their feet, laughing and stretching the stiffness away—a forest of arms reaching outward and upward. The effect was indescribably funny at first, but as it was repeated again and again as the game progressed, the supreme utility of the moment was so apparent that only blessings could be showered at the man who struck upon the novel idea of a "stretching time."

Could this have been the origin baseball's seventh-inning stretch? Buffalo already claimed another first in professional baseball, the printing of scorecards containing business advertisements and selling them for five cents apiece, a precursor to today's game-day program.[21] The holiday game was a success financially and aside from the victory, London went home with a healthy $515 as its share of the gate.

The International Association standings as of May 27 showed Buffalo gaining ground on Syracuse, which continued to lead the loop. Syracuse had 12 wins and one loss in championship matches, while Buffalo was tied for second with Hornellsville with 11 wins and six losses.

Allegheny, which was fighting it out for last place with Hartford, was having a dreadful season. It had lost about 20 games and won only one when the Tecumsehs appeared in Union Park for games on June 5–6. Patronage had been very poor, partly a legacy of suspicion about crooked play from 1877 and partly because of its dismal record. The Allegheny roster included talented infielder Jack Glasscock and noteworthy outfielder Henry Luff, but the last-minute rush to assemble a team had produced a nine that was not competitive. London swept its old rivals by scores of 7–1 and 6–1. On June 7, the Alleghenys welcomed Buffalo to Union Park. The Bisons routed the home club, 12–2. This was the last gasp for Allegheny. The following day, when another game with Buffalo was scheduled, the home team disbanded. It was reported the team was broke because of poor attendance. Several players joined Erie and Cleveland, and those remaining continued as a cooperative nine.[22]

The collapse of one of the founding members of the IA was chilling, but not the last straw for the loop. The departure meant the championship standings had to be adjusted. London lost credit for three wins against Allegheny, while Buffalo lost two and league-leading Syracuse only one. In London, a story was circulated that directors of the Allegheny club wanted to transfer the successful Tecumsehs to their city. The *London Advertiser* printed an item from the *Pittsburgh Leader* saying London was in financial trouble and "hardly able to support a first-class club. It is too far away, is out of line of all base ball travel. Several parties, we understand, have written from this city to the management of the Tecumsehs giving a full account of the status of affairs in this locality, and urging the transfer of the London champions to this city immediately."[23] The London paper, for which long-time Tecumseh director and secretary Harry Gorman was reporter and editor, stoutly denied the club was up for sale, but conceded patronage needed to improve. Rumors of problems for the defending International Association champions were worrisome for the loop, coming so soon after Allegheny had disbanded. But financial problems were dogging several its teams. Before long, the Binghamton Crickets and Worcester, to which Lynn had transferred, would also pull the plug on their nines.

Meanwhile, Buffalo's Steve Libby hit the club's first home run, in spacious Riverside Park in a 3–1 win over Binghamton on June 27, several weeks before the Crickets fell on hard times. His blast into the left field corner came in the tenth inning and brought Dave Eggler home from first base. Home runs were still considered a novelty, and several ladies in the crowd threw bouquets of flowers at the blushing first baseman as he crossed home plate and headed for the Bisons bench.[24] The only other Buffalo homer that season was belted by Pud Galvin in early September, in either Utica or Troy. The ball he launched to center field became lodged in the spring of a carriage parked there. As the fielder struggled to pry it loose, Galvin scampered home.[25]

Just as they had exchanged games on each other's grounds for Victoria Day and Decoration Day, London and Buffalo played another home-and-home series on holidays in July: July 1, Dominion Day, Canada's 11th anniversary as a country, and July 4, Independence Day. Both celebrations usually

6. Joining the Show in Buffalo   77

guaranteed large crowds. On July 1, some brilliant fielding was the feature of the game played at Tecumseh Park before an unexpectedly small crowd of 2,000. Ross Barnes opened the scoring for the Tecumsehs in the third inning with a hit and aggressive running on the base paths. Galvin and Goldsmith both pitched effectively while Dutch Hornung at shortstop and centerfielder Al Hall for the Tecumsehs made some dazzling catches. Dave Eggler for the visitors was a flawless vacuum in center field. No further scoring occurred until the ninth inning, when Dick Allen hit a triple and scored to tie the game on Trick McSorley's single. In the tenth inning, Bill McGunnigle took advantage of a couple of Goldsmith pitches that got past catcher Powers, to score for the Bisons. Dolan followed him in for a 3–1 victory. The visitors were upset at some calls by umpire T. H. Brunton and threatened to play under protest, but the victory ended the controversy. In London, fans complained that the Tecumsehs were developing an unfortunate habit of losing big games on holidays. The crowds on both the Queen's Birthday and Dominion Day were lighter than in previous years when games against rival Guelph attracted as many as 9,000 fans. Buffalo's share of holiday gate proceeds were a slim $75 and $124, respectively.[26]

On their way to the Independence Day game in Buffalo, the same two teams played an exhibition match July 3 in Lockport, a nearby community, where the Bisons pounded out an 11–3 win. The next day, a massive crowd of at least 6,000 jammed into and around Riverside Park. Umpire for the game was C. W. Nicholls, a train brakeman during the winter, who was developing a bit of a reputation among visiting teams as a "homer." His calls were often challenged by visitors, and he was sometimes seen as a tenth man for the Bisons. He relied on the umpiring job for his income in the summer, and it was a job he apparently intended to keep. The Tecumsehs had no quibble with him this day, however. In the top of the first inning, second baseman Ross Barnes touched Galvin for a long hit to right field to score leadoff hitter Al Hall, who had singled. The visitors added to their lead with a run in the fourth when shortstop Mike Burke singled, stole second and scored on a wild throw. In the fifth, Galvin hit a long fly to left field where Dutch Hornung back-pedaled to make a spectacular one-handed catch that drew sustained applause from the appreciative crowd. Dave Eggler scored on the play for Buffalo's only run. The Tecumsehs won the game, 2–1, spoiling the holiday for their hosts, just as they had done on Decoration Day. A rivalry was developing between the teams located barely 150 miles apart, although it was nowhere near as intense as those London had established with Guelph, and Buffalo with Rochester. The four championship games required between the Tecumsehs and the Bisons had been split, 2–2.

Buffalo continued its mostly winning ways through July as it took first place, a game ahead of Syracuse. The standings were published in the *Clipper*,

Today's ballpark in Buffalo is a beautiful facility that seats 17,600. Coca-Cola Field was opened in 1988. The Bisons, today a Triple-A affiliate of the Toronto Blue Jays, play in the Eastern League. The city has a long-standing connection to professional baseball that began in 1877. Its seven-year stint in the National League ended in 1885 (photograph by author).

which complained it would take a "Philadelphia lawyer" to segregate exhibition games from those played for the IA and New York championships.

Trouble was brewing in London after a Tecumseh loss to Syracuse on July 9. London outplayed the Stars in every aspect of the game, but lost, 6–5, as Goldsmith "weakened" in the eighth inning and was replaced by Foghorn Bradley. Syracuse scored three runs in each of the eighth and nine innings to notch the win. General indignation swept London amidst rumors the game had been sold to Syracuse, a team which it was recalled had been involved in crooked play late the previous season. London lost again the next day, 6–3, as Goldsmith sat out. One of the London newspapers said the losses to Syracuse had administered a "deathblow" to baseball in London.[27] Controversy raged in the city and disbanding was considered, but team directors expressed confidence in the nine and agreed to continue their pursuit of a second championship. Things continued to deteriorate at the gate, however, and on August 24, London paid off its professionals in full and finished the season with amateurs. Soon after, Dutch Hornung was signed by Buffalo and Fred Goldsmith joined Springfield, for whom Larry Corcoran was pitching. By then, Binghamton, Hornellsville, Worcester and Manchester had disbanded for lack of fans and money. Rochester was close behind.

Buffalo played London in an exhibition game August 16 at Riverside Park that the Bisons won, 15–10, freely batting Foghorn Bradley as Goldsmith occupied left field and first base. Both Bradley and Galvin used the old-fashioned, straight-armed delivery (in which the elbow cannot bend) in the game, by agreement of both teams. It proved easy to hit. Three days later, Buffalo played host to the Chicago White Stockings, who put 19-year-old Laurie Reis in as pitcher, resting their ace, Terry Larkin. Buffalo scored first in the second inning and Chicago replied with two runs in the fourth. Fulmer tied the game for the Bisons in the eighth, by stealing a base, capitalizing on throwing errors and coming home on a sacrifice hit by Denny Mack. In the 13th inning, Libby connected for a single to left field, advanced to second on a single by Galvin, and capitalized on two fielding errors to win the game, 3–2. Galvin had developed an effective pickoff move and he used it to good effect in the game. He caught five White Stockings runners napping on the base paths that day.

As of the end of August, Buffalo held first place in the International Association standings, with Syracuse a game behind and London, still playing its required championship games, two games back. The final game for the Association championship between Buffalo and Syracuse was played September 14 in Buffalo before a crowd of 3,000 who were delighted to see the Bisons win, 9–1. Buffalo then met the Boston Red Caps, who were on their way to claiming the National League championship. The contest in Boston on October 2 saw the Bisons rely on their bats to defeat the home club and Tommy Bond by a score of 9–5, but it took 12 innings to do so. In their last at-bat, Buffalo erupted for six runs to take the game that was marked by Red Caps errors and their poor base running. The win meant Galvin had at least one victory over each club in the National League. The following day, Buffalo needed 13 innings to defeat the Providence Grays, 6–4, in Providence. Again, the Bisons' bats were strong. Before leaving the east, Buffalo visited Boston yet again, on October 5. They lost, 6–1, to give them two losses and one win against the National League leaders over the season.

On October 8, the Bisons defeated Utica, 3–1, in Buffalo in the final game of the International Association season to claim the pennant. Five days earlier, Syracuse defeated Lowell, 12–1, and made the same claim to the championship. Association records showed both clubs with 24 wins and eight defeats. But Syracuse was counting a forfeit by Rochester as a win. Buffalo argued that Rochester had disbanded at the time, so a forfeit could not be awarded. In their four head-to-head contests counting toward the championship,

In the left field corner of Coca-Cola Field in Buffalo, the successes of the hometown Bisons in various leagues over the years are celebrated. Its first championship came in 1878, when Buffalo won the pennant of the International Association, a rival of the National League. The following year, Buffalo, Syracuse and Troy jumped from the IA to the National League, a move that led to the eventual demise of the National League's rival (photograph by author).

Syracuse and Buffalo had each beaten the other twice. The matter would not be decided until the annual convention of the Association the following February in Utica, where Buffalo's position prevailed and it was awarded the pennant. By then, however, both clubs, along with Troy, the New York State champions, had joined the National League.

The 1878 season had been a bit more difficult financially for Buffalo directors than the previous year. They had expenditures of $21,609, but had only $248.94 in the bank once all bills were paid.[28] By contrast, Syracuse, it was reported, lost $1,600.[29] On the diamond, the Buffalo club had been outstanding. The Bisons won 85 games and lost 32, with three ties.[30] A more recent source puts those numbers at 116 games played, with 81 wins, 32 losses and three ties. They defeated National League teams ten times in 17 meetings.[31] At the end of the season, the *New York Clipper* chose an all-star International Association team, based on fielding averages. Five Bisons were

6. Joining the Show in Buffalo 81

picked: Galvin, Libby, McGunnigle, Force and late-season arrival Dutch Hornung, though largely for his play in London.[32]

For Pud Galvin, the season had been nothing short of extraordinary. Historian Joseph Overfield meticulously tabulated game results from the files of the *Buffalo Express* and credited Galvin with 71 victories overall, but did not report his losses. A more recent source credits Galvin with pitching 101 games and completing 96 of them, with 72 wins and 25 losses with the three ties. He threw 17 shutouts and all ten wins against National League teams.[33] Overfield noted that Galvin's performance hadn't raised eyebrows at a time when teams relied on the arm of one pitcher.[34] In the Bisons' first 23 games, Galvin pitched every inning of every game. It has been estimated that he threw 895 innings that season. He also pitched every inning in 22 consecutive games beginning September 2, late in the season, when other pitchers were complaining of sore arms from overwork. That stretch included wins over the powerful Boston and Providence teams. Baseball-reference.com credits Galvin with only 12 wins and six losses during 1877 and has no numbers for 1878. It considers the International Association a "minor" league, and that is where his record is tucked away. Given the 24 wins recorded by Buffalo in the IA championship race of 1878, he should be credited with 36 for his two years with Allegheny and Buffalo.

Pud Galvin was not a big man, but he was powerfully built and his endurance would become the stuff of legend. He soon had picked up yet another nickname, derived partly from his huffing and puffing as he churned around the base paths: "The Little Steam Engine."

7

A Star Emerges

The loss of its two top teams to the National League marked the beginning of decline for the International Association. For Hulbert and the National League, the move was just the ticket to help the struggling loop for which, again in 1878, only Chicago turned a profit.[1] Milwaukee and Indianapolis had folded so Hulbert was desperate for new members, particularly from the east. Aside from Buffalo, Syracuse and then Troy, the National League added Cleveland to its ranks to create an eight-team organization for 1879. The additions meant an 84-game schedule could be devised to improve revenue for each team and reduce the need for games against teams outside the league to bolster the box office.[2] It also meant the National League was gaining a toehold in the more populous east, could shed its image as a western-based loop, and could begin to squeeze IA teams financially. The baseball landscape was shifting. As baseball historian David Nemec put it: "The consequence was that in 1879, for the first time, playing in the League became a status symbol. [When it] became a stable eight-team circuit, it effectively killed the IA as a worthy rival."[3]

Changes were afoot for the International Association. Without a Canadian member, it was no longer "international." At its February convention in Utica, delegates renamed it The National Base-Ball Association (NBBA), electing L. J. Powers of Springfield as president. Nine clubs signed up to contest the championship: Utica, Manchester, Washington Nationals, New Bedford, Holyoke, Worcester, Springfield, and two clubs from Albany—the Albanys and the Capital Citys. The new season was barely underway when the Capital City club moved to Rochester to become the Hop Bitters, amidst controversy about its commercialized name (taken from a patent medicine) and charges of "crooked play." Manchester, thought to be controlled by gamblers, drew poorly and soon collapsed. Utica, the Hop Bitters and Springfield also disbanded before long. Crowds were light and sometimes unruly in what proved to be a disappointing season all around. In the end, Albany was awarded the NBBA championship.

7. A Star Emerges

The situation continued to deteriorate. Only four teams attended the Association convention, held in New York City in February of 1880: Albany, Washington Nationals, Baltimore and Jersey City. Only the first three decided to enter the pennant race, although 17 other clubs signed on as affiliates. Baltimore disbanded in June, followed by Albany in July. Washington, the last club standing, was awarded the loop's final pennant. The IA/NBBA was dead after four seasons, but only during its first two seasons had it seriously threatened the National League. Historian David Pietrusza explained that its demise was because the Association was "ultimately unsuited to competition with the more-aggressive, better-organized, larger-population-based National League."[4]

Other professional baseball organizations would emerge to challenge the National League and its approach to the game, following in the footsteps of the International Association. Some would last as little as one or two years before collapsing. In all, five more leagues were born out of frustration with the NL: the American Association (1882–1891), Union Association (1884), Players' League (1890), American League (1901-present), and Federal League (1914–1915). All were subsequently accorded "major league" status by baseball and its historians. The definitive ruling was made by Major League Baseball's "special baseball records committee" in 1968–1969. That body denied major league status to the International Association and the National Association because of "erratic schedule and procedures."[5] Only two of the committee's five members were baseball historians. Many years after its demise, the International Association was dubbed the first "minor league" in baseball. Neither the Association nor its players deferred to the National League in any way and would resent being so categorized. With their teams considered to be outside major league baseball, complete player statistics and accomplishments have not been recognized. Pitchers like Pud Galvin and Fred Goldsmith performed in many more games and notched many more wins than currently appear in the official record for the "majors." Yet the discrimination lingers from the baseball establishment.[6]

For its first campaign in the National League, Buffalo kept its roster largely intact. A notable addition was Oscar Walker, 25, a first baseman and outfielder, whose ban on playing had been lifted by the league for his jumping, mid-contract, from St. Paul to Manchester during the 1877 season. A good hitter with a wild swing, Walker collected 79 hits in 72 games with the Bisons for a batting average of .275. Another new man was Hardy Richardson, 24, a third baseman who had played with Binghamton and whose batting average would reach .283. May 1 marked Opening Day, and Buffalo, along with newcomers Cleveland, Troy and Syracuse, were required to charge the league-mandated 50-cent admission charge, double what their fans had previously paid. All four clubs had kicked about the change, but to no avail. For them, it was part of the price of admission to the National League. The Bisons introduced new uniforms for the season, with shirts and pants in white flannel, navy blue stockings, belts, and trim, replacing their old red-and-white color scheme. The team was anxious about its first foray in the National League and was determined to be ready. Pitchers Pud Galvin and Bill McGunnigle and the rest of the team had been practicing indoors at the Buffalo armory and at the Franklin Club on Pearl Street, which became the team clubhouse.

A disappointing crowd of about 500 witnessed Buffalo's first-ever National League game. They saw the Boston Red Caps whitewash the home team, 5–0. Boston began poorly, making three of their four errors in the first inning, but regrouped to score a run on a triple by Jack Burdock in the same inning. The Red Caps added two runs in the seventh inning and two more in the ninth. Three times Buffalo failed to score runners who reached third base, one of them Galvin after he doubled, the others following triples by Eggler and Fulmer. One of the few bright spots for Buffalo was a spectacular one-handed catch made by Dutch Hornung in left field. After the game, first baseman Steve Libby was given his release to join Detroit. The following day, Boston again won, this time, 7–4. The Bisons put themselves in a four-run hole in the first inning when they made three errors on a hit by Boston centerfielder John O'Rourke. To the delight of 600 fans, Buffalo gained back all four runs by the end of the seventh inning. But Boston scored three times in the eighth to win the game, capitalizing on a triple by Sadie Houck and doubles by Charley Jones and O'Rourke. In the third game of their series on May 3, Buffalo finally broke through for a 6–4 win. An error-filled third inning for Boston allowed the Bisons to score four runs and lead the rest of the way to claim its first National League victory. Galvin, with three hits, scored once and held the powerful Boston nine to three hits. Buffalo defeated Providence, 8–5, on May 6 and two days later, 3–2, both games at Riverside Park. In the latter match, Galvin scored the winning run in the ninth inning. He singled, stole second and took advantage of a bad throw, intended to catch him at third, to charge home.

The Bisons easily handled Troy on May 13 in Buffalo, outplaying the visitors in every aspect of the game for a 7–1 win. The Trojans were proving to be a weak addition to the league, but they managed a 1–0 victory over Buffalo on May 16, with a rare win for their pitcher, George Washington Bradley, formerly of Chicago and St. Louis. He was on his way to 40 losses with Troy, the most in the league. The next day, Bradley gave up 17 hits as the Trojans were hammered, 16–9, by the Bisons. Syracuse appeared at Riverside Park on May 20 for the first meeting of the two clubs as National League nines. It was no contest. Galvin gave up six hits but with a stout defense behind him didn't allow a run as Buffalo blanked the Stars, 8–0. Newcomer Hardy Richardson tripled twice and Eggler managed another three-bagger off the usually tough

7. A Star Emerges 85

Harry McCormick, who surrendered 17 hits. Two days later, again in Buffalo, the tables were turned as Syracuse won, 15–11, taking advantage of fielding errors by the Bisons in the first five innings when the Stars counted 11 of their runs. The home team recorded 14 errors. In a non–League game May 26, Buffalo lost, 4–3, to its old rival Rochester before 3,000 fans in that city. The Bisons led, 3–2, until the ninth inning when the Flour City nine's Harry Schafer, the third baseman, drove in two runs to win the game.

During that busy month of May, Pud Galvin became a father. He had married Bridget Griffin shortly before the 1878 season, back in Pittsburgh. James Joseph Galvin was the first of nine children born to the couple, two of whom would die as infants or tots. For a rising star in baseball, with new family responsibilities, the 21-year-old pitcher had plenty on his plate.

Buffalo ended May with an eastern tour that began poorly as Providence defeated the Bisons by scores of 9–2, 4–0 and 13–2 in a three-game series. On June 6, Buffalo lost, 7–1, to Boston in a rain-shortened game. In the first inning, Boston left fielder Charley Jones crushed a Galvin offering over the left-center field fence in South End Grounds for the longest hit ever seen there. The homer was the first of 10 hits Galvin allowed that day. Bill McGunnigle was handed the ball the next day and he came out on top, holding the Red Caps to five hits in a 4–1 Buffalo victory. His win may have prompted McGunnigle to seek more work outside Galvin's shadow. It was reported he wanted his release from the Bisons, but club management refused.[7] By early June, Buffalo was in sixth place in the National League standings with seven wins. Chicago, with 16, led the pack, followed by Providence with 11, Syracuse with 10, and Boston and Cincinnati with nine apiece. Troy had five wins and Cleveland four, to round out the standings.

In a June 20 game with Troy, the Bisons' Oscar Walker became the first major league player to strike out five times in nine innings as Buffalo overcame his underwhelming performance to post an 8–3 win. By mid–June, Buffalo found its stride, downing Syracuse, 5–3, 10–0, and 8–3, and Troy, 3–1 and 4–3. A four-game series with struggling Cleveland ended the month, with each nine picking up two wins. Buffalo traveled to Cleveland, and on July 1 whitewashed the Forest Citys, 9–0, as Galvin gave up a single hit. The Bisons beat them again the next day, 4–2, but back home on Independence Day, Cleveland won, 14–8, before 3,000 fans at Riverside Park. The latter game was marked by poor fielding that gave Cleveland an early lead it did not relinquish. The following day, the Bisons bounced back to defeat the Forest Citys, 9–6, solving Cleveland pitcher Jim McCormick for eight runs in the fourth inning. On July 8, in their ninth meeting, Buffalo again won. The Bisons played Troy twice on July 12 with Galvin pitching in both Buffalo wins of 4–3 and 5–4. He hit a game-winning triple in the second game.

By early July, the National League standings showed that Buffalo had climbed into third place with 17 wins, behind Chicago with 24, and Providence with 22. On July 19, Buffalo defeated Syracuse, 4–3, and went on a ten-game winning tear that took it into August as it repeatedly defeated Syracuse, Providence, Cincinnati, and Chicago. Galvin was ill for games in Cleveland on August 11 and 12 when McGunnigle pitched shutouts of 2–0 in both contests. On August 20, Chicago finally solved Buffalo in the Windy City with an 8–1 victory after White Stockings president William Hulbert "put some ginger in the boys" with a pre-game pep talk.[8] Team manager and star first baseman Cap Anson had just left the team with a liver ailment that sidelined him for the rest of the season, so Hulbert may have felt the need for some personal intervention in Anson's absence.

By August 25, Buffalo had slipped to fourth place. On August 28, Chicago went to Buffalo for a three-game series, the clubs having split their six meetings to that point. The White Stockings' bats were lively and they capitalized on six errors to win, 6–1, in the first clash. Two days later, the same two teams battled for 12 innings before the game was called on account of darkness, tied 5–5. On September 1, they went at it again and this time Chicago prevailed, 4–1. Two days later in Boston, Buffalo hit pitcher Tommy Bond hard and came away with an 8–5 victory. Buffalo scored three of their runs in the ninth inning to take it. Boston downed Buffalo, 9–3, on September 5 when an ailing Galvin was replaced by McGunnigle. With Galvin back the next day, Boston won again, 10–1. Buffalo and Providence split games played September 9 and 10. Meanwhile, on September 9, after a 5–0 loss to Cleveland the Syracuse Stars folded, reportedly bankrupt. Money problems had been rumored for some time and players had been late receiving their pay. Cleveland's share of the gate proceeds at Syracuse for that game was reported as a mere $4.05.[9] The departure of Syracuse required an adjustment in the National League standings, but had little impact on Buffalo. Providence was in the lead with 52 wins, Boston second with 49, Chicago next with 43 and Buffalo still fourth, with 40.

Fred Goldsmith, the curveballer formerly of the Tecumsehs, had started the 1879 season with Springfield of the National Base-Ball Association, but when the club folded he was picked up by struggling Troy for nine games. He pitched for the Trojans in their 8–2 and 10–4 losses at home to Buffalo on September 12 and 13. Galvin was allowed to rest for both games and McGunnigle took his place. Two days later, still in Troy, Galvin faced Goldsmith in a revival of their old Allegheny-Tecumseh pitching duels. Galvin came out ahead this time in the 4–2 Buffalo victory. The following day, Galvin was again rested and McGunnigle claimed a 2–1 victory over Goldsmith and the Trojans.

As the season wound down, Galvin showed no signs of tiring, benefitting from the occasional day off. He completely mystified Cincinnati batters

September 22 in Buffalo's 3–0 win at home, as he allowed four hits. He pitched again the following day in an exciting, come-from-behind 12–7 victory as the Bisons exploded for six runs off pitcher Blondie Purcell in the ninth inning. Cincinnati bounced back September 24 for an 8–5 win over McGunnigle and the next day pounded Galvin for a 10–2 victory. Buffalo played host to Chicago for their final four games of the season. Galvin took a 3–1 loss on September 26, while McGunnigle won a day later in a 17–5 romp over the White Stockings and their pitcher, Frank Hankinson. McGunnigle pitched again on September 29 and 30 as Buffalo won 5–3 and 10–2. Galvin, who had struggled somewhat with the visitors, was given more well-deserved rest after pitching nearly 600 innings in league play.

Providence claimed the National League title with 59 wins and 25 losses. Boston was second with 54 wins and 30 losses. Buffalo finished third with 46 wins and 32 defeats, narrowly edging Chicago, which also had 46 wins but one more loss. Of the four newcomers to the league, Buffalo was clearly the strongest. Cleveland, Syracuse and Troy trailed the eight-member loop, winning 27, 22, and 19 games respectively.

For Pud Galvin, the season's numbers were impressive. He won 37 games and lost 27, with an earned-run average of 2.28. He started 66 games, pitched 593 innings and recorded six shutouts. As a batter, he hit a respectable .249, but he also recorded a league-high 56 strikeouts. Galvin was fourth in wins with 10 fewer than John Montgomery Ward, who had found a home in Providence, where he won 47 games for the league's top club. Tied for second were Will White of Cincinnati and Tommy Bond of Boston, with 43 wins apiece. In complete games, Galvin was second only to the 75 of Cincinnati's White with 65. Galvin was among the top five pitchers in seven of eight major categories, missing the top-five club only on strikeouts. His backup, Bill McGunnigle, was kept on by the Bisons and became manager. McGunnigle recorded nine wins and five losses. Three of those wins came in the final games of the season against Chicago.

Concerned they were not making enough money while players continued to jump from one team to another for fatter contracts, the magnates who controlled the National League held a special meeting September 29 in Buffalo. They wanted to bring some cost-containment to salaries. "It is ridiculous to pay ballplayers $2,000 a year when the $800 boys do just as well," National League president William Hulbert of Chicago fulminated famously.[10] He was the driving force behind the Buffalo meeting and was concerned that League teams had fared little better financially than in 1878. He blamed player pay. The League decided that from this time on, clubs were required to use uniform player contracts and that they were to run from April 1 to October 31 each year. No more advances could be paid to players, who were to be considered part-timers and expected to find other employment during the off-season.

There was more. It didn't become known until the *Buffalo Express* broke the story three days later that the "reserve clause" had also been quietly introduced. That new wrinkle meant that each club could name five players from their existing roster who were protected for the following season, so no other club could speak to them. Some players initially took pride in being so designated, because it guaranteed employment for the following season.[11] But it soon became apparent to them that they could no longer shop around for more money. The list of reserved players would rise to 11 in coming years and it became a sore point among players, feeling they were chained to a team and forced to accept what the team was willing to pay. The reserve clause survived court challenges and was not struck down until 1975.

The ink was barely dry on the new rules governing contracts when Hulbert's Chicago club broke one of them. Fred Goldsmith, who had been pitching for Troy since his Springfield team had disbanded, signed a contract on October 1 to play for the White Stockings in 1880. Troy protested the move as a violation of the new reserve clause by the serial scofflaw Hulbert and his club.[12] But nothing came of the complaint and Goldsmith joined former Buffalo hurler Larry Corcoran in Chicago for the 1880 campaign.

Meanwhile, Galvin, Buffalo catchers John Clapp and Jack Rowe, and Davy Force were invited to join the Cincinnati club, which accompanied Chicago on a 12-week tour of California that began in October. The teams played a series of games against each other as well as local teams on the West Coast. The latter nines fell easily before the eastern clubs, but fans were more interested in seeing the storied National League teams play each other. The tour ended in December, but Galvin was not on the homebound train with the others, having opted to stay behind. Galvin was not signed with Buffalo for the 1880 season and he decided to use California as a bargaining chip in his negotiations with the team. If he didn't get what he wanted, he said, he'd stay in the west. John Sage, the Buffalo president, was among those National League kingpins at the Buffalo meeting where steps were taken to limit player salaries, and he and his fellow directors called Galvin's bluff. Galvin signed a contract with the Athletic Club of San Francisco, a member of the California League. Within two months, that league adopted a strong policy to ensure players honored their contracts. The *San Francisco Bulletin* reported that, generally, "the player is bound by such iron-bound and copper-fastened rules as will make it exceedingly difficult for him to break his contract."[13] The Athletics club Galvin joined was one of the better California nines. Newly installed manager Tom Carey, an infielder and Brooklyn native, had most of his career behind him. He first played professionally with Kekionga (Illinois) of the National Association in 1871 and had been with Baltimore, New York and Hartford in the Association. He jumped to the National League with Hartford, then on to Providence in 1878 and to Cleveland in 1879. In late

April, Galvin's former Buffalo catcher, Tom Dolan, decided to join his old batterymate with the Athletics.[14] Dolan's first game was a 9–0 victory over Bay City on May 9, a game in which Galvin hit a home run "amidst the wildest excitement of the immense audience."[15]

Two weeks into May of 1880, the Bisons wired Galvin and asked him to return to Buffalo. They capitulated and made him an offer he couldn't refuse, but the Athletics wouldn't release him. It was said that his old team was so anxious for his return, they sent his wife Bridget with infant son to California to persuade him to come east. That seems unlikely, but the story received plenty of play and further embellishment. The Bisons, after winning their home opener, 1–0, over Cleveland on May 7, were struggling, riding the arms of Bill McGunnigle and newcomer Tom Poorman. Buffalo grew so anxious for Galvin to return to the fold that they advanced him $300, despite the National League's new ban on pay before play. On May 11, the *Buffalo Courier* announced: "We take great pleasure in being able to state that James F. Galvin has been engaged by the Buffalo management" and would join the Bisons the following week in Cincinnati.[16] Galvin agreed to a contract with Buffalo and immediately found himself in a quandary, having violated the tough new contract rules in California. The story goes that he assumed another identity to slip out of his contract and the state. A rather partisan account appeared in the *Buffalo Express*:

> Naturally enough the Athletics of San Francisco felt rather hard towards Galvin for leaving them and accepting the offer of the Buffalo nine, and according to the papers of that city they tried everything within their power to prevent his joining the latter team. In the issue of the *Chronicle* of the 12th and 13th insts., [instants, that is, May 12 and 13] accounts are given of their arrest of the gentle James on what they term embezzlement, etc. The account says that the mild-mannered pitcher was traveling under the name of James Ryan. The truth of the whole matter, as stated by the parties who should know, is that Galvin went to California with the understanding that if he got anything better in the East during the summer he would take it. The *Chronicle* says that the telegrams from the Buffalos to Galvin were paid for by the Athletics, a statement that is clearly false, as they were both prepaid at this city. The matter was easily enough settled by the liquidation of the indebtedness of Galvin to the club.[17]

There was nothing easy about what happened. Galvin had received his Athletics pay in advance and the club was determined to make him earn it. San Francisco papers said he used some of the money to bribe the authorities who stopped him at some point at the request of team owners. Galvin later told a reporter he had eluded a California detective who was on his trail and had walked 36 miles to a railroad station to catch an eastbound train.[18] His tale of escape improved with time, like fine wine. He told teammate Curry Foley in Buffalo that he had originally boarded a train for the east, then got off to walk 23 miles into Nevada. In crossing the desert to freedom, Galvin nearly burned the shoes off his feet, Foley recalled years later for the *New*

York Clipper.[19] The fugitive hurler escaped without further incident and made it to Cincinnati in time to pitch the Bisons to a 2–1 victory on May 22. Galvin's appearance on the ball field prompted the *Express* to observe that the club he joined was almost as poor as the team of 1877 and would have done much better with Galvin from the outset of the season. It suggested the directors should "weed out the useless material" and change managers to further improve the nine.[20] Two days later, Buffalo was pummeled 17–4 by Cincinnati, despite Galvin's work in the pitching box.

Shortly after that loss, one of the new faces on the Bisons disappeared. Charles "Hoss" Radbourn, 25, who in 1879 played with the topflight nine in Dubuque, Iowa, was a promising pitcher, but he strained his shoulder in spring training for the Bisons. He played six games at second base and in the outfield before being let go, returning to his home in Bloomington, Illinois. The next year, healthy, he caught on with Providence and won 25 games for the Grays. Radbourn spent five years with the Grays and in 1883 and 1884 led the National League in wins with 48 and 59, respectively. Overall, he won at least 20 games nine times, collecting 309 wins in an 11-year career that saw him move to Boston and Cincinnati. He was inducted into the Baseball Hall of Fame at Cooperstown in 1939. This was another talent that Buffalo identified early but allowed to slip away to greener pastures. Had Radbourn stayed with the Bisons, life would have been different for Galvin as a second-stringer, and likely more successful for the team. Denny Mack, a member of the 1878 Bisons, was brought back to cover second base, and McGunnigle was finally given his long-sought release. Poorman continued as the backup pitcher.

On May 25, Galvin made his return to Riverside Park for a game against Chicago. "There was a fine assemblage present," noted the *Buffalo Express*, "and as the picturesque form of the mild-mannered pitcher was recognized loud and continued applause greeted him. A smile illuminated his classic countenance, and with a graceful but unpretentious bow he acknowledged the salute."[21] Fans were hoping Galvin would lift the Bisons out of the lower reaches of the National League standings, but they would be disappointed this day as Cap Anson led the White Stockings to an 8–2 win. Goldsmith pitched for the visitors, his first time back at Riverside Park since his time with the Tecumsehs. He surrendered nine hits, but Galvin gave up a dozen. Galvin buckled down after allowing five runs in the first two innings and his devastating pickoff move kept Chicago runners honest. One of his victims was Anson, who was known for his "kicking," and he didn't like it. "This caused the great warrior to feel much worried and he endeavored in vain to explain to the umpire that he had shoved his foot back on the base," said the *Express*.

The following day, Poorman took the ball for the Bisons, while Larry Corcoran pitched for the White Stockings as the visitors won, 4–2. Anson, the Chicago captain, had introduced what is believed to be the first regular pitching rotation, alternating games between Goldsmith and Corcoran. Things got worse on May 27, when Goldsmith allowed only two Buffalo hits as he shut out the home team, 11–0. Errors were plentiful, and first baseman Oscar Walker had a particularly bad day. The *Express* reporter said of him: "Had a barn been located on the third or second base it would have been difficult for him to hit it."[22] Overall, the report complained, the game was "from the beginning a succession of blunders on the part of the local nine, and never has a crowd left the Buffalo base ball grounds more thoroughly disgusted than did the attendants of yesterday's contest." At the end of May, Buffalo stood last in the National League, with five wins and 12 losses. Chicago led the pack with 14 wins and two losses.

Buffalo's difficult season continued into June. On June 10 against Boston, history was made. The Red Caps were well back of Chicago in the standings, having won fewer than half their games. This day, however, the club had something to cheer about. Boston's leftfielder Charley Jones hit two home runs in the eighth inning as his team routed the Bisons, 19–3. This marked the first time in professional baseball that the two-homer feat was accomplished in a single inning. Poorman was pummeled mercilessly and his defense committed 19 errors. The usually reliable Davy Force, playing second base, was responsible for five of them. The two homers gave Jones a total of four for the year in an era when homers were still a rarity. He would belt only one more that year. Jones had led National League sluggers the previous season with only nine.

Buffalo appeared at the Messer Street Grounds in Providence for a three-game series that began June 16. The Bisons, who played without Force, were swept by the powerful Grays nine, whose pitcher, John Montgomery Ward, the former Bison, was in fine form. Ward hit a double and scored a run as the Grays touched up Galvin for 10 hits in a 5–2 win. In the second game, Ward was perfection itself. He held the visitors hitless and didn't allow a single base runner as the Grays pounded Galvin hard in the 5–0 win. First baseman Joe Start, leftfielder Tom York and third baseman Foghorn Bradley all tripled off Galvin. It marked the second perfect game in National League play in just six days. On June 12 in Worcester, hometown Ruby Legs pitcher Lee Richmond tossed a perfect game as he downed the Cleveland Blues, 1–0. The third Buffalo-Providence game saw Poorman batted around the park in an 8–3 Buffalo loss. Ward's pitching continued to fool batters and he helped himself with three hits and two runs. The Bisons were mired in seventh place among the National League's eight teams when they made the short hop to Rochester to play there on July 12. The independent Hop Bitters featured a young hitting phenomenon from Wappingers Falls, New York, Dan Brouthers, 22. He had already homered in a July 9 exhibition game with the Bisons off backup pitcher Denny Driscoll that Rochester had won, 10–6. Buffalo started strongly in the July 12 game with three earned runs in the first inning thanks to singles by Hardy Richardson and Jack Rowe and a triple by Dutch Hornung. Rochester replied with three runs in the third to tie the game. In the eighth inning, Brouthers connected with a Galvin offering for a homer to give the Hop Bitters a 4–3 win. The performance by the powerful first baseman was duly noted by Buffalo directors and remembered by them when they assembled their roster for 1881.

The Bisons had another crack at third-place Providence, this time at home, on July 16. Spectators witnessed a magnificent pitching duel between Galvin and Ward that lasted 14 innings before a run was scored. The *Buffalo Express* said "the struggle was overflowing with brilliant maneuvres" [sic] and Providence was particularly sharp, playing 13 innings of error-free ball. "Ward and Gentle Jeems twirled the sphere for all they were physically and scientifically worth, and backed by wonderful fielding, the batters did but little with them."[23] In the 12th inning, the Bisons loaded the bases but could not bring in a run. Bill Crowley, the rightfielder for Buffalo, cracked a single off Ward in the 14th inning, advanced on a single by third baseman Hardy Richardson, then took advantage of throwing errors by Foghorn Bradley and shortstop John Peters to score the only run of the game. Another extra-inning struggle took place between Buffalo and Providence at the latter's grounds on July 21 as Galvin and Ward again pitched brilliantly. Buffalo managed a run in the ninth inning to tie the game, 3–3. In the 11th inning, Buffalo lost a scoring chance when base runner Tom Esterbrook was caught napping at third by Ward. In the 12th, Buffalo complained about the baseball, claiming it had been cut by the Grays. It was replaced. Providence batters seemed to like the new one and belted four hits off Galvin in the 15th and capitalized on fielding and throwing errors to score three runs and take the marathon match, 6–3.

The Bisons were still languishing in seventh place in the National League by the middle of August, seven games behind Boston and seven ahead of cellar-dwelling Cincinnati. Despite a disappointing win-loss record, a couple of highlights lay ahead. At home on August 20, Galvin pitched his first no-hitter in the League as Buffalo edged Worcester, 1–0, the Bisons' sole run coming in the first inning when Hornung singled and was brought home on Esterbrook's triple. Rainy conditions made the ball mushy and hard to hit, providing an advantage for both Galvin and Ruby Legs hurler Fred Corey. The weather likely also contributed to the six errors committed by the Bisons that day. And it kept the crowd to about 90 fans. Then, in an August 27 loss of 5–3 to Boston, Buffalo's strong-armed centerfielder, Bill Crowley, threw out four base runners, repeating the four assists he recorded on May 24 in the otherwise forgettable 17–4 humiliation delivered by Cincinnati. Buffalo fortunes did not improve as the season wound down. On September 30, in their last game of the season, the Bisons lost, 10–8, to Chicago, who easily captured the National League pennant. The White Stockings' record was 67 wins to 17 losses, for an impressive winning percentage of .798. Fifteen games back was Providence, followed by Cleveland (47–37), Troy (41–42), Worcester (40–43), Boston (40–44), Buffalo (24–58) and Cincinnati (21–59). For his part, Galvin, held back by a lower-rung team he had joined several weeks into the season, recorded 20 wins and 35 losses, with an earned-run average of 2.78.

In early October, the National League announced that the losses incurred by its eight teams totaled $20,000 in the just-completed season. It blamed continued high player salaries and said some clubs had salary costs that exceeded $14,000. Yet again, only Chicago turned a profit. Henry Chadwick at the *Clipper* blamed the situation on Chicago, which had insisted that the 50-cent admission fee be mandatory for all games. He said Providence lost more than $3,000 and Troy a similar amount. Buffalo, he added, was bankrupt, and Cincinnati had avoided a similar fate only by playing Sunday games at its park and selling beer. The league had just banned all its teams from both activities for the following season, a move seen as targeting the Cincinnati club.

Buffalo's financial condition was indeed precarious, and it was only an infusion of new capital from supporters of the team that kept it going and allowed directors to start planning for an 1881 season they fervently hoped would be more successful.

8

1881–1882:
Prelude to Perfection

It was a new-look Bisons nine that took to the field for the 1881 campaign. With the sale of additional stock in the club, now capitalized at $7,000, directors were able to invest to improve it. The blue-and-white uniforms were replaced by those in brown and white for home games and lavender-blue (a pale violet) and gray for the road. The roster also saw a makeover. With Poorman and McGunnigle gone, a backup pitcher for Galvin was needed. Jack Lynch, 24, of New York, was hired. A rare university-educated player (Fordham), this would be Lynch's first foray in the National League. He had played for New Bedford/New Haven/Hartford in the International Association and for Washington in its successor, the National Base-Ball Association, where he won 20 games in the former IA's final 1880 season.

Galvin and Lynch faced some rule changes made by the National League. The pitcher's box was moved back from 45 to 50 feet, and batters could now draw a walk after seven pitches outside the strike zone, rather than the previous eight. Batters, however, would no longer receive a warning if they failed to swing at a third strike. The warning had given them an additional chance. Combined, both moves tilted things a bit toward batters, adding 15 points to the batting average across the league while walks jumped by 40 percent.[1] Pitchers were still required to use an underhand delivery, and batters could continue to request that pitches be either high or low.

Dutch Hornung had signed with Boston for the 1881 campaign, so Buffalo club directors needed to replace the sure-handed outfielder. Jim O'Rourke, 30, a versatile player from Connecticut, was hired as manager and outfielder. He had been playing professional ball since joining the 1872 Manchester club of the National Association. He moved to the Association's team in Boston and in the National League, and he spent a year with Providence. Famous for making the first hit in the National League, O'Rourke's career spanned 23 years and earned him induction into the Baseball Hall of Fame. O'Rourke attributed his long career to avoiding both alcohol and tobacco. He had a career batting average of .310 with 2,639 hits, and twice recorded the second-best batting average in the National League. The flamboyant O'Rourke sported one of the best handlebar mustaches in baseball, and the well-educated man with a love of long, rhetorical flourishes became known as "Orator Jim." O'Rourke, it was reported, was to be paid $2,000 "just for playing ball." That was considered a large salary at the time, but the *Buffalo Express* defended it, saying: "It should have been at least $400 higher."[2] Also hired was James "Deacon" White, 34, whose long career included stints with Cleveland and Boston in the National Association, beginning in 1871. He joined Chicago's National League team for 1876 and then moved to Boston and Cincinnati. White, who had picked up his nickname for his clean-living ways, led the NA with a .367 batting average in 1875 and then did the same in the National League two years later at .387. In a career of 20 seasons, his batting average was .312, with 2,067 hits and 988 runs batted in. A future Hall of Famer, White was one of the early game's top hitters. Buffalo used him in both the infield and outfield. Another roster addition was Charles "Curry" Foley, 25, an Irish-born rightfielder and first baseman who could also pitch. He had spent his two previous seasons with Boston, where his batting averages had been a solid .315 and .292. A teammate of O'Rourke in 1880, he decided to change scenery at the urging of the new Buffalo manager. John Peters, 31, was the new shortstop to rotate with Davy Force. Peters had played with Chicago in the National Association and then the National League, as well as with Milwaukee and Providence. Picked up after the season began was William "Blondie" Purcell, 27, another backup pitcher and outfielder. He had played with Syracuse, Cincinnati and Cleveland.

Near the end of May, the Bisons signed Dennis "Big Dan" Brouthers, who would become one of the first great sluggers in professional baseball. He earned his nickname honestly, standing six-foot-two and weighing 207 pounds, making him one of the biggest players of his time. Brouthers, 23, played 39 games for Troy in 1879, but only three for the club in 1880 before being released and returning to his home in Wappingers Falls, New York. He began the 1881 season with the New York Atlantics but soon received an offer from the Bisons, who remembered the homers he had crushed against them during his short stint with Rochester. Largely because of the powerful bat of Brouthers, Buffalo had lost three games to Rochester, when he pounded seven hits, including a double and two home runs. He fit into the plans of the new manager, O'Rourke, nicely. "Orator" Jim had a simple approach to winning games: "Overwhelm opponents with heavy hitting."[3] This was a rather novel approach during the era of the dead ball, in which low-scoring games were considered the best by observers, including the "Father of Baseball," Henry Chadwick. Brouthers was at the beginning of a stellar career that saw him lead the National League in batting average twice during his five years as a Bison. He also was the league-leader in hits twice, and once each in triples and runs batted in. In his first season in Buffalo, when he missed nearly all of May, he led the league with eight home runs. Upon arriving in Buffalo, the first baseman's fielding skills needed work, but they improved with time and effort. By acquiring Brouthers, the Bisons had a fourth formidable bat in their lineup and a fourth future Hall of Famer (along with O'Rourke, White and Galvin). Because of their bats, Brouthers, White, Jack Rowe and Hardy Richardson became known as "Buffalo's Big Four." They kept the name when they later moved as a unit to Detroit. The foursome provided solid offense to complement Pud Galvin's outstanding pitching.

Directors of the Buffalo club had done well by adding such potent new talent to the roster in a bid to improve on their disappointing seventh-place finish of 1880. The National League itself was changing. The previous fall, Cincinnati was expelled for the twin vices of allowing Sunday games in its park and selling beer. Detroit had been granted admission in its place, to maintain an eight-team loop.

Buffalo opened the season with a home-and-home series against the Wolverines, beginning May 2 in Detroit. The Bisons disappointed the hometown fans by taking the first game, 6–5, with Lynch pitching. The following day, the Wolverines found Galvin easy to hit and posted a 4–2 win in a nail-biter for their first-ever National League win. To do so, Detroit had to hold off the visitors, who loaded the bases in the ninth inning with none out. The rubber match on May 4 was taken by Buffalo, 4–3, with Lynch again pitching. The teams traveled to the other end of Lake Erie for Buffalo's home opener on May 5, before 1,500 fans. Galvin occupied the pitching box and dominated Wolverine batters. Hard hitting and sharp fielding characterized Bisons play that day as Richardson brought home five runs on his three hits to power Buffalo to an 8–1 victory. The Bisons won again on May 6 and 7, by scores of 3–2 and 6–1, relying on timely hitting. Lynch pitched in the latter game to complete the sweep at home. The Detroit club was struggling without pitcher George Washington Bradley, who was ailing, and used George Derby in his place. Derby was making his debut in the National League after playing in Syracuse, Hornellsville and Washington in the National Base-Ball Association. Bradley played only one game as a Wolverine before signing with Cleveland. Detroit also inserted at shortstop a local 19-year-old amateur, Dan Stearns, for the games in Buffalo. He made two costly errors in the May 6 contest that allowed three runs as Buffalo won by a single tally.

The Bisons were off to a fine start with their tandem of Galvin and Lynch, their powerful batters and strong defense. In a May 20 game that saw Buffalo blank the Worcester Ruby Legs, 7–0, on a Galvin three-hitter, second baseman Davy Force put on a display. He recorded eight assists and two putouts without making an error. Four days later, as Buffalo again downed Worcester, this time 3–2, Force had five assists with seven putouts, again playing error-free ball. By June 7, Buffalo was riding high in the National League standings. With 14 wins, the club trailed only Chicago, which had one more. On June 9, a 13-inning, 1–0 shutout of Boston put Buffalo in a first-place tie with Chicago, giving them 16 wins apiece. Brouthers was a standout both offensively and defensively in the game. He made a running catch in left field that prevented two Boston runs from scoring and, in the 13th inning, he hit a triple that scored the game-winning run. Former Bison Dutch Hornung also had a great day in left field, making nine remarkable catches of Bisons flies. Buffalo didn't stay in first place for very long, however. A 15–4 drubbing by last-place Worcester on June 16 bumped the club back to second.

On June 29, Buffalo hosted Boston in a game marked by heavy hitting by both sides. Buffalo won the slugfest, 16–10. Brouthers connected with a Jim Whitney pitch for a home run in the ninth inning, while Galvin got into the act a few batters later, scorching the ball so far over the left field fence in Riverside Park that it couldn't be found. It was Galvin's first home run in the National League, but his seventh as a professional.[4] The game was delayed until another game ball could be agreed upon and put in play. Galvin was hit heavily by the Red Caps that day, however, giving up 16 hits. The series with Boston continued, with Buffalo winning, 16–10, on June 30 and 7–4 on July 2. The latter loss dropped the once-formidable Boston club to last place in the standings for the first time in its ten-year history.

July would be very good to Buffalo. In its first meeting of the season with league-leading Chicago on July 16, Buffalo won 10–9 at home. Brouthers again made the difference in a tight game. In the eighth inning, he brought in two runs with a triple off Larry Corcoran. The Bisons' hit parade continued on July 19 with an 8–7 victory over the White Stockings, as Brouthers, Richardson, Foley, O'Rourke and Force each recorded two hits and Lynch picked up another win. The next day, Buffalo completed its sweep of the visitors, winning 11–7. The losses cut Chicago's lead over Buffalo to 3½ games.

Buffalo and Chicago began August with two meetings in the Windy City. On August 2, the White Stockings clobbered the visitors, 11–2, in a game that saw the first use of an intentional walk. The Bisons were losing 5–0 in the eighth inning when Chicago's leftfielder, Abner Dalrymple, came to bat. Jack Lynch had loaded the bases with singles by Fred Goldsmith, Silver Flint and Joe Quest. Dalrymple was one of Chicago's best hitters, so rather than risk more damage, Lynch gave him his base on seven successive balls. This scored Goldsmith.[5] Lynch soon regretted his decision. Centerfielder George Gore was next to the plate and he promptly crushed a double to clear the bases. Lynch gave up a total of ten runs on the day he made his contribution to baseball history. On August 4, before a good crowd of 3,000, Corcoran allowed only two hits as the White Stockings won again, this time blanking the visitors, 4–0. Galvin's troubles with Chicago batters continued as he surrendered nine hits. Buffalo was back in Chicago for a three-game series on August 16–18. For the first game, Galvin was unavailable and Lynch was hurt, so Rowe pitched, but fared poorly and was replaced by Foley. The latter did his best, hitting two triples, each of which scored two runs. But the Chicago hitters were too much for him and the home team prevailed, 13–9. Galvin was back in the pitching box the next day, but Chicago played sharp, error-free ball to take the game, 5–1. For the third game, Goldsmith took ill, Corcoran was rested, and third baseman Ned Williamson came in to pitch for the White Stockings. Galvin had a good outing this time and Buffalo came away with a 7–6 victory. By the end of the month, Chicago, with 42 wins, held onto its lead and Buffalo was second with 33, followed by Detroit with 31 and Providence with 30.

The Bisons swept the Wolverines in a three-game series in Buffalo to begin September. In a 14–6 Buffalo win on September 2, Galvin allowed 13 hits but compensated with a hot bat, swatting a single, a double and a triple. The following day, Buffalo won, 5–3, and again, 6–3, on September 5. A highlight for the month came on September 15 in Worcester when Buffalo second baseman Davy Force made two unassisted double plays, aided two other double plays and also started a triple play. Only two other major leaguers have recorded two unassisted double plays in one game.[6] Force maintained his place in the lineup because of his defense, not his bat. Offensively, he struggled with a batting average of .180, just slightly worse than shortstop John Peters at .214. In Boston on September 23, Dutch Hornung set a major league record by converting into outs 11 chances to do so (with 10 putouts and one assist). That record still stands. Galvin's arm was tired by mid–September as he closed in on 500 innings of work, and he won only one game of the last eight he pitched. Buffalo faltered as Blondie Purcell was called upon to pitch the last four games of the year. At the end of the season, Providence edged past Buffalo to take second place with 47 wins and 37 losses. Buffalo went 45–38, while Chicago took the pennant with a 56–28 record. Galvin had 28 wins, good for fourth place among pitchers, pitched 474 innings, also fourth, and had a winning percentage of .538, which tied him for fourth with Mickey Welch of Troy. Lynch had 10 wins and nine losses for the Bisons in his backup role. Purcell won four games and lost one. In hitting, Brouthers led the league with eight home runs and a .541 slugging average. He was fourth in on-base percentage at .361.

Late in 1881, a series of meetings was held by baseball interests from cities unhappy with the National League and interested in creating a new association. Cincinnati, spearheaded by sports editor O. P. Caylor, was the driving force behind the movement. The club was stung by its expulsion from

8. 1881–1882: Prelude to Perfection

the National League for playing games on Sundays and for selling beer in its ballpark. It found sympathetic ears in St. Louis Brown Stockings owner Chris Von der Ahe, a saloon-keeper, and in Pittsburgh, where Denny McKnight was anxious to revive top-flight ball, dormant since the collapse of his Allegheny nine in 1878. McKnight had been among the organizers of the International Association in 1877, and he knew what it took to translate talk into action. He organized a first meeting of the new group in Pittsburgh on October 10. So optimistic was McKnight of a new league that he organized an Allegheny club five days later, raised $5,000 for it and became president. Also pushing for a new league was "Hustling Horace" Phillips of Philadelphia, who was among the leading proponents, but withdrew later when the much-traveled and erratic promoter was fired by his club. Another meeting was held on November 1–2 in Cincinnati that attracted representatives from Louisville, St. Louis, Brooklyn and Philadelphia. Along with Cincinnati and Allegheny, all became members of the American Association.[7] The Brooklyn Atlantics dropped out in early 1882, and were replaced quickly by the Baltimore Orioles to maintain a six-team loop. McKnight was elected president and James A. Williams of Columbus, a moving force in the old International Association and its chief administrative officer, was named secretary-treasurer. Most of the rules of the National League were adopted, except for the reserve clause. Teams were allowed to charge 25-cents admission, play games on Sundays and sell alcohol on their grounds. Because several teams were backed by brewers or saloon owners, the AA soon became known as the "Beer and Whisky League."

The Association included major population centers, but refused to insist on a minimum size for member cities. It appealed to working class fans and immigrants who were familiar with enjoying sport and beer at the same time. The AA thumbed its nose at Hulbert and the Victorian sensibilities with which the National League ran its affairs.[8] Hulbert didn't have to tolerate the upstarts for long, however, and he never saw one of their games. The founder of the National League, and its driving force, died of heart failure in April of 1882, aged 49. The teams of the AA quickly found something Hulbert had sought for so long: profitability. In its inaugural season, Von der Ahe's Cincinnati club turned a profit of $25,000 on an initial investment of $5,000.[9] The Philadelphia Athletics reported a profit of $22,000.[10] All its clubs turned a profit from the start, helped along significantly by the 25-cents admission, Sunday games and beer sales. Meanwhile, in the exclusive National League, only Chicago and Boston made money.[11] It was perhaps just as well Hulbert didn't live to see another organization demonstrate that the keys to prosperity in professional baseball lay in practices he so despised. Cincinnati took the inaugural AA pennant with 55 wins and 25 losses, while McKnight's Allegheny club placed fourth with a 39–39 record.

In Buffalo, two significant additions were made for the 1882 season. Tom Dolan, who had caught for Galvin in Buffalo in 1878 and had followed him to San Francisco in 1880, rejoined the Bisons. He had played in San Francisco and New York in 1881. Never much of a hitter, Dolan was expected to back up the heavy-hitting Jack Rowe behind the plate. The other acquisition was intended to give ironman Pud Galvin some much-needed relief in the pitching box and avert another case of late-season, tired-arm syndrome for him. Hugh Daily, 34, was an imposing figure. At six-foot-two, he was the same height as Big Dan Brouthers, but at only 180 pounds the Irish-born Daily was a towering, lanky figure, with only one hand. Rather swarthy, prone to scowl at batters with beady eyes as he cursed them, he looked fearsome. Daily had a bad attitude and muttonchops as prickly as his personality. His terrible temper, laced with profanity, was directed at teammates who made mistakes, opposition players, umpires, and even fans. He once threatened to kill a newspaper reporter if the game report made much about a fielding error he had made. Daily used a double windmill-type delivery that produced a good curve and a blistering fastball. As a boy, he had lost his left hand in a shooting accident, but that didn't stand in the way of his love of baseball. He used a protective leather "stud" on his stump to trap balls hit toward him and press them against his body. He was known as "One Arm" Daily even though, technically, he was merely one-handed, the first professional pitcher with such a disability.

Daily faced a rule that meant if he wasn't pitching well he could become an additional liability for his team. Before 1890, when pitchers were pulled for doing poorly, they had to be replaced by a player on the field and switch places with him. Managers were understandably reluctant to pull Daily and have him field balls, so he suffered some terrible losses while completing 96 percent of his career starts, a National League record.[12] Daily seldom stayed with any team for long because his abrasive personality turned his fellow players against him. During his 1881 season with the independent New York Metropolitans, he defeated several National League teams, including first place Chicago. After the season, he found himself without a job, replaced in the New York lineup by Buffalo's Jack Lynch. Orator O'Rourke, the Bisons' manager, signed Daily for 1882, saying: "I have batted against Daily, and he is the most perplexing pitcher I ever saw. His delivery is rapid and his curves intricate and peculiar." By signing with Buffalo, Daily for the third time joined a team on which Brouthers played.[13]

Manager O'Rourke decided to showcase "One Arm" before an opening day crowd of 1,500 on a dark and drizzly afternoon when Chicago appeared in Riverside Park. Daily was caught by Tom Dolan and got off to a poor start when each of the three runners he walked in the first inning crossed home plate to score, helped along by errors by shortstop Davy Force. Buffalo bats

The 1882 Buffalo Bisons featured Galvin, along with pitcher "One Arm" Daily and the "Big Four" sluggers, consisting of Dan Brouthers, Deacon White, Jack Rowe and Hardy Richardson. Galvin recorded 28 wins that year before hitting his stride during the following two seasons. At the top is Richardson, below him from left are Charles Foley and Davy Force. Middle two rows, from left, are Rowe, Daily, Manager Jim O'Rourke, Brouthers, and Galvin. Front row: Tom Dolan, Bill Purcell and White (Buffalo History Museum).

roared into action in the second and third innings to score six runs, with doubles by Purcell and White and a triple by Brouthers. Daily himself drove in a run in the third to give the Bisons a 6–3 lead, and the home club added another run for a 7–5 victory over the reigning National League champions. It was a grand start for Daily and for the Bisons. With Galvin pitching on

May 3, Chicago was blanked, 5–0, as Galvin and Force doubled and White Stockings errors led to two runs. On May 5, Buffalo won its third game in row, edging Detroit, 4–3. The Bisons quickly returned to earth, however, losing four in a row, three to Detroit and one to Chicago, before their next win, a 6–2 victory over Chicago on May 17. Daily opened the season 8–4, while Galvin struggled at 2–6. On June 3, Daily complained that his arm was sore after a 6–3 victory over Providence and O'Rourke realized he could no longer count on "One Arm" for any particular game. The bulk of the pitching workload reverted yet again to Galvin, with Daily used mainly for exhibition matches. On June 10 in Troy, the Bisons were forced to borrow a pitcher from a local team as they were hammered, 17–4, and slipped to seventh place in the standings.

On May 25 in Cleveland, Buffalo right fielder Curry Foley became the first major leaguer to hit for the cycle as the Bisons shelled the Forest Citys, 20–1. Foley accomplished the single-double-triple-homer feat off George Washington Bradley. It was the third game in a series in which Galvin sat out, replaced by Daily. "One Arm" pitched again on May 29 as Buffalo prevailed, this time 9–8. During a June 6 game in Providence, heavy showers made the game ball soggy and hard to handle, especially for pitchers Tommy Bond and Pud Galvin. Bisons leftfielder Blondie Purcell took it upon himself to slice open the ball so it could be replaced, giving Galvin a better chance to throw his curve ball. The umpire fined him $10, but the impromptu surgery didn't help Buffalo at all. Providence romped to a 15–7 win with Galvin surrendering 16 hits to the eight allowed by Bond.[14] The next day, Galvin and the Bisons were again pummeled by the Grays, this time 10–0. By July 4, Buffalo had 19 wins and 20 losses, tied with Troy for fifth place in the standings. That day, Galvin won both ends of a doubleheader against cellar-dwelling Worcester, 9–5 and 18–8, the afternoon contest called after seven innings because of darkness. Both games, the latter played in drizzling rain, featured strong hitting by both clubs and sloppy fielding.

"One Arm" Daily led the Bisons to victories over Chicago by scores of 5–4 and 4–3 in July. In the first game, Daily brought the winning run in when he sent the ball over the head of centerfielder George Gore, who was playing him far too shallow. On July 24, Daily hurt several fingers on his only hand when he swung at an inside pitch. He made only four more starts that season, losing three of them. By then, he had alienated his teammates, and the *Buffalo Courier* reported many of them were deliberately playing poorly behind him, hoping he would be released. Daily was gone by late August and eventually signed with Cleveland.[15] With Buffalo, he had compiled a 15–14 record.

Buffalo continued to struggle to get above .500 and by September 4, with 36 wins and 34 losses, was tied for fifth with Cleveland. Wins had been hard to come by and so were good crowds at Riverside Park. On September

8. 1881–1882: Prelude to Perfection 103

7, Orator Jim O'Rourke put on a fine display at the plate, going five-for-five as the Bisons downed the hapless Worcester Ruby Legs, 10–1. With a high-priced roster and slumping attendance, Buffalo transferred its last four home games to Chicago, which had a narrow lead on Providence in a dogfight for first place. Providence protested the move, seen as helping the White Stockings, but to no avail. About 1,500 spectators turned out for the first game of the series on September 26 at Lakefront Park in unseasonably cold weather. Buffalo took an early lead on triples by Galvin and O'Rourke. Galvin, who traditionally had trouble with White Stockings hitters, pitched effectively for six innings, after which he tired. Chicago hitters scored four runs in the seventh and two more in the eighth for the come-from-behind, 8–7 victory. Nearly 3,000 fans showed for the second game the following day when Chicago batters found Galvin had few surprises for them and gave up 17 hits. Chicago won, 8–1.

A close-up of Galvin during his 1882 season with the Buffalo Bisons. In their fourth year in the National League, the Bisons finished tied with Boston for third place. Galvin won 28 games while his backup, the sometimes difficult "One Arm" Daily, collected 15. Galvin's best years were with Buffalo and it is where he returned for an unsuccessful comeback bid (National Baseball Hall of Fame Library, Cooperstown, New York).

O'Rourke put Blondie Purcell in the pitching box for the third game, on September 28. Purcell gave up eight runs in the first five innings and was replaced by Galvin, who surrendered five singles and a home run as Chicago cruised to an 11–3 win.

The fourth and final game attracted 4,000 fans and was the most exciting of the series. Galvin faced Larry Corcoran, who was looking to win his tenth consecutive game since September 1. Corcoran had already won 10 games in a row between June 29 and July 29 and the hometown crowd was looking for a sweep that would give him his second string of 10. They may have been disappointed when captain Cap Anson failed to appear at first base, his usual position. In his place was a 16-year-old local lad, Milt Scott. The Bisons fielded flawlessly for six innings but in the seventh, with Buffalo leading, 5–2, rightfielder Curry Foley made errors that allowed two Chicago runs to cross the plate. Errors by shortstop Davy Force and third baseman Deacon White the next inning allowed Chicago to tie the game. In the bottom of the ninth, Chicago third baseman Ned Williamson doubled off Galvin and made it home on two Buffalo errors to win the game. Young Scott acquitted himself admirably at first base with two hits, and he scored a run. The four-game sweep closed the season and gave Chicago first place in the National League with a record of 55–29, followed by Providence at 52–32. Buffalo had climbed into third place, tied with the Boston Red Stockings with 45–39 records. It had been a disappointing season for Buffalo, hobbled by an overall decline in hitting and an inability to find a reliable backup for Galvin. It was hinted in the *Buffalo Courier* that heavy drinking by the players had also impaired the team's performance.[16]

Pud Galvin tied with Chicago's Fred Goldsmith with 28 wins, for third place in the league. They were just ahead of Goldsmith's teammate, Larry Corcoran, who picked up 27. The top pitcher that year was Cleveland's Jim McCormick with 36 victories in 65 complete games. Gentle Jeems was also third in innings pitched (445⅓) and complete games (48). He had thrown three shutouts and started 51 games, in his worst season since becoming a Bison. Unlike Goldsmith and Corcoran, whose team won

Baseball's first great slugger, Dan Brouthers, was a star on the Buffalo Bisons from 1881 to 1885. A member of the "Big Four," his career batting average stood at .342 but during his Buffalo years it ranged from .341 to .372 (Library of Congress).

8. 1881–1882: Prelude to Perfection 105

nearly twice as many as it lost, Galvin's club had a .536 record, and he was tagged with the fourth-highest number of losses (23).

It had been a breakout season for Big Dan Brouthers, who had league-leading statistics in five categories: batting average, .368; slugging average, .547; on-base percentage, .403; total bases, 192; and hits, 129. He was tied for second in home runs with six, and was alone in second place with 63 runs batted in. In his first full season as a Bison, Brouthers had become one of the most feared hitters in baseball. He also played more games at first base than anyone in the game, and his days of shaky defense were behind him as he recorded the best fielding average for the position, at .974. One of his hits during a 14–3 win over Philadelphia on August 5 had been spectacular. In that game, he belted four doubles, three of which left the grounds but under the ground rules for Recreation Park, they counted only as two-baggers. His last hit was the biggest ever seen in the small park. It sailed 100 feet over the center field fence, flew over the steeple of a small church and came to rest in a cemetery. The feat was recalled for decades.[17]

Storm clouds were on the horizon for teams like Buffalo that faced high salary costs and declining attendance. The *Cleveland Herald* put it this way: "The enormous salaries demanded by league players are going to force several teams to go broke. They are asking for $1,500 to $2,800. Some will get it, but after that there will be scratching among ballplayers for situations in civilian life."[18] Player pay and poor attendance lay behind the decision taken by the National League to toss Worcester and Troy overboard. At a special League meeting September 22, member clubs voted 6–2 to expel the two small-market teams for the following season. "The reason given for kicking out Worcester and Troy was that the patronage in either of these cities is not large enough to give the visiting clubs a share of gate-money sufficient to pay their expenses," said the *New York Clipper*.[19] The League was hoping to replace the two cities with New York and Philadelphia, both of which were anxious for membership. Understandably, Troy and Worcester had resisted, but it did them no good. New York and Philadelphia would fill their places for 1883.

Late in the 1882 season, the American Association began raiding National League teams for talent. Its teams began signing league players to "optional agreements" which committed them to signing formal contracts once the playing season was over. The AA rationalized that because it was not recognized by the National League, it could sign whoever it wanted. Allegheny president Denny McKnight was anxious to improve his struggling nine and persuaded Detroit catcher Charlie Bennett, Chicago third baseman Ned Williamson and Pud Galvin to sign "optional agreements" for the 1883 season. Bennett was paid $100 to do so on the understanding he would sign an Allegheny contract to play for $1,700. When it came time to sign with McKnight's club, however, Bennett suddenly got cold feet and opted to stay with Detroit. Allegheny took him to court to honor his agreement with them and sought $1,000 in damages when Williamson and Galvin also reneged on theirs. The court ruled against Allegheny, finding that the agreement was merely a preliminary one, not a contract itself, and no damages had yet been done to the club. The American Association responded by blacklisting the players.[20]

For Buffalo, it was fortunate Galvin wasn't lured away to Allegheny. Staying put, he was about to put together his best two seasons.

9

Glory Days

For the 1883 season of professional baseball, it seemed as though everything was new. The Buffalo Bisons changed their uniforms yet again. Their shirts and pants were back to blue, with scarlet caps trimmed in white, and red-and-white striped stockings to give a rather patriotic look to the nine. Not everyone was thrilled with the new look. "Galvin objects to the blue suits and says they make his rear view resemble the back of a hack," one newspaper reported.[1] Meanwhile, the National League had two new teams, the New York Gothams and Philadelphia Quakers, replacements for Troy and Worcester. The Boston Red Caps became the Boston Beaneaters, a name they would retain until becoming the Doves in 1907, the Rustlers for 1911 and finally the Braves in 1912. The rule governing pitches was modified to permit sidearm deliveries as well as the traditional underhand technique.

The Bisons signed several new players as directors continued to seek a solid backup pitcher for Galvin, along with fielders and hitters capable of taking the team to the top of the National League. In the course of the season, 10 new players donned the Bisons uniform for varying lengths of time, five of them pitchers. One of them, Walter Burke, pitched only one game, while another, Art Hagan, saw action twice, once at the beginning of the season and once at the end. Ed Cushman, 31, and George Derby, 25, seemed to be the most promising of the new recruits. Cushman, a lefty, won only three games and lost three in his seven appearances, however. Derby appeared to be the best bet. During two seasons with Detroit, he had 46 victories, with the same number of losses. It was hoped he would become the reliable number two hurler that the Bisons so badly needed. But Derby would prove unreliable. Other newcomers who lasted more than a handful of outings included right fielder George "Orator" Shafer, 31, whose career dated back to 1874 with Hartford. He had also played with Louisville, Chicago and Cleveland in the National League. Shafer brought a strong bat to Buffalo. Another new face was the relatively inexperienced Jim Lillie, 21, an outfielder and good hitter who could also pitch. Dave Eggler, the center fielder for the Bisons in 1979, was back, and would appear in 38 games.

A new era in professional baseball began when the National League, the American Association and an invited guest, the Northwestern League, sat down for talks at the Fifth Avenue Hotel in New York City on February 17, 1883. The National League, now under new president Abraham Mills, was willing to recognize the American Association and try to make peace, unlike his predecessor William Hulbert, who had been more inclined to war. They came up with the Tripartite Agreement, as it was called, which contained three key measures. The parties reached a temporary agreement to expand the reserve rule to cover 11 players on each team. Contracts and blacklists in each league would be respected by the others, and any player who signed more than one contract would be expelled by all three organizations. It was a peace treaty intended to stop raids on players and curb the escalation of salaries. The three-hour session that forged the deal was marked by goodwill on all sides, a fact lauded by Henry Chadwick in the *New York Clipper*. He noted: "It was essential to the future existence of both organizations [NL and AA] that the evils of contract-breaking should be at once and forever removed, and also that the penalties inflicted for demoralizing offenses in the ranks [presumably, drinking and gambling] should be mutually observed by both organizations."[2] Some outstanding issues between AA and NL teams were tidied up, including claims made by Association teams on some National League players. Those claims were abandoned, including those of Allegheny for Galvin, Bennett and Williamson.

Buffalo opened the season on May 1 in Cleveland against the Blues. George Derby pitched for the Bisons and was wild. He gave up nine base hits as the 1,800 chilly spectators in the lakeside city were cheered by a 7–4 Cleveland win. The next day, Galvin pitched and held the Blues scoreless, as Brouthers tripled and O'Rourke doubled, powering the Bisons to a 3–0 victory. On May 3, Derby took the ball again as Buffalo lost, 3–1. The home opener for the Bisons was on May 5 when the Blues appeared, to continue the home-and-home series. On a cloudy and cold day before 1,200 fans, Galvin gave up four Cleveland runs by the third inning, including a home run by leftfielder Tom York. Galvin then buckled down and kept batters off the base paths the rest of the way, as Buffalo bats woke up in an 8–4 win. The next day, with Derby pitching, the Bisons had trouble with the timely hitting and sharp base running of the visitors, who took the game, 5–4, in what was described as one of the hardest fought games ever seen at Riverside Park. In the third and final clash of the series, Buffalo won the deciding game, 8–4, cashing in on Blues errors. It marked Galvin's third win in three games, while Derby had lost all three of his starts. The pattern would repeat often throughout the season as Galvin's backups struggled. On May 11, Boston visited Buffalo and with Galvin pitching, the Bisons won, 12–4. The next day, with Derby facing them, the Beaneaters hammered his offerings all over the park in a 16–4 victory.

On Decoration Day, May 30, Buffalo was a team on the move, playing games in two cities on the holiday. In the morning, before 2,000 fans in Providence, the Bisons lost, 4–2, to the Grays, as Galvin gave up eight hits in a contest marked by particularly good fielding. The visitors boarded a train for an afternoon game in Boston before 6,000 fans. The Beaneaters found Derby easy to hit, while the Bisons big bats struggled with Charlie Buffinton, making only four hits off him. Boston won, 2–1.

By early June, Buffalo was finding the going tough. With nine wins and 12 losses, the club was buried in fifth place, tied with Boston and New York. Chicago led the National League with 17 wins, followed by Cleveland, Detroit and Providence, all with 15. Derby had another dreadful performance on June 12 in New York, allowing 20 hits as the Gothams won, 17–8. New York leftfielder Pete Gillespie had his way with Derby, hitting him five times for five runs. Galvin had a bad outing on July 2 in Chicago, as the club with which he so often struggled managed 10 hits off him on the way to a 12–7 win. Second baseman Fred Pfeffer belted a home run, one of his three hits that day. The following day, with the ball in Derby's hand, the White Stockings crushed Buffalo, 31–7. Derby surrendered 32 hits, including two triples and 14 doubles, as he faced 67 batters during a forgettable outing. After Chicago crossed the plate eight times in the first inning, it was apparent the Bisons were just going through the motions on the field, where they made 12 errors. It marked the fourth victory for Chicago in four clashes with Buffalo. The White Stockings were in fourth place in the National League standings, while Buffalo and Detroit were locked in a tie for sixth. The next day, Derby was released. He never again played professional baseball.

The Philadelphia Quakers were by far the weakest team in the National League in 1883, mired in last place when the club rolled into Buffalo on July 17 for four games. Inexplicably, Buffalo had struggled with the Quakers, losing three of their first seven meetings. This time, the Buffalo bats were on fire. O'Rourke and Richardson each managed five hits off Quakers pitcher Tom Coleman, while Brouthers had four, one of them a triple. The Bisons had 24 hits and took advantage of errors for a final score of 21–6. Galvin allowed Philadelphia nine hits. The following day, left-hander Ed Cushman pitched for the Bisons, who collectively made 13 errors to lose, 7–5. The July 19 game saw Coleman shelled again by Buffalo, Brouthers making six successive hits, including two doubles and four singles, and scoring three runs. O'Rourke had five hits, including a home run. The shell-shocked Coleman gave up 27 hits. Galvin had a poor outing, with 10 hits surrendered, but his offense more than compensated for it as the Bisons won, 25–5. In the fourth game on July 21, Buffalo trailed the Quakers until the ninth inning, when it capitalized on some wild throws to tie it up. Doubles by O'Rourke and Brouthers and a single by Deacon White in the tenth inning produced a 7–4 victory.

Fourth-place Boston arrived in Buffalo for a four-game series beginning July 24, and the Bisons won three of them. Cushman took the ball for Buffalo in the first game and came away with the victory, one of his three for the year. He struck out seven Beaneaters, including first baseman John Morrill three times. The next day, with Galvin pitching, Boston roared back for a 9–0 win. Former Bison Dutch Hornung victimized Galvin for a home run, a triple, and a double as Boston played error-free ball. Game three was on July 26, when Cushman started for the Bisons and was hit hard. He was replaced by Galvin after two innings. Sloppy fielding and the Beaneaters' inability to hit Galvin were features of the game. Pitcher Jim Whitney took the 7–4 loss for Boston. The final tilt between the clubs was on July 28, when Charlie Buffinton got off to a rough start for the visitors, allowing 11 hits and seven Bison runs in the first inning. He collected himself, however, and didn't allow any further runs, leaving it to Beaneaters bats to go to work on Galvin. The Bisons held on, however, for a 7–5 win. After losing three of its four games to Buffalo, Boston stepped up its play in August and September to take the National League pennant, four games ahead of Chicago.

Deacon White, a third baseman for the Bisons, was another member of the "Big Four," a key to the team's success although it never finished higher than third place in the National League. His nickname reflected his rather pious habits compared to most other players of his day (Library of Congress).

9. Glory Days

No sooner had Boston left town than Providence, which was leading the league at the time, came to Buffalo for a four-game series beginning July 31. The Grays had been riding the arm of Old Hoss Radbourn, who would record 48 victories in the 76 games he pitched that season. Fans in Buffalo fully expected the local club to fall yet again to the powerful Grays. But Radbourn didn't show and Charlie Sweeney, his backup, took the ball. He presented no challenge for the Bisons batters, giving up 10 runs as his defense committed 11 errors behind him. In the bottom of the third inning, Galvin connected with a Sweeney offering for a home run to score three runs. It was his second homer in the National League, and the eighth of his professional career. The Bisons won the game, 8–1. Galvin pitched well the following day, allowing only four hits, as Providence gave the ball to pitcher Lee Richmond, who fared better than Sweeney. Galvin and Rowe scored doubles off him as their club again downed the Grays, this time 3–1. The third game saw Galvin pitching again and he was very sharp, allowing only three hits as the Grays turned to Sweeney, who surrendered 15. Buffalo won 9–2, and again the following day, when Radbourn finally appeared. Both he and Galvin were freely hit in a come-from-behind, 16–11 Bisons victory to complete its sweep of the front-runners. During the series, Big Dan Brouthers pulled a hidden ball trick to record an out and save shortstop Davy Force from an error. *Sporting Life* reported it this way: "Sweeney was put out at first in one of the Buffalo-Providence games last week by the ball lodging in Brouthers' shirt. It was thrown badly by Force, and but for the accident an error would have been charged the shortstop. Strange things happen on the diamond."[3] On other occasions, Brouthers, who presented a vast acreage of humanity at first base, used the hidden ball trick on purpose, becoming most adept at it. Finding a place to hide the ball on his person was quite a feat in an era when the use of fielding gloves was not widespread.

The Chicago White Stockings came to Buffalo for a series beginning August 11. Galvin, who had only Ed Cushman as backup, always struggled with Cap Anson's club and the series started poorly, with Chicago winning the first two games, 4–2 and 14–8. Its batters hit Galvin freely, 30 times in the two games combined. Cushman started the third game on August 14, but was replaced by "Orator" O'Rourke in the fourth inning. The Bisons earned some hard hits off Larry Corcoran late in the game to win the slugfest, 19–17. The game lasted so long that it had to be called on account of darkness in the eighth inning, the score reverting to that after seven innings. Aside from his three innings pitched, O'Rourke also hit for the cycle. The following day Buffalo won again, this time 4–3, as Galvin held the powerful White Stockings to four hits. Galvin took the ball for the final game on August 16 and came away with another win, also leading the Bisons batters with four hits and scoring a run. Buffalo won, 5–3, and the hard-working Galvin may have been cheered that his usual poor luck against Chicago seemed to be changing.

Chicago returned home from a road trip marked by more losses than wins and on August 23 its first opponent was Buffalo for three games. Fred Goldsmith pitched well for the White Stockings, more than compensating for the nine errors made behind him. Galvin gave up seven hits as Chicago won, 3–1. The following day, Galvin faced Goldsmith again as Buffalo managed ten hits, but had trouble bringing runs home. Brouthers was the final out in four innings, leaving one or two men on base each time. Chicago took the game, 4–1. The final clash of the series was another slugfest as Goldsmith and Galvin were both pounded mercilessly. Superior fielding by the White Stockings made the difference and they won, 18–14. The three consecutive losses may have shattered Galvin's newfound confidence about facing batters from the Windy City.

By early September, Cleveland had a narrow lead in the standings, followed by Providence, Boston and Chicago. Buffalo was fifth with 43 wins and 38 losses. The Bisons faced a tough challenge late in September as they traveled to Boston for a four-game series. The Beaneaters had been in a dogfight for first place, and after defeating Providence September 8 went on a winning streak, taking 13 of their next 14 games on their way to claiming the National League pennant. Whitney and Galvin both pitched well in the first game on September 21. Whitney struck out 10 Buffalo batters and Galvin allowed the powerful opposition only five hits. Buffalo came away with a 3–2 win, its only victory in the series. The next day, Galvin surrendered 13 hits in the first four innings, after which Jim Lillie took over and allowed five more. Buffinton pitched for Boston, which romped to an 18–4 victory. On September 25, Galvin gave up 14 hits to five for Whitney as Boston again won, 8–5. In the final game of the series, Galvin was rested and Art Hagan, recently released by cellar-dwelling Philadelphia, took his place. Brouthers pounded Buffinton for four hits, including a home run described as the longest hit ever made at South End Grounds. Hagan, however, gave up 11 hits to the Beaneaters and the final score was 5–3 for the home team. Even though they had won only once in their final series with Boston, the Bisons could take some comfort from knowing that during the season they had won seven of the 14 games they played against the eventual league champions.

Buffalo finished the season in fifth place, with 52 wins and 45 losses. That was seven more wins than in 1882, when they tied for third. Galvin had been a workhorse in what was his best season to date. He pitched an incredible 656⅓ innings to lead the league, 24 more than second-place Hoss Radbourn. Radbourn had the most wins, with 48, but Galvin was just two behind. Galvin had five shutouts and led all pitchers with 72 complete games, six more than Radbourn. He recorded 279 strikeouts, good for third, and he was also third in lowest on-base percentage at .265. He faced three future Hall of Fame pitchers that season and performed well. Against Radbourn he was 3–2, against Mickey Welch 3–3, and against John Montgomery Ward 1–1.[4] Over in the American Association, the Philadelphia Athletics edged out the St. Louis Browns by a single game to take the pennant. O. P. Caylor's Cincinnati Red Stockings finished third. Denny McKnight's Alleghenys finished a miserable 35 games back in seventh and lost $3,000, in sharp contrast to the profits of other AA teams. The leading AA pitcher, Cincinnati's Will White, had 43 wins.

Yet again, Galvin was forced to work so many innings because Buffalo couldn't find a reliable backup for him. George Derby was not the pitcher he had been with Detroit. Derby started 13 games and lost ten, several of them embarrassments. Cushman won three and lost three, while Hagan lost both late-season games in which he appeared.

In September, the Buffalo club learned that the owner of their Riverside Park grounds, Alexander Culbert, wanted to develop housing on the site and they had to find a new home for the 1884 season. Directors eventually found a suitable property about seven blocks to the east at Richmond Avenue and Summer Street, which would become known as Olympic Park. Owned by semi-retired businessman George Howard, it was a vacant lot that team president Josiah Jewett could see from the back window of his fine home on North Street. A five-year lease was signed at $1,500 annually for four years and $1,800 in the final year. Buffalo had turned a profit of $5,000 for the 1883 season and felt the sum was reasonable and still left directors with enough cash to establish a field and build a covered grandstand.[5] When finished, at a cost of about $6,000, Olympic Park could accommodate 4,000 fans in seats and another 1,000 standing.

On October 27, the National League and American Association gathered to sign a permanent peace settlement between them known as the National Agreement, an update of the Tripartite pact signed in February. The Agreement was intended to make permanent contract provisions such as the reserve clause. But storm clouds were on the horizon. Baseball was becoming a success financially as the economy rebounded from the recession of the 1870s. Other cities wanted in on the action. Meanwhile, players and those who wanted to establish teams had come to resent the reserve clause, which they saw as inhibiting opportunities. Baseball promoters from several cities, led by 26-year-old St. Louis millionaire Henry V. Lucas, gathered in Pittsburgh in September and formed the Union Association of Professional Base Ball Clubs. One of the new loop's founding tenets was opposition to the reserve clause. H. B. Bennett of Washington was elected president (replaced at the end of the year by Lucas), while Tom Pratt of Philadelphia was vice-president. Directors were from Baltimore, Washington, Pittsburgh and Philadelphia.

Among the first items of business was to award franchises to St. Louis, Chicago, Boston, Baltimore, Cincinnati, Philadelphia, Washington and (to make an even number of teams) Altoona, Pennsylvania.

The UA developed a 128-game schedule and decreed that game receipts were to be split 50–50. The new league agreed to respect contracts between players and teams in the National League and American Association, but would not recognize "any agreement whereby any number of ballplayers may be reserved for any club for any time beyond the terms of their contract for such club."[6] In other words, the UA would not respect the reserve clause. The National League was unimpressed by the birth of another rebel league, having just buried its differences with the American Association. In December, the National League threatened to blacklist any player who failed to return his signed league contract within 30 days. The intention was to dissuade players from looking at the sudden, new options presented by the UA. Early the next year, the National League voted to blacklist any player who jumped to the Union Association. For its part, the American Association replied by adding franchises in Washington, Brooklyn, Indianapolis and Toledo, in a bid to reduce the number of players and cities considering the UA.

For 1884, professional baseball would involve three major leagues and a total of 34 teams. There would be plenty of baseball played, and Pud Galvin played some of the best. The last remaining restriction on how pitchers could deliver the ball was dropped by the National League, opening the door to the modern, overhand pitch. Galvin adapted with little difficulty. Others, such as Fred Goldsmith in Chicago, struggled with the new delivery, which he said caused pain in his arm. Goldsmith's arm was tired from years of work and he recorded only nine wins with 11 losses that year as he clung to his underhand technique. He was traded to Baltimore in July, where he picked up three of his wins. At age 29, Goldsmith's career was over when he couldn't find a team for 1885. He discovered the market was flooded with players following the collapse of the Union Association combined with the American Association's decision to revert to eight teams from 12. In his six years in the National League, Goldsmith earned 112 wins and suffered 68 losses.[7] The ruling change on pitching delivery had no impact on Providence hurler Hoss Radbourn, who continued his sidearm technique with remarkable results. In another rule change, the National League reduced the number of balls required for a walk from seven to six. The result of the changes tilted play in favor of pitchers as strikeouts soared and batting averages dropped. The American Association and Union Association opted against the rule changes, staying with the sidearm and underarm delivery, and seven balls for a walk.

Roster changes were few for 1884 in Buffalo. Yet another attempt was made to find a reliable and consistent backup pitcher for Galvin. The latest candidate was Billy Serad, 22, a slightly built right-hander from Philadelphia making his debut in the professional game. He had played with an amateur club in Chester, Pennsylvania, the previous season. At five-foot-seven, Serad was an inch shorter than Galvin, but at 156 pounds weighed at least 30 pounds less than the Bisons' ace, who was beginning to bulk up. Art Hagan, the late-season addition from 1883, was back, but he would make only three starts and lose two of them. Curry Foley was gone, having retired from baseball, while "Orator" Shafer had signed with the St. Louis Maroons of the new Union Association. Newcomers were George Myers, 23, a Buffalo native, who caught but could also play outfield and third base, and Chub Collins, 26, a Canadian, who would play second base and shortstop. Both were making their debuts in the professional ranks.

The 1884 season would prove to be one of the most memorable in baseball history, primarily because of outstanding pitching, but also, paradoxically, for hitting. Hoss Radbourn of Providence was magnificent and set some records expected to last forever. He won 59 games (some sources say 60) and completed 73 of the 75 games he started. He lost only 12 and topped nearly every pitching category. He recorded 441 strikeouts in 678⅔ innings and compiled an earned run average of 1.38. At one point, he won 18 consecutive starts. Other pitchers, including Galvin, had stellar performances. Charlie Sweeney of Providence struck out 19 batters in a game against Boston, while "One Arm" Daily, of the Union Association team in Chicago, did the same against the Beaneaters in an exhibition game. Mickey Welch of the National League's New York Gothams struck out the first nine Cleveland batters he faced on August 28, to set a consecutive strikeout record that lasted until 1970, when Tom Seaver fanned ten straight. Despite the quality pitchers they faced, batters made noteworthy contributions. Fred Dunlap, of the Union Association team in St. Louis, had a record batting average of .412, with 185 hits and 160 runs scored. In the National League, Ned Williamson of Chicago, led the loop with 27 home runs, while his teammate King Kelly had the top batting average at .354. Buffalo's Big Dan Brouthers had the best slugging average at .564, while his teammate "Orator" Jim O'Rourke tied Boston's Ezra Sutton for most hits with 162. Brouthers also set a record by hitting triples during four consecutive games in late July.

Buffalo didn't open its new home park until May 21, after a disastrous start to the new season on the road. Galvin and Brouthers were both ailing. Galvin hurt his back on May 9 after a 3–1 loss to Hoss Radbourn and Providence. It happened when he picked up his suitcase at the Narragansett Hotel and may have been connected to his pitching the previous day in cold weather.[8] He missed eight games. Brouthers, meanwhile, came down with a serious case of influenza, or malaria, in early May, which kept him out for 22 games. The Bisons won only four of their first 15 games, played in Boston, Providence, Philadelphia and New York.

On Opening Day in Buffalo, a smaller than expected crowd of 2,000 turned out on a brilliant, sunny day and were entertained by Poppenburg's Band, a fixture at special events in Buffalo. The Bisons, now in gray and red uniforms, faced the Detroit Wolverines. Galvin, his back still tender, was coaxed to take the ball, to the delight of the home crowd. His appearance also inspired his teammates, who went to town on Detroit pitcher Stump Weidman and won, 12–3. The next day, with Serad pitching, the Bisons held off a late Wolverines rally with a timely strikeout and a brilliant running catch by centerfielder Hardy Richardson to win, 8–7. On May 23, Galvin struck out 14 Detroit batters, including all three in one inning, as Buffalo won, 2–1, to complete the sweep. The White Stockings were next into Olympic Park, and the new facility continued to bring good luck to the home team. Buffalo won, 8–4, on May 24 and 4–0 the next day, with Galvin pitching well in both games. On May 26, he picked up his first shutout of the season, downing Chicago, 4–0. The spell was broken May 27, when Serad appeared in the pitcher's box. Five home runs were sent over the new left field fence, two by Hardy Richardson of the Bisons, but three by Chicago. Two of the White Stockings' blasts came by pitcher Fred Goldsmith, never much of a hitter, whose lifetime batting average was a modest .225. In the fifth inning, Goldsmith connected for the second home run of his career, surprising even himself. Years later, a newspaper account said he laughed so hard at his newfound power that he was barely able to make it around the bases. In the seventh inning, he repeated the feat, this time collapsing at the plate, holding his sides, convulsed with laughter. Captain Cap Anson and his White Stockings teammates eventually persuaded him to get to his feet and circle the bases.[9] The other homer was belted by shortstop Walt Kinzie of the visitors as Chicago won, 14–6.

Big Dan Brouthers returned to the Bisons' lineup on June 6 but didn't fully recover his strength for another week. The layoff reduced his batting numbers for the season, giving him a title only in slugging average. Pitchers continued to fear him, however. On June 19 in Detroit, pitcher Frank Meinke walked him four out of the five times he came to the plate as Buffalo hammered the Wolverines, 18–2. Intentional walks were still quite rare at the time.[10] The Detroit and Cleveland pitchers Brouthers faced from July 23–26 might have considered giving him the same treatment, since he hit triples off them in four consecutive games.[11] Ironically, in the July 24 contest with Detroit, Meinke, apparently feeling somewhat braver than a month earlier, decided to pitch to him. By the end of July, Buffalo had 39 wins and 27 losses, good for fourth place, eight games behind Providence, which was locked in a dogfight for first with Boston.

As Brouthers' bat heated up, Galvin also found his form, which he demonstrated during an early August series in Detroit. When the Bisons appeared at Recreation Park for the first game on August 2, they had already won eight of their 11 games against the Wolverines. Galvin allowed only one hit, issued no walks and struck out seven as he shut out the home team, 2–0, while Brouthers and catcher Jack Rowe belted homers off Stump Weidman. On August 4, Galvin threw a hitless gem, walked no one and struck out nine, although a batter reached first on an error when Brouthers failed to make a catch after a third strike. Rowe, Jim Lillie and Dave Eggler led the Bisons' parade of 22 hits. Every Buffalo player had at least two hits off Meinke, including Galvin, and the Wolverines were blanked, 18–0. In the two games, Galvin had retired 54 of the 56 batters he faced in dominating performances. Rain cancelled games the next two days. The series resumed August 7, and the Bisons picked up where they left off. Galvin gave up only three hits and his club took advantage of Wolverines errors to blank them for the third straight game, this time 9–0. After surrendering a miserly four hits in three games, Galvin was rested for the morning game of the doubleheader on August 8 that completed the series. Bisons batters found pitcher Frank Brill an easy mark, making 16 hits off him. Billy Serad gave up only six hits as Buffalo coasted to a 14–2 victory. Galvin returned for the fifth and final game that afternoon, which proved to be the most exciting clash in the series. Both clubs went scoreless for 11 innings. In the 12th, as he tired, Galvin allowed three singles, and Detroit scored the game's only run on a wild throw by rightfielder Lillie. Meinke took the win for Detroit, having allowed only six hits.

Leftfielder Hardy Richardson was another pillar of Buffalo when it was in the National League. A member of the "Big Four," his batting average hovered around the .300 mark (Library of Congress).

It was Galvin's weakest performance in the series, during which he had surrendered a mere 12 hits and earned three shut outs. He pitched 39 innings, struck out 36 batters, allowed only one run (unearned), didn't issue a walk, and held Detroit to a batting average of .092. The Little Steam Engine was on a roll.

Buffalo was fighting it out for third place with the New York Gothams as September rolled around. Providence had extended its lead over Boston for first as it rode a 20-game winning streak, led by Hoss Radbourn's 18 consecutive wins. Buffalo appeared at the Messer Street Grounds for a series beginning September 9. Galvin held the Grays to four hits in the tightly contested game. No scoring occurred until the fifth inning, when Eggler and Rowe singled and were driven home on a double by O'Rourke. Providence threatened to score in the bottom of the ninth inning when Radbourn hit a fly ball to right field. Lillie made a difficult catch there and quickly threw to second base, doubling off Cliff Carroll, who had advanced, thinking the ball couldn't be caught. Thus ended the Providence winning streak. Salutes were directed to the Bisons and their doughty little pitcher. "Base ball enthusiasts are indebted to James Galvin," one newspaper intoned.[12] Providence quickly recovered its winning ways, downing the Bisons, 8–2, on September 12 with Serad taking the loss. The next day the Grays won, 6–1, this time solving Galvin easily. Providence rolled on to a first-place finish with a record of 84–28 for an incredible winning percentage of .750. Boston was second with 73–38 and Buffalo placed third with 64–47. After the National League and American Association finished their seasons, a series of games was played between their pennant winners to determine an overall professional baseball champion in the first "World Series." Providence defeated the AA champion New York Metropolitans three games straight to claim the title.

This was Galvin's best season ever, his second in a row with 46 wins. Durable and tireless, Galvin led the National League with 12 shutouts. He tossed 71 complete games, second only to Radbourn, who had two more. Galvin was third in wins, behind Radbourn (59) and Buffinton of Boston (48). His 636⅓ innings pitched were second only to Radbourn's 678⅔. He also trailed Radbourn in strikeouts, winning percentage, and earned run average. Galvin's season had been outstanding, but Radbourn eclipsed him with a performance that was other-worldly. Baseball's Hall of Fame, into which Radbourn was inducted in 1939, described his 1884 season, the best of his 11-year, 309-game-winning career, as "unparalleled."[13] Radbourn outperformed Galvin, who enjoyed the best season of his career. Likewise, the Bisons had their best season yet, winning 12 games more than in 1883, their previous best. But they still couldn't rise above third place because Providence and Boston were so dominant. Galvin's backup, Billy Serad, struggled, winning 16 games but losing 20. Had Serad been more successful, Galvin would

9. Glory Days

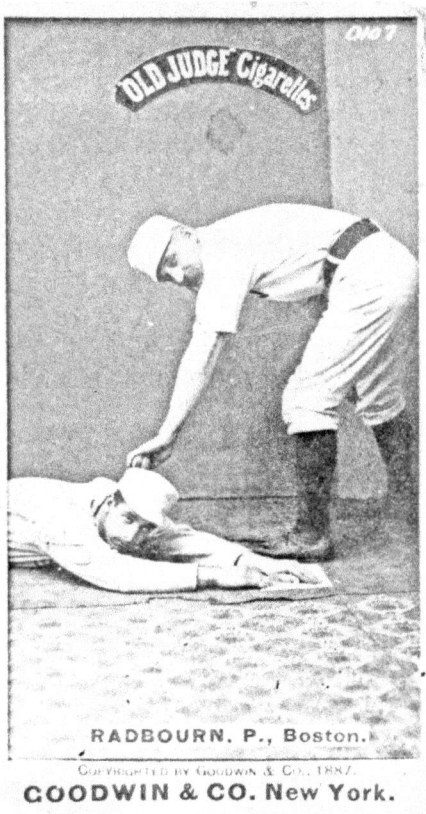

Left: Catcher and infielder Jack Rowe was the fourth member of the "Big Four" that made Buffalo one of the strongest teams of the National League. At the end of the 1885 season, he and the other three Buffalo sluggers were sold to Detroit, where they helped the club to something Buffalo couldn't achieve, the National League pennant *Right:* During his long career, Pud Galvin was overshadowed at times by other pitchers such as Hoss Radbourn. During the 1883 and 1884 seasons, when Galvin won 46 games both years, Radbourn had 48 and an astounding 59, respectively. The accomplishments of other pitchers often caused observers to overlook the diminutive Galvin, also known as "The Little Steam Engine" (Library of Congress).

have seen fewer innings of work and might have been even more effective. And likely Buffalo would have finished higher in the standings.

The season was barely over when Bisons manager "Orator" Jim O'Rourke signed with the New York Gothams, soon to become known as the Giants. It was reported that some friction had been growing between O'Rourke and his fellow Buffalo players, who felt he was too hard on them.[14] He signed with New York for the princely sum of $5,000, an amount unheard-of up to that time. Radbourn and Galvin were among the best-paid players during the 1884 season, earning $3,000 and $2,600 respectively. Even the season's top hitter, King Kelly of Chicago, had been paid only $2,000. New York management was determined to improve their team's performance and prepared to spend what it felt was necessary. With O'Rourke in their roster for 1885, the Giants came within two games of taking the National League pennant.

Buffalo's directors, struggling with the cost of fitting out their new park and concerned that crowds had been thinning, couldn't hope to match that kind of money to keep "Orator" Jim. They turned to their ever-reliable Galvin to fill his shoes. They knew the man, also nicknamed Gentle Jeems, was more easygoing than O'Rourke and was well-liked by his teammates. Besides, Pud Galvin had become the face of the franchise.

10

The Little Steam Engine Changes Gears

The Union Association expired in January 1885, when its driving force, Henry V. Lucas, led his St. Louis Maroons into the National League. His well-financed club had run away with the UA championship, and losing the Maroons to the senior loop saw the UA's remaining members—which hadn't already folded—decide to disband or continue in minor leagues. There had been no real need for the Union Association, historian David Pietrusza has said, so there was no compelling reason for it to survive.[1] Despite its lackluster single year of existence, marked by collapsing and moving franchises, it is nevertheless considered a major league today, unlike the longer-lasting International Association. The National League voted to accept former UA players, overturning its blacklist of them for deserting, but president Denny McKnight of the American Association opposed any such a move. At the end of the 1885 season, however, the AA finally relented and followed suit. With the Union Association relegated to history, the American Association cut back to eight teams from 12. The AA's second-place Columbus Buckeyes had disbanded and were replaced by Brooklyn. In Pittsburgh, new Allegheny manager Horace Phillips swooped into Columbus and signed up most of its roster, including pitchers Ed Morris and Frank Mountain. Morris had won 34 games and lost 13 for the Buckeyes, while Mountain had won 23 and lost 17, while Allegheny's ace Fleury Sullivan had managed only 16 wins against 35 losses. Mountain and Morris were expected to significantly boost their new club, which had finished 11th in the Association, 45½ games behind New York. Also signed was catcher Fred Carroll, who brought with him a respectable batting average of .278. Seven other Columbus players were also added to the Allegheny roster, on which only catcher George "Doggie" Miller and hard-hitting outfielder Charlie Eden were retained.

The National League and American Association again tinkered with the rules for pitchers, insisting that once they began their motion to deliver the ball to the plate, they must continue it, or a balk would be called.[2] The two leagues differed on precise wording, but the essence was the same and would have little impact on Pud Galvin's devastating pickoff move about which competing managers, including Cap Anson, had often complained. In June, the AA dropped the rule that the ball could not be delivered above the pitcher's shoulder, thereby joining the NL in allowing the overhand delivery.

The Buffalo club was little changed from its most successful season ever. Billy Serad was back, as "change pitcher" behind Galvin. After 24 games, 17 of them losses, Galvin happily relinquished his duties as manager, replaced by real estate man George Hughson, secretary-treasurer of the club, who had little experience dealing with hard-nosed ballplayers. Hughson was soon replaced by Jack Chapman, 42, former outfielder with Brooklyn, St. Louis and Louisville, and most recently manager of the National League's last-place Detroit.

The Bisons started their season on the road with a May 1 game in Detroit against the Wolverines. Buffalo was ahead 3–0 after four innings, but the home team solved Galvin to swat 13 hits and score eight runs in an 8–3 victory. The following day, the Wolverines victimized Billy Serad for 16 hits as they again won, this time 10–4. The third game, on May 4, went 11 innings before Detroit belted seven runs off Galvin for another 10–4 win. It was a poor start for a Bisons team coming off such a strong campaign in 1884.

Buffalo's home opener was scheduled for May 6, but rain delayed it for two days. The Bisons played host to Chicago, and Galvin's woes with the White Stockings quickly resurfaced. Buffalo was ahead, 3–2, in the fifth inning, when Galvin allowed six hits to bring nine runners across the plate. The home club's sloppy fielding produced 13 errors as Chicago won, 13–4. In Providence on May 11, with Galvin again pitching, the Bisons lost, 9–4, Buffalo making 12 errors as the Grays recorded 17 hits. The following day, with Serad pitching, the Bisons lost again, 5–1. After six losses in their first six games, the Bisons managed their first victory on May 13 against the Beaneaters in Boston. Hardy Richardson homered for Buffalo, one of 12 hits surrendered by Jim Whitney as the Bisons prevailed, 7–3. Galvin pitched the victory and his defense was much improved, making only three errors. The joy was short-lived as Buffalo lost by identical scores of 3–0 to Providence on May 15 and 16, with Galvin and Serad each picking up a loss. The poor pitching and fielding of the Bisons was highlighted in a May 26 game at the Polo Grounds in New York when the New York Giants, with former Bison "Orator" Jim O'Rourke playing center field, pummeled Buffalo mercilessly. The Giants took an 8–0 lead in the first inning and pounded Galvin for 22 hits, while his team made 17 errors behind him. The final score was an embarrassing 24–0 shutout. Two days later, with Serad pitching, the Giants again whitewashed Buffalo, this time, 11–0. Buffalo's big bats were apparently still

During his eight years in Buffalo, Pud Galvin moved nearly eight times, seldom straying far from Riverside Park or Olympic Park. His last year, 1885, he lived in this building on Vermont Street, pictured today, which housed a saloon on the ground floor. He was known to patronize saloons and after his retirement from baseball operated one of his own, but found it far more difficult to be successful in business than in baseball (photograph by author).

in winter hibernation. Galvin had struggled, and costly errors dogged the Bisons during the first month of the season. By June 1, Buffalo had won only four games and lost 15, good for seventh place, a mere half-game ahead of last-place Detroit. New York, meanwhile, had a comfortable lead, with 17 wins. Over in the American Association, the much-improved Alleghenys were tied for second place, five games behind St. Louis. Left-hander Ed Morris was making a huge impact for Allegheny, becoming the most effective and successful pitcher in the AA.

The Bisons continued to struggle into June. On June 17 they traveled to the Windy City for a four-game series with the White Stockings, who were again among the top National League teams. In the first game on June 17, only Hardy Richardson's home run off Chicago's new pitcher, John Clarkson, kept Buffalo from being blanked in an 8–1 White Stockings victory. Serad took the loss. The next day, Galvin lost as Chicago scored four runs in the first inning in a 7–4 result. Galvin pitched on June 19 and was again hit hard, giving up 12 hits as the Bisons were edged, 9–8. In the ninth inning, Galvin collided with Cap Anson at first base and hurt his ankle, an injury that kept him out of the lineup until June 24 and continued to affect his pitching afterward. The following day, with Serad in the pitcher's box, the White Stockings completed their four-game sweep of the hapless Bisons, blanking them, 5–0, with Clarkson allowing only one hit. Buffalo lost repeatedly to New York and Providence in late June. On June 26, for a game in Buffalo against New York, it was noted that Galvin's injured leg was still swollen as he struggled with both his pitching and hitting.[3] Uncharacteristically, he made three wild throws and two wild pitches, gave up a home run and struck out every time he appeared at the plate. New York won the game, 7–5. By the end of the month the Bisons were still mired in seventh place with 12 wins. Chicago led the league with 35 wins, New York was second with 32, 4½ games ahead of Providence. Buffalo's poor play was compounded by playing so many games in succession against the top teams in the league.

Fans in Buffalo were growing disenchanted with the Bisons, upon whom great hopes had been pinned following their best season ever. Philadelphia appeared at Olympic Park for a four-games series to include the Independence Day holiday on July 4, but crowds were light. On July 3, Buffalo edged the fourth-place Phillies, 6–5, holding off a ninth-inning surge in which the visitors scored three runs. Galvin picked off two runners at first base to take the rare win. July 4 saw the teams play two games, which the Bisons lost by scores of 10–5 and 7–2, Serad and Galvin each losing one. For the series finale on July 5, only 75 fans appeared at the park. Galvin pitched well and Dan Brouthers homered and hit three singles in a 9–3 win. On July 8, Boston snapped an eight-game losing streak by defeating Buffalo, 9–8. The following day, they defeated the Bisons again, 6–2. Galvin took both losses. On July 10,

10. The Little Steam Engine Changes Gears   125

Boston won, 13–6. Finally, on July 11, with Galvin pitching, the Bisons prevailed, 7–3. It was his 13th win in 29 games, a pace far below his stellar 46-win performance the previous season. Directors of the Buffalo club were deeply concerned at the lack of success on the field with the stand-pat roster and the sharply reduced attendance. Free tickets to the comic opera "The Mascot" accompanied each grandstand admission, but that move failed to improve turnout. Since they were still struggling to cover the new lease payments and improvements to Olympic Park, they were as disappointed as the fans that their club was failing to meet lofty expectations. Some of the fans pointed to Galvin, their hero for so many seasons, as the source of the Bisons' troubles. Buffalo's hometown papers had taken to calling the club the "Inglorious" or "Hapless" Bisons. The situation couldn't continue. By July 12, the *Buffalo Courier* was predicting things were about to change.

> There will be shaking up of some of some of the dry bones in the Buffalo Club before long. Manager Chapman goes west this morning, and a new pitcher is the object of the trip. Other players are being looked for and their engagement at an early date is more than probable. It was stated on good authority in Pittsburgh last evening that the Alleghenies [*sic*] of that city had bought Galvin's release from the Buffalos. Some changes in that line are certainly contemplated here, but inquiries last night failed to confirm the rumor.[4]

On July 13, the *Pittsburgh Commercial Gazette* reported that Galvin had indeed been hired by the Allegheny club. In Buffalo, the *Express* hinted that Philadelphia had also been interested in acquiring Galvin, and its president had been in Buffalo trying to sign him. However, Allegheny persuaded Buffalo management to release him for $1,500. Galvin was to be paid another $500 (he would later say it was $700) as part of the transaction and would earn $500 a month with Allegheny, or $3,500 for a year. It was a raise of nearly $1,000 for Galvin. Despite the $500 signing bonus and the pay hike, he was bitter at the turn of events. "They sold me for $2,000 because they can't pay my salary, but they don't remember what I did for them the last seven years. I had a hard time since I was hurt in Chicago, but nobody tried harder than I did," he said.[5] One of Buffalo's directors explained the sale to the *New York Times* in terms that doubtless offended the normally affable Galvin: "The public demanded a change. Both the press and the audiences were growing irritable. We couldn't lose any more games if a pitcher were taken from the grand stand."[6]

The lack of loyalty to Galvin was mind-boggling. He had taken the Bisons so far and had assumed a heavy workload without complaint. No wonder Galvin was upset. Following the two best seasons of his seven spent in Buffalo, he had been dropped after struggling for about two months. Galvin's release came as a surprise, and rumors circulated that the club was about to disband and the rest of its players were for sale. Directors sent telegrams to National League president Nick Young and to *Sporting Life* with reassurances that the club would complete its season and was about to start its eastern trip to play all its scheduled games. *Sporting Life* reported on July 17 that club management had tried to sell off its players, but failed. It claimed directors had sent notices to other club presidents saying Buffalo players were available and they were seeking the best bids for them. Officials from Philadelphia and Boston were among those who replied, indicating their interest for some of the remaining players, but found the asking prices too steep. "Just at this point, however, an unforeseen and insurmountable obstacle arose and the Buffalo management found that their scheme for replenishing their treasury would have to fall through because they could not deliver the goods. The men refused to be sold off to the highest bidders."[7] *Sporting Life* said this meant the Bisons would play out the season, and the directors from other clubs who had been hovering, cash in hand, had returned home empty-handed.

For its part, the *Buffalo Express* acknowledged that a Philadelphia agent was in town, anxious to speak to Dan Brouthers, Hardy Richardson and Jack Rowe, but lost interest when he learned the "fabulous" amount sought for them. It said the players preferred to make their own deals once they were released, and for the time being would continue as Bisons. *Sporting Life* painted a bleak future for baseball in Buffalo: "It may now, however, be set down as certain that this city will not be represented in the League next season. Buffalo has for several years past supported a League club at a financial loss, and this in spite of the fact that it had one of the very best teams in the League." The publication said visiting clubs had received disappointing gate receipts and hadn't complained, but "the fact remained that Buffalo was not a good League city." It took note that Galvin had already been released and had signed with Allegheny, adding: "He always had a hankering after that smoky and dirty town." It further said that players who remained with the Bisons feared management might try to penalize them for not wanting to relocate, by systematically fining them for various offences to make up for revenue their sale could have produced.

Behind the scenes, Frederick K. Stearns, new president and owner of the Detroit Wolverines, one of the least successful National League teams, tried to acquire Buffalo's Big Four hitters of Dan Brouthers, Hardy Richardson, Jack Rowe and Deacon White. But Buffalo president Josiah Jewett felt losing the foursome would be fatal to his club and refused to let the four go. It was suggested that Stearns could buy the entire Buffalo team and move it to Detroit. It is not clear whether Jewett came up with the idea or whether Stearns suggested it to get what he really wanted. Different sources tell different stories.[8] One thing was clear: Jewett was anxious to get out of baseball. His family owned the Jewett Stove Company, and he was also involved in banking and politics, having failed to be elected mayor in 1883. He was tired

10. The Little Steam Engine Changes Gears

of losing money on baseball, and he and his brother Henry were busy establishing a one-mile, covered horse-racing track in the nearby town of Aurora. Once Stearns agreed to buy the entire club, Jewett and his fellow directors okayed what amounted to the first mass sale of players in the history of professional baseball.

Stearns, it was announced on September 17, had purchased the entire operation for $7,000. Detroit planned to add the Big Four to the Wolverines' roster immediately and find replacements for them so Buffalo could complete its league season. The announcement sent shockwaves through the baseball community, and other team owners questioned the legality of the sale. Several wanted an opportunity to sign members of the club, especially the Big Four, if Buffalo was going to disband. There were no rules governing the sale of an entire franchise. Among those most upset were the New York Giants, who faced a four-game series with Detroit and were locked in a dogfight with Chicago for first place. They didn't want to risk losing to a suddenly strengthened Wolverines club, which otherwise might have been easy victims. On September 19, Brouthers, Richardson, Rowe and White appeared in Detroit and were set to join the Wolverines for their game against New York. But National League president Nick Young ordered umpire Bob Ferguson to forfeit the game to the Giants if the foursome played. Sufficiently cowed, Detroit kept them out their lineup and lost, 6–5, to New York. Young had ruled the four were still on the Buffalo roster and the transaction was illegal. He cited the league's Saratoga Agreement, which banned clubs from contacting players before October 20 in any season.[9] The Bisons had to make do without the four players, none of whom appeared in the club's remaining games. Meanwhile, Buffalo losses, on the field and financially, continued to mount.

In Buffalo, manager Chapman found an inexpensive young Canadian, Peter Wood, to replace Galvin. The 18-year-old was playing with the Primrose Club just across the border in Hamilton, Ontario, and was showing great promise. His brother, Fred, 19, a catcher, had played 12 games with Detroit the previous season. Pete Wood appeared in 24 games for Buffalo and won eight of them. For one appearance, September 30 against Boston, Chapman brought in Wood's brother to catch for him. The Bisons lost, 5–3. It marked only the second time in baseball history that a team's battery consisted of brothers.[10] In 1878 in Cincinnati, Will White had pitched to his brother, Deacon, the Bison-turned-Wolverine. Will was 23 and Deacon was 30 at the time. The Wood-to-Wood tandem may have been a late attempt to boost flagging fan interest. It was not repeated after the one game.

The *Buffalo Express* lamented the sale to Detroit, which was a foregone conclusion, but was expected to be delayed until after October 20. "The tone of public sentiment on the deal is decidedly warm," it said.[11] Players were found to replace the Big Four, but crowds of about 100 were not uncommon at Olympic Park as the Bisons' season played out. Boston swept four games at the park between September 29 and October 3, the last contest an 18–0 shellacking of the hapless Bisons. Buffalo pitcher Pete Conway gave up 18 hits and was not relieved. The club's last home games were both played October 7, and it lost, 4–0 and 6–1, to Providence in games limited to five innings to make them official. There was no sense prolonging the misery, the home club felt. Gate receipts amounted to a mere three dollars.[12] The attendance for the doubleheader on a cold day totaled 12 shivering souls. In a bid to salvage some money from the series, another doubleheader of five-inning games was played in Elmira on October 10 to finish the season and end the National League experience for Buffalo. Providence won, 3–0 and 7–3. The latter game marked the 16th straight loss for the Bisons.

It was an ignoble end to eight years of topflight ball in the city. Buffalo had finished third in the National League in 1879, 1881, 1882 and 1884, making it one of the strongest nines during the formative years of the loop. It had won the International Association pennant in 1878, its success there paving the way for its entry into the National League. Buffalo's record in its final season was dismal. The Bisons won 38 games but lost 74, and finished 49 games back of pennant-winning Chicago and just two wins ahead of last-place St. Louis. There had been a glimmer of light in the gloomy picture, however. Dan Brouthers again had the league-leading slugging average at .543, for his fifth year in a row. He was second with 146 hits, second in on-base percentage at .408, and second in doubles with 32. He recorded 15 three-hit games. Despite still-impressive numbers, his inability to hit in the clutch produced some criticism in the press.[13] On a better team, and if he had not sat out the last three weeks of the season amidst the sale controversy, Brouthers' performance would have been even better.

Buffalo may have lost some very good ballplayers, but some would stay connected to the city for personal reasons and investments. In late November, the *New York Clipper* reported: "John C. Rowe, well-known as one of the 'Big Four,' was recently married to a rich and beautiful widow of Buffalo."[14] The following March, *Sporting Life* carried this item about the new Allegheny pitcher and his plans for spring training: "Jimmy Galvin will leave his Buffalo saloon in charge of his brother-in-law, and report for duty April 1."[15]

The Big Four, Galvin, and other players made many good friends during their time in Buffalo. Among them was Grover Cleveland, a former sheriff who served as mayor in 1882. Cleveland became governor of New York for 1883 and 1884, and was elected President of the United States for a term beginning in 1885. In 1888, as he faced a re-election campaign, Cleveland made time in his schedule to welcome the Detroit Wolverines to the White House. The Democratic National Convention was underway in St. Louis, and Cleveland was likely preoccupied with events unfolding there. That he would play

10. The Little Steam Engine Changes Gears 129

host to a baseball team at such a time is a testament to the president's love of the game and affection for some of those who played it. The Wolverines, National League champions in 1887, had defeated St. Louis of the American Association ten games to five in the "World's Series." The Detroit club defeated the Washington Nationals on June 4, 5, and 6, 1888, and afterward met Cleveland. The *New York Times* report went this way:

> **THE PRESIDENT KNEW THEM**
> PITTSBURGH, Penn., June 8.—"How's Jimmy Galvin" said President Cleveland during the Detroit Club's visit to the White House last Wednesday. "He is all right," said Dan Brouthers. "I am glad to hear it," continued the President. "Galvin was a great favorite of mine in Buffalo." The President recognized Brouthers, Rowe, Conway, and "Deacon" White as old acquaintances. After the formalities of introduction were over the players stood in a semicircle in front of the President while he commended their fine athletic appearance and congratulated them upon having won the title of "World Beaters." He expressed his regret that public business has prevented him going to see them play, and alluded to the fact that the Washington team was not making a very credible showing.
> "Do you keep up your hard hitting?" he inquired of Brouthers.
> "I try to," said Dan with a smile. "Deacon" White congratulated the President upon his probable renomination [the St. Louis Convention had not then nominated him] and re-election, for which he returned thanks. After wishing them success in their efforts to return the pennant for a second term the champions withdrew, highly delighted with the pleasant and jovial reception at the White House.[16]

Cleveland was re-nominated, but despite the best wishes of the players, did not win re-election as president, losing to Benjamin Harrison. And Detroit did not repeat as National League champions, placing fifth, well behind winner New York.

After his sale to Allegheny, and while he waited for his paperwork to be completed by the American Association, Galvin umpired an Allegheny game on July 14 which Baltimore won, 5–2. On July 22, he returned to the pitcher's box in Union Park, now known as Recreation Park, after an absence of eight years. The Brooklyn Grays were the opposition and the crowd was good. The *Pittsburgh Commercial Gazette* headlined its account of the game "Good for Galvin."

> "Gentle Jeems" made his first appearance with the Alleghenys yesterday and was on the side of victory at the finish of the game. The popularity of Galvin drew nearly 4,000 people to Recreation Park with high expectations of seeing the team from the City of Churches laid out. The new man pitched a great game, and though the visitors had their most formidable batting nine out they only secured six scattered hits. The "little steam engine" seemed to give encouragement to the home players. They played a splendid game and defeated the Brooklyns with ease.
> The spectators were high in their praise of Galvin, and the opinion now seems to be that the local players will speedily move forward in the score for the championship.[17]

Allegheny won the game, 5–3. The next day, before 2,500 fans, Galvin gave up eight hits as Allegheny defeated Brooklyn again, this time 6–5. He was two-for-two, a promising start. At the time Galvin arrived in Allegheny, it held third place in the American Association, one win ahead of Louisville, two games back of Cincinnati, and ten back of St. Louis. Galvin faced the latter club July 26 and gave up eight hits while his fielders made an equal number of errors as Allegheny was downed, 8–1.

Allegheny wanted Galvin back on its team to work in tandem with lefty Ed "Cannonball" Morris, who was proving to be an effective ace for them. Morris was among the players brought in from Columbus and was becoming one of the top hurlers in the American Association. Frank Mountain, the other pitcher from the Buckeyes, had been hurt. A 23-game winner in 1884, Mountain won only five in Allegheny before being disabled. As a result, Morris was carrying the lion's share of the workload and manager Horace Phillips was looking for help. With Galvin on board, Morris continued to excel. On August 2, in the finale of a three-game series in Louisville, Morris struck out 15 Colonels, an impressive performance. He gave up nine hits, however, and Louisville took the game, 4–1. An inch shorter than Galvin but far less bulky, the durable and dependable Morris, 22, was having a banner year. He led the AA in innings pitched (581), and was also first in complete games (63), strikeouts (298), and shutouts (seven). He was second in wins with 39. Morris stayed with Allegheny until 1889 and amassed 171 wins in his seven-year career. Morris and Galvin got along well and may have crossed paths in San Francisco, where Morris played in 1879 and 1881.

Pitcher Ed Morris became a fast friend of Galvin in the latter part of his career. When Galvin fell on hard times after baseball, Morris hired him to work in his saloon and helped him with accommodation (Library of Congress).

10. The Little Steam Engine Changes Gears   131

Galvin had a short stint there early in 1880 before making his escape for the East. Galvin and Morris alternated appearances at Allegheny, which was referred to increasingly in sporting publications like the *New York Clipper* as Pittsburgh. The team held onto third place, just a couple of games behind Cincinnati. Fourth-place Louisville appeared in Allegheny City for a four-game series that began August 21 and Allegheny took them all to keep the Colonels at bay. In the final game on August 26, Galvin's arm gave out in the second inning and he easily surrendered five hits before backup Pete Meegan came in to salvage a 7–5 victory. It appeared to be a dislocation of some sort suffered by Galvin, the first serious injury suffered by the tireless 28-year-old. Some observers feared the worst, even Galvin, as indicated in this *Sporting Life* report:

> Galvin feels very keenly his disqualification and said to the writer, "I am afraid that I am gone." Just give a few moments' consideration to this man. For ten years he has been, in his different engagements, the hardest working pitcher in the profession. No wonder that his muscles and nerves demand a rest. The little steam engine, that's what he has been, but human nature must succumb sooner or later. Figure up, if you can, the muscular exertion which Galvin has used in his ten years of hard work. He is the oldest pitcher in the profession except Bobby Matthews [Bobby Mathews, of Philadelphia, 33], but the latter has always achieved his best success by head-work, where Jimmy has done it with terrific speed. The old Pittsburgh favorite has probably and simply worn out his muscles and nerves by his smashing work. Jimmy says, "Well, thank God, I have my trade as a gas fitter, which will give me good wages if I can't pitch any more ball." Every admirer of the game will be glad to hear that Galvin will not be left helpless. If ever a man who was knocked out deserves sympathy and a pension from the profession it is this man. However, Galvin's case is not hopeless. He has worked too hard for years. No ball player, or other athlete, can stand such a strain. He is excused from duty and until he gets right and goes to his home in Buffalo tonight to be treated by his own doctor, and while he will not attempt to do any more work this season, he hopes to be his old self next year.[18]

The outlook was not promising. Galvin had just returned to the Alleghenys and within a month had become disabled. But being the scrapper he was, Galvin wasn't about to abandon the season without seeing if rest was all he needed. He joined Allegheny on its trip to New York for a September 18 game against the Metropolitans, and manager Horace Phillips put him in the lineup. The home club jumped on Galvin quickly, however, scoring five runs in the first inning. After allowing three more runs in the fourth inning, he was pulled and replaced by little-used Charlie Eden. Galvin's arm had let him down and he was miserable about it. Allegheny bats swung into action, but it was too late and the lowly Mets won the game, 9–8. Galvin's season was over. It had been his worst year ever, the first time he hadn't won at least 20 games in a season, and particularly dismal after his 46-win years of 1883 and 1884. His record with Allegheny was three wins and seven losses. With Buffalo he had won 13 and lost 19, for a total of 16 victories in 1885. Galvin had pitched

284 innings in Buffalo, and 88⅓ in Allegheny, for a total of 372⅓. That was far short of the 632⅓ recorded in 1883, and 636⅓ in 1884. He may have been thinking his career was over when he spoke to *Sporting Life*. For many other pitchers with 10 years of nearly daily service, it would have been. But James Francis Galvin, the pitcher so good he had earned three nicknames, wasn't a quitter. He returned to his home and saloon in Buffalo for rest and recuperation.

With Galvin gone for the season, the Alleghenys finished third in the American Association standings, winning 56 games and losing 55, putting them a distant 22½ games behind the champion St. Louis Browns. One interesting late-season wrinkle saw Philadelphia pitcher Bobby Mathews (he of even greater seniority than Galvin) strike out four Alleghenys batters in the seventh inning of a September 30 game, two of them managing to get to first base on errors. This was the first time a pitcher needed an extra strikeout to retire a side. Mathews also gave up five hits but held on for a 5–2 win.

In late October, seeds were sown for yet another professional league shortly after Chicago captured the National League championship and St. Louis took the American Association pennant. The National League and American Association set salary caps of $2,000 for players, a move that mobilized lingering resentment about the reserve clause and how professional baseball was minimizing the role and importance of players as its magnates continued to seek higher profits. John Montgomery Ward was among nine New York Giants, including former Bison "Orator" Jim O'Rourke, who banded together to form the Brotherhood of Professional Base Ball Players. Its goal was "to protect and benefit its members collectively and individually, to promote a high standard of professional conduct, and to advance the interests of the 'National Game.'"[19] Ward was named president. A native Pennsylvanian, he had begun his career as a pitcher in 1877 with the Athletics before moving to Providence and the Grays, where he won 47 games to lead the National League in 1879. Ward's pitching arm gave out and he joined the Giants in 1883, where he switched to shortstop and second base. After attending Columbia University law school on a part-time basis, Ward graduated with honors in 1885. He brought his legalistic mind to bear on the problems facing baseball and challenged the validity of the hated reserve clause. Within months, chapters of the Brotherhood were established by players in Detroit, Chicago, Kansas City, Boston, St. Louis, Philadelphia and Indianapolis. Within a year, the Brotherhood could boast it had 107 members, including Hoss Radbourn, Connie Mack, King Kelly and Dan Brouthers. During that first year, it secretly signed up members and proceeded carefully to seek a new deal for players. It would take some time before it became a force with which the National League and American Association were forced to deal.

The tenth annual convention of the National League was held November

10. The Little Steam Engine Changes Gears

18 and 19 in New York, and one of the key decisions facing delegates was the question of Detroit's purchase of the Buffalo club and the "Big Four." Boston, New York and Philadelphia had designs on several of the players and opposed the sale. A committee of neutral directors, including Albert Goodwill Spalding of Chicago, was assigned the task of assessing the situation and recommending a course of action. After six hours of deliberations spread over two days, the committee backed Detroit's claim and by majority vote the convention also endorsed it.[20] It marked the first sale of a franchise in National League history. The decision would produce an immediate improvement in the fortunes for Detroit and fatter pay packets for Dan Brouthers, Deacon White, Hardy Richardson and newlywed Jack Rowe. The following August, *The Sporting News* revealed salaries paid the men in the 1886 season, which were among the highest in baseball. Brouthers received $4,500, the same as second baseman Fred Dunlap, Richardson was paid $4,300, Rowe $4,000 and White, $3,500.[21] The money aspect may not have been quite as important to Rowe, as the others, given his "rich and beautiful" new wife.

For Pud Galvin, the off-season was a time to tend bar in Buffalo and hope that his arm would heal. He was determined to earn his money and justify the faith his old club in Allegheny City had placed in him. The Little Steam Engine was anxious to forget his injury-riddled season of 1885 and get back on track.

11

Back in the Smoky City

When Pud Galvin returned to Allegheny City, he reconnected with the club's founder, Denny McKnight. Their relationship went back to 1877 when McKnight was among the club owners who established the International Association and a young Galvin was his pitching prodigy for the Allegheny club. In 1882, McKnight resurrected first-rate professional baseball in his city with a new Allegheny club, then helped to establish the American Association and became its president. During a difficult 1883 season when Allegheny won only 31 games and lost 67, to place seventh, he resigned the club presidency and was replaced by E. C. Converse. The 1884 campaign was even worse for the Alleghenys and they finished 11th in the expanded American Association with only 30 wins. McKnight tried his hand at managing the struggling club to see if he could make a difference. He couldn't. One of four managers who also failed that year, he was in charge while it won four games and lost eight, before "Hustling Horace" Phillips took over for the last 33 games. McKnight stayed on as AA president throughout, but in 1885 he faced several difficult issues just as the loop was becoming a healthy organization and a viable alternative to the National League. Late in the year, Washington had grown tired of waiting for the National League to respond to its bid for membership and applied to the American Association. At the time, the National League was pondering whether to continue with six teams for 1886 or to replace Buffalo and Providence, both of which had disbanded. But the National League took far too long to decide to suit Washington, so it turned to the American Association. With Washington eager to join, the AA felt it could take another look at a plan by the new owner of the Metropolitans to move from Manhattan to nearby Staten Island. McKnight, in particular, felt the AA needed to keep a toehold in the city and the club should remain in Manhattan. In December, he and his board voted to oust the Mets and replace them with Washington. The new Mets owner replied with an injunction to halt any such eviction. Faced with this challenge, McKnight insisted the AA was not a corporate body, so it had no legal status and could not be pressured this way. A Philadelphia court ruled otherwise, and the Mets were allowed to remain in the Association. While this legal wrangling was underway, other clubs began pilfering players from the Mets, fully expecting the club to fold upon eviction. Brooklyn signed two players, but after the court ruling in favor of the Metropolitans, McKnight intervened to have them returned to the Mets. In the end, the Metropolitans remained in the American Association, while Washington and Kansas City signed on with the National League to fill the openings there.[1]

McKnight had been in the spotlight during the controversy and was subject to criticism from several quarters. He soon landed in even more trouble. The St. Louis Browns decided to sell second baseman Sam Barkley because of his frequent clashes with manager Charlie Comiskey. Allegheny offered $750 for him, but Baltimore upped that to $1,000. Barkley signed a contract with the Orioles, but when the Alleghenys matched the $1,000 offer, Barkley signed with them. McKnight intervened and advised Barkley that his contract with Baltimore was not binding, so he should do the decent thing and remain with St. Louis for the time being at least. Baltimore protested loudly and so did Allegheny, the latter threatening to quit the Association if Barkley was awarded to Baltimore. McKnight found himself in a tough spot as Association president and Allegheny founder and still a shareholder of the club. A special Association meeting was convened to resolve the issue and it included a lawyer from Louisville who was a part-owner of the Colonels of that city. It was ruled that Barkley would be suspended for a year for signing two contracts, but in 1887 he would report to Allegheny. In response, Barkley challenged the suspension order and obtained an injunction from a Pittsburgh court that would prevent any American Association team from playing Allegheny, unless he was on their roster. (By April, the matter was resolved with Barkley allowed to play the upcoming season in Allegheny, which then compensated Baltimore with a first baseman, while St. Louis kept the $1,000 Allegheny paid for Barkley's rights.)

Faced with this legal morass and his conflicts throughout the case, McKnight was asked to resign at a special board meeting held March 20 that he did not attend.[2] He stood accused of partisanship and neglect of duty, and the only vote supporting him came from Allegheny. His failure to deal with the issue impartially, as well as his absence from several important meetings and his delay in acting, had sealed his fate. But McKnight wasn't about to go peacefully. He refused to turn over his papers to his successor, secretary Wheeler Wyckoff, and created an embarrassing standoff. McKnight insisted that he needed them to defend himself, but he eventually relented. He was also stripped of his financial interest in the Allegheny team, which was transferred to William A. Nimick, president of club since 1885, and manager Horace Phillips. He was out of baseball. Nimick, president of the Pittsburgh

Transfer Company, offered McKnight a position overseeing his cattle operation in New Mexico, which he accepted. The prospect of dealing with cowboys must have seemed like a relief for McKnight after dealing with difficult baseball players and owners who couldn't stop signing contracts and hiring lawyers. By 1891, McKnight was back in Pittsburgh and Allegheny City, but he had nothing to do with baseball.[3] He died in 1900, at age 52.

Denny McKnight had been a key figure in the game for an important decade in its history during which he organized two teams and helped establish two professional leagues. McKnight had been owner and president of the Allegheny clubs and was president of the American Association from its inception as the rebel "beer and whisky league," as it grew to become a respected alternative to the National League. Early on, McKnight had also discovered a 19-year-old hurler named Pud Galvin who was just beginning to make a name for himself while pitching ball some 600 miles away in St. Louis. McKnight spotted talent in a young man who would become one of the greats in the game. But while his contributions to baseball had been many, and significant, McKnight's fall was swift.

For 1886, rule changes were made that had an impact on pitchers. The pitching box was lengthened one foot to seven feet, and pitchers were no longer required to have both feet planted on the ground to begin their delivery. This meant pitchers could dance around as part of their windup, or get a short running start. The line from which the ball had to be delivered remained at 50 feet. The National League kept the number of balls before a walk could be issued at seven, but the American Association reduced it to six. Overall, the rule changes favored pitchers and led to a sudden surge in strikeouts. There were no complaints from Allegheny pitchers, who, aside from Morris and Galvin, included two newcomers as relief arms: rookie Jim Handiboe, 19, and John Hofford, 23. The latter was back for his second year with the club. For a second year, former Columbus hurler Frank Mountain would not be a factor, pitching only two games and losing both.

Allegheny spring training took the team to Georgia and Kentucky during March and early April, with Morris and Hofford sharing most of the pitching duties during exhibition games. Galvin did not appear in the box. The home opener was April 14, when 5,000 fans turned out to Recreation Park on a warm and sunny day to see the Alleghenys clash with the newly strengthened Detroit Wolverines. Ed Morris pitched for the home club and struggled with the big bats he faced, particularly Brouthers and Richardson. The former had two doubles and the latter connected for two hits, the second of which brought Brouthers home in the eighth inning. In all, Morris surrendered nine hits as Detroit blanked Allegheny, 3–0. The following day, Galvin appeared, but not in the box. After a 15-minute dispute between the clubs about appointing a suitable umpire, Galvin was selected to do the job. Hofford was pounded hard for nine hits as the Wolverines won again, this time 8–1. No complaints were registered about Galvin's work. St. Louis opened its season at home April 18 by defeating Allegheny and Morris, 8–4. The following day, Galvin took the ball, but his support crew fielded poorly and catcher Dan Sullivan had trouble catching him. Sullivan would not be back. The Browns took the game, 10–3.

Before the month was out, Hofford and Morris lost several more times, as slopping fielding continuing to dog Allegheny, dropping it to last place. On May 1, at home, Allegheny lost an 11-inning struggle with St. Louis, with Morris pitching, while Galvin took the win on May 3 in a 12-inning, 7–6 victory over the Browns. Galvin pitched on May 8 as Allegheny downed Cincinnati, 9–6, and again on May 12 when he sprained his leg running to first base in a 9–7 victory by the Reds. By the end of the month that witnessed few appearances by Galvin, Allegheny had risen to fourth place. Aside from his injured leg, running had become more of a chore for "the little steam engine" once known for his catlike reflexes and agility. His exertion was accompanied by huffing and puffing as he churned around the bases. Galvin was approaching 200 pounds on his five-foot-eight frame, and newspaper accounts had begun to take note of his expanding girth. For instance, after pitching a strong game in a June 2, 6–1 win over the Philadelphia Athletics, the *Pittsburgh Commercial Gazette* headlined its account this way: "Gentle Jeems. The Falstaffian Pitcher Beats the Athletics."[4] He would see many more barbs about his physique in the press before his playing days were over.

By the time Allegheny blanked Cincinnati, 3–0, on June 7, it had risen to second place in the AA standings. Hofford had been injured and Galvin was seeing more action. It was suggested that Galvin had some lucky charms in the pitching box with him that day, as he manhandled Reds batters and easily picked off their base runners. "Galvin pitched in his old Buffalo form. He seemed to have renewed his youth," it was reported.[5] He was helped by some aggressive work on the base paths by his own runners. Galvin's bat was in good form on June 13 during a game played in St. Louis before 10,000 fans. He managed to collect three of the Allegheny hits off Browns pitcher Bob Caruthers that day, but St. Louis prevailed by a score of 2–0. Galvin pitched well in a June 16 loss of 1–0 to St. Louis, striking out ten batters and keeping runners pinned to their bases, in fear of his pickoff move. Allegheny slipped to fourth place briefly but bounced back into second by winning both games in a doubleheader against the struggling Baltimore club on July 5. In the first game, pitched by Galvin and played before 7,000 Pittsburgh fans, Allegheny won in a 15–1 romp. The afternoon game, pitched by Morris, who was becoming one of the top pitchers of the American Association, produced a home win of 13–2.

For his part, Galvin was no slouch as he worked alongside Morris. As

Galvin warmed to his task, the fans in Allegheny City and Pittsburgh warmed to him. He threw a two-hitter at Brooklyn on July 8 as Allegheny won, 8–1. His performance drew praise from one of the Pittsburgh papers:

> There are now many base-ball legends connected with Jimmy Galvin's career as a pitcher. All of them are interesting, and some of them startling. The performance of "Jeems" yesterday will add one more chapter to the many which "The Gentle" has stored away in his phenomenal head. James recalled the days of his youth yesterday and twirled the sphere in a way that not only puzzled the Brooklyn visitors but caused the 4,000 spectators to cheer loudly.[6]

Brooklyn continued to nip at the heels of Allegheny, which clung to second place, and managed to defeat Galvin, 6–3, in Brooklyn on July 25. Allegheny stayed in New York for a three-game series with the Metropolitans, winning 8–1 on July 27 as Galvin pitched, and again, 11–2, on July 29, as Jim Handiboe was the given the ball. In the third game, on July 31, Galvin was tagged for two triples and a double as the Mets won, 7–6. On his day off, July 30, Galvin took in a ball game at the Polo Grounds, where the New York Giants of the National League were playing the deciding game in a three-game series with the St. Louis Maroons. Their game the previous day had been marked by controversy about calls made by umpire John Gaffney. At one point, the veteran Gaffney called a St. Louis runner safe at second base, "to the surprise of everyone," as the *New York Clipper* reported. Not long afterward, Gaffney missed a double play, calling a batter out who was tagged when the New York catcher dropped the ball on the third strike, but missing the fact that the catcher had first touched home plate to force out the runner coming home from third base. A safe hit then brought home two runs that won the game, 5–4, for St. Louis, to the dismay of the Mets. "For a time it looked as if the umpire would be roughly handled, but better judgment prevailed and he left the field unmolested." Gaffney refused to umpire the July 30 game because of the way he was verbally abused the previous day. Someone spotted Galvin in the stands, and the Giants and Maroons prevailed upon him to act as umpire. His work was found satisfactory in the 10-inning contest that New York won, 2–1.[7]

It wasn't all work for Galvin and his teammates during their time in New York. Likely during this same late-July stand, they were caught red-handed as they indulged in some diversions the metropolis had to offer. *The Sporting News* carried a story later in the year in which their team manager, "Hustling Horace" Phillips, recalled that Galvin and his mates had plenty of energy to spare—and perhaps money.

> Horace Phillips, during his recent visit here gave a little glimpse into his managerial experience by relating a story. Said he: "One night last summer, at the Grand Central Hotel in New York City, I caught the members of my team in a neat little trick by which they expected to beat me. Before the clock had struck eleven all of the players were in the hotel.

11. Back in the Smoky City

In a few minutes they started for their rooms to retire. Shortly afterwards I sent a bell-boy up, and he returned with a report that all of them were in bed. As it was a nice, warm evening I concluded to go outside and smoke a cigar before retiring. I drew up a chair and was propped comfortably against the building. I was preparing to enjoy myself when I discovered dark objects coming down the side of the house. I could not make out what they were at first, but it did not take me long to appreciate the fact that the members of my team were trying to make a sneak on me by coming down to the ground on the fire escapes. Fat Jimmie Galvin was the first of the crowd to reach terra firma and as he straightened himself up I stepped out and confronted him. Jimmie took his detection very philosophically.

"'How much will it cost us?' he asked.

"'You are fined $10 each for this trick,' was my reply.

"'Well, it goes,' said Jimmie. 'We're bound for a dance in the Bowery, and a little thing like that won't stop us.'

"They had their fun, but they had to pay for it," was the hustler's parting retort.[8]

Allegheny faltered in August and slipped to third place behind Louisville, which had edged past Brooklyn. By August 30, Galvin's club had regained second, one game ahead of Louisville and nine games back of St. Louis. On October 8 at home, Morris pitched a one-hitter as Allegheny blanked the Metropolitans, 7–0. It marked his 12th shut out of the season, a record for a left-hander. When the American Association season ended on October 15, Allegheny had captured second place, its best finish in its five seasons in the loop. St. Louis, which took the pennant 12 games ahead of Allegheny, went on to defeat the National League champion Chicago White Stockings in the world championship. Chicago had earlier held off the heavy-hitting and much-improved Detroit Wolverines to take the NL flag.

Ed Morris led Allegheny pitchers with 41 wins and 20 losses, for the best record in the AA. Galvin pitched 49 complete games, winning 29 and losing 21, a big improvement from 1885. Galvin had two shutouts, while Morris recorded an Association best of 12. Galvin pitched 434⅔ innings, while Morris amassed 555⅓. As a hitter, Galvin far exceeded Morris with a batting average of .253, compared to Morris' feeble .167. The only other pitchers on the roster to win games were Jim Handiboe, with seven, and John Hofford with three.

In November, a joint rules committee of the National League and American Association convened and made many far-reaching and important changes. Among them was the decision that five balls would draw a walk and four strikes were needed to make an out. Batters were no longer allowed to call for a "high" or "low" pitch, and the strike zone was clarified as being between the top of the shoulder and the knee. The pitcher's box was reduced in size, and the pitching distance was increased from 50 feet. Pitchers were allowed to take only one step forward while making their delivery and were required to have one foot on the back line of the box, which was 55 feet, six inches from home plate. The coin toss was eliminated to determine which team batted last, with the home club entitled to choose. And a batter was entitled to first base if struck by a pitch. The changes were implemented by both leagues.

In another major development, Allegheny withdrew from the American Association and immediately applied to the National League. For some time, directors had been unhappy at the treatment of their former president Denny McKnight on the Barkley issue and no longer felt any loyalty to the rebel league he had helped establish. For its part, the National League was pleased to find a replacement for the Kansas City Cowboys, a club in the throes of disintegration. At the league convention November 18 in Chicago, delegates unanimously approved the application from Allegheny and began steps to expel Kansas City. President William Nimick was elected a league director and he seemed to get on well with Chicago owner and NL pillar Al Spalding.

It has been suggested that the National League welcomed Allegheny by allowing it to acquire two players from Chicago and one from the disbanded St. Louis Maroons to help bolster its roster. Left fielder Abner Dalrymple was released by Chicago, and first baseman Alex McKinnon came from the Maroons. In April, Chicago sold pitcher Jim McCormick to Allegheny for $2,500, while the White Stockings acquired in exchange Allegheny's California pitching prospect, George Van Haltren. Van Haltren, billed as the "California Wonder" for his work on the West Coast, was tending to his ailing mother and didn't join the White Stockings until late June after she passed away. McCormick had won 31 games in 1886, but captain Cap Anson and owner Spalding had soured on him after Chicago lost the world championship series to the St. Louis Browns. For the coming season, the White Stockings would rely on workhorse John Clarkson, a future Hall of Famer, to carry most of their pitching duties, backed by Mark Baldwin. Dalrymple, a left-handed hitter, once wielded a powerful bat and remained a solid outfielder. McKinnon had a .301 batting average with St. Louis and much was expected from him at the plate. With these three additions, along with a few others, manager Horace Phillips felt confident his club would do well in its first foray into the National League.[9]

To replace its founding Allegheny club, the American Association admitted the Cleveland Blues to the loop, but the loss of the Pittsburgh nine, its second strongest team, would be keenly felt.

Allegheny played its first National League home opener on April 30 at Recreation Park, welcoming the reigning champion Chicago White Stockings. Legend has it that sometime before the game, catcher Fred Carroll's pet monkey died and he buried it somewhere near home plate. The animal had followed Carroll everywhere, including the clubhouse, and had become a sort of team mascot. The monkey, the story went, was interred with honors by the players. No newspaper accounts of the event have been found, suggesting it was done surreptitiously—or not at all. There was plenty of time for "monkey business" among the players, however, because rain delayed the opening game for two days. Regardless, the story persists and has been passed down in Pittsburgh baseball folklore.[10] A crowd estimated at from 9,000 to 10,000 crammed into the ballpark and witnessed a game as good as any ever played in the city, the *Pittsburgh Post* reported.[11] Early in the game, Chicago captain Cap Anson complained that Galvin was illegally lifting his right foot during his delivery, contrary to the new rules, but he found no support from umpire Joe Quest and didn't rattle Galvin. The first Allegheny hitter was newly acquired leftfielder Abner Dalrymple, and he victimized his old teammate John Clarkson for a triple. He also scored the first run for the home team. Galvin kept Chicago off the scoreboard until the seventh inning, when Anson singled, advanced on a double and raced home on a long fly ball out. The final score was 6–2 for the home nine, sending the large crowd home happy. So, too were the directors, who saw game receipts of $4,500. Gamblers were not at all pleased, having bet heavily on a Chicago win.

The Detroit Wolverines came to town for a series of games that began May 2. The highly touted Detroiters had won three games already. Galvin pitched and held the big bats at bay, while catcher Fred Carroll hit for the cycle in the first game, won 8–3 by Allegheny. The following day, with Morris pitching, the Big Four and their teammates belted 14 hits as Detroit breezed to a 14–5 win. On May 4, with Galvin in the box, the Alleghenys were edged, 9–8, in 11 innings. Morris was scheduled to pitch on May 9 but refused to do so, and Bill Bishop took his place in a 10–3 Allegheny loss. On May 10, with Galvin pitching, Detroit won, 6–4, but needed 13 innings to do so. Bishop took the ball again for the concluding game of the series on May 11 and was badly rattled in an 18–2 Allegheny loss.

The withdrawal by Morris was noteworthy and immediately the subject of conjecture. He was laid off, without pay, for three weeks. It was said his arm was lame, or that he had simply been afraid to face the heavy-hitting Wolverines and worried that losing to them repeatedly would hurt his record. Some said the lefty was struggling with the new pitching rules that limited his traditional windup as he delivered the ball. There was talk that he would be fined by manager Phillips.[12] Morris did not appear in the pitching box again until May 30, Decoration Day, when Allegheny defeated Philadelphia, 6–4, in the second game of a doubleheader at home. Galvin had to shoulder more work during the layoff, but was doing well. In mid–June, *The Sporting News* compared the work of Galvin and McCormick. "Jimmy Galvin is holding his own with the best of them and is a little dandy under the new rules," it said. "McCormick is pitching good ball for the Smoky City lads, but he receives not the least support from the fielders."[13]

Morris' struggles in the National League may have been connected to his drinking. Horace Phillips had already fined him for doing so, and made Morris sign an agreement that he would abstain from drink or forfeit two weeks of pay if he broke the pledge. Things came to a head when Allegheny appeared in Philadelphia for a doubleheader on July 4. The Phillies won the first game, 9–5, while Allegheny took the second one, 8–4. McCormick pitched the first game and Galvin got the win in the second. Play by both teams was poor.

Management for both clubs had seen enough and suspected heavy drinking was responsible for their dismal records. The Phillies were sitting in fifth place with 25 wins, and Allegheny was sixth with 20. The Philadelphia manager, Harry Wright, and president Al Reach decided to hire detectives to see what their players were up to. They shared their plan and the detectives with Allegheny manager Horace Phillips and president William Nimick. The private eyes confirmed that four Phillies had been drinking on the night of July 4 and they faced being released by management—anxious to send a message to the remaining players. Two of the Phillies never went to bed at all, the detectives reported. The following night, the detectives focused their interest on several Allegheny players who slipped out of their hotel after dark. Two shadowed Morris, outfielder Carroll and team captain Tom Brown, the centerfielder. Another kept his eye on McCormick, shortstop Bill Kuehne, third baseman Art Whitney and second baseman Pop Smith. The detectives lost track of the latter foursome, but Morris, Carroll and Brown received close scrutiny as they entered a saloon and drank their beer as one of the sleuths parked beside them. The trio moved to another saloon for more beer, where another detective settled alongside. After three drinks, the trio returned to their hotel, where Carroll excused himself and went to bed. Morris and Brown sauntered into a billiard hall where they continued to drink as they played. *The Sporting News* reported that "Every time either made a brilliant shot they ordered beer. Pitcher Morris was a good player and made a number of brilliant shots while the detectives stood in Jayne street, a little dark thorough fare [sic], and looked through the windows of the billiard room at the games."[14] One of the detectives fetched manager Phillips from the hotel to witness the scene. He arrived just as Morris and Brown were downing yet another beer. Phillips sent for president Nimick so he, too, could see the pair. The following day, nursing a hangover, Morris allowed 15 hits and walked eight Phillies as Allegheny lost, 9–2.

The Sporting News, which carried on its front page details of the latenight sleuthing by the detectives, reported that a well-known Pittsburgh man staying at the same hotel had asked president Nimick what the problem was with his pitcher, Morris. "'Oh, he is just getting over a drunk,' was the reply. President Nimick added that until the 'boozers' were weeded out of the club the team would not win ball games…. It is said that Capt. Brown is to be released, and that several others are to go." On July 14, it was announced that Morris had been sold to the New York Giants for $2,000. About the same time, the *New York Clipper* reported: "Morris of the Pittsburghs has pitched in eight games in which his club has been defeated, and in only two in which they have won. In fact, he has been a complete failure in the box against League batsmen."[15] By the end of the month, the same publication reported that the deal for Morris had fallen through. "Morris's success against Philadelphia July 22 [a 4–3 win in which he allowed five hits] caused the Pittsburgh management to reconsider their previous action, especially as the local patrons made a great pressure on the club to prevent the departure of Morris."[16] For his part, Brown was traded to Indianapolis a few weeks later.

Tragedy struck the Alleghenys that same month. During the series in Philadelphia, first baseman Alex McKinnon became ill after playing in the morning game on July 4. He felt worse that night, while some of his mates prowled the saloons of Philadelphia, and the following day was sent to his home in Boston to recover. His doctor, wife and mother tended to him, but he died on July 24, a victim of typhoid fever. He was 30. McKinnon had been a positive addition to the club, a non-drinker and very popular with his teammates, who wore black crepe in his memory. His death cast a pall over the struggling club, and the loss of his bat was significant. His batting average had been .340. Phillips had to juggle his infield by moving the .224-hitting second baseman Sam Barkley to fill the sudden opening at first base.[17]

Galvin managed to pull off some wins his club needed and carried the bulk of the workload, but overall, the Alleghenys continued to struggle. On August 27 in Boston, a day after Morris pitched well in a 9–8 loss to the Beaneaters, Galvin was bombarded for 17 hits, including three home runs and three triples, as Boston batters had their way with him. Jocko Fields spelled him for the fifth inning after 21 runs had already been scored. After Boston scored three more runs, Galvin returned to the box. The final tally was an embarrassing 28–14 win for Boston, the worst defeat ever suffered by Pittsburgh's club. Rightfielder King Kelly and shortstop Ezra Sutton each scored six times, a major league record by two teammates in a single game. Kelly also hit for the cycle. Fielding by the visitors was described as "abominable," so it wasn't a bad day just for Galvin. Shortstop Bill Kuehne, first baseman Barkley and third baseman Art Whitney were singled out for play that was "worse than amateurs."[18] By August 29, Allegheny was in sixth place in the National League standings with 38 wins, two ahead of Washington. Detroit and Chicago were locked in a tight battle for first place, while New York and Philadelphia were just behind them.

On September 28, in one of Alleghenys' last games of the disappointing 1887 season, Abner Dalrymple pulled a coup in Chicago against his former team. A hitter once widely feared, who had led the National League with 11 home runs in 1885, Dalrymple had been struggling ever since. His batting average would be .212 for the year. This day, however, the leftfielder hit his only two home runs of the season in the first game of a doubleheader, both off John Clarkson, the league's leading pitcher. The first came in the eighth inning to tie the game, 5–5, and the second in the tenth to win the game, 6–5. It was a statement that no doubt pleased Dalrymple—and Galvin, who picked up the win.

Detroit won the National League pennant in the closest championship race yet. With 79 wins and 45 losses, the Wolverines finished 3½ games ahead of the Phillies and 6½ games up on the White Stockings. Allegheny was sixth, 24 games back. It had been a forgettable season of 69 losses for Pittsburgh's representative. None of its batters finished in the top five of any hitting category. With 28 wins, Galvin was tied for fourth among pitchers. He was third in innings pitched, with 440⅔, fourth in complete games with 47, and had the fifth lowest on-base percentage at .299. Chicago's Clarkson led in most pitching categories, including wins with 38. Detroit went on to win the world championship, defeating the American Association champions, St. Louis.

The joint rules committee of the National League and American Association did away with the four-strikes-for-an-out rule, reverting to three, and did away with the controversial one-

In 1887, Pud Galvin led his club with 28 wins, 18 less than in his sparkling seasons of 1883 and 1884 with Buffalo. It was the beginning of a slow decline for the hurler, who would eventually be credited with 365 wins. In 1888 he recorded his 300th career win (Library of Congress).

season practice of scoring walks as hits. The latter had helped make batters look more successful than necessary and drew widespread criticism. The number of balls for a walk was kept at five. The American Association voted to match the National League by doubling its admission to 50 cents, but by the following August, when it saw the declining attendance that produced, the price of admission returned to 25 cents.

Pud Galvin had proven to be a workhorse yet again as Morris, the team's highest paid player at $2,900, had stumbled, picking up only 14 wins. Meanwhile, McCormick, who was paid $2,500, had also failed to live up to expectations, with 13 wins. McCormick's last appearance was October 7, when he was hit freely by Chicago, but Allegheny still managed a 9–7 win. Soon afterward, McCormick announced his resignation from baseball and said he was returning to his home in New Jersey. No amount of persuasion from manager Horace Phillips could get him to change his mind.[19] A request that McCormick take a cut in pay may have contributed to his decision. At age 30, McCormick's 10-year career came to an end. He had pitched in 492 games, winning 265 times and losing 214. Twice McCormick led the National League with wins, 45 in 1880 and 36 in 1882.

The hunt was on for another pitcher because Allegheny management knew the Little Steam Engine, whose salary had been reduced to a modest $2,100 for the 1887 campaign, couldn't run forever. Galvin had won more than 20 games in nine of his 11 previous seasons in the International Association, the American Association and the National League, to become one of baseball's most reliable and durable performers. At age 30, he had already outlasted most pitchers who were playing when he joined the professional ranks, and many more had come and gone while he continued to perform at a high level.

The question was, how much longer could Pud Galvin last?

12

Making History
Amid the Gloom

Allegheny started 1888 off with a bang, acquiring second baseman Fred Dunlap from the Detroit Wolverines and making him the highest-paid player in baseball. Considered by many the top second baseman in the game, Dunlap, 29, was signed for a salary of $5,000 with a $2,000 signing bonus. His first club had been Cleveland's National League entry in 1880, the Blues, from which he jumped to St. Louis in the Union Association for 1884, with a salary believed to be as high as $3,600. While barely able to read or write, Dunlap was good with numbers and negotiated lucrative contracts throughout his career. He led the UA with a .412 batting average, and in home runs (13), hits (185) and runs (160). He was sold to Detroit by St. Louis (by then in the National League) midway through the 1886 season with guarantees of $4,500 a year for each of the following two years. In 1887, however, he broke a bone in his leg in a collision with Wolverines' rightfielder Sam Thompson and didn't return to the lineup until September. No play meant no pay in those days, so it cost him money. When Dunlap returned, he was pushed hard by team manager Bill Watkins as Detroit won the National League pennant and then the world championship over St. Louis.[1] He grew to hate Watkins, so the Wolverines sold his contract to Pittsburgh for about $5,000, although the *Pittsburgh Press* suggested the amount was closer to $4,000.[2]

Seeing that manager Horace Phillips and president William Nimick were prepared to pry open the vault for Dunlap, Pud Galvin and catcher Doggie Miller were determined to fatten their own pay packets for the upcoming season. Miller held out for several weeks, signing for $2,500 by the middle of February. Galvin sought a salary of $3,000 with $1,000 as an advance. The National League opposed paying advances and the club didn't like them much either. After more dickering, it was agreed Galvin would receive a salary of $3,000 with a $600 advance. It was reported that he received another $1,000 under a personal agreement.[3] Pittsburgh was doing well financially at the time, and club secretary Al Scandrett was quoted as saying he felt the franchise was worth $40,000, with player salaries totaling $30,000.[4] But Galvin, after his 1880 ploy of hanging out in California to get Buffalo to sweeten its offer, had lost his taste for hardball tactics. Over the years, Galvin had proven to be a poor manager of money, and advances meant a lot to him. Even though his salary was many times that of an ordinary workingman, he invariably sought money from team management to tide him over the winter months. Often, club owners learned, they could modify his salary demand by advancing part of it. By now, advances were becoming even more important to Galvin as he and his wife Bridget had five mouths to feed in their growing household. With his signing, Galvin and Miller began training indoors, and Galvin admitted that he wanted to shed some of his 187 pounds. Both he and Miller were looking to drop about 20 pounds. It was noted that Galvin's weight was still below the 212 pounds it was said he carried on his compact frame when he arrived from Buffalo.[5]

Among the newcomers who were early to sign contracts were Billy Sunday and Al Maul. Sunday, 25, an outfielder, had played with Chicago for five seasons and in 1887 had a batting average of .291. A speedster on the base paths and in tracking down fly balls, Sunday was from the same hometown in Iowa as Chicago captain Cap Anson, who had discovered him. He was a decent, clean-living church-goer who rarely drank. The latter trait appealed to his new club, where players continued to abuse alcohol, gamble, and keep late hours. Sunday soon became a fan favorite, on the field and off, joining a local Presbyterian church and teaching Sunday school. After ending his playing days in 1891, the "Baseball Evangelist" became a crusader for temperance and a force in the prohibition movement. He became one of America's leading evangelists, drawing thousands to revival meetings throughout the Midwest and later in the East.[6]

Maul, 22, a pitcher, outfielder and first baseman, was obtained from Philadelphia, where he had earned four wins and two losses in 1887. He pitched only twice for his new club and lost both times, but he appeared in 72 other games as a utility player. In June, in a bid to further strengthen the Alleghenys, who were off to a slow start, Horace Phillips signed pitcher Harry Staley and first baseman Jake Beckley. Staley, 21, had started the season with the St. Louis Whites of the Western Association, while Beckley, 20, came from the same team and brought a powerful bat, sorely needed in a weak-hitting lineup. Beckley would bat .343 for Allegheny. He was beginning a 20-year career that saw him maintain a batting average of better than .300 in 13 seasons, with a lifetime average of .308. Beckley was inducted into the Baseball Hall of Fame in 1971 because of his outstanding offensive output, combined with 23,731 putouts, a record for a first baseman. It was estimated that the combined salaries of newcomers Staley and Beckley came to $4,500.[7]

Pud Galvin, pictured in 1887 with the Allegheny club. Outside newspapers and the National League, which it joined that year, preferred to call the club Pittsburgh (or, for a time, Pittsburg). A good fielder and outstanding pitcher, Galvin was not generally known for his work with a bat. His lifetime batting average stood at .201 (National Baseball Hall of Fame Library, Cooperstown, New York).

12. Making History Amid the Gloom 149

Rule changes were few for 1888 compared to previous seasons. Three strikes returned for an out, and bases on balls were no longer counted as hits. It still took five balls to earn a walk. The scales had been tipped back in favor of pitchers and as a result, batting averages dropped and earned run averages shrank for pitchers. National League hurlers recorded 3,998 strikeouts in 1888 compared to 2,837 in 1887.

Allegheny had a brilliant start to its 1888 campaign as it swept the 1887 league-champion Detroit Wolverines in a three-game opening series at home that began April 20. Morris pitched 12 innings for a 5-2 victory in the first game, Galvin pitched well in a 10-3 win in the second game, and Morris returned for the final game, holding off a late Wolverines push to win again, 10-9. Losses to Philadelphia and Boston quickly brought the club back to earth, and despite the additions made to the roster, the Allegheny club underperformed in the first month of the season. Galvin had a slow start and the team's batters also struggled. By May 28, Allegheny had won 11 games and lost 15, good for sixth place in the standings.

Following their return from Philadelphia, where their club lost three games in early June, with Galvin, Morris and Maul each picking up a loss, Allegheny president William Nimick and manager Horace Phillips decided further steps were needed to strengthen the team. Newcomers Cliff Carroll, an outfielder, and Hardie Henderson, a pitcher, had already been released after five games each, and Phillips was scouting talent in the Eastern League, Western League, and elsewhere. He was supported by Nimick, who, it was said, was tiring of the club presidency and might soon step down. But he was prepared to take bold moves while he remained at the helm. Nimick told *The Sporting News*, which asked him about rumors of further additions: "'I cannot tell you much now beyond the fact that I am negotiating for the release of twelve players, of whom five are pitchers.... All of the men I am trying for are being chosen for their ability as batters and base-runners.'"[8] Nimick, it was noted, "expressed dissatisfaction with Galvin's work." Soon afterward, pitcher Harry Staley and first baseman Jake Beckley donned Allegheny uniforms for the first time. The move paid immediate dividends in the hitting department at least. On June 20, in his debut, Beckley belted a triple and a double, and stole a base in a 5-0 win over Chicago. Staley first took the ball for his new club in the seventh inning of a June 23 game in the same series against the White Stockings, after Morris had been batted all over the field. The previous day the same thing had befallen Galvin in a 12-6 loss when he gave up 15 hits, 11 of them in one inning. In that game, Chicago was down, 2-1, in the sixth inning when Fred Pfeffer, their second baseman, drove in four runs off Galvin with an inside-the-park homer and a single. Staley was given the ball too late in the June 23 game to turn things around, however, as Chicago clobbered Allegheny, 12-1. Staley would see better days ahead, winning 12 and losing 12 by season's end.

The 12–6 pounding of Galvin by Chicago on June 22 prompted the *Pittsburgh Press* to ask on its front page, "Is Galvin Weakening?"

> Brave Jimmy Galvin's best and oldest friends in this city, the men who never before faltered in their allegiance, were at a loss this morning to explain the terrible punishment administered to his delivery at Chicago yesterday in the sixth inning. Some were of the opinion that the old man had temporarily lost his nerve, others went back into the dim misty past and resurrected the score of games to show that it was always Jim's habit to allow opposition to handle him pretty severely in one inning during the game, but that he almost invariably recovered soon afterward. While this may be true to a greater or less extent of Galvin's work in the past, it is generally admitted that it has been specially noticeable in his work this season that single innings of his non-effectiveness lost the game to the home club. On the other hand it is claimed with some show of justice that many of the games he has lost were owing to miserable support and the inability of the home boys to find the ball. Admitting this, Galvin has pitched at least half a dozen games since the opening of the season for whose loss he was personally responsible. It is said that the 11 runs made yesterday are the most made in one inning by any league club this season.[9]

Within days, the newspaper quoted Nimick as saying he had authorized Phillips "to strengthen the club at any cost, and if he does not, then it's about time we were looking for another manager."[10] The newspaper was not alone in wondering aloud if Galvin's time was over. Toward the end of June, after returning from a road trip when it managed only four wins in 19 games, Allegheny was still languishing in sixth place. On July 2, during practice at Recreation Park, team captain Fred Dunlap broke his jaw when struck by a ball, sidelining one of the team's best batters for several weeks.

The long-suffering Allegheny fans found something to cheer about July 13 when the home team made baseball history by winning both ends of a doubleheader, twice shutting out the Boston Beaneaters. The twin victories were especially sweet, coming just two days after Allegheny defeated Boston, 8–6, with Morris pitching. In the doubleheader, timely hitting was credited as a factor as the Beaneaters lost, 4–0, in the first game, with Staley taking the win. In the second contest, Galvin came within a whisker of pitching a perfect game. The only hit he allowed was to Boston third baseman Billy Nash, as he faced 28 batters in Allegheny's blanking of the visitors, 6–0. Sharp fielding by the home club, which committed no errors, contributed to Galvin's win. The three timely victories, especially the two whitewashes of one of the National League's leading clubs, prompted the *Pittsburgh Press* to jump back on the team's bandwagon. "The glory achieved by the Allies in twice shutting out the great Boston team in one day, should live for a while in the memories of those who have been loudest in detracting the boys," it said.[11]

The win was nice and so was the support from the press, but it became apparent that Allegheny had an unhappy clubhouse. Catcher Fred Carroll, *The Sporting News* reported on July 14, "admits that there is trouble in the

12. Making History Amid the Gloom

The 1888 Allegheny Club of Pittsburgh, posing at the South End grounds in Boston. Back row, from left: Jocko Fields, Fred Carroll, Billy Sunday, Al Maul, Pop Smith, Ned Hanlon, Abner Dalrymple. Front row, from left: Ed Morris, Bill Kuehne, Doggie Miller, Pud Galvin, Fred Dunlap (Library of Congress).

team, and that every man has a grievance and would like to get his release. He claims that the management's talk about releasing men causes it.... Dalrymple has asked for his release three times and been refused."[12]

A near-riot broke out after a July 16 home game against Philadelphia, when Allegheny lost, 1–0, on a reversed call by the umpire. Dan Casey, a Phillies pitcher, replaced the scheduled umpire named Daniels, who had taken ill and could not appear. The game was scoreless until the ninth inning, when Phillies centerfielder Ed Andrews came to the plate. Casey called him out on a third strike, then reversed his call to make it a fifth ball, thereby awarding him a walk. Andrews managed to work his way to third base, where it appeared Staley picked him off, but Casey ruled him safe. A hit by second baseman Ed Delahanty brought Andrews home for the winning run. The Alleghenys and their fans were outraged. Casey had to be escorted off the field by police, and spectators pelted the carriages of the retreating Phillies with stones. The next week, Allegheny lost both ends of a doubleheader in Detroit on July 24, by scores of 7–2 and 13–5, to propel the Wolverines into first place. With 26 wins and 38 losses, Allegheny continued to hold down sixth, with Indianapolis close behind.

During August, while his team played in Allegheny City, Chicago captain

Cap Anson, famous for his "kicking" and arguments with umpires, found some time to complain to a local paper about the pitching rules in the National League and specifically about Galvin, who had drawn his ire several times on the field.

> While talking about the irregularities of the present pitching rules, Capt. Anson expressed himself very emphatically that Pittsburgh had a pitcher who had made more balks than any other man in the league, and that Jimmy Galvin was the man. "Why," said he, "as matters stand now there is not a base runner in the country who will take chances in running home on Galvin with [catcher Doggie] Miller behind him. His delivery is plainly illegal under the existing rules. I have called the attention of every league umpire to this peculiarity, but they cannot see it in the same light that I do."
>
> "Gavie's all right," here broke in Horace Phillips. "You will find that he always has his shoulders squarely planted and the ball in sight. It's the peculiarity of the movement that deceives you. Why, nearly every prominent pitcher in the country has tried to copy that little nod of his before he throws the ball."[13]

The same day, Galvin pitched—with all his peculiarities—and Allegheny defeated the White Stockings, 12–8, in the first half of a doubleheader. Morris took the ball for the second game and the home club again won, this time 10–7. A week later in Chicago, Galvin yet again antagonized Anson with his peculiar ways in the pitcher's box during a game Allegheny won, 11–7. It marked the 11th victory for Allegheny in the 20 games they had played against Chicago.

Several days later, on September 5, Allegheny outfielder Billy Sunday made a solo trek to Chicago where he married Helen Thompson, whom he had met while playing in that city. After a wedding ceremony at the bride's home, the bridal party took in a Chicago-Detroit game, sitting in a box donated by White Stockings owner Al Spalding. Chicago second baseman Fred Pfeffer was Sunday's best man. The couple received a carving set from Spalding, a bronze clock from the directors of the Allegheny club, a writing desk and parlor stand from the Allegheny players, and a "handsome" folding bed from the White Stockings. It was hinted, perhaps wistfully, that Sunday might be returning to the Chicago club for next season.[14]

On September 15, Ed Morris, who was having a solid season, pitched his fourth consecutive shutout, a record that would stand until 1968. It came as Allegheny blanked the league-leading New York Giants, 1–0, at Recreation Park. Morris allowed six hits in a hard-fought contest in which the home club scored its only run on a wild throw by Giants third baseman Art Whitney. Morris' previous shutouts were 2–0 and 1–0 against the Phillies on September 8 and 10, and 2–0 against Washington on September 12. His streak ended on September 17, when he gave up three hits to New York in a 1–0 Allegheny loss. Morris won 29 games by the end of the season, good for fourth place in the league. He pitched the most complete games, 54, and was second in innings pitched with 480.

12. Making History Amid the Gloom

Pud Galvin was second in wins for Allegheny with 23 in 49 complete games. But he lost two more games than he won. One particular win, days before the end of the season, made history. It came in the final game of a three-game series in Washington. On October 3, with Harry Staley in the pitching box, the Alleghenys defeated the Nationals, 13–8, to begin the series. The next day, Morris had a bad outing and the host club blanked Allegheny, 5–0. Galvin took the ball for the rubber game on October 5. He faced George Haddock, one of 10 pitchers the struggling Washington club tried during its last-place season. Haddock, 21, had debuted on September 27 and lost, 3–0, to New York, surrendering five hits. This outing against Galvin was the second start of the two Haddock would see. It was duel between an inexperienced rookie and a crafty veteran who had played hundreds of games. "Haddock and Galvin pitched with telling effect," the *New York Clipper* said in its two-sentence report of the game.[15] Haddock allowed four hits and one earned run, while Galvin gave up four hits. Washington committed eight errors to four for Allegheny. The final score was 5–1 for Allegheny. But it wasn't just "another" win for Galvin, despite the scant attention paid to it at the time. It marked his 300th win since his first as a professional at age 19, a 3–2 win by his St. Louis Browns on May 25, 1875. In its report of the victory, the local *Pittsburgh Press* made no mention whatsoever of Galvin. It noted Haddock "did very well" and that he was a brother-in-law of another Washington pitcher, Jim Whitney. Baseball briefs accompanying the game story included items about Billy Sunday leading the league in stolen bases with 73, about new outfielder Sam Nicol and catcher Henry Yaik, league-leading batter Jake Beckley and catcher Fred Carroll's hitting struggles.[16] Not a word appeared about "Gentle Jeems" and his history-making accomplishment.

Historians and baseball statisticians did not consider the 36 wins Galvin pitched in the International Association for Allegheny and Buffalo in 1877 and 1878 in that 300 total. Had they done so, his 300-game benchmark would have been reached a year earlier. Regardless, in an era when pitchers had gone from pitching every day to becoming part of a rotation, no such benchmark of excellence existed. Pitchers were expected to pitch. A lot. Galvin was the first to win 300 times, so he was in uncharted territory. He wouldn't be the last, but only four other pitchers would win more than the 365 he recorded in the fullness of time. The achievement of winning 300 games would later become a sure-fire ticket into the Baseball Hall of Fame, but on this early fall day of 1888 in Washington, D.C., no notice was taken of Galvin's accomplishment. Statistical records were kept in the early days of baseball, but unlike today little heed was paid to them because there was so little history against which to measure them. Baseball history was being written on a weekly or monthly basis. Galvin himself was likely unaware of the significance of that particular win, and he may have gone to his grave without ever knowing it.

The season ended on October 13. New York finished first, a position it had occupied since July 31. Chicago was seven games back. Allegheny, with 66 wins and 68 losses, finished in sixth place for the second season in a row. Overall, it had been another disappointing season for Pittsburgh's National League entry.

Detroit had struggled with injuries, poor attendance, high salaries and a lack of on-field success. The club that took the National League pennant in 1887 managed only a fifth-place finish, 3½ games ahead of Allegheny for 1888. Wolverines owner Fred Stearns stunned the baseball world in October by selling off the team's top players for $45,000 to various clubs, and the remainder of the operation to Cleveland, which planned to join the League. Stearns was a man who favored bold moves. His leaving the National League by selling his team and its players was the mirror image of his controversial move three years earlier, when he acquired the entire Buffalo operation in one fell swoop. Allegheny president William Nimick pounced to sign four of the Detroit stars: outfielder and captain Ned Hanlon, third baseman Deacon White, shortstop Jack Rowe (White and Rowe comprising half of the "Big Four") and backup pitcher Pete Conway.[17] Nimick was still trying to put together a pennant-winner in a bid to create some sort of legacy for himself before leaving the game.

That fall, Albert Goodwill Spalding assembled an All-American team of star players to join his Chicago White Stockings for an around-the-world tour to promote baseball and his financial interests as a supplier of equipment. The Spalding World Tour returned to New York in early April 1889, after playing 28 games in New Zealand, Australia, Egypt, Italy, Paris and London. The trip was a financial disaster—with mixed reviews from its various hosts—but Spalding was pleased that it had provided exposure for his sporting goods business and to the game he would soon be claiming was an entirely American invention.[18]

That year, the National League reduced the number of balls required for a walk to four from five, while strikes remained at three. This would mark the last tinkering with balls and strikes. The league also adopted a salary classification scheme intended to reduce payroll costs for its clubs. There were to be five categories of players under this plan, and salaries could range from $1,500 to $2,000. The announcement of this scheme lit a fire in the bellies of John Montgomery Ward, Dan Brouthers and other members of the Brotherhood of Professional Base Ball Players. They would soon take action.

In December, Deacon White and Jack Rowe purchased a controlling interest in the Buffalo Bisons of the International League and announced they intended to play for the club next year. They were part of an investor group that hoped to bring National League baseball back to Buffalo. The two had begun to think their days as players were numbered and both retained

12. Making History Amid the Gloom 155

a fondness for Buffalo, where Rowe had found his attractive and well-off wife. They had seen how teams were managed during their long careers and wanted to try their hands at it. But their rights had been sold by Detroit to Allegheny, which expected them to play in Pittsburgh. Besides, White and Rowe were barred from playing in Buffalo by the National League's reserve clause, which had just been extended to apply to minor leagues. White, especially, was incensed at being sold to Allegheny against his wishes, disrupting his life. "No man can sell my carcass unless I get half," the normally mild-mannered White thundered. Detroit's former owner, Frederick Stearns, barked back: "White may have been elected president of the Buffalo club or president of the United States, but that won't enable him to play in Buffalo. He'll play in Pittsburgh or he'll get off the earth." Allegheny president William Nimick put it this way: "If they do not want to play in Pittsburgh, they'll play nowhere."[19] After a long standoff to express their displeasure, White and Rowe signed with the Alleghenys, but not until early July.

The 1889 season was still a few months away when the *New York Clipper* carried a feature article about Pud Galvin, highlighting his career and noting that the "steady and reliable" hurler "is pitching just as good ball now as ever he did." It suggested his training as a blacksmith in his hometown of St. Louis is "where he must have developed the muscle which emphasizes his 'cannon ball' curves." This was a rare reference to Galvin throwing the curve. Comment usually focused on his expertise with a knee-buckling fastball and good change-up, along with a wicked pickoff move. One of the Pittsburgh newspapers would later leave the impression that Galvin had no ability to throw the curve. It reported that Galvin told some friends gathered in a bar that as a pitcher he was handicapped by having small hands. "My fingers are too short to enable me to get grip enough on the ball to pitch a deep curve, so that I have been compelled to depend more on drops, straight balls and the different artifices know to pitchers to deceive the batter."[20] Whether it was "deep" enough or not, the reference to a "cannon ball curve" suggested that Galvin was at least able to manage a fast-moving version of the "artifice." The *Clipper* article, which included a large likeness of Galvin, recounted his career in Allegheny and Buffalo and his escape from California in 1880. "His greatest pitching feat for Pittsburgh was shutting out of Boston with a solitary scratch hit July 13, 1888," it concluded. No mention was made of his 300 wins.

Galvin spent part of the winter in St. Louis, where he tended to some business for his mother. In mid–February, upon his return to his home in Allegheny City, he gave an interview to the *Pittsburgh Dispatch* in which he disparaged his hometown as "that city of measles and smallpox." He said that while in St. Louis he had discussed baseball with Browns owner Chris Von der Ahe, a fact which may have contributed to his sour mood. The mercurial and bull-headed Von der Ahe had refused to bet money with him on the outcome of upcoming spring exhibition games between St. Louis and Allegheny, Galvin said. "'I think that we can beat the Browns, and they are champions of the [American] association,'" he said.[21] A few weeks later, Galvin told the same paper that while in St. Louis, he discovered that members of the Browns were doing daily exercise in a gymnasium and he had been asked to join them. Galvin said he declined, because he believed in the value of a few months of idleness during the offseason. "This particularly refers to a pitcher. What he wants is rest." Galvin insisted it didn't take long to get back into shape once muscles have been rested. "Most certainly I recommend a good rest for players of all kinds."[22] A week later, Galvin began exercising to lose weight and get in good shape by April 1, the same paper reported. "He covers 12 miles every morning on the road, and indulges freely in indoor exercise."[23]

As Galvin began his muscle-waking regimen, one of his teammates was arrested by police and charged with running a gambling house in a billiard parlor he operated with another player. Third baseman Bill Kuehne was ordered to appear before Allegheny Mayor Richard T. Pearson on the charge. Kuehne's partner, pitcher Ed Morris, expressed shock at the arrest upon returning from a visit to Michigan. Morris admitted, "the boys occasionally played for cigars and soft drinks in that little back room, but nothing worse." But Morris was also charged. Supporters of the pair claimed they were the victims of a vendetta by Allegheny police. For his part, the *Pittsburgh Press* reported, Kuehne "claims that he never turned a card for money in his life." When the case came to trial several days later, key police witnesses failed to appear and the charges were dismissed.[24] The *Press* found the disappearance of witnesses "rather odd. At all events, Messrs. Morris and Kuehne learned a lesson that they will not soon forget." One is left wondering about the real story behind the story of the duo and who may have pressured whom to do what.

The Allegheny roster was constantly adjusted during the 1889 season, players coming and going with regularity, while president Nimick and manager Phillips struggled to find a winning formula. Aside from Galvin, Morris and Staley, no less than eight other pitchers were tried, two of them appearing only once, another two appearing twice and one of them three times. The best of the bunch was Bill Sowders, who was picked up later in the season from Boston, where he had won 19 games the previous season.

Allegheny opened the 1889 campaign on April 24 at home for the first of three games with Chicago. Galvin pitched the first contest and displayed some rust with wild pitches that allowed three runs in the first inning. But the home bats rescued him in the sixth and seventh innings and Allegheny won, 8–5. The next day, with newcomer Staley in the pitching box, Chicago was edged, 5–4. The White Stockings found Galvin an easy mark in the concluding game April 26, a cold and raw day, and they romped to 7–1 victory.

12. Making History Amid the Gloom 157

Galvin allowed 13 hits in a miserable outing. Morris had been ailing and was considered not yet in shape to join the team. He reported for work on May 6 in Chicago, a day after Galvin was hurt at Indianapolis when he stuck out his foot to stop a hard drive by a Hoosiers hitter. Indianapolis had pounded Galvin and his replacement, Staley, 17–12, led by third baseman Jerry Denny, who went six-for-six that day, including a home run. Morris, nursing a sore arm, sounded somewhat reluctant. "I did not intend to report so soon, as I have been pretty sick," he explained. "However, now that Galvin is knocked out for a time I ought to make an extra effort.... I am satisfied that Galvin's foot is badly hurt, because he will not retire from a game except he is really forced to do so. He offers to stop balls that few men would think of getting in front of."[25]

Manager Horace Phillips was not impressed with Morris and his condition, however, and on May 15 Morris and fellow pitcher Pete Conway were sent home without pay to get in shape. "Until they are in proper shape, they and all others, will condition themselves at their own expense. At present the club is badly in need of pitchers," observed the *Clipper*.[26] Like Morris, Conway was suffering from a sore arm. Morris would return; Conway wouldn't, his career over at age 22. With Galvin hurt, Morris sent home and Conway gone, Phillips' club was indeed in dire need of pitchers. The only bright spot in the month came on May 24 when third baseman Bill Kuehne had three putouts and 10 assists without making an error. His dazzling defense, which established a major league record, helped Allegheny to a 9–7 victory over Washington. By June 3, however, Allegheny had managed only 13 wins for the season and found itself in familiar territory: sixth place. Galvin returned to the lineup later that month and on June 29 threw a 3–0 shutout of Philadelphia. Galvin, it was said, pitched with his youthful form and also hit a double to score a run. "Galvin undoubtedly carried off the honors of the day," said the *Pittsburgh Dispatch* account.[27]

Things looked up in early July when Deacon White and Jack Rowe gave up their fight to play in Buffalo and reported to the Alleghenys. Allegheny was just coming off a winning streak of six games but things would soon change. On July 8, the Alleghenys helped the New York Giants open the new Polo Grounds in New York City, the Giants having forsaken their field on Staten Island where they had drawn poorly. The Giants celebrated the occasion with a 7–5 victory over Galvin, who allowed 14 hits.

July proved to be a difficult month for Allegheny, both on the field and behind the scenes. A depressing 12-game losing streak wasn't snapped until a 7–2 victory in Cleveland on July 22. Along the way, Deacon White and Jack Rowe were benched briefly amid rumors they were playing poorly so they could be released and return to Buffalo where their hearts (and money) were. Galvin had several dreadful outings, including a July 18 loss of 15–0 in

Philadelphia when he gave up 21 hits. Two days later, he surrendered another 21 hits to the Phillies, this time in a 16–1 loss. "Old Sport is Once Again Made a Pitiful Target," the *Pittsburgh Dispatch* said in a headline. It reported that Galvin "possessed plenty of speed and put all the curves in the baseball category across the plate" but the Phillies batters were wise to him. They would have belted even more hits and runs, it said, "but their strength failed them."[28] Meanwhile, help had arrived for the beleaguered Galvin. Horace Phillips signed Boston pitcher Bill Sowders on July 19 after trying and releasing several other hurlers. In the final days of the month, the Alleghenys were able to recoup somewhat by beating Cleveland four more times, climbing back into sixth place after a brief spell in seventh. In the greater picture, however, the team was floundering. *The Sporting News* suggested on July 27 that "a reading of the Riot Act would come in handy." The publication noted that the club had fallen far short of expectations, Galvin had struggled, Morris was hurt again (pulled muscles in his stomach), and White and Rowe were providing "unwilling service." Some fans, it noted, were calling for a new manager. "The results indicate the necessity for a change of some kind."[29]

Horace Phillips was under extreme pressure from president Nimick and club supporters to find a way to turn the club into a contender. He had been shuffling players in and out of the lineup, yet no improvement had resulted. Phillips knew his job was on the line. A rumor had begun that centerfielder Ned Hanlon would be named to replace him as manager. Nimick denied it, however. Another rumor that secretary Al Scandrett denied was that star second baseman and team captain Fred Dunlap was for sale. The club executives found themselves constantly putting out fires. Worse was to come.

Shortly after Phillips acquired pitcher Sowders from Boston, the Allegheny manager began acting oddly around the players. He spoke about some strange and extravagant schemes he had that on July 21 prompted Nimick to grant him a leave of absence for two weeks to rest and collect himself. In less than two weeks, however, Phillips was back at work and traveled to Columbus, where he tried to sell pitcher Ed Morris and substitute catcher Chuck Lauer to the Spiders.[30] Soon after, he traveled to Boston, where he negotiated the sale of infielder Pop Smith for $3,000. On August 1, Phillips checked into the Girard House Hotel in Philadelphia, accompanied by his wife and brother. His behavior became bizarre as he chatted with the hotel clerk while scribbling all over the hotel register. Phillips told the clerk he was worth many millions and that he was in the city looking at investments. He said he was the sole owner of all of the baseball clubs in the country and that he had plans for some innovations to the game. Phillips said he was becoming a partner in the Girard House the following day and that he had already bought several hotels in Washington and New York. Phillips offered to put the clerk in charge of them. That wasn't all. Phillips said he had also invested heavily

12. Making History Amid the Gloom

in theaters. The clerk, realizing his guest was scrambled, persuaded Phillips to return to his room as he fetched a doctor. Dr. Winfield S. Wolford arrived and diagnosed Phillips with "'acute paresis or softening of the brain.'" He concluded: "Phillips's reason is entirely gone." The good doctor said the onset had been sudden and "leaves no hope for recovery."[31] It turned out that Phillips, one of the better managers in baseball, had suffered a complete nervous breakdown, and at age 39 was taken to a private asylum for the insane in New Jersey. His contribution to baseball had been noteworthy and his loss was yet another setback for the team. "He worked like a Trojan for the Pittsburgh club and this year had hoped to reap a fair reward for his efforts," said a sympathetic *Sporting News*. "But strange to say the club has done poorer work this season than ever before and this may have had something to do with Phillip's [sic] illness."[32] After a year of treatment, doctors felt Phillips had been cured, but he suffered a return of hallucinations and was sent back to the asylum. He died at the Philadelphia Hospital for the Insane on February 26, 1896.[33]

Billy Sunday, who had been unable to play in July while being treated for a carbuncle on his hip, was appointed interim manager of the club after the departure of Phillips. Sunday was soon replaced by Ned Hanlon, who proved to be a no-nonsense skipper. After all the turmoil, the Alleghenys, a team that began the 1889 season with so much hope, had slipped to seventh place by August 12, with 35 wins, one less than Indianapolis. To compound their woes, third baseman Deacon White wrenched his back in a collision with catcher Doggie Miller and was out of action for the last two weeks of August, the latest in a long string of injuries that had hobbled the team and dashed its pennant hopes.

The picture was bleak for Pittsburgh, as its Alleghenys slipped toward the basement of the National League.

13

Turning Back the Clock

As Allegheny prepared for a two-game series against Boston set to begin August 13, more changes were made to the team. It marked the 11th meeting between the clubs and Allegheny had lost the previous 10. The Beaneaters remained atop the National League standings, where they had been since May 14, but New York was now nipping at their heels. Allegheny had slipped back into seventh place and made another personnel shuffle as the vaunted Boston club came to town. Fred Dunlap resigned as both field captain and short-term acting manager, and was replaced by Ned Hanlon. Sidelined with an injured finger, Hanlon was expected to assume all responsibilities for the club on and off the field.[1]

Boston was riding the remarkable arm of John Clarkson, who appeared to be on track for his second 50-win season. In 1885, he had led the Chicago White Stockings to the National League pennant with 53 victories, and he was matching that pace in the current campaign. Clarkson and his catcher, King Kelly, had been picked up by the Beaneaters in 1888 for $10,000 apiece as Al

Second baseman Fred Dunlap tried his hand at managing Galvin's club in the 1889 season, with mixed results, and stayed with the Allegheny Club when most of his teammates jumped to the Players' League Pittsburgh Burghers for 1890 (Library of Congress).

160

13. Turning Back the Clock

Spalding cleaned house in Chicago. At the age of 27, Clarkson would fall one short of 50 wins in 1889, but he captured the pitching Triple Crown by also leading in strikeouts with 284 and recording the lowest earned run average at 2.73. In his impressive 12-year major league career he compiled 328 wins, for which he was inducted into the Baseball Hall of Fame. The Allegheny players may have breathed a sigh of relief when they discovered Clarkson was not in the pitcher's box for the August 13 contest. The Beaneaters gave the ball to 21-year-old rookie Bill Daley, a lefty. Daley pitched poorly for four innings, walking seven batters, five of whom scored. For the fifth inning, venerable Hoss Radbourn entered the game and surrendered four more hits and two runs. For his part, Galvin allowed Boston five hits, but all were scattered and none scored as Allegheny triumphed, 9–0. Allegheny's first win against Boston knocked the Beaneaters out of first place and lifted the home club back into sixth. The following day, before a surprisingly small crowd, Boston bounced back, with Clarkson pitching, for a 9–3 win.

Pud Galvin, amid growing concerns at his uneven performance and the criticism he drew for several ugly losses, made some preparations of his own to be at his best for Boston. A day before the Beaneaters arrived in town, he was injected with a solution, popularly known as "the elixir of life," at a Pittsburgh medical college. Its major ingredient was the ground-up testes of animals, in what today would be similar to a performance-enhancing drug called testosterone. The elixir was said to be a rejuvenating treatment, a veritable fountain of youth, and Galvin decided to try it as word of its supposed youth-reclaiming properties spread across North America. Newspapers had been full of testimonials about its value. "Old Men Made Young," blared a headline in the *St. Paul Daily Globe* that summer, while the *Boston Globe* on August 11 proclaimed, "Old Men Made as Frisky as the Friskiest Boys."[2] On August 13, the same day Galvin faced Boston with the elixir his system, the *Washington Post* began a three-part series that examined the potion and claims about it with stories headlined: "Live for Centuries"; "The Elixir of Life: Old Age Yearns for Youth"; and "Old Age Seeks Youth." A paralyzed Memphis man reportedly felt so much better after taking the elixir that he discarded his crutches. Extravagant claims were being made about the effects of the miracle potion, in the days when extravagant claims were made about all sorts of patent medicines and cure-alls. However, not everyone was persuaded of the value of the new elixir that had been developed by Dr. Charles E. Brown-Sequard, a respected neurologist and physiologist. Leading American orthopedic surgeon Dr. Lewis Sayre, for instance, told the *New York Herald* he had his doubts.

> I know Doctor Brown-Sequard of course. He is an eminent physician, one who has done great service to his profession and to the world, but I am sorry to say that his eagerness in new lines of research and in the interpretation of results sometimes gets the better of his

judgment. He is often a little wild in his conclusions, and besides he is getting pretty well along in years.... I have so small an opinion of its importance that I think that any time spent in experiments would be wasted.[3]

On June 1, 1889, Brown-Sequard made a presentation to the Paris Biological Society (of which he was president), in which he shared his research about the potion he claimed had demonstrated dramatic rejuvenating properties. He said he had injected himself with it and, at age 72, found he became sharper mentally, stronger physically and had also developed a better appetite. Brown-Sequard was no quack. Today he is considered one of the founders of modern endocrinology, a branch of medicine concerned with the structure, function, and disorders of endocrine (internally secreting) glands. His research encouraged other scientists to undertake early work in organotherapy, the injection of testes-based potions and the use of animal or human testes to treat patients for a wide range of diseases and conditions. Nothing proved as popular as his concoction that promised to recapture youth. By the end of 1889, more than 12,000 physicians were reportedly administering Brown-Sequard's "elixir of life." Chemists and doctors had grown wealthy meeting public demand for it.[4] Brown-Sequard himself charged nothing for the potion he distributed widely to physicians who asked for it.

Brown-Sequard also wrote about his discovery and the effects of his formula on himself in the July 20, 1889, edition of *The Lancet*, the respected British medical journal. He said he created the fluid because he believed there is a connection between a man's power and the energy produced by his testicles. He attributed the weakening of men as they age to "the generally diminishing action of the spermatic glands." So Brown-Sequard developed a liquid with a small amount of water, to which he added blood from testicular veins, semen, and juice extracted from the crushed testicles of a dog or guinea pig. To this recipe he added some distilled water, and the concoction was then filtered through paper. He injected himself 10 times between May 15 and June 4, the first five times using a potion derived from a dog and the last five with the concoction derived from guinea pigs. Brown-Sequard said the strength he enjoyed as a younger man "had gradually diminished during the last ten or twelve years." Things soon changed dramatically. "The day after the first subcutaneous injection, and still more after the two succeeding ones, a radical change took place in me, and I had ample reason to say and to write that I had regained at least all the strength I possessed a good many years ago." He said he could stand for longer periods at his laboratory bench and was no longer tired when he returned home at night. After supper, he could do further work, a contrast to his usual routine of going to bed exhausted. "For more than twenty years I had never been able to do as much," he said. He was able to resume his former habit of bounding up stairs, while dynamometer tests showed he had gained strength in his limbs. Even his "jet" during urination had improved significantly and his chronic constipation was cured, he noted. After discontinuing the injections, the positive benefits lasted for a good four weeks, he said, but gradually "I have witnessed almost a complete return of the state of weakness which existed before the first injection." He noted that a fellow researcher had injected three older men with the same potion and found similar results. Brown-Sequard concluded that his elixir "possesses the power of increasing the strength of many parts of the human organism" and he suggested further research was needed.[5]

Brown-Sequard's work produced a sensation. Man has always hunted for the "Fountain of Youth," and the public wanted to believe him. After all, Brown-Sequard wasn't some traveling patent-medicine salesman rolling through town armed with bottles of magic potion and a well-rehearsed sales pitch like some flim-flam man. He had presented to the prestigious Paris Biological Society and was published in *The Lancet*, both significant accomplishments in the field of medicine. He had a pedigree, even if some thought him a bit eccentric. The Mauritius-born son of an American sea captain and a Mauritian woman, Brown-Sequard's work was well known in America. He was acclaimed for the originality of his ideas, but he also faced the criticism and ridicule they inevitably attracted. His medical legacy is the Brown-Sequard Syndrome, a condition that relates to damage to the spinal cord and leads to paralysis and the loss of the sensations of touch and temperature. The researcher had taught and worked in New York and Boston, and was a member of the American Academy of Arts and Sciences, the National Academy of Sciences, and a Fellow of the Royal Society, a British-based sort of club for the world's leading scientists.

Soon after word of Brown-Sequard's work became known, the *New Haven Register* was among those newspapers to suggest his concoction might be of interest to baseball players. "The discovery of a true elixir of youth by which the aged can restore their vitality and renew their bodily vigor would be a great thing for baseball nines. We hope the discovery ... is of such a nature that it can be applied to rejuvenate provincial clubs."[6]

It is unclear whether Galvin approached the Pittsburgh medical college or researchers there approached him. Either way, he made an ideal subject. His pitching relied on fastballs that required strength, which was beginning to wane as he approached the age of 33. Galvin was growing concerned about the number of bad performances he had delivered and worried about how much longer he could play baseball. He was anxious to continue pitching because the comparatively fat paychecks enjoyed by ballplayers were many times what he could bring home to his growing family as a plumber, blacksmith, steamfitter, or saloon-keeper. On August 12, Galvin was injected with the Brown-Sequard potion in his thigh. Other subjects were part of the same test, although none were believed to be ballplayers. Galvin may have felt there was nothing to lose. After Allegheny's 10 straight losses to Boston, he was willing to try anything to end that embarrassing streak.

In the August 13 game, Galvin played like a man possessed. "Old Jeems once more was a youngster full of fun, power and tricks," the *Pittsburgh Dispatch* reported in its story headlined: "Galvin, the Great."[7] Aside from his shutout, with only five hits allowed the powerful Boston batters, he belted a double and a triple. The *New York Times* led off its account of the game with: "Galvin pitched one of the best games of his life today."[8] The *Pittsburgh Commercial Gazette* reported that a smiling Galvin doffed his cap to the crowd that cheered his work with the bat that day.[9] The *Washington Post*, which had written extensively about the elixir and claims surrounding it, also took note of Galvin's performance in its "Base Ball Notes."

Galvin was one of the subjects at a test of the Brown-Sequard elixir at a medical college in Pittsburgh on Monday. If there still be doubting Thomases who concede no virtue to the elixir, they are respectfully referred to Galvin's record in yesterday's Boston-Pittsburgh game. It is the best proof yet furnished of the value of the discovery.[10]

Galvin continued to play well for several weeks, but took no further injections of the testosterone-based potion, as far as can be determined. His next outing came August 17 at home against New York. He scored one run on two hits and, although he allowed 13 hits, he led Allegheny to a 15-10 win. Galvin won his next four starts (rotating with Ed Morris, Harry Staley and Bill Sowders), beating Cleveland, Chicago, Indianapolis and then Chicago again. In a 6-2 win over Chicago on August 28, the *Pittsburgh Dispatch* said Galvin was particularly effective silencing the White Stockings' bats. "Galvin, who is usually rather good eating on the home grounds, at this time of year, was surprisingly effective today. He swung his big fat arms with much vehemence, and laughed merrily as the sweat rolled off his globular face, and, dropping into the box, rose above the tops of his shoes."[11] On August 31, Galvin came in to relieve a struggling Staley against Chicago, but the game was tied and called on account of darkness after 13 innings. He came back to earth on September 2, his next start, when New York beat Allegheny, 9-5. Galvin had enjoyed an unusually productive three weeks in what had been a sometimes difficult season.

Had the *Dispatch* hinted at one point at what would later be dubbed "'roid rage" in the hurler, along with his excessive sweating? Was Pud Galvin the first "juicer" in baseball? It has been argued that he was.

In his book *The Dark Side of the Diamond: Gambling, Violence, Drugs and Alcoholism in the National Pastime*, published in 2007, law professor Roger I. Abrams drew attention to Galvin's use of the Brown-Sequard elixir as he enumerated the many vices in which baseball players have indulged over the years. Abrams' book was published during the controversy about whether modern players who took performance-enhancing drugs (PEDs) should be allowed into the Baseball Hall of Fame. The majority sentiment expressed by writers and others was that they had cheated, so they should be barred from induction. But supporters of players such as Mark McGwire, Barry Bonds and Jose Canseco latched onto the revelation by Abrams to show that Galvin had taken a similar substance yet was already in the Hall. So the precedent had been set, they asserted, and the door should not be slammed shut on modern players.

Not nearly as well known as Abrams' book was a 2002 article in the *Medical Journal of Australia* by scientists who decided to test the Brown-Sequard elixir, using modern scientific techniques. Abrams didn't mention their work in his book. Australian researchers carefully replicated the elixir as prepared by the 19th-century doctor in a bid to test its effectiveness. "In recent years," they noted, "the hypothesis that the aging process in men arises from testicular insufficiency has re-emerged." Testes were obtained from five healthy dogs of various breeds which were undergoing castration surgery, and the tissues were stored and then crushed according to Brown-Sequard's formula. The liquid was filtered and carefully analyzed for testosterone concentration. The scientists found that the "canine testicular extract" with which Brown-Sequard injected himself was four times less than the amount that would be needed simply to replace the testosterone in men suffering from inadequate testosterone production, a condition known as hypogonadism. "The favorable response he reported was therefore clearly a placebo effect," they concluded, referring to Brown-Sequard's observations. In other words, there was too little testosterone in the concoction to have any biological effect on a subject. They did note the potential feel-good effect of taking something that a subject thinks has value. "Brown-Sequard's experience demonstrates that the placebo effect can be powerful, even in a highly educated physician who was well aware of its existence," they said.[12] Modern science had debunked all those claims about an injectable fountain of youth made more than a century ago.

So it was all in Brown-Sequard's head. And in Galvin's, too. The pitcher *believed* the potion helped him perform. And because he did, it did. The performance enhancement came from his mind, not from any injection. The elixir of life faded from public consciousness after about two years, the fad having burnt itself out in a veritable hula-hoop of experimental medicine. For his part, the free-thinking and colorful Brown-Sequard died in 1894. He has been lauded for his pioneering experiments that led to hormonal replacement therapy and organ transplants, but, as one of his biographers noted, "his ideas sometimes superseded reasoned judgment, leading to unrealistic expectations by the general public and chilling disenchantment by the scientific and academic communities, which suspected that much of his work was based on the shifting sands of self-delusion."[13]

It's not known if other baseball players heeded the advice from the *New Haven Register* and other papers that promoted the elixir as a "great thing" for baseball and tried it themselves. But given the rage it became and the number of doses administered, it seems likely other players tried it, especially those looking to combat the decline that comes with age. To date, however, the only documented user has been Pud Galvin. And it appears he used it only once.

Back on the baseball field, Allegheny was in sixth place as September began and was still there at the end of the month. On September 26, Galvin had a terrific game at Recreation Park against Philadelphia. He got off to a bad start, allowing a Phillies run in the first inning, loading the bases by giving up three singles. But then he settled down to work, striking out a batter as his defense threw out runners at home plate and first base to end the inning. "Galvin never received better support in his life than he did in yesterday's game," said the *Pittsburgh Dispatch*. Despite his girth and age, the hurler also used his legs to help the Allegheny cause. In the third inning, Galvin reached first on a fielder's choice, advanced around the bases, taking advantage of errant throws, and finally "ran and puffed his way home amid cheers." In the fifth inning, with two men on base, Galvin again came to the plate and worked pitcher Dave Anderson for three balls.

> Jeems got his big bat fairly on to the nose of a nice ball, and with a biff, bang, the ball went sailing over Fogarty's head into the long grass in deep center field. An ordinary runner would have reached home on the hit, but the old sport was happy to reach third, where he sat cheerfully down on the bag to mop his brow. After he had regained his wind he showed a little more of his sprinting by scoring on Miller's sacrifice hit."[14]

The newspaper observed that had he been able to run as fast as he once had, he would have scored his first home run in Recreation Park since 1877. It would have been Galvin's sixth in his career in the National League. The newspaper continued:

> He nearly made a home run. He would have done so had he been able to run as fast as molasses from a jar. The old man, however, made a three-bagger and his effort at getting to third was so exhausting that Miller delayed the game until Jeems was restored to his wonted vigor.... He also pitched a fine game, and altogether it was the old man's day.

Allegheny, because of the hitting, pitching, and running of their "old man," won the game, 9–2. Galvin's club was going to play spoiler again as New York and Boston continued to battle it out for first place in the dying days of the 1889 season. Allegheny would play both teams and help determine who would bring home the pennant. New York came to town on September 30 for a three-game series, clinging to first place a half-game ahead of Boston. With Galvin pitching for the first meeting, the teams were tied, 3–3, when the rain-delayed game had to be called on account of darkness. The next day,

Allegheny downed the Giants, 7–2, when Staley pitched well and his batters tallied 13 hits off Mickey Welch. The loss knocked New York out of first place and allowed Allegheny to slip into fifth. Boston, which defeated Cleveland, 8–5, moved to the top of the league. Notwithstanding the home club's disappointing season, the *Dispatch* noted, "there is still an opportunity for Pittsburgh to gain a goodly amount of glory yet, and it lies in the fact of killing the championship aspirations of such clubs as New York and Boston."[15] New York bounced back on October 2 to win, 6–3, against Sowders. In Cleveland, the Spiders defeated the Beaneaters, 7–1, so Boston dropped back to second. A feature of the game was the behavior of Boston's star King Kelly, who was drunk while in uniform and did not play. He verbally abused the opposition, his own teammates and the umpire. Police ejected Kelly from League Park when he tried to hit umpire John McQuaid in the sixth inning after he called a Boston runner out at home plate.

The next day, October 3, Boston came to Recreation Park while New York appeared in Cleveland. Beaneaters pitcher John Clarkson was again outstanding, collecting his 49th win of the season. Galvin, who also pitched well, received little support from his teammates, however, in the 7–2 loss. In Cleveland, meanwhile, New York defeated the Spiders, 9–0, to remain in first. Boston edged Allegheny, 4–3, on October 4, while New York again defeated Cleveland, this time 6–1, to stay in first place. The final games of the closest-ever National League championship race were set for October 5. When it became known that Galvin would be called upon to take the ball that day, New York manager Jim Mutrie wired him a promise of $100 if he beat the Beaneaters, a victory that would ensure the Giants took the pennant. That day, Galvin again faced Clarkson, who was looking for his 50th win. The pitcher upon whom Boston had relied heavily for its success all year occupied the box for his fifth start in six days, and was likely tired. He was wild this day, giving up four hits as Galvin and the Alleghenys took the game, 6–1. Galvin surrendered five hits, three of them to King Kelly, including a double in the sixth inning to score the only run for the visitors. In Cleveland, New York swept its third game from the Spiders, 5–3, to claim its second straight National League championship. Galvin and Allegheny had not only played a pivotal king-making role, but had edged past Cleveland in the process to claim fifth place, one spot ahead of the position where it had languished during its first two years in the league. An added bonus for Pud Galvin was the $100 sweetener from Mutrie. The promise of money may have affected his mind, much like the elixir, that inspired him to beat Boston.

The Sporting News was quick to credit Galvin for winning the game that ended the exciting pennant race and disappointed the Beaneaters and their fans. It went on to praise his work throughout the season and his longevity.

Jimmy Galvin's work in the box this year has been phenomenal, not for any strike-out record or big achievements in the matter of low base hits, but for splendid headwork, strategy and good generalship. Galvin has lived long enough and been in harness for a period that has outgrown many another that has started in which he did, but he is still there, driving them in and causing people to stop and wonder in amazement.... The secret of Galvin's success, like many another in this world, is an abundance of pluck and strict attention to business.[16]

At the close of the season, Clarkson, with his 49 wins, was 21 games better than Tim Keefe of New York and Charlie Buffinton of Philadelphia, who tied for second among pitchers. Galvin was fifth with 21 wins, while his teammate Harry Staley was two behind, but had the back luck to lead the league with 26 losses. The frequently hurt Ed Morris managed only six wins in 21 starts. Galvin logged 341 innings, the last year in which he exceeded 300. His earned run average had jumped to 4.17, his worst ever. Yet again, Galvin had been the workhorse for his club. After the season, he returned to the laundry business he had opened on Chartiers Street, close to his home, where he used a white horse to pull a wagon to collect soiled linen from his customers.[17] For some reason, he liked to tell onlookers the animal was a goat. He also kept an eye on the newspapers because of significant developments that were about to shake up the baseball world.

The fall of 1889 saw great turmoil as John Montgomery Ward and the Brotherhood of Professional Base Ball Players swung into action. On November 4, Ward and his allies, which included many of the best players in the National League and some from the American Association, severed relations with the National League and announced they had formed the "Players' League." The name was chosen to recognize that the new organization was a creation of players, many of whom had invested money in their clubs. The new league would consist of teams in Boston, New York, Chicago, Pittsburgh, Philadelphia, Cleveland, Brooklyn and Buffalo. For the latter franchise, partners Deacon White and Jack Rowe each subscribed for $1,000 worth of stock. Catcher Cornelius McGillicuddy, better known as Connie Mack, jumped from Washington to Buffalo and bought $500 in shares in the Bisons. Ned Hanlon, team captain and manager of the Alleghenys, acquired stock in the Pittsburgh club, to be called the Burghers. Even Pud Galvin, who seldom had money to spare, found $500 to buy shares in the new club.[18] The Players' League established a profit-sharing scheme and attracted no shortage of capitalists who had seen how profitable the National League had been during the 1889 season and eagerly bought in. For rules, the PL elected to use the more lively Keefe ball than the Spalding version used in the NL and AA (likely to improve offense), instituted a two-umpire system and lengthened the pitching box. Pitchers had to begin their delivery from the back of the box, which was 57 feet from home plate, 18 inches farther than in the National League.

13. Turning Back the Clock   169

The Pittsburgh Allegheny ball club moved from its longtime home at Union/Recreation Park to Exposition Park in 1891, about the same time the team became known as the Pirates. Still in Allegheny City across from downtown Pittsburgh, the low-lying grounds were subject to flooding of the Allegheny River. It was used by the Alleghenys for three seasons in the early 1880s. This image is from about 1900. It was located between today's PNC Park and football's Heinz Field (Library of Congress).

Like the National League, but unlike the American Association, the Players' League banned Sunday games and the sale of alcohol in its parks. New ballparks were found to accommodate the new teams. In Pittsburgh, Exposition Park was chosen. It had been used by the Allegheny club during its 1882, 1883 and 1884 campaigns in the American Association. The club abandoned it because its major drawback was its low-lying location alongside the north bank of the Allegheny River that made it subject to springtime flooding.

The Players' League was popular with both players and fans, and it outdrew the older loops in the 1890 season. It had attracted the top players of the day who were tired of being treated by club magnates like cattle and chafed at the reserve clause that kept them chained to clubs against their wishes. The latter provision had led to the inevitable suppression of salaries because players could no longer shop their talents around. The players had not shared in the additional profits the successful 1889 season had generated. Among those who found it easy to leave their teams was Pud Galvin, even though he conceded he had been generally well-treated by management over the years. Most of his fellow Alleghenys, except Billy Sunday and three others, decided to sign with Hanlon and the Burghers. Sunday originally expressed interest in jumping to the new team, but changed his mind, feeling he had made a commitment to the management of the existing nine. He would be rewarded with the captaincy. Many of the top stars in the American Association, including Charlie Comiskey, the player-manager in St. Louis, also opted for the Players' League. Comiskey was appointed manager of the Chicago franchise, which adopted the name "Pirates."

Most prominent among the National League players to stay put and criticize the new organization was Chicago player-manager Cap Anson. In his autobiography, Anson, who owned shares in the White Stockings and was friends with owner Al Spalding, was completely dismissive of Ward and his breakaway group, saying they were motivated simply by greed. "I felt bound in honor to stand by my friends, even if I sank with them, and at that time the skies did look remarkably dark," he wrote. " The fact that the majority of the League clubs had the season before made a great deal of money excited the cupidity of certain capitalists, and they, finding the players dissatisfied over some minor grievances, incited them to revolt."[19] Anson changed his tune about the Players' League after Spalding dumped him from the Chicago club when it reorganized in 1893, a move Anson felt was a betrayal. By 1900, Anson was among the leading members of the baseball fraternity who took steps to create yet another league, the New American Association, to rival the National League. He had changed his tune and insisted that competition would actually benefit both leagues.[20] Anson and his associates failed to get their loop off the ground, but a year later others succeeded, establishing the American League. Also anxious to stay loyal to his friends, most of whom had jumped to the Players' League, was fan favorite King Kelly, the right fielder of the Boston Beaneaters. He had signed to become the playing manager of the PL's Boston Reds. Chicago's Al Spalding offered him a stunning $10,000 to turn his back on the upstart league and return to the National League, but Kelly rejected it, saying: "I can't go back on the boys."[21]

The Players' League created financial hardship for the American Association in particular, and rough going for some National League teams like the Alleghenys in Pittsburgh. The club had so many untried rookies that it became widely known as the "Innocents" for the 1890 season. Aside from Sunday, the only other players with much experience were catcher Doggie Miller, pitcher Bill Sowders, and second baseman Fred Dunlap. William Nimick held on as president while an associate, J. Palmer O'Neill, ran the club

13. Turning Back the Clock

and hired former Louisville pitcher Guy Hecker as manager. During the course of the 1890 season, a total of 52 players wore the Allegheny uniform as Hecker scrambled to field a competitive team. Meanwhile, aside from Galvin and Hanlon, the Players' League Burghers included Fred Carroll, Ed Morris, Harry Staley, Jake Beckley, Jack Glasscock, Al Maul, Jocko Fields, Bill Kuehne, and pitcher John Tener. The latter was treasurer of the Brotherhood, a future governor of Pennsylvania and president of the National League. Tener had pitched for Chicago in 1889, when he won 15 games and lost 15. In all, nearly 80 players jumped to the new organization from the National League and nearly 20 from the American Association.[22]

In 1890, professional baseball would again have three major leagues. But unlike 1884, when the Union Association appeared, the third league would prove more attractive and viable. Because it featured the biggest stars in the game, attendance at most Players' League parks was strong, at least to start the season. Like the old National Association, it would be player-centered. Players had turned back the clock to create a league in which they would make key decisions, not the capitalists they found to bankroll the operation. The National League fought back by setting a schedule that matched game dates already picked by PL clubs in cities where both leagues operated.[23] That meant they had to fight to fill the seats in their parks on the same day. As a result, both suffered.

In January 1890, once he secured Exposition Park for the season, Burghers manager Hanlon let contracts for construction of new grandstands, demolition of old ones and for new fill to raise the low-lying field. He hired Galvin as superintendent to oversee the work.[24] The pitcher liked the extra income, but had his hands full as he managed a crew trying to update the park.

In late February, it was reported in the *Pittsburgh Commercial Gazette* that the National League had tried to persuade Galvin to forsake the rebel team and rejoin the League, a not surprising effort, given Spalding's attempt to lure King Kelly back into the fold.

> The report which was current on Saturday that the National League bribery agent was in the city and was going to work on Jimmy Galvin made the veteran pitcher mad. "Do you think he will come after me?" said Jimmy to a friend yesterday. "Well, if he does he must be a pretty good, stout man, or I'll give him a thump in the nose that'll take him some time to forget. Just let him tackle me on the subject of desertion and he'll get a dose of Brotherhood knuckles that will make him sick. I ain't got any time to argue the question.[25]

Galvin was a promoter for the new venture by the Brotherhood, even though he had not been among its most ardent proponents. He was there for his "brothers" and became a willing foot soldier once the Players' League was up and running. A story would later surface that he was offered a significant inducement to abandon his brothers, but resisted it as well. Early in the season, shortly before the first home game for the Burghers, *Sporting Life* sought Galvin's views on the situation to date. As always, he provided good copy:

> Pittsburgh, April 14.—"Well, we are still together and our salaries are being paid with the same punctuality as if we were still playing in the National League," said old Jim Galvin, Saturday, as he flourished his check for two weeks' salary before the eyes of the writer. "Come and see us if you want to see the difference between professional and amateur ball. Hecker and his crowd are not in it, I tell you, and Galvin never told a lie in his life. I tell you Nimick and [Allegheny club secretary Al] Scandrett will be awful tired two months from this date, when we are paying dividends and they are making assessments to keep a minor league grade club in the field. We have the people with us and you can gamble we are not going to disappoint them. The League people said we would not keep together until the opening of the season. We have done so and lie number one is nailed. They said we would have to wait on gate receipts to pay salaries, so lie number two is disposed of to the satisfaction of all reasonable men, for this check is the proof of it. We will keep right on and by acts, not words, convince the public that base ball players are fit and able to govern themselves."[26]

Galvin did his best to ensure that Exposition Park was ready for Opening Day, April 19. But he found himself on a tight schedule, often delayed by heavy rains and occasional flooding. When the gates opened to the public, some work was not yet finished. A grandstand seating 4,000 had been completed but another to seat 3,000 was still being erected. Both the Burghers and Innocents opened their seasons the same day and held competing parades from different hotels to their respective parks, where concerts were scheduled. An estimated 8,500 spectators crammed into Exposition Park to see Galvin and the Burghers face the Chicago Pirates of Charlie Comiskey. About 1,550 appeared at Recreation Park to see Billy Sunday's Alleghenys take on the Cleveland Spiders of Henry Larkin in the National League game.

The poor condition of the playing field at Exposition Park led to multiple errors, especially by the home team. Galvin started strongly but toward the end of the game was hit hard. He surrendered 10 hits to seven for Silver King and Chicago won the game, 10–2. A few blocks north at Recreation Park, the Innocents edged Cleveland, 3–2. On April 21, the Burghers defeated Chicago, 5–2, before only 474 fans under threatening skies and cold winds. Galvin again pitched, this time "one of his old-time games," and found strong support from his fielders.[27] The Alleghenys, meanwhile, edged Cleveland, 11–9. The following two days, the Burghers and Alleghenys split their remaining opening-series games with Chicago and Cleveland, respectively. In their April 23 contest with Cleveland, the crowd for the Alleghenys numbered 17, of which only six paid for their tickets. The Innocents won, 20–12. Before the end of the month, the Burghers and some other PL clubs dropped the price of admission from 50 cents to 25 cents, in a bid to undercut National League teams playing at home on the same dates. In Pittsburgh, the Burghers were already outdrawing the Innocents by a ten-to-one margin.[28] By the beginning

13. Turning Back the Clock

The Pittsburgh Players' League team of 1890, to which most of the Alleghenys switched for the season. From top, clockwise, outer circle: Harry Staley, Jake Beckley, Jocko Fields, Jerry Hurley, Bill Kuehne, Ed Morris, Yank Robinson, Al Maul, Joe Visner, Tommy Corcoran, Tom Quinn. Inner circle, clockwise from top: Ned Hanlon, Fred Carroll, Pud Galvin, John Tener (Carnegie Library of Pittsburgh).

of May, both the Players' League and National League clubs in Pittsburgh were in fifth place in their respective loops.

Pittsburgh, a blue-collar, working-class city of more than 240,000, and its sister Allegheny City, with another 105,000, were more disposed toward a local team in which players, rather than capitalists, called the shots. Residents sympathized with those who opposed the reserve clause, a form of economic slavery. Memories of mine and railroad strikes, especially the 1877 railroad strike and the violence that claimed more than 40 lives in Pittsburgh, were still fresh. Labor favored the players and the upstart Burghers.

The Burghers entertained the Buffalo Bisons of Deacon White and Jack Rowe on May 2 with Ed Morris appeared in the pitching box. The Pittsburgh club outplayed the Bisons in every respect and came up with a 4-1 win. The next day, before a crowd of about 3,000, the largest since Opening Day, Galvin took the ball and completely mastered the Bisons batters. He allowed only five scattered hits in a 6-2 win. In the third inning, the pudgy Galvin did something he had not done in quite some time: he stole a base, catching pitcher George Haddock by surprise as he scampered to third. "The crowd went wild and Jimmy was compelled to make his bow in front of the grand stand before he again took his place in the pitcher's box," said the *Pittsburgh Dispatch*.[29] After the game, a disappointed Jack Rowe was quoted as saying: "Well, you have a better club than I anticipated. I knew it was good one, but I thought, and still think, that we have a better [one]. Of course, your club was at home and we were visitors, which makes a great difference, as any base ball man can tell you."

On May 5 in Chicago, the Burghers disappointed fans of the Pirates on their opening day, winning by a score of 13-5, with Staley pitching. The next day, Galvin had a poor outing, giving up 14 runs as Chicago bounced back for a decisive 14-6 victory. A Pittsburgh paper said Galvin "appeared out of sorts," unable to limber up his arm on a cold day.[30] On May 19, both the Burghers and Alleghenys came out on the short end of big scores in Philadelphia and Brooklyn, respectively. With Galvin pitching, the Players' team was blasted, 16-3, by the Quakers, while the Nationals' team was hammered, 18-2, by the Bridegrooms. The losses kept the Burghers in sixth place in the eight-team PL and Allegheny seventh in the eight-team National League. The Burghers played three games in Buffalo in early June and won two of them, despite Rowe's assurances earlier in Allegheny City that home field made all the difference to success. It marked Galvin's first pitching in that city since he left five years earlier. On June 3, he pitched well in a second Burghers victory, 7-3, and seemed anxious to impress the crowds before which he had performed so well in a Bisons uniform. "Pitcher Galvin used to be a Buffalo player, but was thrown overboard, and he determined to goose the present Buffalos if possible," the *Pittsburgh Dispatch* said. "He nearly succeeded, and only special intervention of Providence allowed the Buffalos to score. Outside of his superb pitching Galvin batted out two timely hits."[31] Back in Buffalo again for a doubleheader on June 14, the Bisons batters had their revenge, hitting Galvin hard and winning the opening game, 9-6. The two clubs met again in Allegheny City on June 19, when Galvin pitched a strong game and helped himself with two hits. The Burghers pounded the visitors, 19-6, helped along by homers from Beckley, Hanlon and Carroll.

13. Turning Back the Clock 175

By the end of June, as the Innocents fell to last place in the National League and continued to struggle at the gate, acting president J. Palmer O'Neill announced that games slated for July 4 in Brooklyn would instead be moved to Recreation Park to boost the club financially. The Burghers continued to outdraw his team, and money was growing tight. By late July, O'Neill agreed to play all his club's remaining 23 games on the road. In early August, the Alleghenys lost four straight games to Brooklyn, losses which put the Bridegrooms in first place and kept the Pittsburgh nine in the National League basement. This was part of a string of 23 straight losses for the hapless Innocents/Alleghenys. Fred Dunlap, the team's best-paid player, was released to save money and because of his weak bat. He replied by angrily accusing manager Guy Hecker of drunkenness and poor pitching. It was not a happy clubhouse.[32] In August, the popular Billy Sunday was traded to the Philadelphia Phillies for two lesser players and $1,100 cash as O'Neill fought to stay afloat. This marked Sunday's last season before he turned to preaching. By the end of the 1890 campaign, the National League club had managed only 23 wins with 113 losses, a record of futility. That put them 66½ games back of the pennant-winning Brooklyn Bridegrooms.

Meanwhile, attendance had begun to slip for the Burghers, and other Players' League teams were feeling the pinch financially. The baseball war being waged by three leagues had proven costly all around. Toward the end of the year, it was estimated that the National League lost $231,000, while the PL lost $125,000. Pittsburgh's J. Palmer O'Neill put his club's deficit at $5,700.[33] The American Association was also struggling, but numbers were not readily available.

The Burghers remained in sixth place through late July and early August, losing games it was expected to win, as crowds thinned. At the tail end of July, the fickle nature of the club's fans was becoming apparent. When he pitched, Galvin was sometimes the object of cat-calls and chants of "Put Morris in the box," when the fault really lay in poor fielding behind him, as the *Pittsburgh Dispatch* noted in early August.[34] The Burghers had begun to play better than in previous weeks, but its record stood at 37 wins and 42 losses. Meanwhile, the Innocents/Alleghenys remained in the National League cellar with 18 wins and 66 losses. On August 6 in Cleveland, a rookie pitcher named Cy Young appeared for the National League Spiders in a game against Cap Anson's White Stockings. Young, 23, started what would become a Hall of Fame career by allowing only three hits as the Spiders won, 8–1. He would win 510 more by the time his career ended in 1911, making him the winningest pitcher of all time. Two days later, in Pittsburgh, Ed Morris was released for heavy drinking and being out of condition to play baseball. Seven members of the club were implicated, including Galvin and Carroll—who didn't deny the allegation—but only Morris was released. Galvin had an outstanding performance on August 18 at home when he led the Burghers to 5–3 win over the Cleveland Infants. His pitching was effective and Cleveland scored its only run on errors. But Galvin's work with the bat was special that day. He hit a single in his first at-bat and crushed a triple in the eighth inning, "and every one of the 1,325 people present got up on their toes and shouted," noted the *Dispatch*.[35]

By the end of August, it was generally agreed that the warfare among the three leagues must come to an end and talk was beginning about the following season and consolidating efforts. Despite being released in early August, Ed Morris continued to practice with the Burghers and told a reporter he was looking to hire a lawyer because he was unhappy at being made a scapegoat for the woes of the club. On September 1 in Brooklyn, the Innocents and Bridegrooms played what is believed to be the first triple-header in major league history. With losses of 10–9, 3–2, and 8–4, the visitors extended their losing streak to 22 games. The streak would reach 24. The club's dismal record of 23–113 was the worst in the major leagues until the Cleveland Spiders eclipsed it in 1899 with a 20–134 mark. In late September, Ned Hanlon was insisting the Players' League Burghers would return for 1891, while at the same time papers were reporting the National League team was dead and would not return.[36] It was estimated that the Innocents/Alleghenys had attracted a mere 16,064 fans during the season, for an average home attendance of 411, while the Burghers drew 117,123. Only the National League teams in Brooklyn and Philadelphia had outdrawn their PL counterparts. Overall, the Players' League drew 980,611 to 813,678 by the National League.[37]

Galvin was spotted on the streets of Buffalo in late October by an enterprising newsman who sought his thoughts on the season past and what the future held for him and the Buffalo Bisons. Under the headline, "Galvanized Wisdom," the report went this way:

> For some time past Galvin has been inhaling the ozone of Buffalo to regain his health again. "Gentle Jeems," who is fair, fat and forty, but claims to be only seventeen, was interviewed by a Buffalo reporter.
> "What do you think of the outcome of the base ball war, Mr. Galvin?" he was asked.
> "Impossible to form any idea. One thing is certain, something must be done to make the great national game more interesting next year. A continuation of the fight during the past season between the Brotherhood and National League, means ruination to both."
> "Going to stay in Pittsburgh again this winter, or coming back to Buffalo?"
> "Don't know. I reside in Allegheny City at present, and while I am in Buffalo on a visit I might go into business here if I can find a good opening."
> "How many children have you?"
> "Only eight boys." (Laughing.)
> "Why not organize a nine of your own?"
> "That would be a galvanized team! Good idea."
> Mr. Galvin thinks that Buffalo is one of the best base ball cities in the country, if

13. *Turning Back the Clock* 177

This image of Recreation Park, taken two years after Galvin died, shows the configuration of the park, the proximity of fans to outfielders and the dirty air that prompted the steel city of Pittsburgh to earn the sobriquet "Smoky City" (Library of Congress).

represented by a winning club, and this is the general opinion of many other leading players. But as the speculation now stands it is idle talk to speculate upon the future. One thing seems settled. Buffalo will be represented in some league next year, and time will reveal the name of the organization. For the present base ball enthusiasts must be contented to wait for developments.[38]

Fans in Buffalo hoping for a return to major league baseball would be disappointed. The club had placed last in the Players' League, with a record of 36 wins and 96 losses, 46½ games back of the pennant-winning Boston Reds. For 1891, the Bisons joined the Eastern Association.

After peace talks were initiated in November, it became clear that the Players' League would not survive, as some of its backers and teams suddenly pulled out. The men who bankrolled the teams had expected dividends quickly and were not prepared to wait and underwrite another year of costly diamond warfare. By the end of the year, Pittsburgh and New York amalgamated their National League and Players' League clubs. Other teams took other steps. Some simply expired, like Cleveland and Buffalo. In Chicago, Al Spalding bought the Players' League Pirates in a deal valued at $25,000.[39]

Galvin spoke to a writer from *Sporting Life* late in November when it was clear the Players' League was being relegated to history. His remarks were in sharp contrast to those he shared with the same publication in April when he painted a rosy picture of the Burghers and their new league. "If there is any ball player who is glad the great struggle is over it is the veteran," began the story. "And one will not laugh when they are told that Galvin refused a house and lot to jump the Players' League some time during the fall—August or thereabouts—although by that time he had come to the conclusion that he had made a bad play by jumping the National League." The offer of a house for Galvin to jump back to the National League came as a revelation. The story continued:

> "I tell you what it is," said Jeems, as he stood in a crowd of base ball people yesterday afternoon, "I'm kinder [sic] glad it's over. I knew I had put my foot in it not long after I signed, but what could I do? They talk about slaves. Every time they sold me I benefited by the operation. When Buffalo sold me to Pittsburgh I received $700 cash and had my salary raised $1,000. That wasn't so bad, was it? And I know dozens of men who were benefited by their sale." Jeems is a National League man with all his heart now, and to hear him talk you would think he had about 100 shares of stock in the organization.[40]

John Montgomery Ward, the leading light in the Brotherhood, was terribly disappointed at the collapse of the league and blamed it on "stupidity, avarice and treachery."[41] He recalled failing to persuade the money men to agree to change the schedule so playing dates wouldn't conflict with National League games, but he had met stiff resistance from the new capitalists determined to thwart more established ones, a hawk-like attitude which hurt both sides.[42] A particularly insightful post-mortem was penned by historian Charles Alexander. He wrote: "It was a unique episode in baseball history ... an experiment ... [that] might have changed the entire sport's structure.... The ballplayers had tried something drastic to redress what they saw as a gross imbalance in their circumstances vis-à-vis their employers. The serf's revolt didn't work."[43]

Pud Galvin finished his season with a disappointing 12 wins and 13 losses. He pitched 217 innings, recorded one shutout, and had a lofty 4.35 earned run average. It was the worst performance of his career, and tongues began wagging that it was time for the old man to pack it in. Harry Staley had been the best pitcher for the Burghers, winning 21 games but losing 25. Al Maul picked up 16 wins with 12 losses, while Ed Morris, with his limited duty of 15 starts, had eight wins and seven losses in what would be the lefty's final season. For pitchers, it had been a challenge to put up good numbers on a team as weak as the Burghers, whose overall record was 60 wins and 68 losses.

Despite some outstanding performances during the year, Galvin had an increasing number of bad ones. His days appeared to be numbered. But the "Old Sport" felt he still had some life left in his arm. He had been pitching for 16 years and would turn 34 on Christmas Day, 1890. He had grown older, wiser and heavier—and rather flexible about for whom he was willing to play.

But Pud Galvin wasn't a quitter.

14

"The action ... was piratical."

Following the collapse of the Players' League, all parties agreed that players who had jumped to its teams from the National League or American Association could return to their former clubs without penalty. In Pittsburgh, the merger of the Alleghenys with the Burghers produced a reorganization under the name Pittsburgh Athletic Company, with J. Palmer O'Neill as president. A decision was made early on to use Exposition Park, the updated facility on which Pud Galvin and his crew had worked so hard, as home field for the club still known locally as the Alleghenys.

Seven members of the Brotherhood team opted to sign with the club: pitchers Pud Galvin, Harry Staley and Al Maul; catchers Fred Carroll and Jocko Fields; first baseman Jake Beckley, and centerfielder Ned Hanlon. Only Galvin, Maul and Beckley would last the entire season, which would prove to be an unexpectedly difficult campaign. Hanlon was the playing manager. Pitcher John Tener opted to retire from baseball after only three years in the professional game, to pursue banking and other interests that would see him elected as a U.S. congressman, governor of Pennsylvania and then president of the National League. Among the new faces was Connie Mack, a catcher who played with the Brotherhood club in Buffalo after jumping from Washington.

The new team in Pittsburgh would play a key role in hastening the demise of the American Association, which expired at the end of 1891. The AA had been buffeted by collateral damage during the war between the Players' League and the National League. Attendance at its games suffered the most, and several key players like Charlie Comiskey had bailed for Brotherhood teams. Late in 1890, Allan W. Thurman, a minority shareholder in the Columbus Solons of the American League, proposed that the Players' League, National League, and American Association should be rolled into two organizations. His notion became the basis of the settlement that was eventually reached, bringing an end to the war. For this, he picked up the nickname

"The White Winged Angel of Peace," and became president of the American Association. Thurman was also asked to chair a three-member "arbitration board" to sort out any issues that arose between the National League and the American Association. "White Wings," as he was also known, would soon be tested to his limits.[1]

As clubs in the National League and American Association began to sign players for the 1891 campaign, they discovered that the Players' League interlude had made business such as the reserve list more confusing than in previous years. Philadelphia was a case in point. During the 1889 season the city had two teams, the Phillies of the National League and the Athletics in the American Association. In 1890, those two clubs were joined by the Quakers, the Players' League club (several years earlier, the Phillies had played under that name). At the end of 1890 and the collapse of the Players' League, the American Association expelled the insolvent Athletics and replaced them with the Quakers. For 1891, owners of the Quakers hired the principals of the former Athletics to assemble their team for the AA, to be called the Athletics. Through a clerical error in all the changes, committed, apparently, by the former management of the Athletics, two of their players were omitted from the team's reserve list: star second baseman Louis Bierbauer and hard-hitting leftfielder Harry Stovey, an accomplished base stealer. In 1890, Bierbauer had jumped to the Ward's Wonders PL club in Brooklyn, while Stovey was with the PL's Boston Reds. The oversight was spotted by Pittsburgh manager Ned Hanlon, president J. Palmer O'Neill and former manager Guy Hecker, and they decided to pursue Bierbauer, a native of Erie, Pennsylvania. On January 19, 1891, the same day the Players' League officially expired, Hanlon signed Bierbauer to a contract for $4,500, giving him an advance of $1,000. It had been no easy task, as Alfred Spink, founder of *The Sporting News*, recalled in his 1911 book, *The National Game*. Bierbauer, an outdoorsman, had been enjoying some rest and relaxation in a remote shack along Lake Erie, far from baseball.

> Ned Hanlon, then managing Pittsburgh, went to Erie in the depth of the Winter to secure a contract from Bierbauer. He found him on Presque Isle Peninsula, his favorite "hang out." Hanlon had to cross the ice on the harbor in a bitter storm, but he finally reached Bierbauer's shack and before leaving had secured his signature to a contract to play with Pittsburgh.[2]

For his part, Stovey attracted the attention of the Boston Beaneaters of the National League, who signed him to a deal. Pittsburgh and Boston defended signing the players, saying both were free agents because neither had been reserved by the deadline to do so by their former club. The American Association howled at what had happened. It argued that both players were property of the Athletics and should be returned to them. The failure to reserve the pair had been a mere oversight, its officials said. Pittsburgh

14. "The action ... was piratical." 181

The signing of second baseman Louis Bierbauer of the American Association's Philadelphia Athletics by the Alleghenys for the 1891 National League season produced outrage from the AA and a cry that the move was "piratical." The team was soon known as the Pirates, and the Allegheny name was consigned to history (National Baseball Hall of Fame Library, Cooperstown, New York).

president O'Neill stood his ground as the controversy escalated. In February, with both sides dug in, the matter was turned over to the arbitration board on which AA president "White Wings" Thurman sat, along with Philadelphia Phillies owner John I. Rogers and Louis Krauthoff, president of the Western Association and a former executive with the AA Kansas City Cowboys. The board, for which the AA magnates had high hopes because two of its three members were considered sympathetic to the Association, was asked to consider the cases of five players in all, including another Pittsburgh signee, Connie Mack, whose rights were claimed by the Association team in Boston.

In arguing the case that Bierbauer should stay with the Athletics and that Pittsburgh had acted improperly, an unnamed American Association representative exploded in rage with an accusation that would make baseball history: "The action of the Pittsburgh club in signing Bierbauer was piratical."[3] As Frederick G. Lieb, author of *The Pittsburgh Pirates*, noted: "Somehow, no one around the Pittsburgh club seemed ashamed, and it wasn't long before the piratical Pittsburgh club became known as the Pirates."[4]

After deliberations that lasted until 3 a.m. on February 14 at a Chicago hotel, the arbitration board decided Pittsburgh could keep Bierbauer and Mack, while Boston was awarded Stovey.

In summing up, the board said: Undoubtedly Pittsburgh has the legal right to the men, but morally it has not. It ought withdraw [sic] its claim, but as it does not we must reluctantly decide in favor of Pittsburgh. The case of H. G. Stovey was exactly the same as Bierbauer except that he was claimed by Boston and the board was compelled to decide in favor of Boston. Connie Mack was given to Pittsburgh.[5]

The National League's much-loathed salary limitation plan was reinstated, alongside the reserve clause. The arbitration board, by suggesting a lack of morality in Pittsburgh's behavior, managed to stoke the fires of those who believed the club had acted like pirates. The decision had an odor that lingered. None more so than for Thurman, whose vote to support the claims of the National League clubs prompted calls for his resignation by indignant members of the American Association. As the *New York Clipper* reported, their surprise was mixed with anger. "The American Association stood by the National League all through the latter's fight with the Players' League, and it certainly did not expect, nor was it prepared for such a seemingly unfair deal as it has received. It is to be hoped, for the sake of fair play, that the National League will decline to accept the decision."[6] The publication urged the league to "right what apparently is a wrong" to avoid a conflict between "two great organizations." But neither Pittsburgh nor Boston, nor the National League, was willing to backtrack. On February 18, the American Association ousted president Thurman and renounced the National Agreement under which the AA and NL had respected the contracts of players

14. "The action ... was piratical."

signed by either league. The war with the Players' League was over, but a new round of hostilities had broken out with an old friend turned adversary.

On March 1, under the saucy headline "Talk About Pirates," the *Pittsburgh Dispatch* noted that shortly after the arbitration board decision, the American Association club in Chicago had wired its blunt assessment of the situation to the Boston AA team: "It is war. Sign all the good League players you want." The newspaper also quoted Thomas Kalbfus, secretary of the Association club in Washington, as saying: "We are now pirates and have hoisted the black flag against the National League for the good of baseball."[7] Pittsburgh, which had sparked the war, unfurled its own Jolly Roger and began to raid the Association for even more talent. President O'Neill signed third baseman Charles Reilly from Columbus and pitcher Mark Baldwin of the expired Chicago PL club, formerly of Columbus. Baldwin, a Pittsburgh native, had already signed with Columbus, but readily succumbed to O'Neill's blandishments. Shortly after signing on, Baldwin went to St. Louis at the behest of O'Neill, in a bid to recruit the Association club's pitcher Silver King, along with King's former catcher Jack O'Connor, over in Columbus.

St. Louis Browns owner Chris Von der Ahe was outraged. He pressed charges against Baldwin and had him arrested for conspiring with others to induce King to break his contract with the Browns. The case was dropped, then resurrected, then dropped again, but Pittsburgh was allowed to keep King. Litigation between St. Louis and Baldwin (and Pittsburgh) continued for years before Baldwin ultimately prevailed. O'Connor signed with Pittsburgh, but jumped back to Columbus, claiming Baldwin obtained his signature after getting him drunk.[8] He said the $750 he was given to sign the contract was a "bribe" and didn't plan to return it, in a bid to teach Pittsburgh a lesson.[9] O'Neill wasn't done there, however. He became branded as J. "Pirate" O'Neill, or "the Pirate," for his continued predations.[10] He and an associate, Frank Chamberlain of Chicago, described as O'Neill's "dummy" by the *New York Clipper,* purchased the Cincinnati club of the American Association for $30,000 to bring it into the fold of the National League.[11] It was later acknowledged by National League president Nick Young that O'Neill had acted for the league in the successful, but difficult, negotiations.[12] Before he was done, the "piratical" O'Neill also signed pitcher Silver King, formerly of the St. Louis Browns, and leftfielder Roger "Pete" Browning, a slugger from Louisville. Browning would leave for a greener outfield in Cincinnati partway through the season.

Poaching and pirating continued as the better-financed National League clubs were able to recruit players they wanted without worrying about the niceties of contracts they had signed with American Association clubs. Historian David Pietrusza said the AA quickly came out the loser:

It was a war to the death, and the Association cracked apart almost immediately. Milwaukee, Columbus and Louisville were total financial disasters. As early as June, Columbus was mumbling about peace. In August, Boston desperately cut admissions to 25 cents, a violation of an agreement made when [the National League Beaneaters president Arthur P.] Soden and company allowed Tim Prince [and his Reds] into Boston. To forestall desertions of individual franchises ... the majority of stock in each club was transferred to the Association itself.[13]

The loop struggled to finish the year in which the Boston Reds captured the last championship of the so-called "Beer and Whisky League." The AA had gone head to head with the National League for 10 seasons, becoming by far its most successful rival. In December, peace talks with the National League produced an agreement whereby four of the strongest AA teams were brought into the National League: Baltimore, Louisville, Washington and St. Louis. This made for a 12-team loop, to be called the National League and Association. It marked the fifth time the league had triumphed over a rival professional organization with which it had battled for top playing talent (the National Association, International Association, Union Association, and Players' League being the other four). Players on the teams not part of the new organization were considered free agents and sought work wherever they could find it.

In March of 1891, as Pittsburgh president O'Neill was still scooping up players from the AA, he had to fend off a rumor that Pud Galvin was to be released. "A few days ago," the *Pittsburgh Dispatch* reported on March 16, "Mr. O'Neill stated emphatically that Galvin would be on the team. If any of the officials are desirous of getting rid of Jimmy they should remember that he is one of the most popular players in Pittsburgh."[14] The next day, St. Patrick's Day, the same newspaper reported that Galvin, along with former manager and first baseman Guy Hecker, and center fielder/catcher John Henry "Tun" Berger, were issued their walking papers by the club. Galvin sought his release when he was offered $2,500 to play, less money than he had earned the previous year, believed to be about $3,000. O'Neill, having signed new pitchers Mark Baldwin and Scott Stratton, along with the returning Harry Staley, was prepared to let Galvin go, saying the pitching situation had changed since he had assured everyone the aging hurler would be back. The *Dispatch* lamented the loss of Galvin in particular, saying: "It is difficult to think of a local team minus 'Gentle Jeems,' and many a glorious day he has made for the enthusiastic crowds that used to be packed into Recreation Park."[15] Galvin and manager Ned Hanlon continued to dicker about his services for the upcoming season, however, and on March 26 it was announced that a deal had finally been struck, under which Galvin would receive $2,500 and a bonus of another $500, provided he pitched "a satisfactory number of winning games."[16] It was widely surmised that club management yielded to

14. "The action ... was piratical." 185

PNC Park is just a few steps east of Exposition Park, where Pud Galvin and his teammates played, and like its predecessor affords a fine view of downtown Pittsburgh across the Allegheny River. Once known as Allegheny City, the area is today known as the North Side. On game day, the adjacent Roberto Clemente Bridge spanning the Allegheny River becomes a pedestrian walkway to connect downtown to its ballpark (photograph by author).

public pressure when it agreed to bring "Old Sport" back for yet another season.

This year the Pittsburgh club was among the first in baseball to travel to Florida for spring training. The team was sent to St. Augustine in late March and played exhibition games there and in Jacksonville against Cleveland in early April. Three games were arranged in Havana and another at Key West, as the club prepared for Opening Day back home.[17] On April 3, in an exhibition game against Cleveland, the battery of Pud Galvin and Connie Mack was particularly impressive as Pittsburgh downed the Spiders, 5–3. Staley also pitched, but it was Galvin who drew praise. "Galvin pitched in the old-time fashion," the *Pittsburgh Dispatch* reported about the game in the sunny south.[18]

Galvin was handed the ball for the Opening Day game on April 22 at Exposition Park against Chicago, which had adopted the nickname the Colts, or Anson's Colts, during the 1890 season. A grand parade that included the visiting team began at a hotel in Pittsburgh, then stopped at city hall, where civic employees gathered on the front steps to wish the hometown club good luck. "Every street the procession passed was crowded with people. Every pedestrian, from the banker to the bootblack, stopped to look into the faces of the Chicago team and to gossip on the result of J. Palmer O'Neill's piracies," it was reported. The parade crossed the bridge to Allegheny City and the ballpark, where Mayor James Wyman and many other civic officials were among the 6,500 in attendance. They included, it was noted, city coroner Heber McDowell, who "viewed each play as seriously as if it had been a part of the testimony of an inquest." Also present were leading businessmen, doctors and lawyers, and others from law enforcement, including Allegheny County Sheriff W. H. McCleary. The *Dispatch* reported comments from excited fans who obviously had embraced the new name for the club and its president: "The Pirate certainly has a fine looking set of men," said one, while another said: "There goes J. Palmer, the Pirate." Hopes were riding high because after so many mediocre seasons for their team, fans seemed to think the predatory practices of club management might produce the winner they so badly wanted. Upon hearing umpire Phil Powers, the former catcher for the London Tecumsehs, call "play ball," the newspaper said: "In response, the Pirate King's forces and the chieftain of the West commenced hostilities."[19]

The Chicago bats went to work early and "touched up" Galvin for five runs by the sixth inning, when the Pittsburgh hitters replied and put six runs across the plate to lead, 6–5. Chicago added another run in the ninth inning to force extra innings. In the tenth, Chicago third baseman Bill Dahlen led off with a triple and was brought home by rightfielder Cliff Carroll, who singled, for a 7–6 Chicago win. The following day, April 23, with Staley pitching, the Colts again won, this time, 9–2. Pittsburgh edged Chicago, 11–8, on April 24 for its first win, but lost a ten-inning contest, 8–7, the next day as Baldwin pitched poorly and handed the ball to Galvin, who then passed it to Staley. Pitcher Silver King arrived in Pittsburgh just before the month ended, to become yet another arm for the Pirates. At $5,000, his salary led the club, $1,300 more than Baldwin and twice that of Galvin. As if motivated by the arrival of King and determined to prove his own worth, Galvin was outstanding on April 27, and Pittsburgh downed Cleveland, 7–1, at home, with Galvin giving up six hits. The *Pittsburgh Dispatch* said Galvin was "in great form.... Jeems was out in his glory."[20] On May 1, he led Pittsburgh to a 5–2 victory over Chicago at its home opener before 7,000 spectators. Galvin hadn't originally been expected to pitch, given his frequent problems with the boys from the Windy City, but as the *Dispatch* noted: "As soon as today's contest opened came the first disappointment. The scorecards had it either King or Staley for Pittsburgh, but at the last moment the 'Pirates' put in old horse Galvin.

14. "The action ... was piratical."

The old man lifted his hat to the smiling audience. Neither side sent a run over the plate until the fourth. Then the 'Pirates' helped themselves [to four runs]."[21]

The *Chicago Times* took it upon itself to describe the appearance of the aging hurler as he faced down the young and fresh-faced Colts in their home opener. The *Dispatch* picked it up and reprinted it for the benefit of readers in Pittsburgh:

> As he appeared yesterday on the grounds Galvin was the antithesis of the ideal ball player. He is only about 5 feet nothing in height, but he displaces more cubic feet of air than Anson. He is so fat that his cheeks stand out like a pair of toy balloons and his calves hang over his shoe tops. But the Chicagos could hit him safely but six times, and he kept those six hits well scattered. At the bat he made the first hit in the game and scored the first run.[22]

Noteworthy in the report of the opening game in Chicago was the use of the term "Pirates" for the Allegheny team by a local newspaper back in Pittsburgh. Papers in other cities had been using the term in a derogatory fashion, but it was slowly becoming a source of pride in Pittsburgh. The reports of two more games in Chicago, which the Colts won by single runs, saw the *Pittsburgh Dispatch* use the term four times in one game report and five times in another. On May 5, with Galvin pitching, Pittsburgh was blanked, 1–0, by Chicago's Ed Stein. The latter game featured the first triple play of the season when Pete Browning bunted too hard and the ball was caught on the fly by second baseman Fred Pfeffer. He threw it to shortstop Jimmy Cooney, who covered second and relayed it to Cap Anson at first, retiring base runners Jake Beckley and Fred Carroll. The new team name made it into headlines in a report of a May 7 game in Cincinnati when Staley pitched well against the Reds. The *Dispatch* headlined the story: "Of the Very Finest. The Pirates Get Down to Good Work and Defeat the Reds in a Great Argument." The club's new, unofficial name was no longer drawing quotation marks as the Alleghenys name was quietly retired. But bad press continued. On their arrival in Cincinnati, the *Dispatch* noted, a local paper, the *Post*, headlined the story: "Men of dishonor. Baseballists who disgrace the diamond represented in J. Palmer O'Neil's [sic] Pittsburgh pirates. Can they play honest ball? the public asks." The Cincinnati paper added: "To-day O'Neil's [sic] pirates, Pittsburgh's all star aggregation, or as best named, the contract jumper team, will make their appearance at the League park for four games."[23] The paper reminded its readers about several of the Pittsburgh players who had jumped to the club while still under contract elsewhere.

The Pirates had just left Cincinnati when the Brooklyn Bridegrooms arrived for a series of games with the Reds. On May 14, history was made when Cincinnati pitcher Hoss Radbourn shut out the Bridegrooms, 4–0, allowing only four hits. It marked his 300th victory. Radbourn, 36, would play for only three more months, with 10 more wins, before ending his career. As usual in those days, no fuss was made about his achievement, likely because no one was keeping track and besides, it wouldn't have been seen as anything special. He was the fourth pitcher to hit the 300-win mark in two years. Pud Galvin accomplished it first on June 4, 1888. Next was Tim Keefe, pitching for Syracuse of the American Association on June 4, 1890, and the third was New York Giants hurler Mickey Welch, on August 11, 1890. Late in the 1892 season, John Clarkson was next to reach 300, while pitching for Cleveland.

In May, *The Sporting News* carried an item about the state of affairs in the Smoky City as the Pirates recovered from a poor start to climb from sixth place to fourth. The publication took note of what it called "Galvin's rejuvenation," noting the pitcher "has the clean well fed appearance which indicates that all is going well with him. His rejuvenation has been complete as he has lost the aldermanic proportions that seemed to indicate his ball playing days were nearly over."[24] Within a few days, however, Galvin failed to show up at practice and missed a scheduled start as rumors began to swirl that he and manager Ned Hanlon were feuding, although Hanlon denied any such thing. Soon afterward, pitcher Harry Staley, who had also quarreled with Hanlon, was released and signed by the Boston Beaneaters for $3,250, an increase from the $2,700 Pittsburgh paid him.[25]

By early June, the Pirates had slipped back to seventh place, as diminutive catcher Doggie Miller struggled when moved from behind the plate to the infield, where he made numerous errors and was blamed for several losses. Problems continued between Hanlon and the players, but the board of directors supported him and urged the manager to make any changes he felt were needed. Drinking, tardiness and suggestions of a "clique" determined to bring down Hanlon continued to afflict the team, and wins were hard to come by. Despite the poor performance, fans remained loyal. Attendance at games continued to average a bit more than 2,300.

When Galvin faltered in the seventh inning of a June 18 game in Pittsburgh, allowing Cincinnati to win, 4–3, the Pirates slipped to last place. This prompted an uncharitable observation from the *Sporting Life*, which opined: "In spite of his big outlay of money for players and the wholesale indulgence in contract-breaking, J. Palmer O'Neill and his pirates are at the tail end of the League pennant race. Is this retribution?"[26] On June 29, yet another Pittsburgh loss allowed Chicago pitcher Bill Hutchison to earn his 13th straight win over the Pirates, an 8–3 victory. By early July, the Pirates had edged past Cincinnati into seventh place, with 23 wins and 32 losses, continuing the poor showing for a team from which so much had been expected. Fans began to lose heart, and on July 29 only 400 of them turned out watch Cincinnati beat the Pirates, 8–2. About the only bright spot was the fact that Doggie

14. "The action ... was piratical."

Miller was playing better, but pitching continued to be weak. Silver Flint, the $5,000 arm, was proving to be a major disappointment. At the end of July, with the Pirates again in last place, manager Ned Hanlon was sacked and replaced by Bill McGunnigle. McGunnigle, a former pitcher, had played with Galvin in Buffalo from 1878 to 1880, and had found later success as a manager. In 1890, he had led the Brooklyn Bridegrooms to the National League pennant, and a year later managed the same team to the pennant of the American Association. McGunnigle was the only manager to win back-to-back pennants in competing major leagues. It was thought that his experience with winning teams was just what the Pirates needed, and McGunnigle was granted the authority to take all steps he felt were needed. At the same time, directors sought the resignation of president O'Neill and, when he refused, they curtailed his powers. Louis Bierbauer, the second baseman whose acquisition had given the club its new name, was named captain.[27] By the end of August, however, Bierbauer was demanding his release as the Pirates continued to struggle. "He says connection with the club is damaging his reputation," it was reported. But manager McGunnigle refused to let him go.[28]

Galvin had one of his worst outings of the season in a 7–1 loss to Boston at Exposition Park on August 25. He allowed six runs in the first inning and at the start of the second, after Beaneaters right fielder Harry Stovey took him over the left field fence for a home run, Galvin threw down the ball in disgust and walked off the field. "He was in no condition to pitch," one of the newspapers observed.[29] It was getting to the point that manager Bill McGunnigle wasn't certain what to expect from his aging hurler from one outing to the next. But true to the form he had demonstrated in his career, Galvin bounced back from a rocky performance to a good one. On September 4, Galvin was brilliant in the first game of a three-game series with the Brooklyn Bridegrooms, now managed by John Montgomery Ward. He allowed eight hits as he shut out Brooklyn, 6–0. The *Dispatch* was moved to comment:

> For the last day or two there has been a timidity relative to putting Old Sport Galvin in to pitch. It was thought that the old man would be knocked out of the box, but the Jeems [sic] showed the timid ones where they were wrong yesterday. He faced the Brooklyns and they did not get a good run, which means that Galvin put up a first-class article of ball pitching. In the aggregate there were probably enough hits made by the Brooklyn people to score some runs, but Old Sport kept these hits so far apart that tallying was not in the order of things.[30]

The Pittsburgh defense was sharp behind him, with only two errors, both by Bierbauer, while Galvin singled to left field and scored in the ninth inning. He again pitched well on September 14, leading the Pirates to a 4–3 win over the New York Giants and prompting the *Dispatch* to remark, after joking about his age: "He is still one of the foremost boxmen of the country, and seems to improve with age and rotundity."[31] Not to be outdone, Mark

Baldwin won both ends of a September 12 doubleheader in Brooklyn, 13–3 and 8–4, allowing a total of 11 hits in the two games. The second victory was his fourth in six days. Overall, however, wins were hard to come by for the Pirates in the closing weeks of the season.

Galvin was griping by mid-September that he was owed $500 by the club, the additional bonus that had been promised by former manager Ned Hanlon back in March if he pitched "a satisfactory number of winning games." He said: "I have won more games than either Baldwin or King, and one receives $3,700 and the other $5,000, while I only draw $2,500, Now, that is pretty rocky, isn't it? They thought I would be laid on the shelf before the close of the season, but here I am, feeling better than ever and pitching pretty good ball."[32] He conceded the $500 bonus was not spelled out in his contract, and J. Palmer O'Neill seized upon that omission to profess ignorance of the deal struck by his former manager. In what might have been a timely effort to put the squeeze on the Pirates for the money he said he was owed, Galvin helped the club climb to sixth place with a 12–3 shellacking of Cleveland on September 23. The *Dispatch* praised his effort in allowing only four hits: "Old Sport Galvin can step out yet and turn a trick just as gay as the youngest and most brilliant of the pitchers now before the world."[33] It did note, however, that the veteran had recently been generating some anxiety among fans: "It is, indeed, singular to note how general the fear of defeat is when Jimmy comes into the box, and yet he is one of the best winners in the business." So popular for so long, Galvin was likely dismayed to see some dissatisfaction setting in among the fans.

By late September, club officials were thoroughly tired of Silver King, the "golden" arm they had hired for $5,000 but who had pitched so poorly. They left him at home for a road trip to Chicago and decided not to reserve him for the following season when King refused to accept a reduction in pay to $3,700, the same amount they were paying Baldwin. Club directors said they carried an onerous payroll and hoped to break even for the year. As a bargaining ploy while his negotiations dragged on, Galvin threatened to bolt to the American Association team in Chicago.[34] In early November, about the same time Silver King signed with New York, Galvin came to terms with club director William W. Kerr, a principal in the Arbuckle Coffee Company and a future president of the Pirates. The contract would pay Galvin $3,000 for the 1892 season.[35] Late that same month, it was reported that J. Palmer O'Neill had sold his last stock in the club and was replaced as president by William C. Temple, a lumber, coal and citrus baron.

Galvin's numbers for the season were marginally better in 1891 than he had posted the previous year, but he was still performing far below his peak in the mid-1880s. He ranked third among Pirates pitchers, completing 31 of 33 games. He logged 246⅔ innings, won 14 games and lost the same number.

He threw 46 strikeouts and had an earned run average of 2.88. Mark Baldwin had won 22 and lost 28 (second-most in the league) and pitched 437 innings. Baldwin struck out 197 batters and had an earned run average of 2.76. Silver King had won 14 games but lost 29, the most recorded by any league pitcher. King struck out 160 batters in his 384 innings and recorded a team-high earned run average of 3.11.

Yet again, the Pittsburgh club had been a lower-rung team, finishing with 55 wins and 80 losses, placing them one game behind Cincinnati and 30.5 games behind pennant-winner Boston.

Shortly before Galvin's 35th birthday at Christmas, the nine-team American Association formally expired and four of its clubs joined the National League. Galvin, contract in hand for 1892, had every reason to believe he could continue his playing string for an 18th season of professional baseball. He was no longer pitching as well as he once had, but it was still good enough to keep playing the game he loved.

15

Final Innings

For 1892, major league baseball was again a monopoly, now operating as the League-Association, a name it would use for several years before reverting again to the National League. In late 1891, while the American Association was being negotiated into history, National League teams raided its members for talent, the most seriously targeted being the St. Louis Browns of Chris Von der Ahe. He lost every member of his starting nine to teams that would become his new competitors.[1] So Von der Ahe was busier than most other club owners throughout late winter and early spring, finding and signing replacements. The League-Association decided that for 1892, it would split the season into two parts, the first half beginning on April 12, the second on July 15. With 12 teams, a split season was seen as one that could produce new hope and a fresh start midway through the summer for lower-rung teams, in a bid to keep fan interest high. The AA was gone, but its legacy lingered because the League-Association liberalized its operating rules and copied many of its practices. Admission of 25 cents, half the usual amount, could be charged by any team that chose to do so; Sunday games were allowed where not forbidden by local law; and each team could decide whether to sell alcoholic beverages in its home park.

In Pittsburgh, manager Bill McGunnigle was let go following the last-place finish of the Pirates. His golden touch at winning pennants had failed as the club managed just 24 wins and 33 losses under his watch. He was replaced by Al Buckenberger, who had managed the Columbus Solons of the American Association to a second-place finish in 1890. A hard-working and conscientious sort, the Detroit native had never played in a major league, but he had a good eye for talent and was able to cobble together a lineup with some new and promising faces. Among them were pitchers Charley "Duke" Esper from Philadelphia and Phil "Red" Ehret from Louisville. Galvin and Baldwin were back for another campaign and so was catcher Connie Mack. Several new outfielders were signed, among them George Van Haltren, the

15. Final Innings

former pitcher for Chicago. William C. Temple became president in 1892, but he squabbled constantly with new director William W. Kerr, the coffee nabob who took such an active role in club affairs that it verged on meddling.

Galvin worked hard to get in shape for the season, determined to prove he could still play the game at its highest level. His efforts produced early dividends. In an April 1 exhibition game between the "first nine" and "second nine" of the Pirates, he attracted special attention for both his pitching and his work in the field. The *Pittsburgh Dispatch* said:

> Why, nobody could believe that it was the Galvin of many, many years ago. The old man was really there as a worthy example of the youngsters who took part in the game. His form was indeed pleasing to his old friends, in view of the many insinuations that have been made about his not taking care of himself. He is capable of showing many of them a trick or two yet.

After five innings, Galvin left the pitching box for the outfield, where he scampered around like a teenager, prompting the paper to note:

> The two thousand onlookers were satisfied there was a "ringer" in the field. But it was no ringer, it was the perennial young man Galvin, and he hopped about the outfield like a lively lawn tennis player in his suit of white. Old Sport really made a remarkable catch, in fact, two of them, and both from [catcher Doggie] Miller's bat, which performance made George very, very weary.[2]

The Pirates opened their season on April 12 in Cincinnati. Mark Baldwin was handed the ball and delivered a 7–5 win that disappointed the 7,500 Reds fans in attendance. During warm-ups, outfielder Ned Hanlon suffered a leg injury while chasing a fly ball. It was sufficiently serious to end his playing career and force him into managing full-time. Smart and aggressive, Hanlon proved to be a terrific skipper, winning five pennants with Baltimore and Brooklyn by 1900. He was inducted into baseball's Hall of Fame as a manager.

The following day, still in Cincinnati, Galvin posed no challenge for the Reds batters, but the Pirates still managed an 8–7 win.

Opening Day in Pittsburgh was April 22, and the Pirates welcomed St. Louis to town. Galvin appeared in the pitching box under leaden skies that kept the crowd to about 2,500. The home club batters teed off on Browns pitcher Ted Breitenstein in the first inning for 12 runs, chasing him from the box. Meanwhile, Galvin held the opposition bats in check until the fifth inning, when two runs scored. He helped himself by making two hits. The score was 14–3 for the Pirates when the skies opened up and the game was called after seven innings. Yet again, the *Dispatch* was moved to praise Galvin's performance:

> And Old Jeems, that good, that glorious twirler of many generations, was there, just as brimful of vigor, deception and joviality as he was many years ago, when lots of the

Downtown Pittsburgh today, as seen from Mount Washington. No longer known for its steel, the city has reinvented itself but still does most of it work downtown and crosses the Allegheny River to what is now known as the North Side for its sports. To the left of the first bridge is Heinz Field, home of the NFL Steelers. Between it and the second bridge, named after Pirates star Roberto Clemente, is PNC Park, home of the Pirates. Exposition Park was located midway between these two venues (photograph by author).

present old people were young. Jimmy is not a reed that can be shaken by the wind even though it blows a hurricane, and when he was presented with a gold-beaded cane by the Fifth Ward Allegheny Independent Fishing Club he responded by banging out one of his famous hits. Phenoms may come and phenoms may go, the gentle Jeems goes on forever.[3]

The opening series was profitable, with St. Louis' Von der Ahe taking home $2,300 as his share of the gate from the two games. Pirates manager Buckenberger said such an opening proved that Pittsburgh was one of the best baseball cities on earth. It was further suggested by the *Dispatch* that a "vast amount of money" could be earned "if the team can only win games and keep near the front."[4] On the field, however, pitching proved worse than expected. In May, a six-foot-two, left-handed rookie named Fred Woodcock was signed in a bid to turn things around for Pittsburgh, mired in seventh place at the time. On May 18, at home, Galvin had a dreadful outing, surrendering nine hits in an 8–3 loss to Cincinnati. He was shelled during the second inning when seven Reds runs crossed the plate. About the same time, it was announced that club directors were pursuing Tommy Burns, the former third baseman from Chicago, to become captain. Notoriously gruff and uncompromising, Burns had been mentored by the hard-bitten Chicago manager, Cap Anson, and was seen as just the tonic needed to get the Pirates performing better.

Galvin had a strong game on May 21 in Chicago, when he allowed just three hits, but Anson's Colts blanked the Pirates, 1–0. He was poorly supported by the men behind him. At one point, after making a hit and advancing to third, Galvin tried to make it home on a line drive by Bierbauer, but was thrown out at the plate. The *Pittsburgh Press* accused Galvin of "laziness ... [he] might have scored if he had used a little exertion and slid."[5] The criticism stung, but it wouldn't be the last the rotund pitcher would face this season. The win was the 13th straight by Chicago over the Pirates. Two days later, on May 23, that streak was ended when Mark Baldwin led Pittsburgh to a 5–4 victory. By the time of an eastern road trip in late May with Tom Burns in control as captain, the team's fielding and hitting had become anemic. In Washington May 27, Galvin was pulled from the box while the Nationals belted 14 hits in a 6–4 win. The lefty Woodcock, from whom much was expected, was released after losing two games and winning just one.

The Pirates ended May on a winning note, however, with Baldwin pitching both games of a doubleheader on Decoration Day, May 30. The games had been moved from Baltimore to Pittsburgh to take advantage of large crowds, temporarily interrupting an eastern swing by the Pirates. It was a good decision because a total of 14,000 fans attended the two games, which the Pirates won, 11–1 and 4–3. Afterward, both teams, their coffers fattened, boarded the evening train for Baltimore for the concluding game in the series the next day. Barely 1,000 spectators turned out to watch the last-place Orioles. After a rough first inning in which the home club put two runs across the plate, Galvin settled down and pitched well. The Pirates were able to hit Charlie Buffinton but were unable to score, leaving 13 men on base. Pittsburgh tallied two runs in the fourth inning and another in the fifth, but Baltimore won the game, 4–3. During the fifth inning, Galvin was hurt when he tried to stop a hard grounder off Buffinton's bat and split open his right forefinger. The severity of the injury, it was suggested, would keep him out of the box for "some time."[6] At the end of May, club president William C. Temple surprised his fellow directors by resigning from his post, citing business interests he said did not allow time for baseball. It was presumed that vice-president William Kerr would succeed him, but instead, manager Buckenberger was named a director and was asked to become interim president.

With 21 wins and 19 losses, the Pirates began June in sixth place in the League-Association. The *Pittsburgh Press* took note of Galvin's situation at the beginning of the third month of play:

> The father of seven has been singularly unfortunate recently, the Pittsburghs throwing away by errors the nicest game he pitched this season. Jimmy's best work was done early in the season, when he was the wheel horse of the team. Baldwin seems to hold that relation to the club at present. Then came Jim's accident to a finger.... He will remain at home until he can pitch his game.[7]

Baldwin, known for his inconsistency, was now pitching well. But club officials continued to hunt for additional arms, unable to rely on Baldwin to string together some much-needed victories to get the club out of its funk. "Pitching is the great feature this year," the *Dispatch* noted, "and that is just where the Pittsburghers are weak."[8] In the meantime, another rookie pitcher, Winfield Camp, was released. The club was still carrying a large roster and pressure was growing to reduce it. At a special meeting of league magnates, a decision had been made that clubs must carry no more than 13 men on their rosters to cut operating costs. The deadline to comply was July 2, and it meant the Pirates would have to shed five men, a move that would not be good for Galvin. On June 15, the *Dispatch* reported that St. Louis wanted to acquire Galvin in a three-way deal with New York, which would send three players to Pittsburgh.[9] A Pittsburgh official confirmed that Galvin had been released to St. Louis, the city where he had started his pitching career and where his mother and siblings still lived. Under the deal, the Pirates were to receive pitcher William "Adonis" Terry, rightfielder Patsy Donovan and Frank Genins, an outfielder, shortstop and third baseman. Galvin, who was about to return from his injury, was devastated. He had established strong roots in Allegheny City and had many friends throughout the Pittsburgh area. Besides, he had seven children and he wasn't anxious to move back to the city of his birth, about which he had made unkind remarks, or to play for the outspoken and unpredictable Chris Von der Ahe.

"Yes, I have been released, I suppose," a downcast Galvin told the *Pittsburgh Press*. "It was news to me when Manager Buckenberger told me a trade had been made. Well, I am still here, and here I am going to stay until things are arranged somewhat to my satisfaction." He added that Buckenberger had told him he was being let go because he was getting hurt too often.[10] At one point, Galvin said he would prefer to go into the plumbing business than report to St. Louis. But on June 16, after learning that his failure to report could cost him $1,000 in salary, he and Von der Ahe came to terms and Galvin signed a contract to pitch for the Browns. He agreed to accept $3,300, a slight improvement on his pay as a Pirate. Aside from everything else, he couldn't have been happy about leaving an eighth-place club for one sitting in 11th, a move likely to make wins even harder to come by. "Galvin was offered to 11 clubs and but one wanted him," a club official told the *Dispatch*. "I was greatly surprised.... Galvin is good for five years' pitching yet, and will pitch well outside of Pittsburgh or as soon as he gets away from some of his jolly friends here." The newspaper wished Galvin well. "He has been a great card in Pittsburgh for a long time, and is a good pitcher yet," it said.[11] Later cited as key reasons for his release were his "social habits" and constant carrying-on with his buddies (the "jolly friends") in the lower reaches of Allegheny City when he needed to pay more attention to his playing condition (weight).[12]

Galvin had barely arrived in St. Louis on June 17, when later that same day he received tragic news from Allegheny City. His seven-year-old son Eugene had fallen into a hot water vat at the Union Salt Works near the family's Beaver Avenue home and was badly scalded. The boy died the next day, never regaining consciousness. Galvin, his string of bad luck never seeming to end, was beside himself with grief as he raced back home, where he and Bridget oversaw funeral arrangements.[13] As they mourned, the sporting editor of the *Dispatch* paid tribute to Galvin on the end of his career in Pittsburgh.

> In the general shakeup, and a shakeup that public opinion had clamored for a long time, our dear old friend Galvin has been released and has gone to St. Louis. There is not a person in Allegheny county regrets the departure of Jimmy more than I do. He has certainly been one of the most faithful and one of the best workers the club has ever had. While scores of younger players have fallen by the wayside unable to bear the brunt of battle, Jimmy, like the sturdy oak, has successfully weathered all the storm and withstood all the onslaughts that have been made on him. A more honest player or a more generous worker never set foot in the diamond than Jimmy Galvin. But he has been released and what can we do about it? Nothing illegal has been done, and it would be unreasonable to say that anything unfair has been transacted. Galvin has bettered himself financially, and the local club helped him do this. Doubtless Captain Burns is working with the object of getting a good team together for the second season of the year [to begin July 15], and it is only fair to await results before we deal out censure all round. At any rate I'm sure we can all wish Galvin the best possible success in St. Louis. There is a deal of good work in Jimmy yet, and I will be surprised if many teams do not find it out.[14]

Galvin made his first appearance for the Browns on June 25 in the second game of a doubleheader at St. Louis. He drew hearty applause from a crowd estimated at 4,500, the fans no doubt hoping he could help push the club higher in the standings. "Never was a grander or more spontaneous ovation received by a ball player than that tendered Galvin in St. Louis, last Saturday, on his first appearance with the St. Louis team," *Sporting Life* said. "The spectators arose to a man and for fully a minute vied with each other in expressing their appreciation and regard for the old war horse. Jimmie lost the game but not the goodwill of the spectators."[15] Galvin struck out three Cleveland batters and allowed seven hits, but the Browns came up short, losing 3–2. Galvin and his new team prepared to face the Pirates two days later for a pair of games. Von der Ahe, never one to miss an opportunity to pique fan interest, announced that Galvin would pitch the first game, on June 27. Galvin himself had asked for the ball, like any ballplayer anxious to defeat a team that had traded him away. In Pittsburgh, anticipation of seeing Galvin pitted against his old team in St. Louis was high, but victories were predicted in both games because Pittsburgh was on a bit of roll. Pitching for the Pirates would be Mark Baldwin, their inconsistent ace.

Old Sport was motivated and pitched a "masterly game," it was reported, demonstrating "all his old-time skill and twirling abilities, which have made him famous, shone out mightily as he sent Pittsburgh from the grounds defeated."[16] He worked well with his catcher, Dick Buckley, no mean feat for a new battery. The game was hard fought and neither team gave an inch, with brilliant fielding by both clubs. The still-deceptive Galvin picked off two Pirates base runners napping at first base, neither man accustomed to worrying about the master of the move. Galvin also singled to drive in a run during the second inning. For Pittsburgh, Baldwin became a little wild in the same inning and the Browns scored two runs. Two more runs crossed the plate in the third inning for the Browns, while Baldwin continued to issue walks, six in all in the game. Pittsburgh replied with two runs in the fourth and one more in the fifth to complete the scoring. Galvin and Baldwin each allowed seven hits, but on this day the Old Sport came out on the winning end of a 4–3 score. The following day, with Kid Gleason pitching for the Browns against Adonis Terry, the Browns again won, 7–3, racking up five runs in the first inning alone.

While in St. Louis, the Pirates learned that Browns owner Von der Ahe had lied to them about the status of third baseman Frank Genins, who had been included in the Galvin deal. Genins had been released by the Browns on May 15, well before the deal was made, and was now playing in Cincinnati. Von der Ahe had had no right to trade a man he had already released. Upset, Pittsburgh directors said they planned to complain to League-Association president Nick Young. Pittsburgh had not only lost two games they expected to win in St. Louis but also a player on whom they were counting.[17]

Galvin did not play in three games the Browns lost in Louisville, but took the ball for a July 1 game at home against the Brooklyn Bridegrooms. He pitched St. Louis to a come-from-behind, 5–4 victory over the second-place Brooklyn nine. Dan Brouthers, his old teammate from Buffalo, made three hits off him and scored once in a losing cause. Galvin also pitched the first game of a July 4 doubleheader at home against third-place Philadelphia that attracted 4,000 fans. The St. Louis bats teed off on Phillies pitcher Tim Keefe in the first inning, scoring four runs. The final score was 9–2 for St. Louis. The Phillies roared back in the afternoon game to win, 6–3, as Browns pitchers Kid Gleason and Ted Breitenstein struggled. Philadelphia pitcher Kid Carsey, meanwhile, allowed a single St. Louis hit. Galvin next appeared

15. Final Innings 199

in a 6–1 loss on July 9 at home to Washington, when the Senators touched him up for 10 hits. Two days later, it was reported that Galvin was seeking his release from the Browns. No reason was given. The next day in Pittsburgh, Mark Baldwin also sought his release, anxious to go to Brooklyn. Neither request was granted by their respective clubs and both men continued to pitch. Galvin was back in the box July 12 for a 13–1 St. Louis romp over cellar-dwelling Baltimore, helped by the Browns' bats, which exploded for 15 hits. The game was the second in a doubleheader with the Orioles, the first of which the Browns also won, 4–3.

In its July 16 edition, the *New York Clipper* reported that problems had beset St. Louis. Chris Von der Ahe cut player salaries, prompting protests. Four of his players, including pitcher Kid Gleason and catcher Dick Buckley, refused to accept the cuts and sought time to consider their options. "Pitcher Galvin and Von der Ahe disagreed over a matter of discipline and the former was given his unconditional release," it said, noting that the Browns owner was pursuing pitchers from Columbus of the disbanding Western League and from the Southern League. Von der Ahe, it added, planned to release three men from his roster.[18] For his part, Galvin was apparently ill or hurt and clashed with Von der Ahe about his ability or willingness to play. The release, sought by Galvin himself, was soon recalled, however. He joined the Browns for a trip to Boston for a game against the Beaneaters, and the dispute appeared to be resolved. *The Sporting News*, based in St. Louis, reported that everyone "was sorry that the trouble occurred and glad that it was settled so as to allow Galvin to remain a member of the Browns. He is a great favorite here and has been pitching good ball since he joined the club. There are no pitchers idle at present who are Galvin's equal."[19] In the same edition, *TSN* said: "Galvin is too good a man to let go. He has won four of the six games he has pitched for the locals. The best base-watching battery in the country is Galvin and Buckley."

On July 19 in Brooklyn, Galvin took the loss when the Browns were shut out, 1–0, by the Bridegrooms, George Haddock earning a win. Galvin pitched well, but in the fifth inning was tagged for a triple by catcher Tom Kinslow, who was brought home when Haddock singled. Two days later in Philadelphia the Browns were again shut out, this time 2–0 by the Phillies. Galvin was in generally good form in the game but surrendered six hits, one of them a homer by centerfielder Ed Delahanty. The game was an historic matchup, but neither fans nor players would appreciate it at the time. Phillies pitcher Tim Keefe, 35, a future Hall of Famer, collected his 326th win that day. His career dated back to 1880 with Troy in the National League, when he had faced Galvin, then pitching for Buffalo. Keefe would retire at the end of the 1893 season with a total of 342 wins. On this day in Philadelphia, he faced Galvin who, at age 36, had already earned 364 wins. The next time that 300–

game winners would face each other in major league baseball was 94 years later, June 6, 1986, when Cleveland Indians pitcher Phil Niekro shut out the California Angels and Don Sutton, 2–0.[20] Both American Leaguers became Hall of Famers, knuckleballer Niekro with 318 wins and Sutton with 324. Galvin threw poorly on July 23 in New York and was driven out of the box after three innings by the hard-hitting Giants. His replacement, Bob Caruthers, fared even worse, and New York rolled to a 12–4 win. In Washington two days later, Galvin was again handed the ball, this time to face the Nationals. He got off to a shaky start, allowing five hits in the first inning and four runs. With his traditional bad inning out of the way early in the game, Galvin allowed only five more hits, all well scattered, and the Browns won, 7–4. This win was number 365, Galvin's last for St. Louis and the final one in his career.

In Baltimore on July 27, Galvin was pounded mercilessly by the lowly Orioles, who blanked the Browns, 12–0. They collected 15 hits off Old Sport that day and he suffered a rocky seventh inning, giving up a homer and four triples. To add insult to injury, the following day an amateur named Dick Hawke, 22, appeared in the box for St. Louis and allowed Baltimore only four hits as the Browns prevailed, 2–1. Von der Ahe signed Hawke to a contract after the game.

Galvin's poor showing may have been connected to personal matters. On July 28, he filed a lawsuit against the owners of the salt company in whose vat his son Eugene had fallen a month earlier. He was seeking $10,000 in damages, alleging that Haller, Beck and Co. failed to have the dangerous area fenced off.[21] For St. Louis, however, the entire month of July had been a struggle and it was already in last place early in the second half of the split season, with only two wins. Von der Ahe was grumbling about the performance of his team and warning that changes were coming if play didn't improve. The Browns were not alone in their troubles. Back in Pittsburgh, club directors released their hard-nosed captain, Tommy Burns, amidst player discontent and poor play. Burns soon filed a lawsuit, saying his multi-year contract had been ironclad, and he sought $13,000 in damages. President Al Buckenberger resumed his former responsibilities as manager in the wake of Burns' departure.

Galvin started an August 2 game in Cleveland but the Spiders' batters quickly drove him from the box. He was replaced by Caruthers, who was also pounded before being relieved, in turn, by Dick Hawke. The game was a display of batting power by both sides with Cleveland swatting 17 hits to 10 for St. Louis. Cleveland won, 12–10. The following day Galvin was released, along with third baseman George Pinkney. Von der Ahe complained bitterly about the eastern road trip, calling it "the most disastrous trip I have ever had during my career in baseball." He confirmed that Galvin and Pinkney had been let go. "I have nothing to say against them. They have played their best, but their work has not been good enough to satisfy me, and I must try to improve my team."[22] Von der Ahe was still pursuing more pitchers as the Browns remained in the basement of the League-Association with six wins and 14 losses.

Galvin's fans in Pittsburgh were disappointed when he didn't appear with the Browns, who came to town for games on August 9 and 10. St. Louis had Hawke in the box for the first game and he was batted around Exposition Park in a 12–1 Pittsburgh victory. The following day, with Breitenstein pitching, the Pirates again won, this time, 3–2. The *Pittsburgh Dispatch* put the crowd at 1,200 in the first game and blamed the low turnout on Von der Ahe for not having Galvin pitch, unaware he'd been released. "Hundreds were eager to see Jimmy face his old colleagues and in not doing so Von der Ahe lost several hundred dollars."[23]

As word spread of Galvin's departure, speculation mounted that the erratic Von der Ahe might be persuaded to take him back. But it was not to be, and some fans, still known as "cranks" in the press, lamented his departure. One of them tried to put Galvin's lengthy career into some sort of historical perspective in a musing that was printed in *Sporting Life* and other publications:

> A Louisville crank on reminiscences figures that the veteran pitcher, Galvin, has pleased and displeased 800,000 people in his 17 years pitching, has travelled 112,000 miles or about four and a half times the circumference of the earth, has taken part in about 500 games in which on an average 35 men went to the bat per game, and that four balls were pitched to each. That will make a total of 70,000 throws and balls pitched by Galvin. But during a large part of Galvin's career seven balls instead of four sent a man to first base. That runs the total up to, perhaps an even 100,000, and these balls have travelled 2000 miles, and in pitching these 100,000 balls Galvin expended sufficient strength to carry them 30,000,000 feet, or about 6000 miles.[24]

Galvin was a spectator at a local game in Allegheny City on August 17 and confided to a local reporter that he was unhappy at his treatment by Von der Ahe. The St. Louis magnate, he said, had docked him $70 in pay for leaving the team to rush back home when his son was so badly hurt and staying for Eugene's funeral.[25] At the end of August, Mark Baldwin was released by Pittsburgh, but the club made no effort to reach out to Galvin, who, it was said, was considering a job as an umpire. "The Pittsburgh players are all great friends of Jimmy and they would like to see him back on the team," noted *The Sporting News*. "They always worked harder to win Jim's games than any other pitcher Pittsburgh ever had, and he is the most popular ball player who ever wore a Pittsburgh uniform."[26] As it turned out, Baldwin was recalled by manager Buckenberger and the Pirates gradually rose to second place in the standings. Galvin was unable to secure an umpiring job, and his longtime Pirates friends, accepting that his career was over, began planning a benefit game for him at the end of the season.

The magnates of the League-Association met in New York in early October to consider money problems related to their purchase of the old American Association teams, a total debt standing at $132,000. To deal with that obligation, they decided to cut expenses, namely salaries. The salary classification scheme was back that sharply reduced the pay packets of top players, with the top rate at $2,400. This ceiling would produce salary cuts of 30–40 percent or more for top players. Some clubs, like St. Louis, Washington and Louisville, began releasing players before the season was over to cut expenses. The league also decided to shorten the season for next year and scrap the split-season concept. Lower than expected attendance in many cities was attributed to low-scoring games, so to tilt the game back in favor of batters, the pitching distance, which had been 55-and-a-half feet, was increased to 60 feet, six inches for 1893. It marked the last change made to the distance, and the pitcher's box was replaced by a foot-long rubber slab.

Boston won the pennant that fall of 1892, with Pittsburgh yet again claiming sixth. St. Louis finished in 11th place, 46 games back of Boston and 8.5 games ahead of Baltimore. Galvin's record stood at five wins and six losses in the 12 games in Pittsburgh, with exactly the same number of games, wins and losses in St. Louis. His earned run average was 2.63 for the Pirates, but 3.23 for the Browns. He pitched 96 innings for Pittsburgh and 92 for St. Louis. His 10 victories for the season produced a lifetime record of 365 wins against 310 losses. When he retired, no pitcher had won more games.

On October 17, the benefit game was played for Galvin. He and his old teammates split into opposing nines, with lefty Ed Morris in the box facing him. A large and enthusiastic crowd included several prominent local dignitaries, some of whom paid as much as $25 for tickets to salute the popular hurler. Galvin pitched well and his team won the game, 7–6, with the event producing $1,800 for him.[27] Meanwhile, Galvin failed in his bid obtain a saloon license, when a judge ruled that his proposed transfer came too soon after another transfer of the same license and appeared to amount to mere speculation. By late November, he and partner Jacob Becker had obtained a license for a property at 32 Sixth Street in Pittsburgh. In the interim, Galvin had considered returning to the laundry business, *Sporting Life* said in late October as it recorded his retirement and looked back on his career. It also hinted at the reason to his longevity in baseball.

> He was one of the original below-the-shoulder or "under-hand" pitchers as it was incorrectly called. When the full arm throw came into vogue and was legitimized, Galvin was effective as ever though he sprinkled his delivery with the less wearing below-the-shoulder motion, and this relief from the monotonous strain of constant ball pitching saved his arm. As a watcher of the bases and adept in the art of catching base-runners "napping" Galvin never had an equal.[28]

15. Final Innings

The Roberto Clemente Bridge linking downtown Pittsburgh to the North Side, once known as Allegheny City, is bathed in light from PNC Park, home of the Pirates, late in a recent game. Pittsburgh still loves its Pirates, who started life as the Alleghenys several blocks to the north in 1876 at Union Park (photograph by author).

During the winter, items appeared in various publications suggesting that Galvin might yet again appear in a Pirates uniform. One rather bizarre suggestion, attributed to Galvin himself, was that he would pitch only in home games, provided he could do so without jeopardizing the operation of his saloon.[29]

Galvin spent 1893 busy with his upscale establishment, the Pirates apparently uninterested in retaining a part-time hurler for home games only. His Sixth Street saloon was one of the biggest bars in the Pittsburgh area, and he had nine bartenders, including former teammates catcher Tun Berger and pitcher Harry Staley. The location was a good one, but the rent was a steep $2,400 annually, as much as Galvin had earned some years in baseball. His license cost a further $1,000.[30] He enjoyed the people, but was overly generous to his customers and had trouble managing his staff, freely admitting later that he was a poor businessman. Galvin and his partner Becker had a falling out and, according to Galvin, all that Becker brought into the business was 40 cents worth of carpet. Becker owed the operation $2,600 and Galvin opted to pay him a further $584 to dissolve their partnership.[31] Overall, Galvin had little business acumen and was hopeless at keeping the books.³² Within a year, he was bankrupt, owing $6,129.37, when the sheriff stepped in to lock the doors in January of 1894. "'Old Sport' is disconsolate," said *Sporting Life* as it recounted the failure of yet another baseball player to succeed in the saloon business:

> When asked how saloonkeeping compared with ball playing as an occupation, the "Old Sport" looked as if it were almost a sacrilege to mention the two in the same breath.
> "The ball field," he said, "is all velvet. Go over in the morning, put on a suit for an hour, come back, go over in the afternoon for an hour and a half and the rest of the day is yours. Then you have a comfortable feeling on pay day. In the saloon business you're there day and night. It's all right when everything is moving along in a smooth way, but in these times there's nothing in it."³³

It was said that nearly all of the nine bartenders he employed went off to open successful saloons of their own, while Galvin himself found work in other establishments. "Jeems lost heavily in the saloon venture, and must begin his savings over again," *Sporting Life* noted in March when it said he had turned to former Allegheny sheriff McCleary to help him land a job as a National League umpire.³⁴ Friends said Galvin told them he lost about $3,300 on the venture.³⁵

Early in January 1894, the same month the doors were slammed shut on his saloon, Galvin and three companions travelled to Cleveland to visit a friend who was ailing. "After putting him on the road to recovery," Galvin later told a reporter, "we thought it no harm to take in a little of a certain cure against sickness ourselves." While fortifying themselves at a local watering hole, the four friends were disrupted by an inebriated and rather obnoxious tailor named H. W. Hubbard. After tolerating the man through four bottles of beer, Galvin said he and his companions "adjourned to another place for the express purpose of getting rid of him." He said Hubbard showed up at the second venue, accompanied by several policemen, accusing Galvin and his associates of taking a $250 diamond and $125 gold watch from him. Among the officers, Galvin said he recognized George Strief, a second baseman against whom Galvin played while Strief was with Cleveland and Philadelphia. The baseball connection didn't help. Galvin and his associates were charged with theft. They were locked in a jail cell with 27 other prisoners until 10 a.m. the next day, when they appeared before a judge and the charge was dropped because the "victim" didn't show and no evidence was presented. Angry, Galvin and his companions sought out Hubbard in a bid to confront him about the false accusations. When they found him in the company of "seventeen relations and a deputy sheriff," Galvin threatened to sue the tailor for damages, after which he and his companions did the prudent thing and left.³⁶ Nothing came of his threat, nor from Galvin's suit against the salt company in Allegheny City. No court records can be located for the latter, suggesting it was likely dropped or settled privately.³⁷

On February 10, *The Sporting News* reported that Galvin was anxious to return to baseball. He missed the "velvet" ball field, apparently. He said he was "not averse" to playing for a minor league team like Erie or Buffalo and he had been doing exercises to lose weight in a bid to "catch on" with a team.[38] Jack Chapman, the Buffalo rightfielder who had managed Galvin in his last season with the Bisons, had returned to manage the club in 1893 and decided to take a chance on Gentle Jeems—now 37 and weighing about 250 pounds. Buffalo was playing in the Eastern League, and fans in the city recalled Galvin fondly. Chapman was willing to gamble on the old overweight hurler as he managed a miserable team and was desperate to find some kind of winning formula. The Bisons were losing as many games as they were winning and the newspapers were putting heat on team management to make changes. The *Buffalo Express* was particularly outspoken in its assessment. "It is bad enough for a first-class city to be in a second-class league, but to be represented by such a conglomeration of misfits in such a league is scandalous." The newspaper didn't pull any punches and included the beleaguered manager in its withering criticism:

> The distinguished Mr. Chapman in the perfection of his baseball wisdom, has succeeded in getting together an aggregation of butter-fingered, white-livered, awkward and bow-legged young and old men who play as is they were each aged 102 years and had never seen a contest at [*sic*] One Old Cat or Handy Andy Over, to say nothing of a professional game. They cannot bat and they cannot field.[39]

When fans in Buffalo learned that Galvin signed a contract, they hoped for a return to better times, even though he hadn't played a game in nearly two years and was in poor shape. Galvin made his first appearance, a sort of cameo, in the last inning of a May 21 game in which the Bisons defeated Troy, 9–2. He hit the first batter he faced, gave up two singles and allowed a run as the visiting batters teed off on him. It wasn't a promising start. The following day, he faced Springfield at Olympic Park. Galvin started the game and it was acknowledged he still possessed "a goodly supply of speed, his curves are as winding as ever, and that slow ball is a teaser."[40] He started poorly, however, allowing a single, a double and two more singles that scored two runs for the visitors. Buffalo replied with a run in the bottom of the first. Neither team scored in the next three innings. Springfield then adopted a strategy that proved to be the winning formula by taking advantage of the pudgy hurler they faced. "Every man tried to bunt the ball to Galvin, who has not quite got down to weight yet, and had considerable difficulty in fielding in his territory."[41] To compensate for Galvin's immobility, Bisons third baseman Pete Gilbert played closer to home plate than normal. Playing out of his normal position, Gilbert made two wild throws to first base, the errors giving Springfield a come-from-behind, 5–4 win. Galvin was replaced late in the game by Bill Hoffer. Rather than blame the loss on Galvin, the 1,800 spectators and the newspapers preferred to pin it on Gilbert and his miscues.

Old Sport's third game was on May 27, when the Bisons played host to the last-place Providence Grays, also known as the Clam Diggers. The 3,000 fans were hoping Galvin would show the outstanding form for which he was remembered. But Galvin was dreadful, unable to fool the visiting batters. Two Providence runs scored in the first inning and nine more in the second, and Buffalo replied with a single tally. In the fourth inning, Galvin was touched for three singles and a double for three more runs. In the fifth, he allowed a double and two singles for another run. In the seventh, after two Grays flied out, he gave up six singles for five more runs. Galvin pitched the entire game in which the visitors recorded 27 hits. In his own last at-bat, Galvin hit a home run, but by then it was too little, too late. And somewhat out of character for a player whose lifetime major league batting average was .201 with five homers. The final score was 21–8 for Providence, and after the game he was released. "Jimmy Galvin justly received his walking papers after his exhibition of pitching yesterday," the *Buffalo Evening News* said. "Old Galvin has for many years held down heavy batters of the big league but could not place a ball over the plate yesterday where the tail-enders could not connect with it."[42] The *Buffalo Express* lamented that "the once great and renowned James Galvin crawled out of the game with his reputation torn to shreds. The Grays uncovered the true extent of the Gentle Jeems's pitching powers in the most unmerciful manner."[43] Despite the cruel words about his effort, the newspapers of Buffalo wished him well in the future and thanked him for the pleasant memories he had provided fans of the game in the city over the years.

Back home in Allegheny, Galvin became a regular spectator at Exposition Park for Pirates games and occasionally pitched for saloon-based teams. He worked as a National League umpire during the 1895 season, but didn't enjoy it. The easygoing and likeable Galvin hated the abuse that was heaped on him, like all umpires of the day. He returned to tending bar and briefly tried his hand as foreman for a contracting firm. Galvin then moved his family into the Oakland area east of downtown Pittsburgh and took jobs at several bars, but migrated back to Allegheny City by 1900, where his old pal Ed Morris put him to work in his saloon. Overweight, in poor health, ruined financially, with the four youngest of his six children still to support, Galvin and his wife Bridget struggled to get by. Several years after he died, an old friend from his Buffalo days, Dave Kerr, recalled failing to persuade Galvin to save money from his big pay checks for "a rainy day." Kerr said: "The Little Steam Engine made a fortune for the ball clubs but his bit frittered away despite the efforts of his good wife, who tried hard to induce her good-natured husband to lay up some cash for stormy times."[44]

15. Final Innings 207

Those stormy times had arrived. On Thanksgiving Day, 1901, he contracted pneumonia and was confined to bed, unable to work. Some of his friends opened their wallets to the penniless Galvin, whose family had moved into a small, four-room rooming house at the rear of 414 East Lacock Street, not far from the banks of the Allegheny River and several blocks east of Exposition Park. It was located in a notorious section of Allegheny known locally as "Little Canada." The area provided refuge for lawbreakers in Pittsburgh chased across the Allegheny River bridges from that city by Pittsburgh police whose jurisdiction ended mid-span, not unlike an international border.[45] With the annexation of Allegheny City in 1907, the sanctuary for lawbreakers ceased to exist, and the city became known as the North Side. Galvin turned 45 on what must have been a far-from-merry Christmas Day in the Galvin household. His health deteriorated further when he contracted "catarrh of the stomach," a gastro-intestinal malady, and as the weeks passed, it became apparent that the wasted, pale shell of a man would not recover.

On March 3, with the city inundated by floodwaters that washed up his street to his door, the *Pittsburgh Press* reported "the news that the veteran is passing away causes genuine regret. The once-great pitcher was an artist in his own profession, but he was not a financier and although in his time, he earned a small fortune, not a cent of the money is left." Friends and fans had been helping Galvin and his family with money for food, rent and medical bills. A letter to the newspaper from James W. Platt included $50 intended for Galvin. Platt wrote: "I am one of the many Pittsburghers who was often entertained by him in the old days of baseball and take this way of showing my sympathy for him now."[46] From his retirement home in California, Albert Goodwill Spalding wired $100.[47] James Mason, a friend, announced plans for a "monster benefit" for the pitcher and his family on March 22 at Allegheny's old city hall, which would feature boxing matches, dancers, and a talent show.[48]

About 3 p.m. on March 7, Galvin slipped into unconsciousness, and four hours later was dead. Aside from Bridget, he left behind five sons and a daughter: James J., 23; William, 20; Mark, 17; Walter, 14; Joseph, 12; and Marie, 11. The two oldest boys returned from the west, where they had been working. His funeral service was conducted at St. Peter's Roman Catholic Church, where Galvin was a member. It attracted a large crowd of ballplayers and fans, and his pallbearers included four former Pittsburgh players: Tun Berger, Ed Swartwood, Tom Quinn and Sam Gillen. Gillen was a late replacement for Ed Morris, grieving the loss of his wife, who had died the day before Galvin. Afterward, a procession travelled across the bridge into Pittsburgh and a few miles east to Galvin's final resting place atop a slope in Calvary Cemetery in Greenfield. A simple, flat stone marker, befitting a man of little means, would mark the spot. It bears a passing resemblance to a pitching rubber.

The March 22 benefit became a major event to provide much-needed funds for Galvin's family. The *Pittsburgh Press* called it a "huge success," noting that 37 different acts, boxing matches, vaudeville performers and singers participated. It was a large, good-natured crowd, and police officers present had little to do. The amount raised was not released publicly, but it was said to be enough to "keep the wolf from the door" of the Galvin household. "Everybody was happy," reported the *Press*. "And those that were present not only had their money's worth, but had the added satisfaction of knowing that they were helping the widow of a man who had afforded them much solid entertainment in years gone by."[49]

One of the more eloquent tributes to mark Galvin's passing appeared in the *Pittsburgh Leader*, which recalled the legacy of the man variously—and affectionately—known as Gentle Jeems, The Little Steam Engine, and Old Sport:

With a heart as big as himself, he never refused aid to anyone in need, he was everyone's friend and in his death the community loses an athlete who helped lift baseball to its present unparalleled prominence, who was a diamond marvel in his day, a loyal comrade under any conditions, and affectionate and indulgent husband and father, and, in all that the world implies, a man.[50]

It had been quite the run for Pud Galvin. But memories of his contributions would prove short.

Epilogue

Pud Galvin was the winningest pitcher of all time when he retired in 1892. He was the Cy Young of baseball before Cy Young. Young would soon put up the numbers that made him a legend as the best pitcher that baseball has ever seen. In 1892, when Galvin earned his last win, Denton True Young, 25, nicknamed "Cyclone" for his fast delivery, was in the early stages of an amazing career. He was in his third year in the National League, playing with the Cleveland Spiders. Young's 36 wins led the league that year, along with the top winning percentage of .750 and earned run average of 1.93. Nine years later, at the end of the 1901 season, with Galvin at death's door, Young had already matched Old Sport's 365 wins. Young pitched for 22 years in all, before age and weight caught up to him, amassing 511 wins and 316 losses in the 7,356 innings he pitched. In his 749 complete games, he recorded 76 shutouts, and he amassed 2,803 career strikeouts. Young appeared in 906 games in total, and the six-foot-two, right-hander was a model of consistency, winning 30 or more games five times and 20 or more in 15 seasons. Young's career earned run average was 2.63. He made such an impression that he was elected to the Hall of Fame in 1937, two years before the Hall opened. Baseball's top award for pitching was named after him in 1956, for good reason. It is safe to say his numbers will never be topped.

Cy Young was not alone in eclipsing Galvin and his accomplishments. New York's Christy Mathewson pitched win number 300 in 1912 and earned 73 more before retiring. Washington's Walter Johnson joined the 300-win club in 1920, on his way to 417 victories. And Grover Cleveland Alexander won game 300 in 1924, retiring with 373, tying him with Mathewson for third all-time. Young, Mathewson, Johnson and Alexander all benefited from the poor offense that characterized the "deadball era" in the first two decades of the 20th century. Yet again, history was not kind to Galvin. While other pitchers had their turn in the limelight, he quickly slipped from public consciousness, seen as a man from the previous century. Even during his own era, he often played in the shadow of pitchers Hoss Radbourn, John Clarkson and Tim Keefe, all of whom had outstanding seasons during solid careers and were inducted into the Hall of Fame in 1939, 1963 and 1964 respectively.

Pud Galvin pitched for 18 seasons in five different leagues: the National Association, International Association, American Association, Players' League and the National League. He was given credit in some quarters for his work in the National Association, but nowhere for his time in the International Association. He was forced to adjust to repeated changes in the counts for balls and strikes and a continued tinkering with the pitching distance. Yet he never pitched from today's 60 feet, six inches, the distance established in 1893, the year after he retired, when the pitching box in which he had worked was replaced with a rubber slab. When he first pitched, it was from 45 feet, and he needed three strikes to record an out and nine balls before walking the batter. The number of balls for a walk was not settled at four until 1889. A 50-foot pitching distance was implemented in 1881. That increased to 55 feet, six inches in 1887, and stretched to 57 feet in the 1890 Players' League, but reverted to 55 feet, six inches after the rebel league expired. In 1887, four strikes were required for an out, but that was quickly rescinded, along with the controversial scoring of walks as hits. Pitching was underhand, or sidearm, until all restrictions were lifted in 1884 when an overhand delivery was permitted. Galvin, unlike fellow hurlers such as Fred Goldsmith, made the change easily and used both deliveries in his arsenal. Until 1887, Galvin and all pitchers faced batters who were able to call for a "low" or "high" pitch, giving an edge to the man with the bat. Most importantly, he straddled the eras in baseball when a single pitcher did all his team's pitching, to the use of two pitchers in the early 1880s and to being part of a rotation of several hurlers by the time his career ended.

Pitching every inning of every game helped produce big numbers, both in the win and loss columns. Galvin's best single season was 1884 with Buffalo, followed by a long and slow decline. He threw the first perfect game on record. In 10 campaigns he won more than 20 games, in 1879 he had 37 victories, and in 1883 and 1884 he recorded 46. Galvin didn't enjoy the success or acclaim he might have seen if he had played for a pennant winner. The only year his team took a championship was 1878, when the Buffalo Bisons did so in the International Association, a league that historians won't recognize as a major one. The previous year with Allegheny he pitched for the second-place finisher in the IA, and then again in 1886 with Allegheny when it placed second in the American Association. The rest of his teams were middle-of-the-pack clubs; the Buffalo, Allegheny/Pittsburgh and St. Louis clubs finished third, fifth, sixth, seventh, eighth and 11th. Galvin lived to see the Pirates win the National League pennant for the first time in 1901. They became a powerhouse and repeated the feat in 1902, 1903 and 1909, in the latter year also winning the World Series. One has to wonder how much better his numbers would have been had he played on teams that won more games than they lost (like Cy Young). And how much more acclaim he would have received had his teams represented major cities like Chicago, New York, Philadelphia or Boston.

Despite the generally poor teams on which he played, Galvin is the fifth-most successful pitcher of all time, with 365 wins, or tied for sixth all-time with Kid Nichols, if the 361 number that discounts his National Association wins is used. His plaque in the Hall of Fame in Cooperstown recognizes him for 365. If his 36 wins earned in the International Association were added, he would be comfortably third, with 401. Regardless, he trails only Cy Young in complete games, with 646 to Young's 749. He is also second in innings pitched with 6,003⅓, to Young's 7,356. Galvin is also second only to Young in losses, with 310 to Young's 316.

In the years after Galvin died, a parade of hitters including Babe Ruth, Ty Cobb, Honus Wagner, Tris Speaker and Napoleon Lajoie claimed the spotlight in baseball, and Pud Galvin's 19th-century pitching accomplishments continued to fade into obscurity. His name surfaced briefly in 1942 when *Brooklyn Eagle* writer Bill Gottlieb related pitching feats from the past in the March 8 edition of the paper. He said that during a September 23, 1886, game played in Pittsburgh, Galvin walked three Brooklyn batters in a row with none out, then methodically picked off each of them on the bases to retire the side. This was the first telling of the story. Galvin was famous for his ability to catch runners napping, but Gottlieb's account cannot be verified. The *Eagle* covered the game but its report made no reference to the feat. Neither did other sporting publications of the day. The game was played in Brooklyn, not Pittsburgh. The widely published box score doesn't support the story. Galvin walked only two batters that day, with no wild pitches or hit batters. And the three batters supposedly walked were held hitless in Pittsburgh's 8–2 win. The game couldn't be confused with the only other one played that year when Galvin faced Brooklyn. On July 8, the order of Brooklyn batters was different, and he issued only one walk. The story would seem to be yet another myth in a game rife with myths. Galvin's name surfaced again in 1952 when facts were stretched to make a better story. That year, cartoonist-showman Robert Ripley drew a passable likeness of Galvin with his trademark handlebar mustache and proclaimed that Galvin pitched four no-hit big league games and "weighed 300 pounds."[1] While there is a nice symmetry to saying a 300-game winner tipped the scales at 300, it was a fine bit of exaggeration about the girth of Galvin, whose weight was closer to 250 pounds when he left the game.

Among the few who would have laughed at Ripley's depiction of Galvin was a Buffalo man named Joe Overfield. Since the late 1940s, Overfield had developed a keen interest in the Buffalo Bisons of days gone by and especially in Galvin, that city's first superstar in sport. A title searcher by occupation and baseball historian by avocation, Overfield stumbled across a financial report for the 1878 Buffalo Bisons club in the Erie County clerk's office. He became fascinated by the club that went on to capture the second pennant of the International Association, largely on the strength of Galvin's arm. Overfield eventually became vice-president of the Monroe Abstract Corporation, but he never lost his passion for uncovering information about the Bisons and Galvin. Beginning in 1953, Overfield began publishing the fruits of his research, in newspapers and elsewhere, opining that Galvin was one of baseball's most underrated pitchers.[2] Overfield dug into newspaper microfilm and reconstructed the eight seasons Galvin spent in Buffalo, in seven of which the Bisons contended in the National League. Overfield became official historian of the Bisons and was a founding member of the Society for American

The hard work of researcher Joe Overfield led to Pud Galvin's being inducted into the National Baseball Hall of Fame at Cooperstown in 1965. Shown here during the induction ceremony with baseball commissioner Ford Frick are Galvin's children, Walter Galvin and Marie Wentzel. His family was thrilled at the honor they felt was overdue (National Baseball Hall of Fame Library, Cooperstown, New York).

Baseball Research. He became a recognized authority on Buffalo baseball history and in 1985 published *The 100 Seasons of Buffalo Baseball,* a book in which he chronicled the feats of baseball greats who graced the diamonds of his native city, beginning at the Rhode Island grounds that became Riverside Park.

The more he learned about Pud Galvin, the more Overfield felt "Gentle Jeems" ought to be enshrined in the Baseball Hall of Fame, where other 300-game winners were recognized. He compiled the evidence to support his contention about Galvin's career, especially his little-known, iron-man exploits in 1878 in the International Association when Galvin won 72 games, of which 24 were scheduled contests for the IA championship. Galvin, he noted, was 10–5 when pitted against National League teams that same year, with 17 shutouts overall as he pitched between 895 and 905 innings. Overfield lobbied for recognition of the pitcher whom he dubbed "Baseball's Forgotten Man" and "Buffalo's First Superstar."[3]

Overfield made a persuasive case and in 1965, the Baseball Hall of Fame's Committee on Veterans elected Galvin unanimously as inductee number 102. The move was seen as long overdue. Hall of Fame historian and *Sporting News* columnist Lee Allen wrote: "It is difficult to recall when a player elected to membership in the Hall of Fame brought more robust qualifications."[4] A couple of observers were not impressed, however. Charles O. Finley, outspoken owner of the Kansas City Athletics, told the United Press: "It is the height of stupidity for the veteran's committee to name a man who has been dead for 63 years." Joe Falls, a sportswriter from Detroit, was also puzzled and asked: "Who ever heard of Jim Galvin?" unwittingly underscoring Overfield's argument that Galvin was a forgotten man in baseball.[5]

Overfield was able to track down Pud and Bridget Galvin's two surviving children, Walter, their fifth-born, and Marie, their seventh. Walter Galvin, 77, lived in Geneva, Ohio, while Marie Wentzel, 74, was in Amarillo, Texas. Upon learning of the honor for her father, Marie told *The Sporting News*: "We had nine boys and two girls in the family [four had died as infants] and there was so much to be done at home that we didn't get very many chances to see my father pitch."[6] They and other family members were in Cooperstown for the induction ceremony on July 28, 1965, before a crowd of about 3,500. Baseball Commissioner Ford C. Frick gave Marie and Walter a replica of the plaque to be mounted in the Hall of Fame. In what was described as a brief and touching acceptance speech, Walter said: "Thanks for remembering my father. I've been waiting a long time."[7] He went on to say his father "was lucky to earn $300 a year in his best baseball season." Walter's memory may have faded or he was operating under some bad information because his father earned far more than that, even in his worst season, ranging from a bit less than $1,000 a year to more than $3,000.[8]

Epilogue 215

After Galvin's induction, his name again slipped from the headlines for nearly 40 years until the revelation that he had used chemical help to improve his performance. His use of the steroid-like substance derived from animal testes sparked renewed interest in Galvin and his remarkable career. If Pud had enhanced his performance, supporters of "juicers" like Jose Canseco, Sammy Sosa, Mark McGwire and others argued, they should also not be barred from recognition by the Hall of Fame. But scientific analysis found there was no physiological impact on Galvin from his injection, ensuring his place in the Hall of Fame is secure and that modern-day juicers will have to make other arguments. No evidence has been uncovered to suggest that Galvin tried the "elixir of life" more than once.

Throughout all the decades of forgetting, remembering, forgetting and remembering again, Galvin's tiny, cracked headstone in Pittsburgh's Calvary Cemetery has endured, a tangible but modest reminder of one of the greatest pitchers from the formative years of professional baseball.

He deserves a better memorial, befitting the charter member of baseball's 300-win club.

But the easygoing man they called Gentle Jeems would be the last to complain.

Opposite, top and bottom: Pud Galvin died a pauper in early 1902 at the age of 45. He left behind a widow and six children. His friends in Pittsburgh and Allegheny City held a benefit to assist his family. His grave marker is a simple one on a hillside in Calvary Cemetery in Pittsburgh. It is hard to find and not what is expected for a member of Baseball's Hall of Fame and the charter member of pitching's 300 wins club (photograph by author).

Appendix One:
The Wins of Pud Galvin

Year	Team	League	Wins
1875	St. Louis Browns	National Association	4
1876	St. Louis Reds	unaffiliated	not tallied
1877	Allegheny	International Association	12
1878	Buffalo	International Association	24
1879	Buffalo	National League	37
1880	Buffalo	National League	20
1881	Buffalo	National League	28
1882	Buffalo	National League	28
1883	Buffalo	National League	46
1884	Buffalo	National League	46
1885	Buffalo/Allegheny	National League/AA	16
1886	Allegheny	American Association	29
1887	Allegheny	National League	28
1888	Allegheny	National League	23
1889	Allegheny	National League	23
1890	Pittsburgh	Players' League	12
1891	Pittsburgh	National League	15
1892	Pittsburgh/St. Louis	National League	10
		Total	401

Total for which he is credited 365, or 361

Source: Most sources credit him with the four games won in the National Association, even though it is not considered a major league. No sources credit him with the 36 games won in the International Association, also not considered a major league.

Appendix Two: The 300 Wins Club

Rank & Pitcher	Date of 300th	Total Wins
1. Cy Young	July 3, 1901	511
2. Walter Johnson	May 14, 1920	417
3. Grover Cleveland Alexander	September 20, 1924	373
4. Christy Mathewson	June 28, 1912	373
5. Pud Galvin	**June 4, 1888**	**365**
6. Warren Spahn	August 11, 1961	363
7. Kid Nichols	September 7, 1900	361
8. Greg Maddux	August 7, 2004	355
9. Roger Clemens	June 13, 2003	354
10. Tim Keefe	June 4, 1890	342
11. Steve Carlton	September 23, 1983	329
12. John Clarkson	September 21, 1892	328
13. Eddie Plank	September 11, 1915	326
14. Nolan Ryan	July 31, 1990	324
15. Don Sutton	June 18, 1986	324
16. Phil Niekro	October 6, 1985	318
17. Gaylord Perry	May 6, 1982	314
18. Tom Seaver	August 4, 1985	311
19. Charles Radbourn	May 14, 1891	310
20. Mickey Welch	August 11, 1890	307
21. Tom Glavine	August 5, 2007	305
22. Randy Johnson	June 4, 2009	303
23. Lefty Grove	July 25, 1941	300
23. Early Wynn	July 13, 1963	300

Source: Baseball-Reference.com, which does not count 36 wins earned by Galvin in the International Association in 1877–1878.

Appendix Three: Pud Galvin's Changing Working Conditions During His Career, 1875–1892

1875: Pitchers were restricted to a box, the closest point to the batter being 45 feet. Restricted to underhand delivery. Nine balls constituted a walk. After two strikes, the batter would be issued a warning if he failed to swing at a ball in the strike zone. A third strike was called if he failed to swing at another good pitch. Batters could call for pitches to be either "high" or "low."

1879: Eight balls for a walk. Warning before called third strike remains.

1881: Pitching distance increased to 50 feet. Seven balls for a walk. Warning by umpire if batter failed to swing at third strike is eliminated.

1883: Shoulder-high pitching delivery now permitted. Error charged to pitcher for a walk.

1884: End of restrictions on pitch delivery, overhand now permitted. Six balls for a walk.

1885: Seven balls for a walk.

1887: Pitchers must start delivery with one foot on back line of pitching box, which is 55 feet, six inches from home plate. Five balls for a walk. Error no longer charged to pitcher for a walk. Four strikes for an out, and a walk is scored as a hit. Hit-by-pitch gives batter first base. Batter no longer allowed to call for "high" or "low" pitch. Strike zone set at top of shoulder to bottom of knee.

1888: Three strikes for an out. Walks no longer recorded as hits.

1889: Four balls for a walk.

1890: Pitching distance in Players' League set at 57 feet. More lively ball adopted by PL than that used in National League.

1891: Return to National League and 55-foot, six-inch pitching distance. Free substitution allowed, a move that allows relief pitchers and pinch hitters. Previously, if relieved, a pitcher had to assume another position on the field.

Today's pitching distance of 60 feet, six inches, was established in 1893, the year after Galvin retired. Also, at the same time, the pitcher's box was eliminated and replaced by a 12-inch slab.

Sources: The Pitcher, *by John Thorn and John Holway (London: Sports Pages by Simon and Schuster, 1987), BaseballAlmanac.com, and www.19cbaseball.com.*

Chapter Notes

Chapter 1

1. Derek Zumsteg, *The Cheater's Guide to Baseball* (New York: Houghton Mifflin Company, 2007).
2. "Throwback Thursday: Curveballs," *The Harvard Crimson*, November 7, 2013, accessed December 23, 2014, http://www.thecrimson.com/article/2013/11/7/throwback-thursday-baseball/.
3. "Rogers Hornsby Quotes," in Baseball Almanac, accessed December 20, 2014, http://www.baseball-almanac.com/quotes/Quohorn.shtml.
4. Roger I. Abrams, *The Dark Side of the Diamond: Gambling, Violence, Drugs and Alcoholism in the National Pastime* (Burlington, MA: Rounder Books, 2007), 15–16.
5. "Mickey Mantle," SABR player biography, accessed Dec. 21, 2014 http://sabr.org/bioproj/person/61e4590a.
6. Abrams, 104.
7. "Canseco Regrets Naming Names in His Book About Steroids," ESPN.com: Baseball, accessed December 21, 2014, http://espn.go.com/espn/print?id=3655031.
8. "It's Over There, Commissioner," Baseball—The Tenth Inning, accessed November 3, 2014, http://www.pbs.org/baseball-the-tenth-inning/dark-days/over-there-commissioner/.
9. "Baseball; McGwire Stopped His Use of Andro Four Months Ago," *New York Times*, August 6, 1999, accessed November 3, 2014, http://www.nytimes.com/1999/08/06/sports/baseball-mcgwire-stopped-his-use-of-andro-four-months-ago.html.
10. "HHS Launches Crackdown on Products Containing Andro," Health and Human Services press release, March 11, 2004, accessed December 22, 2014, http://www.fda.gov/NewsEvents/Newsroom/PressAnnouncements/2004/ucm108262.htm.
11. "MLB Bans Use of Androstenedione," MLB.com, accessed November 3, 2014, http://mlb.mlb.com/content/printer_friendly/mlb/y2004/m06d29/c783595.jsp.
12. "Congress Opens Hearings on Steroid Use in Baseball," by Maria Newman, *New York Times*, March 18, 2005, accessed December 22, 2014, http://www.Nytimes.com/learning/teachers/featured_articles/20050318friday.html.
13. "McGwire Offers No Denials at Steroid Hearings," by Duff Wilson, *New York Times*, March 18, 2005, accessed December 22, 2014 http://www.nytimes.com/2005/03/18/sports/baseball/18steroids.html.
14. "Rules for Election," *National Baseball Hall of Fame and Museum 2014 Yearbook* (Lynn, MA: H.O. Zimman Inc., 2014), 138.
15. "Why I'll Never Vote for a Known Steroids User for the Hall of Fame," by Tom Verducci, SportsIllustratedwww, January 8, 2013, accessed December 23, 2014, http://www.si.com/mlb/2013/01/08/hall-fame-ballot-steroids-mark-mcguire-barry-bonds-roger-clemens.
16. "Bonds (and Everyone) Strikes Out," by Tyler Kepner, *New York Times.com*, January 9, 2013, accessed Dec. 23, 2014, http://www.nytimes.com/2013/01/10/sports/baseball/no-players-elected-to-baseball-hall-of-fame.html.
17. "Hall of Fame Vote Means Baseball Is, Finally, Emerging from the Steroids Era," Thomas Boswell, *Washington Post*, January 6, 2015, accessed January 8, 2015, http://www.washingtonpost.com/sports/nationals/hall-of-fame-vote-means-baseball-is-finally-emerging-from-the-steroids-era/2015/01/06/

fcb7c858-95db-11e4-8005-1924ede3e54a_story.htm.
18. "Baseball Hall of Fame Must Have Steroid Era Wing," by Darren Rovell, CNBC.com, accessed October 8, 2014, http://www.cnbc.com/id/47877888.
19. "Tony La Russa Says That Steroid Cheats Should Be in Baseball Hall of Fame—With Asterisks," *New York Daily News*, July 26, 2014, accessed October 15, 2014, http://www.nydailynews.com/sports/baseball/tony-la-russa-put-steroid-cheats-baseball-hall-of-fame-asterisks-article-1.1880787.
20. "Such Hypocritical Voting for the Baseball Hall of Fame," by Bob Nightengale, USA Today Sports, *Detroit Free Press*, January 6, 2015, accessed January 8, 2015, http://www.freep.com/story/sports/mlb/2015/01/06/baseball-hall-fame-voting/21338275/.
21. "Baseball Hall of Fame Makes a Huge Change That Will Screw Players Linked to Steroids," *Business Insider*, July 29, 2014, accessed October 8, 2014, http://www.businessinsider.sg/baseball-hall-of-fame-voting-rules-change-2014-7/#VDWXwyje7Hg.
22. "So Who's the Hall of Fame 'Roider Tom Boswell Mentioned Last Night?," by Craig Calcaterra, NBCSports.com, September 29, 2010, accessed October 15, 2014, http://hardballtalk.nbcsports.com/2010/09/29/so-whos-the-hall-of-fame-roider-tom-boswell-mentioned-last-night/.
23. Abrams, 105.
24. Ibid., 106.
25. For instance, "Baseball's Hall of Fame Already Has One Known Steroid User," by Cork Gaines, BusinessInsider.com, January 10, 2013, accessed October 15, 2014, http://www.businessinsider.com/baseballs-hall-of-fame-already-has-one-known-steroid-user-2013-1 and "Reminder: There Are Already Steroid Users in the Hall of Fame," by Craig Calcaterra, NBCSports.com, January 9, 2013, accessed October 8, 2014, http://hardballtalk.nbcsports.com/2013/01/09/reminder-there-are-already-steroids-users-n-the-hall-of-fame/.

Chapter 2

1. "Gone to America," Irish Potato Famine, The History Place, accessed December 28, 2014, http://www.historyplace.com/worldhistory/famine/america.htm.
2. "Physical Growth of the City of Saint Louis," St. Louis City Plan Commission 1969, accessed December 28, 2014, http://www.museum.state.il.us/RiverWeb/landings/Ambot/Archives/History69/.
3. Mullanphy-Clemens Family, St. Louis University, Libraries Special Collections, Archives and Manuscripts, accessed December 28, 2014, http://archon.slu.edu/?p=creators/creator&id=56.
4. Stefene Russell, "Of Cabbages and Kings. One of St. Louis' Most Irish Neighborhoods, the Kerry Patch Was All but Gone 100 Years Ago—But Its Memory Refuses to Fade," *St. Louis Magazine*, July 24, 2014, accessed November 21, 2014, http://www.stlmag.com/arts/history/of-cabbages-and-kings/.
5. "The Kerry Patch and St. Louis Irish History," St. Louis Irish, by John B. McGinnis, March 6, 2007, accessed January 19, 2015, http://stlfire8.loudclick.net/home.aspx.
6. A birthdate of December 25, 1855 is given by sources such as the U.S. Census of 1900 and the Biographical Dictionary of American Sports. So, too, do his obituaries in the *Pittsburgh Press* and *Pittsburgh Gazette*. But Baseball-reference.com, the National Baseball Hall of Fame and the Find a Grave Index use December 25, 1856. The SABR BioProject profile on Galvin and the Joe Overfield biography of Galvin at the Buffalo History Museum use both 1855 and 1856.
7. A steamfitter, according to "Pud Galvin," by Charles Hausberg, SABR BioProject, accessed March 3, 2014, http://sabr.org/bioproj/38c553ff, but blacksmith in "J. F. Galvin," *New York Clipper*, February 8, 1889, 769.
8. Joe Overfield, "'Gentle Jeems' Jim Galvin: Buffalo's First Superstar," Bisontales, in *Bisongram*, a publication of the Buffalo Bisons Professional Baseball Club, February/March 1993, 26.
9. Rich Westcott, *Winningest Pitchers: Baseball's 300-Game Winners* (Philadelphia, PA: Temple University Press, 2002), 4.
10. "Physical Growth of the City of Saint Louis," 13.
11. Jeffrey Kittel, "19th Century St. Louis Baseball Clubs," in This Game of Games: St. Louis Baseball in the 19th Century," 2, accessed December 29, 2014, http://www.thisgameofgames.com/19th-century-st-louis-baseball-clubs.html.
12. "Sportsman's Park," ballparksofbaseball.com, accessed December 29, 2014, http://www.ballparksofbaseball.co/past/SportsmansPark.htm.

13. Kittel, 5.
14. "A Bad Beating. Westerns Paralyzed the Red Stockings," Edmund Tobias, *The Sporting News,* February 1, 1896, 5.
15. "The St. Louis Club," *New York Clipper,* January 30, 1875, 347.
16. "The Professional Gathering of 1875," *New York Clipper,* March 13, 1875, 397.
17. Paul Batesel, *Players and Teams of the National Association, 1871–1875* (Jefferson, NC: McFarland, 2012), 203–205.
18. "The Brown Above the Red and the White," *New York Clipper,* May 15, 1875, 50.
19. Ibid.
20. Charlton's Baseball Chronology, 1875, BaseballLibrary.com, accessed August 24, 2014, http://www.baseballlibrary.com/chronology/byyear.php?year=1875.
21. "Baseball," St. Louis vs. Chicago, *New York Clipper,* May 22, 1875, 61.
22. "The Championship Official Record," *New York Clipper,* May 15, 1875, 50.
23. "Chicago Vs. St. Louis Reds. the Best Game on Record," *New York Clipper,* May 22, 1875, 58.
24. "Paid Players. Professional Clubs More Numerous in 1874," Edmund Tobias, *The Sporting News,* January 18, 1896, 5.
25. Ibid.
26. "Baseball," Chicago vs. St. Louis, *New York Clipper,* May 29, 1875, 69.
27. "Baseball," St. Louis vs. Western," *New York Clipper,* June 5, 1875, 74.
28. "Sporting News. Fourth Game of the Whites and Browns," *Chicago Tribune,* May 23, 1875, 13.
29. "Sporting News. News in St. Louis," *Chicago Tribune,* May 23, 1875, 13.
30. Ibid.
31. "St. Louis Vs. Boston. Defeat of the Champions," *New York Clipper,* June 12, 1875, 83.
32. Charlton's Baseball Chronology, 1875.
33. "St. Louis Vs. Chicago," *New York Clipper,* July 17, 1875, 123.
34. Batesel, 210, and Charlton's Baseball Chronology, 1875.
35. "St. Louis Vs. Atlantic," *New York Clipper,* July 17, 1875, 123.
36. "Baseball. Philadelphia Vs. St. Louis," *New York Clipper,* August 21, 1875, 162.
37. "Baseball. the New St. Louis Team," *New York Clipper,* October 9, 1875, 229.
38. "Baseball. St. Louis Vs. Mutual. Two Good Contests," *New York Clipper,* October 30, 1875, 245.
39. "Baseball. Philadelphia Vs. St. Louis," *New York Clipper,* October 30, 1875, 245.
40. "Baseball. Athletic Vs. St. Louis," *New York Clipper,* November 6, 1875, 250.
41. "Baseball. Mutual Vs. St. Louis," *New York Clipper,* November 6, 1875, 253.
42. "Pud Galvin," written by Charles Hausberg, SABR BioProject, accessed June 1, 2014, http://sabr.org/bioproj/person/38c553ff.

Chapter 3

1. "Nineteenth Century Stars, 2012 Edition, Ed. by Robert L. Tiemann and Mark Rucker (Phoenix, AZ: Society for American Baseball Research, 2012), 92.
2. Paul Batesel, *Players and Teams of the National Association, 1871–1875* (Jefferson, NC: McFarland, 2012), 206–208.
3. Rich Westcott, *Winningest Pitchers: Baseball's 300-Game Winners* (Philadelphia, PA: Temple University Press, 2002), 4.
4. "The St. Louis Reds," *New York Clipper,* July 22, 1876, 131.
5. "The Campaign of 1876. a Retrospective Commentary," *New York Clipper,* October 28, 1876, 245.
6. "A Glorious Victory for Our Reds," *St. Louis Globe-Democrat,* July 5, 1876, 8.
7. Charlton's Baseball Chronology, 1876, BaseballLibrary.com, accessed January 7, 2015, http://www.baseballlibrary.com/chronology/byyear.php?year=1876.
8. "The Tournament," *Ionia Sentinel,* August 18, 1876, 1, from the Joseph Overfield Collection, Buffalo History Museum, Buffalo, New York.
9. "The Tournament," *Ionia Sentinel,* August 25, 1876, 1, from the Joseph Overfield Collection, Buffalo History Museum, Buffalo, New York.
10. "Pud Galvin," by Charles Hausberg, SABR BioProject, accessed June 1, 2014, http://sabr.org/bioproj/person/38c553ff.
11. "Diamond Dust," *New York Clipper,* August 26, 1876, 171.
12. "Diamond Dust," *New York Clipper,* September 2, 1876, 179.
13. Charlton's Baseball Chronology, 1876.
14. David Nemec, *The Great Encyclopedia of 19th Century Major League Baseball* (New York: Donald I. Fine Books, 1997), 86 and "Pete Alexander," by Jan Finkel, SABR BioProject, accessed January 8, 2015, http://sabr.org/bioproj/person/79e6a2a7.
15. Nemec, 88.

16. "A St. Louis Revolver," *New York Clipper,* August 19, 1876, 168.
17. "Baseball," *New York Clipper,* Sept. 16, 1876, 197.
18. "The St. Louis Reds' Record," *New York Clipper,* November 25, 1876, 277.
19. David Piestrusza, *Major Leagues: The Formation, Sometimes Absorption and Mostly Inevitable Demise of 18 Professional Baseball Organizations, 1871 to Present* (Jefferson NC: McFarland, 1991), 38.
20. *Ibid.,* 47.
21. John N. Ingham, "Iron and Steel in the Pittsburgh Region: The Domain of Small Business," Business and Economic History, second series, vol. 20, 1991, 108, accessed January 19, 2015, http://www.thebhc.org/sites/default/files/beh/BEHprint/v020/p0107-p0116.pdf.
22. Frederick G. Lieb, *The Pittsburgh Pirates* (Carbondale: Southern Illinois University Press, 2003), 3–4 (Writing Baseball series edition reprint of 1948 edition by G.P. Putnam's Sons).
23. *Ibid.,* 4.
24. *Baseball's First Stars,* edited by Frederick Ivor-Campbell, Robert L. Tiemann, and Mark Rucker (Cleveland, OH: The Society for American Baseball Research, 1991), 106, and *Directory of Pittsburgh and Allegheny Cities 1878–1879,* 462, accessed January 10, 2015, http://digital.library.pitt.edu/cgi-bin/t/text/pageviewer-idx?c=pitttextdir&cc=pitttextdir&idno=31735054778604&node=31735054778604%3A1.26&frm=frameset&view=image&seq=464.
25. "Record of the Allegheny Club," *New York Clipper,* November 11, 1876, 259.
26. "A New Movement Out West," *New York Clipper,* October 21, 1876, 235.
27. The Campaign of 1876. A Retrospective Commentary," *New York Clipper,* October 28, 1876, 245.
28. "A New National Association," *New York Clipper,* November 4, 1876.
29. "The International Association," *New York Clipper,* January 20, 1877, 339.
30. "The International Association," *New York Clipper,* January 27, 1877, 346.
31. William J. Ryczek, *Blackguards and Red Stockings: A History of Baseball's National Association, 1871–1875* (Wallingford, CT: Colebrook Press, 1992), 226.
32. "The International Association," *New York Clipper,* March 10, 1877, 394.
33. "The International Association," *New York Clipper,* March 3, 1877, 387.
34. "Candy Cummings," by David Fleitz, SABR BioProject, accessed January 15, 2015, http://sabr.org/bioproj/person/99fabeSf.
35. Pietrusza, 48.

Chapter 4

1. *London (Ontario) Advertiser,* April 30, 1877.
2. "The Allegheny Club of Pittsburgh," *New York Clipper,* January 13, 1877, 331.
3. Brian Martin, *The Tecumsehs of the International Association: Canada's First Major League Baseball Champions* (Jefferson, NC: McFarland, 2015), 53–70.
4. *Ibid.,* 104–105.
5. Ted Vincent, *Mudville's Revenge: The Rise and Fall of American Sport* (Lincoln: University of Nebraska Press, 1981), 146.
6. David Pietrusza, *Major Leagues: The Formation, Sometimes Absorption and Mostly Inevitable Demise of 18 Professional Baseball Organizations, 1871 to Present* (Jefferson, NC: McFarland, 1991), 48.
7. "William Hulbert," by Michael Haupert, BioProject of the Society for American Baseball Research, accessed February 5, 2014, http://sabr.org/bioproj/person/38c553ff.
8. Charlton's Baseball Chronology, 1877, BaseballLibrary.com, accessed January 24, 2015, http://www.baseballlibrary.com/chronology/byyear.php?year=1877.
9. David Q. Voigt, *American Baseball* (Norman: University of Oklahoma Press, 1966), 76.
10. Pietrusza, *Major Leagues,* 48–49.
11. "Ball Notes. an Auspicious Beginning," *Pittsburgh Commercial Gazette,* April 20, 1877.
12. "Base Ball. Allegheny Vs. Star," *New York Clipper,* May 5, 1877, 42.
13. "The Giants Laid Low," *Pittsburgh Commercial Gazette,* April 26, 1877.
14. As quoted in "Base Ball. Allegheny Vs. Boston," *New York Clipper,* May 12, 1877, 53.
15. "Once More, for the Boys," *Pittsburgh Commercial Gazette,* May 3, 1877, 1.
16. "Memphis Vs. Allegheny," *New York Clipper,* June 16, 1877, 91.
17. "Boston Vs. Allegheny," *New York Clipper,* June 23, 1877, 99.
18. Charlton's Baseball Chronology, 1877.
19. "And Yet Another Victory," *Pittsburgh Commercial Gazette,* July 5, 1877.

Chapter 5

1. "Base Ball," *Pittsburgh Commercial Gazette,* July 21, 1877.

2. Joe Overfield, "'Gentle Jeems' Jim Galvin: Buffalo's First Superstar," from "Bisontales" in the (Buffalo) *Bisongram*, February, March, 1993, 26, and Charlton's Baseball Chronology, Baseballlibrary.com, accessed February 5, 2015, http://w.w.w.baseballlibrary.com/chronology/byyear.php?year=1877.
3. "The Next Page: The Railroad War," post-gazette.com, the *Pittsburgh Post-Gazette*, accessed February 4, 2015, http://www.post-gazette.com/opinion/Op-Ed/2007/07/06/The-Next-Page-The-Railroad-War/stories/200707060327.
4. "The Great Railroad Strike," Digital History, accessed February 4, 2015, http://www.digitalhistory.uh.edu/disp_textbook.cfm?smtID=2&psid=3189.
5. Dan Rooney and Carol Peterson, *Allegheny City: A History of Pittsburgh's North Side* (Pittsburgh: University of Pittsburgh Press, 2013), 82.
6. "Base Ball," *Pittsburgh Commercial Gazette*, July 31, 1877.
7. "Base Ball," *Pittsburgh Commercial Gazette*, August 3, 1877.
8. "Base Ball Notes," *Pittsburgh Commercial Gazette*, August 6, 1877.
9. "Departure of the Alleghenys on Their Western Trip—Schedule of Games—McKelvy to Go to Indianapolis Next Season," *Pittsburgh Commercial Gazette*, August 14, 1877.
10. "Indianapolis Vs. Allegheny," *New York Clipper*, August 25, 1877.
11. Paul Batesel, *Players and Teams of the National Association, 1871-1875* (Jefferson, NC: McFarland, 2012), 22, 28.
12. "Base Ball Notes," *Pittsburgh Commercial Gazette*, August 29, 1877.
13. "Base Ball," *Pittsburgh Commercial Gazette*, September 10, 1877.
14. "The Pittsburgh Tournament," *New York Clipper*, September 22, 1877, 202.
15. "Base Ball," *Pittsburgh Commercial Gazette*, September 17, 1877.
16. "Base Ball," *Pittsburgh Commercial Gazette*, September 24, 1877.
17. "Base Ball," *Pittsburgh Commercial Gazette*, September 25, 1877.
18. "Short Stops," *New York Clipper*, September 29, 1877, 210.
19. "Crow Out Loud! the Tecumsehs International Champions," *London Advertiser*, October 3, 1877, 1.
20. "The Championship Match," *London Free Press*, October 3, 1877, 1.
21. Ibid.
22. "The Championship Lost," *Pittsburgh Commercial Gazette*, October 3, 1877.
23. "The International Championship," *New York Clipper*, October 13, 1877, 226.
24. "Base Ball Notes," *Pittsburgh Commercial Gazette*, October 8, 1877.
25. "International Championship," *New York Clipper*, October 20, 1877, 234.
26. "The Allegheny's Claims and Charges," *New York Clipper*, November 3, 1877, 251.
27. "The International Convention," *New York Clipper*, March 2, 1878, 386.
28. David Nemec, *The Great Encyclopedia of 19th Century Major League Baseball* (New York: Donald I. Fine Books, 1997), 101.
29. "Short Stops," *New York Clipper*, November 3, 1877, 251.
30. "Base Ball Talk," *New York Clipper*, November 24 1877, 274.
31. The *Syracuse Courier*, as quoted in "Base Ball," the *London Advertiser*, October 24, 1877.
32. David Pietrusza, *Major League: The Formation, Sometimes Absorption and Mostly Inevitable Demise of 18 Professional Baseball Organizations, 1871 to Present* (Jefferson, NC: McFarland, 1991), 39.
33. "Allegheny (Pa.) Club," *New York Clipper*, December 8, 1877, 293, and "The Canadian Champions. the Tecumseh Club Record," *New York Clipper*, November 10, 1877, 261.
34. The final official standing for Allegheny in the International Association as reported in newspapers at the time, including the *New York Clipper*, showed the club with 11 wins. That record was confirmed later at the annual convention of the IA as it awarded the championship to London. But Baseball-reference.com nevertheless indicates 12 wins for Galvin.
35. Joseph M. Overfield, "It All Began with a Pitcher's Duel," *Buffalo Courier-Express*, May 8, 1977, 20.
36. Charlton's Baseball Chronology, 1877.

Chapter 6

1. Copy of telegram in the Joseph Overfield Collection, Research Library, Buffalo History Museum, Buffalo, New York.
2. "Short Stops," *New York Clipper*, November 3, 1877, 251.
3. Joseph M. Overfield, *The 100 Seasons of Buffalo Baseball* (Kenmore, NY: Partners' Press, 1985), 17.
4. Richard C. Brown and Bob Watson,

Buffalo: Lake City in Niagara Land (Buffalo, NY: Windsor Publications, 1981), 108–120.

5. *Buffalo Courier* of August 2, 1877, quoted by Joe Overfield in season notes, Overfield Collection, Buffalo History Museum, Buffalo, New York.

6. Joseph M. Overfield, "It All Began with a Pitchers' Duel," *Buffalo Courier-Express*, May 8, 1977, 18.

7. "Base Ball," *Buffalo Courier*, August 4, 1877.

8. "Base Ball," *Buffalo Express*, August 4, 1877.

9. "Indianapolis Vs. Buffalo," *New York Clipper*, September 22, 1877, 205.

10. Overfield, "It All Began with a Pitchers' Duel," 20, and Overfield's detailed notes of *Buffalo Courier* coverage of the 1877 season in the Overfield Collection, Buffalo History Museum, Buffalo, New York.

11. Letter from W.A. Cummings to Directors of the Buffalo Base Ball Association, dated December 20, 1877, Overfield Collection, Buffalo History Museum, Buffalo, New York.

12. David Pietrusza, *Major Leagues: The Formation, Sometimes Absorption and Mostly Inevitable Demise of 18 Professional Baseball Organizations, 1871 to Present* (Jefferson, NC: McFarland, 1991), 49–50.

13. Ted Vincent, *Mudville's Revenge: The Rise & Fall of American Sport* (Lincoln: University of Nebraska Press, 1994), 147.

14. Charlton's Baseball Chronology, Baseballlibrary.com, accessed February 11, 2015, http://www.baseballlibrary.com/chronology/byyear.php?year=1878.

15. David Nemec, *Major League Baseball Profiles 1871–1900. Volume 1: The Ballplayers Who Built the Game* (Lincoln: University of Nebraska Press, 2011), 456.

16. Overfield, *The 100 Seasons of Buffalo Baseball*, 19.

17. "Out-Door Sports," *London Advertiser*, April 27, 1878. In his *100 Seasons*, Overfield said, in error, the score was 5–3.

18. Joseph M. Overfield, "Professional Baseball in Buffalo—How It Began," *Niagara Frontier Magazine 1, No. 2* (Spring 1954), 34.

19. "Ball and Bat. London's Day Off!," *London Advertiser*, May 25, 1878.

20. "Out Door Sports," *London Advertiser*, May 31, 1878.

21. Overfield, "Professional Baseball in Buffalo—How It Began," 32.

22. "Buffalo Vs. Allegheny," *New York Clipper*, June 15, 1878, 90.

23. "Out-Door Sports," *London Advertiser*, June 17, 1878.

24. Overfield, *The 100 Seasons of Buffalo Baseball*, 19.

25. In his *The 100 Seasons of Buffalo Baseball*, Joseph Overfield said it was September 9, in Utica. But *New York Clipper* box scores show Buffalo played in Troy on September 9 and in Utica on September 6. The Bisons won both games, 6–2 and 3–2 respectively and Galvin is shown as having one hit and one run in both contests.

26. "Out-Door Sports," *London Advertiser*, July 8, 1878.

27. "Out-Door Sports, *London Advertiser*, July 11, 1878.

28. Annual Statement of the Financial Condition of the Buffalo Base Ball Association at the Close of the Season November 1, 1878, in the Overfield Collection, Buffalo History Museum.

29. "The Stars of Syracuse," *New York Clipper*, February 1, 1879, 354.

30. Overfield, "Professional Baseball in Buffalo—How It Began," 34.

31. "Pud Galvin," by Charles Hausberg, SABR BioProject, accessed June 1, 2014, http://sabr.org/bioproj/person/38c553ff.

32. Overfield, *The 100 Seasons of Buffalo Baseball*, 19.

33. "Pud Galvin," Hausberg.

34. Overfield, "Professional Baseball in Buffalo—How It Began," 34.

Chapter 7

1. Ted Vincent, *Mudville's Revenge: The Rise and Fall of American Sport* (Lincoln: University of Nebraska Press, 1981), 149.

2. David Nemec, *The Great Encyclopedia of 19th Century Major League Baseball* (New York: Donald I. Fine Books, 1996), 121.

3. Ibid., 121.

4. David Pietrusza, *Major Leagues: The Formation, Sometimes Absorption and Mostly Inevitable Demise of 18 Professional Baseball Organizations, 1871 to Present* (Jefferson, NC: Mcfarland, 1991), 60.

5. Historian John Thorn in his Major League Baseball blog "Our Game," May 4, 2015, accessed May 10, 2015, http://ourgame.mlblogs.com/2015/05/04/why-is-the-national-association-not-a-major-league-and-other-records-issues/.

6. For a more complete discussion of the impact of "Minor League" status on the Inter-

national Association and its players, see Brian Martin, *The Tecumsehs of the International Association: Canada's First Major League Baseball Champions* (Jefferson, NC: McFarland, 2015), 236–239.
  7. "Later Baseball Notes," *New York Clipper,* June 14, 1879, 90.
  8. Charlton's Baseball Chronology, 1879, Baseballlibrary.com accessed February 16, 2015, http://www.baseballlibrary.com/chronology/byyear.php?year=1879.
  9. "Baseball Notes," *New York Clipper,* September 20, 1879, 202.
  10. Pietrusza, *Major Leagues,* 43.
  11. Ibid., 43.
  12. "Baseball Notes," *New York Clipper,* October 11, 1879, 229.
  13. *San Francisco Bulletin,* February 11, 1880, as quoted in "Pud Galvin," by Charles Hausberg, a SABR BioProject, accessed June 1, 2014, http://www.sabr.org/bioproj/person/38c553ff.
  14. "Later Baseball Notes," *New York Clipper,* May 8, 1880, 50.
  15. "The California League," *New York Clipper,* May 22, 1880, 66.
  16. "Base Ball," *Buffalo Courier,* May 11, 1880.
  17. *Buffalo Express,* May 22, 1880.
  18. "About a Pitcher," *New York Clipper,* May 29, 1880, 77.
  19. "J.F. Galvin," *New York Clipper,* February 9, 1889, 769.
  20. "Utterly Demoralized," *Buffalo Express,* May 24, 1880.
  21. "More Misery," *Buffalo Express,* May 26, 1880.
  22. "Another Game Lost," *Buffalo Express,* May 28, 1880.
  23. "A Famous Victory," *Buffalo Express,* July 17, 1880.

Chapter 8

  1. David Nemec, *The Great Encyclopedia of 19th Century Major League Baseball* (New York: Donald I. Fine Books, 1997), 148.
  2. Joseph M. Overfield, *The 100 Seasons of Buffalo Baseball* (Kenmore, NY: Partners' Press, 1985), 21.
  3. Roy Kerr, *Big Dan Brouthers: Baseball's First Great Slugger* (Jefferson, NC: McFarland, 2013), 29.
  4. His earlier home runs: May 2, 1877, with Allegheny versus Boston, at Allegheny (exhibition); May 24, 1877, with Allegheny versus Philadelphia Athletics at Allegheny (exhibition); August 20, 1877, with Allegheny versus St. Louis, at St. Louis (exhibition); October 3, with Allegheny versus London Tecumsehs, at London (International Association league game); September 6 or 9, 1878 with Buffalo, versus Utica or Troy, at Utica or Troy (IA league or exhibition); May 9, 1880, with San Francisco versus Bay City, at San Francisco.
  5. "Intentional Bases on Balls Records," Baseball Almanac, accessed February 22, 2015, http://www.baseball-almanac.com/recbooks/rb_wk3.shtml.
  6. Charlton's Baseball Chronology, 1881, Baseballlibrary.com, accessed February 3, 2015, http://www.baseballlibrary.com/chronology/byyear.php?year=1881.
  7. David Pietrusza, *Major Leagues: The Formation, Sometimes Absorption and Mostly Inevitable Demise of 18 Professional Baseball Organizations, 1871 to Present* (Jefferson, NC: McFarland, 1991), 62, 63.
  8. David Nemec, *The Beer and Whisky League: The Illustrated History of the American Association—Baseball's Renegade Major League* (New York: Lyons and Burford, 1994), 21–25.
  9. Pietrusza, *Major Leagues,* 69.
  10. Charlton's Baseball Chronology, 1882, Baseballlibrary.com, accessed February 17, 2015, http://www.baseballlibrary.com/chronology/byyear.php?year=1882.
  11. Ted Vincent, *Mudville's Revenge: The Rise and Fall of American Sport* (Lincoln: University of Nebraska Press, 1981), 164.
  12. "Hugh Daily," by Frank Vaccaro for the SABR BioProject, accessed February 24, 2015, http://sabr.org/bioproj/person/8d8c99e4.
  13. Ibid.
  14. Charlton's Baseball Chronology, 1882.
  15. "Hugh Daily," Vaccaro.
  16. Kerr, *Big Dan Brouthers,* 37–38.
  17. Ibid., 37.
  18. Overfield, *The 100 Seasons of Buffalo Baseball,* 22–23.
  19. "The Late League Meeting," *New York Clipper,* September 30, 1882, 448.
  20. Harold Seymour and Dorothy Seymour Mills, *Baseball: The Early Years* (New York: Oxford University Press, 1989 reprint of 1960 edition), 142.

Chapter 9

  1. *Cleveland Herald,* as quoted in the *Buffalo Express,* May 3, 1883, notation found in

1883 season notes by Joseph M. Overfield, Manuscript Department, Buffalo Historical Society, Buffalo, New York.
 2. "The Work of the Conference," *New York Clipper*, February 24, 1883, 790.
 3. *Sporting Life*, August 6, 1883, as quoted in Roy Kerr, *Big Dan Brouthers: Baseball's First Great Slugger* (Jefferson, NC: McFarland, 2013), 39.
 4. "Pud Galvin," by Charles Hausberg, SABR BioProject, Society for American Baseball Research, accessed June 1, 2014, http://sabr.org/bioproj/person/38c553ff.
 5. "Professional Baseball in Buffalo," by Joseph M. Overfield, *Niagara Frontier, Volume 1, Numbers 1-4*, Winter 1953—Spring, Fall, Winter, 1954, Published by the Buffalo Historical Society, Buffalo New York, 30.
 6. David Pietrusza, *Major Leagues: The Formation, Sometimes Absorption and Mostly Inevitable Demise of 18 Professional Baseball Organizations, 1871 to Present* (Jefferson, NC: McFarland, 1991), 82.
 7. Brian Martin, *The Tecumsehs of the International Association: Canada's First Major League Champions* (Jefferson, NC: McFarland, 2015), 198.
 8. "Pud Galvin," by Charles Hausberg, SABR BioProject.
 9. "Fred Goldsmith," by David Fleitz, SABR BioProject, Society for American Baseball Research, accessed January 8, 2014, http://sabr.org/bioproj/person/99c4a5f5.
 10. Roy Kerr, *Big Dan Brouthers: Baseball's First Great Slugger* (Jefferson, NC: McFarland, 2013), 43.
 11. "A Memorable Year—1884 a Memorable Performer—Jim Galvin," by Joseph M. Overfield, SABR Research Journals Archive, accessed June 3, 2014, http://research.sabr.org/journals/jim-galvin.
 12. *Providence Evening Telegram*, September 10, 1884, as quoted in "Pud Galvin," by Charles Hausberg, SABR BioProject.
 13. *National Baseball Hall of Fame Yearbook 2014* (Lynn, MA: H.O. Zinman, 2014), 110.
 14. *Sporting Life*, July 16, 1884, as quoted in Kerr, *Big Dan Brouthers*, 44.

Chapter 10

 1. David Pietrusza, *Major Leagues: The Formation, Sometimes Absorption and Mostly Inevitable Demise of 18 Professional Baseball Organizations, 1871 to Present* (Jefferson, NC: McFarland, 1991), 98.
 2. "The League Umpires' Meeting," *New York Clipper*, May 9, 1885, 116.
 3. *Sporting Life*, July 1, 1885.
 4. *Buffalo Courier*, July 12, 1885, as quoted in Roy Kerr, *Big Dan Brouthers: Baseball's First Great Slugger* (Jefferson, NC: McFarland, 2013), 44.
 5. Joseph M. Overfield, *The 100 Seasons of Buffalo Baseball* (Kenmore, NY: Partners' Press, 1985), 25.
 6. "A Pitcher Changes Clubs," *New York Times*, July 14, 1885, 2.
 7. "The Bisons. They Will Stick," *Sporting Life*, July 22, 1885, 1.
 8. Even the esteemed Buffalo historian Joseph M. Overfield couldn't resolve the issue. In his "Professional Baseball in Buffalo" history published in 1954, he said the idea came from Detroit. But in his later *The 100 Seasons of Buffalo Baseball*, he said it was Jewett's idea. See: "Professional Baseball in Buffalo," by Joseph M. Overfield, *Niagara Frontier, Volume 1, Numbers 1-4*, Winter, 1953—Spring, Fall, Winter, 1954 (Buffalo, NY: Buffalo Historical Society, 1954), 22 and Joseph M. Overfield, *The 100 Seasons of Buffalo Baseball*, 25.
 9. "The Buffalo-Detroit Deal," *New York Clipper*, September 26, 1885, 442.
 10. Charlton's Baseball Chronology—1885, Baseballlibrary.com, accessed March 1, 2015, http:///www.baseballlibrary.com/chronology/byyear.php?year=1885.
 11. "The Glory Has Departed," *Buffalo Express*, September 18, 1885, 2.
 12. Overfield, *The 100 Seasons of Buffalo Baseball*, 25.
 13. Roy Kerr, *Big Dan Brouthers: Baseball's First Great Slugger* (Jefferson, NC: McFarland, 2013), 47.
 14. *New York Clipper*, November 28, 1885, 587.
 15. "Notes and Comments," *Sporting Life*, March 2, 1886, 3.
 16. "The President Knew Them," *New York Times*, June 9, 1888, 2.
 17. "Good for Galvin," *Pittsburgh Commercial Gazette*, July 23, 1885, 8.
 18. "Jimmy Galvin Knocked Out for the Rest of the Season, and Perhaps for Good," *Sporting Life*, September 2, 1885, 4.
 19. Pietrusza, *Major Leagues*, 99.
 20. "The League Convention," *New York Clipper*, November 28, 1885, 585-586.
 21. *Sporting News*, August 23, 1886, 5.

Chapter 11

1. David Nemec, *The Beer and Whisky League: The Illustrated History of the American Association—Baseball's Renegade Major League* (New York: Lyons and Burford, 1994), 109, 110.
2. "American Association Meeting," *New York Clipper*, March 27, 1886, 26.
3. *Baseball's First Stars* (Cleveland: The Society for American Baseball Research, 1996), 109.
4. "Gentle Jeems. the Falstaffian Pitcher Beats the Athletics," *Pittsburgh Commercial Gazette*, June 3, 1886, 8.
5. "Base Stealing. an Art Which Puts the Alleghenys Up to Second," *Pittsburgh Commercial Gazette*, June 8, 1886, 8.
6. "Only Two Hits. Galvin Shows the Brooklyns Where They Are Wrong," *Pittsburgh Commercial Gazette*, July 9, 1886, 8.
7. "New York Vs. St. Louis," *New York Clipper*, August 7, 1886, 324.
8. *Sporting News*, November 13, 1886, 4.
9. Frederick G. Lieb, *The Pittsburgh Pirates* (Carbondale: Southern Illinois University Press, 2003), 11. Writing Baseball series reprint of original 1948 edition by G.P. Putnam's Sons.
10. John McCollister, *The Bucs!: The Story of the Pittsburgh Pirates* (Lenexa, KS: Addax Publishing, 1998), 26.
11. *Pittsburgh Post*, May 2, 1887, as quoted in *The Pirates Reader*, edited by Richard Peterson (Pittsburgh: University of Pittsburgh Press, 2003), 33.
12. "Ned Morris on the Shelf," *Sporting News*, May 14, 1887, 1.
13. "Caught on the Fly," *Sporting News*, June 11, 1887, 4.
14. "Shadowed by Detectives. the Pittsburgh and Philadelphia Boys Under Surveillance," *Sporting News*, July 9, 1887, 1.
15. *New York Clipper*, July 16, 1887, 281.
16. *New York Clipper*, July 30, 1887, 314.
17. "The Late Alexander J. Mckinnon," *New York Clipper*, July 30, 1887, 313.
18. "From the Hub," *New York Clipper*, September 3, 1887, 394.
19. McCollister, *The Bucs!*, 26.

Chapter 12

1. *Major League Baseball Profiles. 1871–1900, Volume 1: The Players Who Built the Game*, compiled and edited by David Nemec (Lincoln: University of Nebraska Press, 2011), 352–354.
2. "Is It Freeze Out? Dickenson's Impressions of Allegheny Methods," *Pittsburgh Press*, January 4, 1888, 3.
3. "Jimmy Joins. The Favorite Pitcher Signs and the Club's Troubles End," *Pittsburgh Commercial Gazette*, February 14, 1888, 8.
4. "Stray Sparks from the Diamond," *New York Clipper*, July 21, 1888, 302.
5. "Jimmy Joins," *Pittsburgh Commercial Gazette*, February 14, 1888, 8.
6. "Billy Sunday," by Wendy Knickerbocker, SABR BioProject, accessed January 3, 2015, http://sabr.org/bioproj/person/7fae24bc.
7. "Sporting," *Pittsburgh Press*, June 20, 1888, 3.
8. "New Blood for Pittsburgh," *Sporting News*, June 16, 1888, 1.
9. "Is Galvin Weakening?," *Pittsburgh Press*, June 23, 1888, 1.
10. "Nimick Defines His Stand. Manager Phillips Must Either Strengthen Club or Resign," *Pittsburgh Press*, June 25, 1888, 2.
11. "Sporting," *Pittsburgh Press*, July 14, 1888, 3.
12. "Caught on the Fly," *Sporting News*, July 14, 1888, 5.
13. "Open to America," *Pittsburgh Press*, August 21, 1888, 1.
14. "Sporting," *Pittsburgh Press*, September 6, 1888, 3, and *New York Clipper*, September 8, 1888, 413.
15. "Washington Vs. Pittsburgh," *New York Clipper*, October 13, 1888, 498.
16. "Sporting," *Pittsburgh Press*, October 6, 1888, 4.
17. Frederick G. Lieb, *The Pittsburgh Pirates* (Carbondale: Southern Illinois University Press, 2002), reprint of G.P. Putnam's Sons 1948 edition, 15.
18. John Thorn, *Baseball in the Garden of Eden: The Secret History of the Early Game* (New York: Simon & Schuster, 2011), 234.
19. Lee Lowenfish, *The Imperfect Diamond: A History of Baseball's Labor Wars* (Lincoln: University of Nebraska Press, 2010), 33.
20. "Still Undecided," *Pittsburgh Press*, January 12, 1890, 5.
21. "Old Galvin Returns," *Pittsburgh Dispatch*, February 17, 1889, 6.
22. "Galvin's Training Methods," *Pittsburgh Dispatch*, March 3, 1889, 6.
23. "Galvin Getting Ready," *Pittsburgh Dispatch*, March 9, 1889, 6.
24. *Pittsburgh Press*, March 8, 12, 15, 1889.

25. "Ready for Work," *Pittsburgh Dispatch*, May 6, 1889, 6.
26. "Stray Sparks from the Diamond," *New York Clipper*, May 25, 1889, 179.
27. "Gracefully Done," *Pittsburgh Dispatch*, June 29, 1889, 6.
28. "Keeping Up the Fun," *Pittsburgh Dispatch*, July 21, 1889, 6.
29. "Pittsburgh's New Twirlers," *Sporting News*, July 27, 1889, 4.
30. "Caught on the Fly," *Sporting News*, August 3, 1889, 4.
31. "Horace D. Phillips Insane," *New York Times*, August 2, 1889, 1.
32. *Sporting News*, August 10, 1889, 4.
33. "Horace Phillips Found," Society for American Baseball Research, Biographical Research Committee, January/February 2011 Report.

Chapter 13

1. "Stray Sparks from the Diamond," *New York Clipper*, August 24, 1889, 395.
2. "Baseball's First Fountain of Youth," by Christopher Klein, History in the Headlines, accessed March 1, 2015, http:///www.history.com/news/baseballs-first-found-of-youth.
3. "Don't Believe in It," *Washington Post*, August 13, 1889, 4.
4. "A Brief History of Testosterone," by Erica R. Freeman, David A. Bloom and Edward J. McGuire, department of surgery, University of Michigan, from the Journal of Urology, American Urological Association, Vol. 165, 371–373, February 2001, as appearing at Masters Men's Clinic, accessed June 26, 2014, http://www.mastersmensclinic.com/history_of_testosterone_htm.
5. "The Effects Produced on Man by Subcutaneous Injections of a Liquid Obtained from the Testes of Animals," by Dr. Brown-Sequard, F.R.S. &c., *The Lancet*, July 20, 1889, 105–107, accessed June 26, 2014, http://www.sciencedirect.com/science/article/pii/S0140673600641181.
6. Roger I. Abrams, *The Dark Side of the Diamond: Gambling, Violence, Drugs and Alcoholism in the National Pastime* (Burlington, MA: Rounder Books, 2007), 106–107.
7. "Galvin, the Great," *Pittsburgh Dispatch*, August 14, 1889, 6.
8. "Pittsburgh 9; Boston, 0," *New York Times*, August 14, 1889, 3.
9. Abrams, *The Dark Side of the Diamond*, 107.
10. "Base Ball Notes," *Washington Post*, August 14, 1889, 2.
11. "Fooled Mr. Tener," *Pittsburgh Dispatch*, August 25, 1889, 6.
12. "Brown-Sequard Revisited: A Lesson from History on the Placebo Effect of Androgen Treatment," by Andrea J. Cussons, John P. Walsh, Chotoo I. Bhagat and Stephen J. Fletcher, *Medical Journal of Australia 2002: Vol. 177 (11)*, 678–679, accessed July 7, 2014, https://www.mja.com.au/journal/2002/177/11/brown-sequard-revisited-lesson-history-placebo-effect-androgen-treatment.
13. Michael J. Aminoff, *Brown-Sequard: An Improbable Genius Who Transformed Medicine* (New York: Oxford University Press, 2010), 6,7.
14. "That Gay Old Sport," *Pittsburgh Dispatch*, September 27, 1889, 6.
15. "Ah! We Downed Them," *Pittsburgh Dispatch*, October 2, 1889, 6.
16. "Jimmy Galvin Did It," *Sporting News*, October 12, 1889. 3.
17. "Base Ball Notes," *Pittsburgh Commercial Gazette*, November 19, 1889, 6.
18. "May Buy Jimmy's Stock," *Pittsburgh Dispatch*, November 21, 1890, 6.
19. Adrian Constantine Anson, *A Ball Player's Career* (Gloucester, UK: Dodo Press, 2008 reprint of original 1900 edition), 251.
20. Ibid., 291.
21. David Pietrusza, *Major Leagues: The Formation, Sometimes Absorption and Mostly Inevitable Demise of 18 Professional Baseball Organizations, 1871 to Present* (Jefferson, NC: McFarland, 1991), 115.
22. "A Very Significant List," *Pittsburgh Dispatch*, December 17, 1889, 1.
23. Pietrusza, *Major Leagues*, 112.
24. "Base-Ball Notes," *Pittsburgh Commercial Gazette*, January 24, 1890, 6.
25. *Pittsburgh Commercial Gazette*, February 24, 1890.
26. "Staunch Galvin," *Sporting Life*, April 19, 1890, 8.
27. "The Old Man's Day," *Pittsburgh Dispatch*, April 24, 1890, 6.
28. "Twenty-Five Cents," *Pittsburgh Dispatch*, April 29, 1890, 6.
29. "Galvin Stole a Base," *Pittsburgh Dispatch*, May 4, 1890, 6.
30. "Too Cold for Jeems," *Pittsburgh Dispatch*, May 7, 1890, 6.
31. "Two in Succession," *Pittsburgh Dispatch*, June 4, 1890, 6.
32. Pietrusza, *Major Leagues*, 118.

33. "Stray Sparks from the Diamond," *New York Clipper*, December 6, 1890, 617.
34. "The Tide Turning," *Pittsburgh Dispatch*, August 4, 1890, 6.
35. "It Was Galvin's Day," *Pittsburgh Dispatch*, August 19, 1890, 6.
36. "Stray Sparks from the Diamond," *New York Clipper*, September 27, 1890, 457.
37. Pietrusza, *Major Leagues*, 121.
38. "Galvanized Wisdom," *Sporting Life*, November 1, 1890, 4.
39. "Stray Sparks from the Diamond," *New York Clipper*, November 22, 1890, 585.
40. "A Veteran on Anti-Abolitionism," *Sporting Life*, November 22, 1890, 5.
41. "Stray Sparks from the Diamond," *New York Clipper*, December 6, 1890, 617.
42. Lee Lowenfish, *The Imperfect Diamond: A History of Baseball's Labor Wars* (Lincoln: University of Nebraska Press, 2010), 51.
43. Charles Alexander, *Our Game* (New York: Henry Holt, 1991), 58, quoted in Roy Kerr, *Big Dan Brouthers: Baseball's First Great Slugger* (Jefferson, NC: McFarland, 2013), 90.

Chapter 14

1. Donald Dewey and Nicholas Acocella, *The Biographical History of Baseball* (Chicago: Triumph Books, 2012), 423.
2. Alfred H. Spink, *The National Game*, Second Edition (St. Louis: The National Game Publishing Company, 1911; reprint, Carbondale: Southern Illinois University Press, 2000), 191–192, as quoted in "We Are Now Pirates: The 1890 Burghers and Alleghenys," by Craig Britcher, *Western Pennsylvania History*, Spring 2014, 49.
3. Frederick G. Lieb, *The Pittsburgh Pirates* (New York: G.P. Putnam's Sons, 1948; reprint Carbondale: Southern Illinois University Press, 2002), 21.
4. Ibid., 21.
5. "On Top This Time," *Pittsburgh Dispatch*, February 15, 1891, 6.
6. "The National Board Meeting," *New York Clipper*, February 21, 1891, 793.
7. "Talk About Pirates," *Pittsburgh Dispatch*, March 1, 1891, 6.
8. "Mark Baldwin," by Brian McKenna, SABR BioProject, accessed January 18, 2015, http://sabr.org/bioproj/person/41f65388.
9. "Diamond Field Gossip," *New York Clipper*, March 28, 1891, 47.
10. Harold Seymour and Dorothy Seymour Mills, *Baseball: The Early Years* (New York: Oxford University Press, 1960, reprint 1989), 251.
11. "Diamond Field Gossip," *New York Clipper*, March 14, 1891, 12.
12. "Diamond Field Gossip," *New York Clipper*, March 28, 1891, 48.
13. David Pietrusza, *Major Leagues: The Formation, Sometimes Absorption and Mostly Inevitable Demise of 18 Professional Baseball Organizations, 1871 to Present* (Jefferson, NC: McFarland, 1991), 127.
14. "Old Sport Galvin," *Pittsburgh Dispatch*, March 16, 1891, 6.
15. "Jimmy Galvin Released," *Pittsburgh Dispatch*, March 17, 1891, 6.
16. "The Old Man Signs," *Pittsburgh Dispatch*, March 26, 1891, 6.
17. "Diamond Field Gossip," *New York Clipper*, March 28, 1891, 47.
18. "Sporting," *Pittsburgh Dispatch*, April 4, 1891, 3.
19. "Day of the Diamond," and "We Nearly Won It," *Pittsburgh Dispatch*, April 23, 1891, 1 and 6.
20. "We Called a Halt," *Pittsburgh Dispatch*, April 28, 1891, 6.
21. "The Gay Old Sport," *Pittsburgh Dispatch*, May 2, 1891, 6.
22. "Describing Old Jimmy," *Pittsburgh Dispatch*, May 4, 1891, 6.
23. "A Weakling's Wail," *Pittsburgh Dispatch*, May 7, 1891, 6.
24. "In the Smoky City," *Sporting News*, May 23, 1891, 2.
25. "Diamond Field Gossip," *New York Clipper*, June 6, 1891, 221.
26. *Sporting Life*, June 20, 1891, 2.
27. "O'Neill Triumphs," *Sporting Life*, August 1, 1891, 1.
28. "Local and General Gossip," *Sporting News*, August 22, 1891, 4.
29. "Knocked Jeems Out," *Pittsburgh Dispatch*, August 26, 1891, 6.
30. "Jeems in His Glory," *Pittsburgh Dispatch*, September 5, 1891, 8.
31. "Too Tough to Kill," *Pittsburgh Dispatch*, September 15, 1891, 6.
32. "Diamond Field Gossip," *New York Clipper*, September 19, 1891, 475.
33. "Up a Notch Higher," *Pittsburgh Dispatch*, September 24, 1891, 6.
34. "Jeems May Leave Us," *Pittsburgh Dispatch*, November 7, 1891, 8.
35. "Powers Gets King," *Pittsburgh Dispatch*, November 11, 1891, 8.

Chapter 15

1. David Nemec, *The Great Encyclopedia of 19th Century Major League Baseball* (New York: Donald I. Fine Books, 1997), 469.
2. "Started Off Well," *Pittsburgh Dispatch*, April 2, 1892, 8.
3. "Started in Style," *Pittsburgh Dispatch*, April 23, 1892, 8.
4. "Willing to Put Up," *Pittsburgh Dispatch*, April 25, 1892, 6.
5. "An Awful Costly Error," *Pittsburgh Press*, May 22, 1892, 4.
6. They Were Unlucky," *Pittsburgh Dispatch*, June 1, 1892, 8.
7. "Sporting," *Pittsburgh Press*, June 3, 1892, 4.
8. "A Review of Sports," *Pittsburgh Dispatch*, June 5, 1892, 15.
9. "St. Louis Wants Galvin," *Pittsburgh Dispatch*, June 15, 1892, 12.
10. "The Pittsburgh Club Releases Two Players and Wants Three," *Pittsburgh Press*, June 15, 1892, 4.
11. "He Signed with St. Louis," *Pittsburgh Dispatch*, June 17, 1892, 8.
12. "Pittsburgh Chaff," *Sporting News*, August 27, 1892, 3.
13. "Fell into Salt Vat," *Pittsburgh Dispatch*, June 18, 1892, 2.
14. "A Review of Sports," *Pittsburgh Dispatch*, June 19, 1892, 15.
15. "Editorial Views, News, Comment," *Sporting Life*, July 2, 1892, 2.
16. "Jeems Got Revenge," *Pittsburgh Dispatch*, June 28, 1892, 8.
17. "Von Der Ahe's Latest," *Pittsburgh Dispatch*, June 29, 1892, 8.
18. "Diamond Field Gossip," *New York Clipper*, July 16, 1892, 298.
19. "The St. Louis Browns," *Sporting News*, July 16, 1892, 1.
20. Charlton's Baseball Chronology—1892, Baseballlibrary.com, accessed February 7, 2015, http://www.baseballlibrary.com/chronology/byyear.php?year=1892.
21. "Pitcher Galvin Sues," *Pittsburgh Dispatch*, July 28, 1892, 9.
22. "Diamond Field Gossip," *New York Clipper*, August 13, 1892, 362.
23. "So Very, Very Easy," *Pittsburgh Dispatch*, August 10, 1892, 8.
24. "Galvin's Work," *Sporting Life*, August 13, 1892, 1.
25. "The Diamond," *Pittsburgh Dispatch*, August 20, 1892, 8.
26. "Pittsburgh Chaff," *Sporting News*, August 27, 1892, 3.
27. "Jimmy's Good Benefit," *Pittsburgh Dispatch*, October 18, 1892, 9.
28. Ibid., 9.
29. "Personals," *Sporting Life*, December 10, 1892, 1.
30. "Pittsburgh Pencillings," *Sporting Life*, December 3, 1892, 4.
31. "Old Sport's Troubles," *Sporting Life*, January 27, 1894, 1.
32. "Pud Galvin. Allegheny's Forgotten Hall of Famer," by Emilia Boehm, *Reporter Dispatch: Journal of Old Allegheny History and Lore*, Number 49, Allegheny City Society, Pittsburgh, Spring 2010, 3.
33. "Old Sport's Troubles," *Sporting Life, Ibid.*
34. "Another Change," *Sporting Life*, March 3, 1894, 3.
35. "Pittsburgh Points. a Noted Veteran Has Answered the Last Summons," *Sporting Life*, March 15, 1902, 2.
36. "Galvin's Ordeal," *Sporting Life*, January 13, 1894, 1.
37. "Pud Galvin. Allegheny's Forgotten Hall of Famer," by Boehm, *Ibid*.
38. "Caught on the Fly," *Sporting News*, February 10, 1894, 3.
39. "Need a New Team," *Buffalo Express*, May 14, 1894, 9.
40. "Couldn't Blame Jeems," *Buffalo Courier*, May 23, 1894, 8.
41. "Two Wild Throws," *Buffalo Express*, May 23, 1894, 9.
42. "An Awful Roast," *Buffalo Evening News*, May 28, 1894, 4.
43. "Gentle Jeems. He Made a Monkey of the Home Team in Yesterday's Game," *Buffalo Express*, May 28, 1894, 9.
44. "Jeems Galvin's Days," *Sporting Life*, September 26, 1908, 9.
45. "Little Canada," in "North Side: Across the River," Carnegie History of Pittsburgh, accessed May 22, 2015, www.clpgh.org/exhibit/neighborhoods/northside/nor_n41.htm.
46. "One Check for Jimmy Galvin," *Pittsburgh Press*, March 3, 1902.
47. "Funeral Today," *Pittsburgh Press*, March 9, 1902, 23.
48. "Benefit for Galvin Sure to Be a Hummer," *Pittsburgh Press*, March 6, 1902.
49. "Galvin Benefit a Huge Success," *Pittsburgh Press*, March 23, 1902, 21.
50. *Pittsburgh Leader*, as quoted in "Pud Galvin. Allegheny's Forgotten Hall of Famer,"

by Emilia Boehm, *Reporter Dispatch. the Journal of Old Allegheny History and Lore.* Number 49. Allegheny City Society, Pittsburgh, Spring 2010, 4.

Epilogue

1. "Ripley's Believe It or Not," May 1, 1952.
2. "When Baseball Came to Richmond Avenue," by Joseph M. Overfield, *Niagara Frontier, Volume 1, Numbers 1-4,* Winter 1953–Spring, Fall, Winter, 1954, published by Buffalo Historical Society, Buffalo, N.Y., 29.
3. "Jim Galvin, Baseball's Forgotten Man" and "Jim Galvin, Buffalo's First Superstar," by Joe Overfield, Joe Overfield Collection, Box 9, Folder 6, Buffalo History Museum, Buffalo, N.Y.
4. "Galvin Carried Credentials for Hall of Fame," in Cooperstown Corner by Lee Allen, *Sporting News,* February 20, 1965, 6.
5. "Jim Galvin, Baseball's Forgotten Man," by Overfield.
6. "Vets Group Selects Galvin for Shrine," *Sporting News,* February, 13, 1965, 10.
7. "Baseball Honors $300-A-Year Man," *New York Times,* July 27, 1965.
8. From Major League pitching statistics and salaries, at baseballreference.com.

Bibliography

Books

Abrams, Roger I. *The Dark Side of the Diamond: Gambling, Violence, Drugs and Alcoholism in the National Pastime.* Burlington, MA: Rounder Books, 2007.
Alexander, Charles. *Our Game.* New York: Henry Holt, 1991.
Aminoff, Michael J. *Brown-Sequard: An Improbable Genius Who Transformed Medicine.* New York: Oxford University Press, 2010.
Anson, Adrian Constantine. *A Ball Player's Career.* Reprint of original 1900 edition. Gloucester, UK: Dodo Press, 2008.
Batesel, Paul. *Players and Teams of the National Association, 1871–1875.* Jefferson, NC: McFarland, 2012.
Block, David. *Baseball Before We Knew It.* Lincoln: University of Nebraska Press, 2005.
Brown, Richard C., and Bob Watson. *Buffalo: Lake City in Niagara Lan.* Buffalo, NY: Windsor, 1981.
Dewey, Donald, and Nicholas Acocella. *The Biographical History of Baseball.* Chicago: Triumph, 2012.
Ivor-Campbell, Frederick, and Mark Rucker, eds. *Baseball's First Stars.* Cleveland, OH: Society for American Baseball Research, 1996.
Kerr, Roy. *Big Dan Brouthers: Baseball's First Great Slugger.* Jefferson, NC: McFarland, 2013.
Lieb, Frederick G. *The Pittsburgh Pirates.* Reprint of 1948 edition by G. P. Putnam's Sons. Carbondale: Southern Illinois University Press, 2003.
Lowenfish, Lee. *The Imperfect Diamond: A History of Baseball's Labor Wars.* Lincoln: University of Nebraska Press, 2010.
Martin, Brian. *The Tecumsehs of the International Association: Canada's First Major League Baseball Champions.* Jefferson, NC: McFarland, 2015.
McCollister, John. *The Bucs! The Story of the Pittsburgh Pirates.* Lenexa, KS: Addax, 1998.
National Baseball Hall of Fame and Museum 2014 Yearbook. Lynn, MA: H.O. Zimman, 2014.
Nemec, David, ed. *The Beer and Whisky League: The Illustrated History of the American Association—Baseball's Renegade Major League.* New York: Lyons and Burford, 1994.
_____. *The Great Encyclopedia of 19th Century Major League Baseball.* New York: Donald I. Fine, 1997.
_____. *Major League Baseball Profiles, 1871–1900: Volume 1: The Players Who Built the Game.* Lincoln: University of Nebraska Press, 2011.

Overfield, Joseph M. *The 100 Seasons of Buffalo Baseball.* Kenmore, NY: Partners' Press, 1985.
Pietrusza, David. *Major Leagues: The Formation, Sometimes Absorption and Mostly Inevitable Demise of 18 Professional Baseball Organizations, 1871 to Present.* Jefferson, NC: McFarland, 1991.
Rooney, Dan, and Carol Peterson. *Allegheny City: A History of Pittsburgh's North Side.* Pittsburgh: University of Pittsburgh Press, 2013.
Ryczek, William J. *Blackguards and Red Stockings: A History of Baseball's National Association, 1871–1875.* Softcover reprint of 1992 McFarland edition. Wallingford, CT: Colebrook Press, 1999.
Seymour, Harold, and Dorothy Seymour Mills. *Baseball: The Early Years.* Reprint of 1960 edition. New York: Oxford University Press, 1989.
Spink, Alfred H. *The National Game.* Second edition. Reprint of 1911 edition by the National Game Publishing Company. Carbondale: Southern Illinois University Press, 2000.
Thorn, John. *Baseball in the Garden of Eden: The Secret History of the Early Game.* New York: Simon & Schuster, 2011.
Tiemann, Robert L., and Mark Rucker, editors. *Nineteenth Century Stars.* Phoenix, AZ: Society for American Baseball Research, 2012.
Vincent, Ted. *Mudville's Revenge: The Rise and Fall of American Sport.* Lincoln: University of Nebraska Press, 1981.
Voigt, David Q. *American Baseball: From Gentleman's Sport to the Commissioner System.* Norman: University of Oklahoma Press, 1966.
Westcott, Rich. *Winningest Pitchers: Baseball's 300-Game Winners.* Philadelphia: Temple University Press, 2002.
Zumsteg, Derek. *The Cheater's Guide to Baseball.* Boston: Houghton Mifflin, 2007.

Articles

Allen, Lee. "Galvin Carried Credentials for Hall of Fame." In Cooperstown Corner (column) by Lee Allen, *Sporting News,* February 20, 1965.
Boehm, Emilia. "Pud Galvin. Allegheny's Forgotten Hall of Famer." *Reporter Dispatch: Journal of Old Allegheny History and Lore,* Number 49, Allegheny City Society, Pittsburgh, Spring 2010.
Boswell, Thomas. "Hall of Fame Vote Means Baseball Is, Finally, Emerging from the Steroids Era." *Washington Post,* January 6, 2015, accessed January 8, 2015, http://www.washingtonpost.com/sports/nationals/hall-of-fame-vote-means-baseball-is-finally-emerging-from-the-steroids-era/2015/01/06/fcb7c858-95db-11e4-8005-1924ede3e54a_story.htm.
Brown-Sequard, Charles E. "The Effects Produced on Man by Subcutaneous Injections of a Liquid Obtained from the Testes of Animals." *The Lancet,* July 20, 1889, 105–107, accessed June 26, 2014, http://www.sciencedirect.com/science/article/pii/S0140673600641181.
Britcher, Craig. "We Are Now Pirates: The 1890 Burghers and Alleghenys." *Western Pennsylvania History,* Spring 2014.
Calcaterra, Craig. "Reminder: There Are Already Steroid Users in the Hall of Fame." NBCSports.com, January 9, 2013, accessed October 8, 2014, http://hardballtalk.nbcsports.com/2013/01/09/reminder-there-are-Already-Steroids-Users-N-The-Hall-Of-Fame/.
_____. "So Who's the Hall of Fame 'Roider Tom Boswell Mentioned Last Night?" NBCSports.com, September 29, 2010, accessed October 15, 2014, http://hardballtalk.nbcsports.com/2010/09/29/so-whos-the-hall-of-fame-roider-tom-boswell-mentioned-last-night/.

"Canseco Regrets Naming Names in His Book About Steroids," ESPN.com: Baseball, accessed December 21, 2014, http://espn.go.com/espn/print?id=3655031.

Curry, Jack. "Baseball; McGwire Stopped His Use of Andro Four Months Ago," *New York Times*, August 6, 1999, accessed November 3, 2014, http://www.nytimes.com/1999/08/06/sports/baseball-mcgwire-stopped-his-use-of-andro-four-months-ago.html.

Cussons, Andrea J., Walsh, John P., Bhagat, Choo I., and Fletcher, Stephen J. "Brown-Sequard Revisited: A Lesson from History on the Placebo Effect of Androgen Treatment." *Medical Journal of Australia 2002: Vol. 177 (11)*, 678–679, accessed July 7, 2014, https://www.mja.com.au/journal/2002/177/11/brown-sequard-revisited-lesson-history-placebo-effect-androgen-treatment.

Fleitz, David. "Fred Goldsmith." SABR BioProject, accessed January 8, 2014, http://sabr.org/bioproj/person/99c4a5f5.

Freeman, Erica R., Bloom, David A. and McGuire, Edward J. "A Brief History of Testosterone." Department of surgery, University of Michigan, from the *Journal of Urology, American Urological Association*, Vol. 165, 371–373, February 2001, as appearing at Masters Men's Clinic, accessed June 26, 2014, http://www.mastersmensclinic.com/history_of_testosterone_htm.

Gaines, Cork. "Baseball Hall of Fame Makes a Huge Change That Will Screw Players Linked to Steroids," *Business Insider*, July 29, 2014, accessed October 8, 2014, http://www.businessinsider.sg/baseball-hall-of-fame-voting-rules-change-2014-7/#VDWXwyje7Hg.

———. "Baseball's Hall of Fame Already Has One Known Steroid User," *Business Insider*, January 10, 2013, accessed October 15, 2014, http://www.businessinsider.com/baseballs-hall-of-fame-already-has-one-known-steroid-user-2013-1.

"Gone to America," Irish Potato Famine, The History Place, accessed December 28, 2014, http://www.historyplace.com/worldhistory/famine/america.htm.

"The Great Railroad Strike," *Digital History*, accessed February 4, 2015, http://www.digitalhistory.uh.edu/disp_textbook.cfm?smtID=2&psid=3189.

Haupert, Michael. "William Hulbert." SABR BioProject, accessed February 5, 2014, http://sabr.org/bioproj/person/38c553ff.

Hausberg, Charles. "Pud Galvin." SABR BioProject, accessed June 1, 2014, http://sabr.org/bioproj/person/38c553ff.

"Horace Phillips Found," Society for American Baseball Research, Biographical Research Committee, January/February 2011 Report.

Ingham, John N. "Iron and Steel in the Pittsburgh Region: The Domain of Small Business." *Business and Economic History*, second series, vol. 20, 1991, 108, accessed January 19, 2015, http://www.thebhc.org/sites/default/files/beh/BEHprint/v020/p0107-p0116.pdf.

"It's Over There, Commissioner," Baseball—The Tenth Inning, accessed November 3, 2014, http://www.pbs.org/baseball-the-tenth-inning/dark-days/over-there-commissioner/.

Kepner, Tyler. "Bonds (And Everyone) Strikes Out." *New York Times.Com*, January 9, 2013, accessed Dec. 23, 2014, http://www.nytimes.com/2013/01/10/sports/baseball/no-players-elected-to-baseball-hall-of-fame.html.

Kittel, Jeffrey. "19th Century St. Louis Baseball Clubs." *This Game of Games: St. Louis Baseball in the 19th Century*, accessed December 29, 2014, http://www.thisgameofgames.com/19th-century-st-louis-baseball-clubs.html.

Klein, Christopher. "Baseball's First Fountain of Youth." History in the Headlines, accessed March 1, 2015, http:///www.history.com/news/baseballs-first-found-of-youth.

Knickerbocker, Wendy. "Billy Sunday." SABR BioProject, accessed January 3, 2015, http://sabr.org/bioproj/person/7fae24bc.

Bibliography

"Little Canada," in "North Side: Across the River," Carnegie History of Pittsburgh, accessed May 22, 2015, www.clpgh.org/exhibit/neighborhoods/northside/nor_n41.htm.

McGinnis, John B. "The Kerry Patch and St. Louis Irish History," *St. Louis Irish*, March 6, 2007, accessed January 19, 2015, http://stlfire4.loudclick.net/home.aspx.

McKenna, Brian. "Mark Baldwin." SABR BioProject, accessed January 18, 2015, http://sabr.org/bioproj/person/41f65388.

"MLB Bans Use of Androstenedione," MLB.com, accessed November 3, 2014, http://mlb.mlb.com/content/printer_friendly/mlb/y2004/m06d29/c783595.jsp.

Newman, Maria. "Congress Opens Hearings on Steroid Use in Baseball." *New York Times*, March 18, 2005, accessed December 22, 2014, http://www.Nytimes.com/learning/teachers/featured_articles/20050318friday.html.

Nightengale, Bob. "Such Hypocritical Voting for the Baseball Hall of Fame." USA Today Sports, *Detroit Free Press*, January 6, 2015, accessed January 8, 2015, http://www.freep.com/story/sports/mlb/2015/01/06/baseball-hall-fame-voting/21338275/.

Overfield, Joe. "'Gentle Jeems' Jim Galvin: Buffalo's First Superstar." Bisontales, in *Bisongram*, a publication of the Buffalo Bisons Professional Baseball Club, February/March 1993.

Overfield, Joseph M. "It All Began with a Pitcher's Duel." *Buffalo Courier-Express*, May 8, 1977.

———. "A Memorable Year—1884 a Memorable Performer—Jim Galvin." SABR Research Journals Archive, accessed June 3, 2014, http://research.sabr.org/journals/jim-galvin.

———. "Professional Baseball in Buffalo—How It Began." *Niagara Frontier Magazine 1*, No. 2 (Spring 1954).

"Physical Growth of the City of Saint Louis," St. Louis City Plan Commission 1969, accessed December 28, 2014, http://www.museum.state.il.us/RiverWeb/landings/Ambot/Archives/History69/.

Rovell, Darren. "Baseball Hall of Fame Must Have Steroid Era Wing." CNBC.com, accessed October 8, 2014, http://www.cnbc.com/id/47877888.

Russell, Stefene. "Of Cabbages and Kings. One of St. Louis' Most Irish Neighborhoods, the Kerry Patch Was All but Gone 100 Years Ago—But Its Memory Refuses to Fade." *St. Louis Magazine*, July 24, 2014, accessed November 21, 2014, http://www.stlmag.com/arts/history/of-cabbages-and-kings/.

"Sportsman's Park," ballparksofbaseball.com, accessed December 29, 2014, http://www.ballparksofbaseball.co/past/SportsmansPark.htm.

"Throwback Thursday: Curveballs," *The Harvard Crimson*, November 7, 2013, accessed December 23, 2014, http://www.thecrimson.com/article/2013/11/7/throwback-thursday-baseball/.

Tobias, Edmund. "A Bad Beating. Westerns Paralyzed the Red Stockings." Edmund *The Sporting News*, February 1, 1896.

"Tony La Russa Says That Steroid Cheats Should Be in Baseball Hall of Fame—With Asterisks," *New York Daily News*, July 26, 2014, accessed October 15, 2014, http://www.nydailynews.com/sports/baseball/tony-la-russa-put-steroid-cheats-baseball-hall-of-fame-asterisks-article-1.1880787.

Vaccaro, Frank. "Hugh Daily." SABR BioProject, accessed February 24, 2015, http://sabr.org/bioproj/person/8d8c99e4.

Verducci, Tom. "Why I'll Never Vote for a Known Steroids User for the Hall of Fame." SportsIllustratedwww, January 8, 2013, accessed December 23, 2014, http://www.si.com/mlb/2013/01/08/hall-fame-ballot-steroids-mark-mcguire-barry-bonds-roger-clemens.

Wilson, Duff. "McGwire Offers No Denials at Steroid Hearings." *New York Times*, March

18, 2005, accessed December 22, 2014 http://www.nytimes.com/2005/03/18/sports/baseball/18steroids.html.

Baseball Periodicals
Bisongram
New York Clipper
Sporting Life
The Sporting News
Sports Illustrated

Newspapers
Buffalo Courier
Buffalo Courier Express
Buffalo Evening News
Buffalo Express
Chicago Tribune
Detroit Free Press
Ionia (MI) Sentinel
London (Ont.) Advertiser
London (Ont.) Free Press
New York Daily News
New York Times
Pittsburgh Commercial Gazette
Pittsburgh Dispatch
Pittsburgh Post
Pittsburgh Press
St. Louis Globe-Democrat
Washington Post

Other Publications
Business and Economic History
Business Insider
Harvard Crimson
Niagara Frontier Magazine
St. Louis Magazine
Western Pennsylvania History

Journals
Journal of Urology, American Urological Association
The Lancet
Medical Journal of Australia
Reporter Dispatch: Journal of Old Allegheny History and Lore
St. Louis Irish

Online Resources
ancestry.com
baseballalmanac.com
baseball-reference.com
bioproj.sabr.com
retrosheet.org

Index

Numbers in **_bold italics_** refer to pages with photographs.

Abrams, Roger I. 8, 15–16, 164–165
Alaskas of New York 40
Albany Capital Citys 82
Albanys of Albany, New York 82
Alexander, Charles 178
Alexander, Grover Cleveland 209
Alexander, Pete 34
Alleghenys of Pittsburgh 49, 50, 52, 54, 56–57, 63, 65, 72, 74–76, 99, 121, 125, 129, 134, 140, 146, **_151_**
Allen, Dick **_71_**, 72, 77
Allen, Lee 213
American Association 44–45, 83, 99, 105–106, 108, 113–114, 121, 134–136, 139–140, 170–171, 179–180, 182–184, 191–192, 202, 210
American League 83, 170
Anderson, Dave 166
Andrews, Ed 151
androstenedione, "andro" 10, 11
Anson, Cap 15, 86, 90, 103, 116, 122, 124, 140–141, 152, 170, 175, 187, 195
Anson's Colts 186–187, 195

Bagwell, Jeff 14
Baldwin, Mark 140, 183–184, 186, 189–193, 195–196, 198–199, 201
Balk 121, 122
Baltimore Orioles 99, 135
Barkley, Sam 135, 143
Barnes, Ross 27, 30, 33–34, 73, 77
Barnie, Bill 66–67
Baseball Writers Association of America 12
Battin, Joe 57
Becker, Jacob 202–203
Beckley, Jake 147, 149, 153, 171, **_173_**, 174, 179, 187
"Beer and Whisky League" 99, 136, 184
Bennett, Charlie 105, 108
Bennett, H.B. 113

Berger, John Henry "Tun" 184, 203, 207
Bielaski, Oscar 24
Bierbauer, Louis 180, **_181_**, 182, 189, 195
"Big Four" 126–128, 133, 141, 154
Biggio, Craig 13
Binghamton Crickets 76
Birrell, W.H. 62
Bishop, Bill 141
"Black Sox" scandal 8
Blong, Joe 57–58
Blyleven, Bert 15
Bond, Tommy 31, 47–48, 55, 79, 86–87, 102
Bonds, Barry 9, 12–16, 165
Borden (or Josephs), Joe 28
Boston Beaneaters 107, 109–110, 112, 122, 150, 160–161, 180
Boston Red Caps 47–48, 50, 55, 64, 79, 84, 97
Boston Red Stockings 22, 27
Boswell, Thomas 13, 15
Bradley, George H. "Foghorn" 44, 62–63, 78–79, 92
Bradley, George Washington 23, 25–34, 50–51, 57, 68, 84, 91, 96, 102
Breitenstein, Ted 193, 198
Brill, Frank 117
Brooklyn Atlantics 28, 44, 99
Brooklyn Bridegrooms 174, 176
Brooklyn Grays 128
Brotherhood of Professional Baseball Players 132, 154, 168, 171, 173, 179
Brouthers, Dan 91–92, 95–98, 100, 101, **_101_**, **_104_**, 105, 108–111, 115–117, 124, 126–128, 132–133, 136, 154, 198
Brown, Tom 142–143
Brown-Sequard, Dr. Charles E. 161–165
Browning, Roger "Pete" 183, 187
Brunton, T.H. 77
Buckenberger, Al 192, 194–196, 200–201

239

Buckley, Dick 198–199
Buffalo Base Ball Club 64–65, 67, 93, 113, 120, 125, 128
Buffalo Bisons 60, 65, 68–69, *71*, 73, 84, 94, *101*, 107–110, 112, 116, 118, 128, 177, 212
Buffinton, Charlie 109–110, 112, 118, 168, 195
Bulkeley, Morgan 45–46
Bunning, Jim 12
Burdock, Jack 84
Burke, Mike 61–62, 77
Burke, Walter 107
Burlingtons, of Hamilton, Ontario 66
Burns, Ken 15
Burns, Tommy 195, 200

Calcaterra, Craig 15
California League 88
Caminiti, Ken 13
Camp, Winfield 196
Canseco, Jose 3, 9, 12, 15, 165, 215
Carey, Tom 88
Carroll, Cliff 118, 149, 186
Carroll, Fred 121, 140–142, 150, *151*, 153, 171, *173*, *174–175*, 179, 187
Carsey, Kid 198
Caruthers, Bob 200
Casey, Dan 151
Cass Club of Detroit 32–33, 38, 67
Caylor, O.P. 98
Chadwick, Henry 34, 38–40, 63, 70, 74, 93, 95, 108
Chamberlain, Frank 183
Champion Cities of Springfield, Ohio 53, 55
Chapman, Jack *26*, 27, 122, 127, 205
Chicago Pirates 170, 172
Chicago White Stockings 23–26, 28, 30, 33, 50–51, 57–58, 68, 79, 86–88, 90, 93, 97–98, 103, 109, 111–112, 116, 122, 139–140, 152, 154, 160, 170
Cincinnati Red Stockings 21–22, 37, 44, 50
Clapp, John 88
Clarkson, John 124, 140–141, 144, 160–161, 167–168, 188, 210
Clemens, Roger 9, 12–16
Cleveland, Pres. Grover 128–129
Cleveland Blues 108, 140, 146
Cleveland Forest Citys 85, 102
Cleveland Infants 176
Cleveland Spiders 175–176
Coates, William 49
Cobb, Ty 15, 211
Coca-Cola Field in Buffalo *78*, *80*
Coleman, Tom 109
Collins, Chub 115
Collins, Dan 31, 34–35
Columbus Buckeyes 40–41, 44, 47, 51, 56, 60, 121
Columbus Solons 179, 192
Comiskey, Charlie 135, 170, 172, 179
Compton Avenue Grounds, St. Louis 22, 24
Converse, E.C. 134

Conway, Pete 128, 154, 157
Cooney, Jimmy 187
Corcoran, Larry 60, 64, 67–68, 70, 79, 88, 90–91, 97, 103–104, 111
Corcoran, Tommy 173
Corey, Fred 92
Craver, Bill 64
Creamer, George 43, 48, 60
Crowley, Bill *71*, 72, 74, 92
Culbert, Alexander 113
Cummings, William A. "Candy" 41, 46, 49–50, 70
Cushman, Ed 107, 109–111, 113

Dahlen, Bill 186
Daily, Hugh "One Arm" 100–101, *101*, 102, 115
Daley, Bill 161
Dalrymple, Abner 97, 140–141, 143–144, *151*
Dehlman, Dutch 29
Delahanty, Ed 151, 199
Denny, Elizabeth O'Hara 36
Denny, Jerry 157
Derby, George 96, 107–109, 113
Detroit Wolverines 96, 116–117, 122, 126, 128, 144, 146, 154
Devlin, Jim 23, 47, 58, 64
Dinnen, Mike 44, 61
Dolan, Tom 30, 43, 49, 55–56, 60, 62, 64, *71*, 72, 77, 89, 100, *101*
Donovan, Patsy 196
Doscher, Herm 44, 75
Doubleday, Abner 1
Driscoll, Denny 92
Dunlap, Fred 115, 133, 146, 150, *151*, 158, 160, *160*, 170, 175

Eastern Association 177
Eastern League 149, 205
Eden Charlie 121, 131
Eggler, Dave *71*, 72, 76–77, 84, 107, 117–118
Ehret, Phil "Red" 192
Eliot, Charles W. 7–8
"elixir of life" 16, 161, 215
Empire Club of St. Louis 24–27
Eries of Erie, Pennsylvania 48
Esper, Charles "Duke" 192
Essex Club of Buffalo 40
Esterbrook, Tom 92
Exposition Park in Pittsburgh *169*, 169, 171–172, 185, 189, 201, 206

Fairbanks of Chicago 40
Falls, Joe 213
Federal League 83
Fehr, Donald 12
Ferguson, Bob 127
Field, Sam 67–68, 179
Fields, Jocko 143, *151*, 171, *173*
Finley, Charles O. 213
Fisher, Cherokee 28, 33
Fleet, Frank 25–26, 28

Flint, Frank "Silver" 22, 24, 30, 97, 189
Foley, Curry 89, 95, 97–98, *101*, 102, 104, 115
Force, Davy 57, *71*, 71–72, 81, 88, 91, 95–98, 100, *101*, 104
Frick, Ford C. *212*, 213
Fulmer, Chick 412, 58, 60,-62, 64, 66, *71*, 72–73, 79, 84

Gaffney, John 138
Galvin, Bridget 89, 147, 206–207
Galvin, Eugene 197, 200–201
Galvin, James Francis "Pud": birth 20; children 85, 197, 200–201, 207; comeback bid 205–206; death 207; first-ever no-hitter 31; first League home run 99; first League no-hitter 92; first perfect game 33; first professional game 26; images *16*, *71*, *101*, *103*, *144*, *148*, *151*, *173*; induction into Baseball Hall of Fame 213; injects elixir of life 163; sale to Allegheny 125; sale to Buffalo 125; sale to St. Louis 196; 300th win 153; win number 365, 200
Galvin, James, Jr. 85, 207
Galvin, Joseph 207
Galvin, Marie 207
Galvin, Mark 207
Galvin, Martin 18–20
Galvin, Walter 207, 212–213
Galvin, William 207
Genins, Frank 196, 198
Gilbert, Pete 205–206
Gillen, Sam 207
Gillespie, Pete 109
Glasscock, Jack 76, 171
Gleason, Jack 32
Gleason, William "Kid" 198–199
Glenn, John 24
Goldsmith, Fred 43–45, 48–49, 52, 56, 61–63, 65, 70, 74–75, 77–79, 83, 86, 88, 91, 97–98, 104, 112, 114, 116, 210
Goodman, Jake 43, 55, 60–62
Gore, George 97, 102
Gorman, Harry 39–41, 43, 61, 76
Gottlieb, Bill 211
Graffen, Mase 32
Grand Avenue Ball Grounds 21, 23, 25
Great Railroad Strike of 1877 53–55
Griffin, Bridget 85
Griswold, Merritt 21
Guelph (Ontario) Maple Leafs 41, 43, 49, 63–64, 72

Haddock, George 153, 174, 199
Hagan, Art 107, 113, 115
Hague, Bill 27
Haldeman, W.N. 34
Hall, Al 77–78
Hall, George 64
Hamilton (Ontario) Primrose Club 127
Hamilton (Ontario) Young Canadians 66
Handiboe, Jim 136, 138–139

Hankinson, Frank 87
Hanlon, Edward "Ned" *151*, 154, 158–160, 168, 170–171, *173*, 174, 176, 179–180, 184, 188–190, 193
Hartford Dark Blues 31, 34, 41, 47, 49, 55
Hartranft, Gov. John 54–55
Hastings, Scott 24, 45
Hawke, Dick 200–201
Hecker, Guy 171, 175, 180, 184
Henderson, Hardie 149
Henderson, Rickey 7
Higham, Dick 24, 59
Hoffer, Bill 205
Hofford, John 136–137, 139
Holbert, Bill 42, 55–56, 61
Hornells of Hornellsville, N.Y. 68
Hornsby, Rogers 8, 10
Hornung, Joe "Dutch" 43, 62, 75, 77, 79, 81, 84, 92, 94, 98, 110
Hotaling, Pete 51
Houck, Sadie 54
Hubbard, H.W. 204
Hughson, George 122
Hulbert, William 30, 33, 45–46, 70, 72, 82, 86–87, 99, 108
Hurley, Jerry 173
Hutchison, Bill 188

Indianapolis Blues (or Blue Legs) 49, 56, 58
International Association of Professional Base Ball Players (later National Base-Ball Association) 2, 32, 40–41, 43–47, 50, 52, 56, 60, 62–65, 70, 72, 74–76, 79–83, 99, 121, 153, 184, 210–211
International League 154
Ionia, Michigan, baseball tournament 32

Jackson, "Shoeless Joe" 8
Jewett, Josiah 126
Johnson, Randy 13
Johnson, Walter 209
Jones, Charley 84–85, 91

Kalbfus, Thomas 183
Kansas City Cowboys 140, 182
Keefe, Tim 168, 188, 199, 210
Kelly, Mike "King" 44–45, 60, 115, 120, 132, 143, 160, 167, 170–171
Kennedy, Doc 45
Keokuk Westerns 25–27
Kerr, Dave 206
Kerr, William 195
Kerry, William W. 190, 193
Kerry Patch of St. Louis 18–19
King, Silver 172, 183, 186, 190–191
Kinslow, Tom 199
Kinzie, Walt 116
Knowdell, Jake 44
Krauthoff, Louis 182
Kuehne, Bill 142–143, *151*, 156–157, 171, *173*

Lajoie, Napoleon 211
Lakefront Park in Chicago 103
Larkin, Henry 172
Larkin, Terry 79
La Russa, Tony 10, 14
Latham, Warren "Juice" 43–44
Lauer, Chuck 158
League Alliance 47, 56–59, 64, 67, 70
Leonard, Andy 48
Libby, Steve *71*, 72–76, 79, 81, 84
Lieb, Frederick 182
Lillie, Jim 107, 112, 117
Live Oaks of Lynn, Massachusetts 28, 40–41, 49–50, 60, 76
London (Ontario) Tecumsehs 32, 38, 41, 43, 48, 52, 61–63, 65, 72–79
Louisville Colonels 135
Louisville Grays 33–34, 42, 44, 47, 51, 58, 64
Louisville Grays Scandal of 1877 8, 51, 64
Louisville Reds 68
Lucas, Henry V. 113, 121
Luff, Henry 76
Lynch, Jack 94, 96–98, 100

Mack, Connie 168, 179, 182, 185, 192
Mack, Denny 32, *71*, 72, 79, 90, 132
Manchesters 41, 52
Manfred, Rob 11
Mantle, Mickey 9
Maris, Roger 10
Martinez, Pedro 12
Mason, James 207
Mathews, Bobby 44, 51, 132
Mathewson, Christy 209
Maul, Al 147, 149, *151*, 171, *173*, 178–179
McCleary, Sheriff W. H. 186, 204
McCormick, Harry 47, 49, 51, 73, 85
McCormick, Jim 47, 49, 51, 73, 85
McDowell, Heber 186
McGeary, Mike 57
McGunnigle, Bill *71*, 72, 74–75, 77, 81, 84–87, 89–90, 94, 189, 192
McGwire, Mark 3, 9, 12–16, 165, 215
McHenry, Patrick T. 12
McKelvy, Russ 35, 37, 43, 48–50, 56–58, 60–62
McKinnon, Alex 140, 143
McKnight, Harmar Denny 35, 38–43, 46, 54, 63, 99, 105, 113, 134–136, 140
McKnight, Robert 36
McLean, Hugh 43
McNeary, Thomas 34
McQuaid, John 167
McSorley, John "Trick" *71*, 72–73, 77
McTigue, Bridgette 18–20
McVey, Cal 27, 30, 33, 68
Meegan, Pete 131
Meinke, Frank 116–117
Memphis Blues 50
Miller, George "Doggie" 121, 146–147, *151*, 159, 170, 188

Miller, Tom 28, 29
Mills, Abraham 108
Mitchell Report 14
Morgan, Daniel "Pidge" 31
Morrill, John 110
Morris, Ed 121, 124, 130, *130*, 131, 136–137, 139, 141–143, 145, 149–150, *151*, 152–153, 156–158, 164, 168, 171, *173*, 174–176, 178, 202, 206–207
Mountain, Frank 121, 130, 136
Mountain Cities of Altoona, Pennsylvania 40
Mullanphy, John 18–19
Murnan, Tom 50
Mutrie, Jim 167
Mutual Club of Jackson, Michigan 32–33
Myers, George 115
Myler, Theo 39

Nash, Billy 150
National Agreement 113, 182
National Association of Professional Base Ball Players 22, 27, 30, 41–42, 44, 46, 72, 83, 184, 210–211
National Base-Ball Association (formerly International Association) 82–83, 86
National Baseball Hall of Fame 3–5, 12, 14–16, 45, 69, 90, 94, 118, 153, 161, 165, 209, 213, 215
National League 30, 40–41, 44–47, 57, 64, 70, 72, 74, 80, 82–83, 87, 93, 99, 108, 113–114, 121, 132–135, 139–140, 168, 170–171, 175–176, 178–180, 184, 192
Nelson, John "Candy" 42, 47, 56–57, 60, 62
Nemec, David 82
New American Association 170
New Havens of New Haven, Connecticut 37, 70, 72, 94
New York Giants 119, 122, 127, 138, 157
New York Gothams 107, 109, 119
New York Metropolitans 100, 134–135
New York Mutuals 29, 35, 42
New York State League 80
Niagaras of Buffalo 66
Niagaras of St. Louis 24, 26–27
Nicholls, C.W. 77
Nichols, Al 42, 47, 51, 58, 64
Nichols, Kid 211
Nicol, Sam 153
Niekro, Phil 200
Nightengale, Bob 14
Nimick, William 135, 140, 142, 154
Northwestern League 108, 146, 149–150, 155–156, 158, 170, 172

O'Connor, Jack 183
Olympic Park in Buffalo 113, 116, 124–125, 128
O'Neill, J. Palmer 170, 175, 179–180, 183–184, 186–190
O'Rourke, Jim "Orator" 27, 94–97, 100, *101*, 102–103, 109–111, 115, 118–120, 122, 132
O'Rourke, John 84

Index 243

Overfield, Joseph 81, 211–213
overhand pitching allowed 114

Palmeiro, Rafael 9, 12–13
Pearce, Dickey 27, 32
Pearson, Mayor Richard T. 156
Peters, John 28, 51, 92, 95, 98
Pfeffer, Fred 109, 149, 152, 187
Philadelphia Athletics 29, 31, 35, 49–50, 99, 180
Philadelphia Pearls 28
Philadelphia Phillies 180, 182
Philadelphia Quakers 107, 109, 174, 180
Phillips, Horace 68, 99, 121, 130–131, 134–135, 138, 140–143, 145–147, 149–150, 156–159
Piazza, Mike 14
Pietrusza, David 45, 83, 121, 183
Pike, "Lip" 27, 29
Pinkney, George 200
Pittsburgh Burghers *160*, 168, 170–172, *173*, 174–178
Pittsburgh Innocents 170, 172, 175–176
Pittsburgh Pirates 182–183, 186–188, 195, 210
Platt, James W. 207
Players' League 45, 83, 168–171, 175–180, 182–183
PNC Park in Pittsburgh *185*, *194*, *203*
Pond, N.P. 41
Poorman, Tom 89–91, 94
Powers, L.J. 82
Powers, Phil 43, 48, 61–62, 73–74, 77, 186
Pratt, Tom 113
Providence Grays 79, 90–92, 109, 111, 118, 122, 206
Purcell, William "Blondie" 87, 95, 98, *101*, 101, 103
Purrington, John 67
Purroy, Charles 65

Queen Cities Club of Buffalo 66
Quest, Joe 97, 141
Quinn, Tom *73*, 207
Quinton, Marshall 61–63

Radbourn, Charles "Hoss" 90, 111–112, 114–115, 118–120, 132, 161, 187, 210
Rankin, A.B. 41, 71
Reach, Al 142
Readings of Reading, Pennsylvania 40
Recreation Park in Allegheny City 5, *37*, 129, 136, 140, 150, 152, 166–167, 172, 175, *177*
Recreation Park in Philadelphia 105
Redmond, Billy 31
Reilly, Charles 183
Reis, Laurie 79
Resolutes of New Jersey 40
Rice, Jim 15
Richardson, Hardy 83–84, 92, 96–97, *101*, 109, 116, *117*, 122, 124, 126–127, 133, 136
Richmond, Lee 91, 116
Ripley, Robert 211

Riverside Park in Buffalo *69*, 73, 76–77, 79, 84–85, 90, 97, 100, 102, 108, 113
Robinson, Yank 173
Rochester Flour Cities 67–68, 85
Rochester Hop Bitters 82, 91–92
Rochesters of Rochester, New York 41, 49, 58, 74, 79
Rodgers, John I. 182
Rodriguez, Alex 3, 13
Rogers, W.P. 39
Rose, Pete 8, 14
Rovell, Darren 13
Rowe, Jack 88, 92, 96, 98, 100, *101*, 111, 117–119, 126–128, 133, 154–155, 157, 168, 174
Ruth, Babe 211

Sage, John 88
St. Louis Brown Stockings 21–13, 25–35, 37, 44, 47, 57–58, 99, 135, 144, 196–200
St. Louis Maroons 115, 121, 138, 140
St. Louis Red Stockings 22–23, 28, 30–38, 41, 72
San Francisco Athletics 88–89
Saratoga Agreement 127
Say, Lou 45–46, 161
Sayre, Dr. Lewis 161
Scandrett, Al 147, 158
Schilling, Curt 12
Scott, Milt 103
Seaver, Tom 115
Selig, Bud 11
Serad, Bill 114, 116–118, 122, 124
Seward, George 26, 28
Shafer, George "Orator" 107, 115
Sheeran, R.B. 39
Sleeman, George 41, 64
Smith, Pop 142, *151*, 158
Smith, Tommy 62
Smoltz, John 13
Soden, Arthur P. 184
Solari, August 199
Somerville, Ed 44, 61–62
Sosa, Sammy 9, 12–13, 215
Southern League 199
Sowders, Bill 156, 158, 164, 167, 170
Spalding, Albert Goodwill 1, 27, 30, 33–34, 50–51, 140, 152, 154, 160–161, 170, 177, 207
Spalding World Tour 1889 154
Spaulding, Edward R. 67
Speaker, Tris 211
Spencer, Elihu 61
Spink, Alfred 180
Sportsman's Park in St. Louis 21
Staley, Harry 147, 149, 150–151, 153, 156–157, 164, 168, 171, *173*, 174, 178–179, 184–186, 188, 203
Start, Joe 91
Stearns, Dan 96
Stearns, Frederick K. 126–127, 154–155
Stein, Ed 187
Steroid Era 10, 13–15

steroids 9–17
Stovey, Harry 180, 182, 189
Stratton, Scott 184
Strief, George 204
Sullivan, Dan 137
Sullivan, Fleury 121
Sunday, Billy 147, *151*, 152–153, 159, 170, 172, 175
Sutter, Bruce 15
Sutton, Don 200
Sutton, Ezra 115, 143
Swartwood, Ed 207
Sweeney, Charlie 111, 115
Syracuse Stars 46–47, 49, 51, 55, 58–59, 64, 73, 78–79, 84–86

Tecumseh Park in London, Ontario 61, 77
Temple, William C. 190, 193, 195
Tener, John 171, *173*, 179
Terry, William "Adonis" 196, 198
testosterone 1, 3, 4, 9, 16, 161, 164–165
Thomas, Frank 13
Thompson, Helen 152
Thompson, Sam 146
Thompson, Tommy G. 11
Thurman, Allan W. 179, 182
Tobias, Edmund 24
Tripartite Agreement 108
Troy Trojans 84, 86
Turner Club of St. Louis 24

Union Association 44–45, 83, 113–115, 121, 171, 184
Union Park 5, 36, *37*, 46, 49, 51–53, 55, 58–59, 75–76
Uticas of Utica, New York 79

Van Haltren, George 140, 192
Verducci, Tom 13
Vincent, Ted 44
Visner, Joe 173
Voigt, David Q. 46
Von der Ahe, Chris 99, 155, 183, 192, 194, 196–201

Wagner, Honus 211
Waite, L. C. 35, 38–42
Walker, Oscar 45, 83, 85, 91
Ward, John Montgomery 68–70, 87, 91–92, 113, 154, 168, 178, 189
Washington Nationals 28, 83, 153
Waterman, Fred 44
Watkins, Bill 146
Weidman, Stump 116–117
Weiner, Michael 14
Welch, Mickey 98, 113, 115, 167, 188
Wentzel, Marie *212*, 213
West End Club of Milwaukee 38
Western Association 182
Western League 199
White, Jim "Deacon" 27, 30, 33, 95–96, 101, *101*, 104, 110, *110*, 126–127, 133, 154–155, 157, 159, 168, 174
White, Warren 24, 27
White, Will 87, 113, 127
Whitney, Arthur 142–143, 152
Whitney, Jim 97, 110, 112, 122, 153
Williams, J.A. 41, 99
Williamson, Ned 43, 56–57, 62, 98, 104–106, 109, 115
Wilstein, Steve 10
Wolford, Dr. Winfield S. 159
Wood, Fred 127
Wood, Pete 127
Woodcock, Fred 194–195
Worcester Ruby Legs 91, 96, 103
Wright, George 50
Wright, Harry 142
Wyckoff, Wheeler 135
Wyman, Mayor James 186

Yaik, Henry 153
York, Tom 91, 108
Young, Cy 175, 183, 198, 209, 211
Young, Nick 127, 183, 198

Zettlein, George "Charmer" 23–25, 28